PEASANT
METROPOLIS

Studies of the Harriman Institute

Columbia University

The Harriman Institute, Columbia University,
sponsors the Studies of the Harriman Institute in
the belief that their publication contributes to
scholarly research and public understanding. In
this way, the Institute, while not necessarily
endorsing their conclusions, is pleased to make
available the results of some of the research
conducted under its auspices. A list of the Studies
appears at the back of the book.

PEASANT METROPOLIS

Social Identities in Moscow, 1929–1941

David L. Hoffmann

Cornell University Press

Ithaca and London

STUDIES OF THE HARRIMAN INSTITUTE

THIS BOOK HAS BEEN PUBLISHED WITH THE AID OF A GRANT

FROM THE HULL MEMORIAL PUBLICATION FUND OF CORNELL UNIVERSITY

First published 1994 by Cornell University Press
First printing, Cornell Paperbacks, 2000

Library of Congress Cataloging-in-Publication Data
Hoffmann, David L. (David Lloyd), 1961–
    Peasant metropolis : social identities in Moscow,
1929–1941 / David L. Hoffmann.
        p.   cm. – (Studies of the Harriman Institute)
    Includes bibliographical references and index.
    ISBN 0-8014-2942-0 (cloth : alk. paper)
    ISBN 0-8014-8660-2 (pbk. : alk. paper)
    1. Working class—Russia (Federation)—Moscow—History—20th
century.   2. Urbanization—Russia (Federation)—Moscow—
History—20th century.   3. Moscow (Russia)—Population—
History—20th century.   4. Rural-urban migration—Russia
(Federation)—Moscow—History—20th century.   I. Title.
II. Series.
    HD8530.2.Z8M674   1994
    305.5'62'09473120904—dc20   94-10913

BK
$5.98

Printed in the United States of America

Cornell University Press strives to use environmentally responsible
suppliers and materials to the fullest extent possible in the publishing
of its books. Such materials include vegetable-based, low-VOC inks and
acid-free papers that are recycled, totally chlorine-free, or partly
composed of nonwood fibers. Books that bear the logo of the FSC (Forest
Stewardship Council) use paper taken from forests that have been
inspected and certified as meeting the highest standards for environmen-
tal and social responsibility. For further information, visit our website
at www.cornellpress.cornell.edu.

1   3   5   7   9   Cloth printing   10   8   6   4   2

1   3   5   7   9   Paperback printing   10   8   6   4   2

For my parents

Contents

Illustrations and Maps

Acknowledgments

Support for my research has been very generous, and I am grateful to the institutions that provided it. The Cornell University Society for the Humanities, the Harvard University Russian Research Center, and the Hoover Institution of Stanford University (with funds provided by the Title VIII Soviet–Eastern European Research and Training Act) each awarded me a postdoctoral fellowship. The International Research and Exchanges Board (with funds provided by the Andrew W. Mellon Foundation, the National Endowment for the Humanities, and the U.S. Department of State) sponsored two of my research stays in Moscow. An additional grant from the National Endowment for the Humanities made possible a third research trip. Fellowships from the Social Science Research Council and the Mellon Foundation funded several years of preliminary work. I also received a short-term grant from the Kennan Institute. None of these organizations is responsible for the views expressed in this book.

As far as research in Soviet archives is concerned, I seem to have been born at the right time. During the fourteen months I spent in Moscow between 1988 and 1992, one archive after another opened its doors to foreign researchers. I became the first Western scholar ever admitted to the Moscow Party Archive, a boon for which I thank Dmitrii Mikhailovich Dankin and the archival assistant there, Marina Evgen'evna Minaeva. I also thank the staffs of the Central Party Archive, the Central State Archive of the October Revolution, the Central State Archive of the National Economy (especially Tat'iana

Feliksovna Bavarova), the Archive of the Soviet Academy of Sciences, the Moscow Oblast Archive, and the Moscow City Archive (especially Galina Alekseevna Shorokhova). At the archive of the Hammer and Sickle plant, Raisa Nikolaevna Nagikh aided me enormously both by procuring materials and by arranging interviews with retired workers—people who generously shared memories of their migration to Moscow in the 1930s.

I am grateful to the staffs of the Lenin Library, the library of the Museum of the History of Moscow, the Moscow University Library, and the library of the Institute for Scientific Information in the Social Sciences, all in Moscow; the Widener Library of Harvard University, the Hoover Institution Library, the Stanford University libraries, the Columbia University libraries, the New York Public Library, and the Library of Congress. Special thanks go to Eugene Beshenkovsky, Slavic bibliographer at Columbia University. I also benefited from the assistance of archivists at the Hoover Institution Archives, the Bancroft Library at the University of California at Berkeley, the Bakmeteff Archive at Columbia University, and the United States National Archives.

Many scholars have helped me with advice and comments, and I thank them as well. My greatest debt is to those who read the entire manuscript at one stage or another. They include Timothy Colton, Frederick Corney, Robert Davies, Leopold Haimson, Michael Hanagan, Peter Holquist, Oleg Khlevniuk, Stephen Kotkin, Yannis Kotsonis, Hiroaki Kuromiya, Robert Lewis, Roberta Manning, Elena Osokina, Lewis Siegelbaum, Mark von Hagen, and Richard Wortman. Among others who have read portions of my work and offered their suggestions for improving it are Robert Argenbright, William Chase, Viktor Petrovich Danilov, Aleksa Djilas, Jonathan Elkind, Terence Emmons, Laura Engelstein, Cathy Frierson, Larry Gringlas, Robert Johnson, Walter Pintner, Christine Ruane, Nobuaki Shiokawa, Kenneth Straus, Jeremy Telman, Elizabeth Wood, Glennys Young, and Reginald Zelnik.

Several scholars offered their expertise during consultations. To Sheila Fitzpatrick and Moshe Lewin I owe not only thanks for their advice but also an intellectual debt—they were the first to highlight the importance of rural-to-urban migration in Soviet history. Others who have discussed aspects of my research with me include Eric Brian, Natalia Degteva, Vladimir Zinov'evich Drobizhev, Igor'

L'vovich Kornakovskii, Irina Koznova, Tat'iana Mironova, Timothy Mixter, Iurii Orlov, Aleksei Ovsiannikov, Anastasiia Mikhailovna Panfilova, Blair Ruble, Evsei Irmovich Shkaratan, Andrei Konstantinovich Sokolov, and Lynne Viola.

Part of Chapter 2 appeared as "Moving to Moscow: Patterns of Peasant In-migration during the First Five-Year Plan," in *Slavic Review* 1991 no. 4, and I thank the American Association for the Advancement of Slavic Studies for permission to use this material here. I am grateful to Iulia Trubikhina for translating the peasant songs in the text, to Christopher Brest for drawing the maps, and to Pilar Wyman for compiling the index. Also deserving of my gratitude is the staff of Cornell University Press, especially its director, John Ackerman, who has shown a genuine interest in my work, and Barbara Salazar, who edited the manuscript. Lastly, I thank my sisters, Jill and Karen, and most of all my parents for their constant support and encouragement.

D. L. H.

Ithaca, New York

Abbreviations

AAN   Arkhiv Akademii Nauk SSSR (Archive of the Academy of
          Sciences of the USSR); now renamed Arkhiv Rossiiskoi
          Akademii Nauk

MPA   Moskovskii Partiinyi Arkhiv (Moscow Party Archive); now
          renamed Moskovskii Gosudarstvennyi Arkhiv
          Obshchestvennogo Dvizheniia

TsGAMO   Tsentral'nyi Gosudarstvennyi Arkhiv Moskovskoi Oblasti
          (Central State Archive of Moscow Oblast); now merged with
          TsGAORgM as Moskovskii Gosudarstvennyi Arkhiv

TsGANKh   Tsentral'nyi Gosudarstvennyi Arkhiv Narodnogo Khoziaistvo
          SSSR (Central State Archive of the National Economy of the
          USSR); now renamed Rossiiskii Gosudarstvennyi Arkhiv
          Ekonomiki

TsGAOR   Tsentral'nyi Gosudarstvennyi Arkhiv Oktiabr'skoi Revoliutsii
          SSSR (Central State Archive of the October Revolution of the
          USSR); now renamed Gosudarstvennyi Arkhiv Rossiiskoi
          Federatsii

TsGAORgM Tsentral'nyi Gosudarstvennyi Arkhiv Oktiabr'skoi Revoliutsii
          goroda Moskvy (Central State Archive of the October
          Revolution in the City of Moscow); now merged with
          TsGAMO as Moskovskii Gosudarstvennyi Arkhiv

TsPA   Tsentral'nyi Partiinyi Arkhiv (Central Party Archive); now
          renamed Rossiiskii Tsentr Khraneniia i Izucheniia
          Dokumentov Noveishei Istorii

Introduction

To Moscow, to Moscow, to Moscow!
CHEKHOV, *Three Sisters*, Act II

When eighteen-year-old Evgenii Mikhailovich stepped off a train in Moscow in 1931, he gaped in awe at the bustling metropolis that surrounded him. To a peasant lad the sights and sounds of the city were at once fascinating and unsettling. Evgenii Mikhailovich felt overwhelmed by the throngs of people, not a familiar face among them. He still recalls his astonishment at the height of the buildings, the loud screech of tramcars, and the general commotion of the city. Yet his adjustment to urban life proved much less difficult than his initial encounter had led him to expect. Relatives housed him, fellow villagers found him a job, and an acquaintance showed him around town. And unlike most peasant in-migrants of earlier generations, he went on to become a highly paid steelworker and a permanent resident of Moscow.[1]

Evgenii Mikhailovich was one of at least 23 million Soviet peasants who moved permanently to cities between 1926 and 1939—a rate of rural-to-urban migration unprecedented in world history. So rapid was peasant in-migration that by the end of the 1930s, 40 percent of the Soviet urban population consisted of former peasants who had

---

[1] Interview with Evgenii Mikhailovich Kostin at the Hammer and Sickle metallurgical plant, Moscow, May 16, 1989. See also the initial impressions of Moscow recounted by two peasants who became Stakhanovites: Aleksandr Kh. Busygin, *Moia zhizn' i moia rabota* (Leningrad, 1935), pp. 8–13; Ivan Gudov, *Sud'ba rabochego* (Moscow, 1974), pp. 3–4.

moved from the countryside within the decade.[2] Most of these peasant in-migrants joined the industrial workforce and provided labor crucial to the industrialization drive. The number of industrial workers in the USSR doubled during the First Five-Year Plan alone, and the great majority of new workers were former peasants.[3]

The massive migration of peasants to cities, a consequence of collectivization and industrialization, transformed the population in a way that widened the potential base of social support for the Communist Party. Since the Revolution, Party leaders had agonized over their predicament as Marxist rulers of an overwhelmingly peasant country. They hoped and even declared that industrialization would promote "the socialist transformation of the peasant."[4] The millions of peasants who joined the industrial workforce during the 1930s seemed to offer them the cadres they needed to create a large, politically supportive proletariat.

To pursue this opportunity, Party leaders initiated extensive political and cultural education programs to transform the newcomers from recalcitrant peasants into loyal workers. Some of these programs resembled the efforts of nineteenth-century Western European capitalists to inculcate punctuality, sobriety, cleanliness, and labor discipline in new industrial workers. Soviet ideology, of course, remained antithetical to capitalism. Whereas the bourgeoisie in Western Europe had envisioned a fully competitive, individualist world of private property and laissez-faire economics, Communist Party leaders championed a state-run, state-controlled economy, ruled by the Party in the interests of the workers and drawing upon their unanimous support. Workers of the new generation were to be taught, in the words of one Moscow Party secretary, "to shoulder all the burdens of organizing socialism."[5]

Yet the peasants who entered Soviet industry, like the newly pro-

[2.]Frank Lorimer, *Population of the Soviet Union* (Geneva, 1946), pp. 149–150; Robert A. Lewis and Richard H. Rowland, *Population Redistribution in the USSR* (New York, 1979), p. 214; Eugene M. Kulischer, *Europe on the Move* (New York, 1948), p. 107.

[3]A. I. Vdovin and V. Z. Drobizhev, *Rost rabochego klassa SSSR, 1917–1940 gg.* (Moscow, 1976), p. 97; R. P. Dadykin, "O chislennosti i istochnikakh popolneniia rabochego klassa SSSR (1928–1937 gg.)," *Istoricheskie zapiski* no. 87 (1971), pp. 46–49.

[4]*Torgovo-promyshlennaia gazeta*, November 9, 1926, as quoted in Anne D. Rassweiler, *The Generation of Power: The History of Dneprostroi* (New York, 1988), p. 55.

[5]MPA f. 634, op. 1, d. 221, l. 53.

letarianized workers in nineteenth-century Western Europe, resisted official ideology and drew upon their preindustrial culture and traditions to develop an alternative vision and understanding of the world.[6] When they migrated to the city, peasants brought with them village forms of organization and community, task-oriented work habits, their own modes of cultural expression, and an attitude of circumspection toward authority. Through this alternative culture and worldview, former peasants in the city resisted Party leaders' efforts to fashion industrial society according to the state's needs and the Party's ideology.

Party and government functionaries recognized that new workers of peasant origin did not share their vision or agenda, and labeled them "backward" workers who had not yet achieved political consciousness.[7] One commentator complained that former peasants "do not know the love of a worker for his factory."[8] Underlying these assessments was the ideologically based assumption that peasants who moved to the city and began work in industry would necessarily become model proletarians once they attained full "political consciousness" (defined by Party leaders as support for the Soviet state).

Since the Marxist-Populist debates of the 1880s, Russian thinkers had pondered the true identity of peasants who entered the urban workforce. According to Populist scholars and publicists, Russian workers of peasant origin continued to own land and maintain families in their native villages, engaging in industrial work only to supplement their earnings in agriculture. As a result, they retained a peasant mentality and social identity despite the time they spent in the city.[9] Marxists, in contrast, argued that workers from the countryside inexorably shed their rural ways and became genuine proletarians.

[6]E. P. Thompson, *The Making of the English Working Class* (New York, 1963), p. 194. On resistance to industrial capitalist ideology in developing countries, see Frederick Cooper, ed., *Struggle for the City: Migrant Labor, Capital, and the State in Urban Africa* (Beverly Hills, Calif., 1983), pp. 17, 29.

[7]TsGAOR f. 5469, op. 15, d. 4, l. 45; *Sputnik kommunista* 1930 no. 6, pp. 50–51; S. E. Chaiko, *Kak vesti kul'trabotu sredi stroitelei* (Moscow, 1930), p. 3; A. Khain and V. Khandros, *Kto oni—novye liudi na proizvodstve?* (Moscow, 1930), pp. 3–4.

[8]L. Gan, *V zavodskom kotle* (Leningrad, 1930), p. 47.

[9]V. P. Vorontsov, *Sud'by kapitalizma v Rossii* (St. Petersburg, 1882), pp. 30, 310–311; N. A. Karyshev, "Russkaia fabrichno-zavodskaia promyshlennost' v 1885–1891," *Russkoe bogatstvo*, November 1894, pp. 3–4.

Their studies indicated that mechanized production and the division of labor, as well as the "fascination of life in the city," served to alienate former peasants from the land and allowed them to develop a proletarian consciousness and identity.[10]

To move beyond the confines of the Marxist-Populist debate, it is important to avoid discussion of peasants and workers as reified social types, and to discard the assumption that they represented successive stages on some evolutionary path. Peasants who moved to the city did not remain rural prototypes, and they did not become model workers. Nor did they constitute a hybrid form, the peasant-worker, existing somewhere on a continuum between ideal types.[11] The variegated world of peasant in-migrants encompassed both the village and the city, and their sense of social identity was accordingly complex and variable. Moreover, the urban environment they entered was itself constantly changing (in part because of their massive influx) and presented no stable, unadulterated urban culture to which they could assimilate.[12] Peasants who migrated to the city drew upon elements of both peasant and urban culture, taking from each the parts that best corresponded to their needs and experiences, to reach an understanding of the world that gave meaning to their new surroundings.

To investigate the social identity of these new city dwellers, it is necessary to examine the migration process as a whole. The character of rural-to-urban migration depended on the reasons peasants left the village and the means by which they located work and housing in the city, and these factors in turn influenced the experiences and outlooks of the peasants who made this transition. Had Soviet authorities regulated in-migration, they would have exercised control over which peasants left the village, what cities they settled in, and where they

[10]Mikhail Tugan-Baranovsky, _The Russian Factory in the Nineteenth Century,_ Arthur and Claora Levin, trans. (Homewood, Ill., 1970), pp. 299–307, 356–361, 410 (quoting studies of Dement'ev and Zhbankov); Georgii Plekhanov, _Selected Philosophical Works,_ vol. 1 (Moscow, 1977), pp. 235–236.

[11]Semen Ivanovich Kanatchikov, _A Radical Worker in Tsarist Russia: The Autobiography of Semen Ivanovich Kanatchikov,_ Reginald E. Zelnik, ed. (Stanford, 1986), p. xviii.

[12]See Janet Abu-Lughod, "Migrant Adjustment to City Life: The Egyptian Case," in _Arab Society in Transition,_ Saad Eddin Ibrahim and Nicholas S. Hopkins, eds. (Cairo, 1977), p. 392.

found employment. Had in-migration been a chaotic process that up-rooted peasants from their villages and thrust them unprepared into an urban environment, then disorientation and social dysfunction might have resulted.[13]

Instead migration traditions and village networks guided peasants to the city and eased their transition to urban life. These traditions and networks determined patterns of employment and settlement, per-petuated village-based associations and elements of peasant culture, and continued to inform in-migrants' worldview and social identity. Only through an examination of the process of in-migration and the particular conditions of Soviet industrialization is it possible to iden-tify features of peasant culture (in partial or metamorphosed form) which provided new city dwellers with a basis for understanding the city and the place they occupied in it.[14]

It would be impossible, however, to deduce social identities solely from an objective description of in-migration and the urban envi-ronment. One must also consider what may be termed the politics of social identity. Soviet authorities in particular, but also technical elites and established workers, categorized new workers and pre-scribed the identities and behaviors they wished them to adopt. Even as they drew upon peasant culture, first-generation city dwellers were obliged to define themselves in relation to the people and social hier-archies they encountered in the city, and in relation to the definitions Soviet authorities sought to impose upon them.

Because systems of classification construct societal reality as much as they express it, social categories become crucial stakes in any political struggle.[15] The degree to which the new arrivals established

---

[13]Nineteenth-century Western European sociologists characterized peasants in cities as uprooted, alienated, and prone to irrational violence—an assessment that allowed authorities to dismiss the legitimacy of urban unrest and to use repressive measures against it. More recent studies have demonstrated, on the contrary, that tradi-tions of migration and kinship networks eased the transition for peasants who moved to Western European cities. See Charles Tilly, "The Chaos of the Living City," in *An Urban World*, Tilly, ed. (Boston, 1974), pp. 88, 91–95.

[14]Lynn Lees, *Exiles of Erin: Irish Migrants in Victorian London* (Ithaca, 1979), pp. 16, 170–191; John Bodnar, *The Transplanted: A History of Immigrants in Urban America* (Bloomington, Ind., 1985), pp. 208–209.

[15]See Pierre Bourdieu, *In Other Words: Essays toward a Reflexive Sociology*, Matthew Adamson, trans. (Stanford, 1990), p. 134.

social identities and understandings of the world different from those prescribed by Soviet authorities therefore held great significance for the Soviet system that took shape in the 1930s. The fact that these former peasants refused to accept the concept of a working-class state and their role as loyal proletarians serving that state thwarted the efforts of Party leaders to construct a social and political order that corresponded to their Marxist-Leninist ideology. Peasant in-migrants' alternative constructions of social identity, divergent value systems, and rejection of official goals and myths provoked conflicts with Soviet authorities, who responded with further coercive measures and eventually were obliged to make ideological retreats and accommodations.

Implicit negotiation and struggle between former peasants and Soviet officials helped to shape important aspects of the emerging Soviet order, including the parameters of public behavior, the spheres of public and private, gender roles, the rights and obligations of various social groups, the expected functions of government, and forms of political expression and activity. Of course interaction between new workers and Soviet authorities was only part of this process by which the Soviet system took shape during the 1930s. Other social groups also interacted with one another and with Soviet officialdom, itself divided into various Party, police, and bureaucratic agencies, each with its own priorities and methods. The pace of the industrialization drive, the levels of coercion employed to mobilize resources and to fight purported class enemies, the hostile international environment, Russian traditions of political authoritarianism, and Party leaders' own predilections and practices all contributed to the character of what became Soviet socialism. This book focuses primarily on Soviet officials' efforts to delineate the social identity of peasant in-migrants and the resistance of these former peasants as they continued to draw upon their preindustrial traditions, networks, and culture.

Moscow, as the nation's capital and its largest industrial center, offered a wide range of employment opportunities for new workers. It was also a city rich in institutions and traditions—churches, peasant markets, shop-floor culture, and migration networks—that predated the Soviet industrialization drive and continued to influence and shape events and behaviors during the immense changes of the 1930s. In this respect, Moscow and other established cities may be contrasted with the new Soviet cities built in the 1930s, which lacked any preexisting structures.[16]

Moscow was among the fastest-growing urban areas during the historical period that began with collectivization and industrialization in 1929 and ended with the Nazi invasion of the Soviet Union in 1941. Its growth was particularly rapid during the First Five-Year Plan, when its population increased from 2.2 million to 3.7 million. In the span of only two years, 1931 and 1932, the number of Moscow residents grew by nearly one million. The rate of peasant in-migration slackened somewhat during the Second and Third Five-Year plans, and consequently the city's population rose less rapidly—to 4.1 million by 1939.[17] When the growth of Moscow's suburbs during the 1930s is taken into account, the metropolitan area absorbed roughly 2 million peasants and increased its population to 4.5 million by the end of the decade.[18]

Moscow's workforce expanded in tandem with the industrialization drive and with the city's overall development. The number of industrial workers jumped from 186,500 to 433,900 during the First Five-Year Plan, and reached 614,000 by the end of the Second Five-Year Plan. During the Third Five-Year Plan the size of the industrial workforce hardly changed, though military mobilizations necessitated recruitment of new workers to replace those drafted into the armed forces.[19] Sixty-eight percent of all new industrial employees during the First Five-Year Plan were peasants. For the remainder of the decade slightly over half of all newly recruited employees

[16]Soviet officials may have exercised more power in the new cities simply because fewer alternative traditions existed to compete with state authority. See Stephen Kotkin, "Magnetic Mountain: City Building and City Life in the Soviet Union in the 1930s: A Study of Magnitogorsk" (dissertation, University of California, Berkeley, 1988).

[17]TsGAORgM f. 126, op. 10, d. 47, l. 16. While in-migration accounted for the great bulk of population growth, natural increase accounted for 18 percent of Soviet urban growth in the 1930s. See Michael F. Hamm, "The Modern Russian City: An Historiographical Analysis," *Journal of Urban History* 4 no. 1 (1977), pp. 53–54.

[18]Municipal authorities annexed little new territory during the 1930s, so the enormous growth of Moscow's suburbs did not register in Moscow's official population. See O. A. Konstantinov, "Geograficheskie razlichiia v dinamike gorodskogo naseleniia SSSR," *Izvestiia Vsesoiuznogo Geograficheskogo Obshchestva* 1943 no. 6, p. 12; *Vsesoiuznaia perepis' naseleniia, 1937 g.* (Moscow, 1991), pp. 70–71.

[19]See Appendix I.

were peasants, as urban women filled part of the demand for industrial labor.[20]

It is helpful to put rural-to-urban migration of the 1930s into
the broader chronological context of Russian and Soviet industrialization. Collectivization and peasant in-migration ended the long-
standing gulf between urban and rural Russia, between urban society
and officialdom on one side and the vast mass of peasants on the other.
This gulf had predated the Revolution, and though tsarist authorities
and educated elites had identified peasant autarky as a problem, they
had never agreed on a program to integrate peasants into the country's larger political and economic structures. Much of the provincial
nobility opposed the industrialization drive of the 1890s as well as
other efforts to modernize the country and its population.

After the 1917 Revolution, both the gulf between urban and rural
Russia and the problems of underdevelopment persisted. Once again
there was little agreement within the ruling elite or society as a whole
regarding the pace and course of industrialization, though the Communist Party was certainly more committed to modernization than
the tsarist nobility had been. The fact that Party leaders ultimately extended administrative control over the peasantry and industrialized
the country very suddenly and coercively meant that the Soviet order
formed in the 1930s was not based on broad societal consensus and
did not result in a high level of social and political integration.

With the launching of the First Five-Year Plan (in the last quarter
of 1928 for selected branches of industry and in January 1929 for the
economy as a whole), the Soviet Union embarked upon a crash industrialization drive, characterized by "bacchanalian" planning and
ruthless administrative measures.[21] The optimal variant of the original First Five-Year Plan called for a 77 percent increase in industrial
output, and in late 1929 plan targets were revised upward to call
for a 145 percent increase, to be accomplished in not five years but
four.[22] Such unrealistic targets resulted in enormous disorganization,

[20]*Izmeneniia sotsial'noi struktury sovetskogo obshchestva 1921–seredina '30-kh
godov* (Moscow, 1979), p. 199; Vdovin and Drobizhev, pp. 115–116; Dadykin, pp. 46–49.

[21]See Hiroaki Kuromiya, *Stalin's Industrial Revolution: Politics and Workers, 1928–
1932* (New York, 1988), pp. 17–23.

[22]Alec Nove, *An Economic History of the USSR* (New York, 1982), p. 190. See also
Naum Jasny, *Soviet Industrialization, 1928–1952* (Chicago, 1961).

shortages, and human suffering. They also promoted ever-increasing administrative pressure and the widening use of police coercion to compel the sacrifices required of the population.

Party leaders forced not only the pace of industrialization but its direction: they promoted heavy industry and prohibited private property and free markets. Party ideology opposed the capitalist ventures and profit taking of a market economy. More fundamentally, the First Five-Year Plan called for levels of investment simply irreconcilable with market relations. The administrative-command system marshaled resources and quadrupled the level of investment in industry without the benefit of foreign loans or overseas colonies (indeed, carrying out industrialization "in one country").[23]

Much of the First Five-Year Plan was devoted simply to construction. Huge new plants sprouted in Moscow and existing factories were expanded to double or triple their original size. Overambitious planning, however, led to countless malfunctions and hardships. Economic disorder and decline became especially severe in the summer of 1930 as the available raw materials, labor, and capital fell far short of the levels dictated by the plan. Industrial stoppages and low-quality production resulted.[24] A special campaign at the end of 1930 succeeded in overcoming this economic downturn, but it was followed at the end of the First Five-Year Plan by a much more serious crisis, centered on agriculture. The collectivization of agriculture, like the command economy as a whole, served to mobilize resources, but collectivization and forced requisitioning of grain led to a grievous famine in several regions of the country by 1932–33. Industry also entered a year of crisis at this time, as economic growth slowed nearly to a standstill. Officials declared the First Five-Year Plan to be complete at the end of 1932, but in reality many production goals had not been met, and Party leaders felt compelled to moderate the rate of industrialization.

[23]The share of Soviet national income reinvested in industry in the 1920s never surpassed 10 percent; as in most societies, over 90 percent went for consumption. In 1930 the share of national income reinvested climbed to 29 percent, and in 1932 it reached 44 percent. See L. A. Gordon and E. V. Klopov, *Chto eto bylo? Razmyshleniia o predposylkakh i itogakh togo, chto sluchilos' s nami v 30–40e gody* (Moscow, 1989), pp. 52–68.

[24]R. W. Davies, *The Soviet Economy in Turmoil, 1929–1930* (Cambridge, Mass., 1989), pp. 370–372.

The Second Five-Year Plan set much more reasonable goals for industrial growth. By 1933 most construction had been completed, so planners concentrated on bringing factories into production and getting workers to master the technology already in place. The result of these efforts proved quite favorable, as productivity grew and industrial output increased substantially during the "good" industrial years 1934–36.[25] The Second Five-Year Plan also allowed for a rise in the living standard. As planned levels of reinvestment became more moderate, a greater proportion of national income went for consumption. The moderate industrial policies of the Second Five-Year Plan were eventually interrupted in late 1935 by the Stakhanovite movement, which substituted record mania and political pressure for rationalized and systematic production.[26]

Far more disruptive than Stakhanovism to normal industrial and societal functioning were the Great Purges of 1936–38. The arrest and execution of countless officials, engineers, and workers left a legacy of fear and distrust that lingered well into the Third Five-Year Plan.[27] This plan (1938–41) was further hampered by military mobilization. Soviet leaders devoted ever-greater resources to military production, and the armed forces doubled in size. The living standard consequently began to fall once again, and severe shortages of consumer goods became common by 1940. The prewar five-year plans overall increased steel and weapons production enormously, while the manufacture of consumer goods lagged well behind.[28]

Industrialization undeniably augmented Soviet military power, but its impact on society and its implications for the country's political unity were far more questionable. Party leaders considered industrialization an integral part of building socialism, and indeed the peasant in-migration that accompanied industrialization offered them the opportunity to create a large proletariat on which the socialist order could be based. In this sense the 1930s represented a moment of truth for the Bolshevik Revolution—a Marxist revolution in an overwhelmingly peasant country. But did the Soviet system transform

---

[25]Donald Filtzer, *Soviet Workers and Stalinist Industrialization: The Formation of Modern Soviet Industrial Relations, 1928–1941* (New York, 1986), pp. 126–128.

[26]Lewis H. Siegelbaum, *Stakhanovism and the Politics of Productivity in the USSR, 1935–1941* (New York, 1988), pp. 76–84.

[27]See O. V. Khlevniuk, "1937 god: Protivodeistvie repressiiam," *Kommunist* 1989 no. 18.

[28]Nove, pp. 228–229, 257–260.

the peasants, or did peasants transform the Soviet system? The confrontation in the 1930s between Soviet officialdom and the mass of peasant in-migrants forced each party to reach accommodations with the other.

Nowhere was interaction between urban officials and former peasants more intense than in Moscow. As the Soviet capital, Moscow represented an important symbol of socialism and socialist achievement. Stalin and other Party leaders took a personal interest in the city's industrial and urban development, and the heavy concentration of Party functionaries, economic planners, and government bureaucrats intensified official efforts to reshape not just the city but also the 2 million peasants who became its new residents. Yet while the ruling elite controlled all ideological resources and wielded enormous political power, it soon discovered the limits of directed social transformation. Peasant in-migrants had means with which to resist official attempts to define their identity and behavior. Generations of peasant migration to Moscow had established village networks and urban settlement patterns that authorities could not easily reverse. Former peasants drew on these migration traditions as well as on peasant culture and its modes of passive resistance to blunt the efforts of Soviet officials to control them. The extent to which they formulated their own social identity and thwarted official efforts to fashion a loyal working class figured prominently in the formation of the Soviet system and its level of political cohesion and stability.

1

Moscow and
Its Hinterland

Evgenii Mikhailovich and other new arrivals during the 1930s were of course not the first peasants to migrate to Moscow. Peasants had been moving to Moscow for centuries, and the tide had swelled in the late imperial period. A peasant named Semen Ivanovich Kanatchikov, who moved to Moscow in 1895, shared many characteristics with Evgenii Mikhailovich. He too came from a village not far from Moscow, initially felt overwhelmed by the size and bustle of the city, relied on the help of a fellow villager to secure a job, and eventually became a well-paid metalworker. Yet ultimately Kanatchikov's fate was very different from that of first-generation workers of the 1930s. He became involved in revolutionary activity, joined the Bolshevik Party, suffered arrest and exile, and after 1917 became a Soviet official of high standing.[1]

Similarities and differences between peasant in-migrants of the 1890s and the 1930s reflect both continuity and change in Moscow's history. In addition to long-standing traditions of peasant migration, Moscow possessed a rich legacy of associations and social networks, economic structures and institutions, and political conflicts and revolutions. Though it is impossible even to summarize this legacy here, it is important to describe certain aspects of it, particularly those that pertain to peasant in-migration and working-class formation.

[1] See Kanatchikov.

The Prerevolutionary Period

Moscow was the center of the oldest industrial area of the Russian empire—the Central Industrial Region, which included Moscow province and the provinces immediately surrounding it. The distinctive rural economy of this region shaped the experiences and perspectives of the peasants who lived there. Flax and vegetables were extensively grown in the region, and because cultivation of these crops was considered women's work, male peasants were free to take nonagricultural jobs.[2] The large amounts of land devoted to potatoes and other vegetables especially in Moscow province reflected the proximity of a large urban market for these products. Extensive commercial agriculture based on the marketing of produce in Moscow existed from at least the eighteenth century, and continued to prosper throughout the prerevolutionary period and into the 1920s.[3] Peasants who traded at urban markets were shaped by their experiences—travel to the city and commercial exchange became familiar to them well before many of them would move permanently to Moscow in the 1930s.

Equally important in villages of the Central Industrial Region was nonagricultural production. The rural economy had never been purely agricultural, because peasants had always constructed their homes, repaired their tools, and made their clothing. Cottage industry in its most rudimentary forms—processing flax, weaving cloth, and carving wood—had been prevalent in Russia from the Middle Ages. Peasants developed cottage industry to an especially high level in the Central Industrial Region, because its poor soil made agriculture less productive there than in other regions. Over 90 percent of peasant households in Moscow province in 1899 reported one or more members employed in nonagricultural labor. Peasants produced glass beads, buttons, abacuses, wooden utensils, straw hats, gloves, boots, spectacle frames, clocks, and furniture. As these skills were passed down from one generation to the next, an entire stratum of artisans and

[2]Iu. P. Bokarev, *Biudzhetnye obsledovaniia krest'ianskikh khoziaistv 20-kh godov kak istoricheskii istochnik* (Moscow, 1981), p. 209.

[3]*Moskovskii kraeved* 1930 no. 5 (13), p. 56; Bokarev, pp. 228–229; N. M. Sazonova, *Kuda idet derevnia (po pis'mam krest'ian Moskovskoi gubernii)* (Moscow/Leningrad, 1928), p. 126.

handicraft laborers developed in the villages of the Central Industrial Region.[4]

Specialization developed over time, as peasants of certain villages or regions concentrated on particular handicraft industries. In one district of Tver province literally thousands of peasants made shoes, while in another (a district with several lakes) a sizable percentage were either blacksmiths or fishermen. In yet another district, peasant artisans specialized in the manufacture of knives, locks, and other small metal implements. Peasants in Moscow province displayed similar specialization by district and village.[5]

Peasants of the Central Industrial Region also benefited from opportunities to work in rural factories. Small factories and workshops in rural areas of Moscow province dated from the eighteenth century, and textile mills spread throughout several provinces during the nineteenth century.[6] Located often simply at the ends of rail spurs, these mills became the centers of industrial villages. Peasants around them continued to own and cultivate land, while some members of their households worked part of the year in the mill.

Industry in Moscow itself dated from the early eighteenth century, when Peter the Great first constructed factories there. In contrast to factories in Western Europe, these enterprises were manned by serfs, who remained legally bonded to their lord and to the land in their native villages despite the fact that they worked in Moscow. Some serfs were assigned to specific factories by their lords; others received permission to leave on their own and seek work in Moscow. Serfs who worked in the city were required to return home periodically and pay a large percentage of their earnings to their owners as quit-rent (obrok).[7] The urban status of Moscow factory workers remained

[4]V. P. Danilov, "Krest'ianskii otkhod na promysly v 1920-kh godakh," *Istoricheskie zapiski* no. 94 (1974), p. 55; Judith Pallot and Denis J. B. Shaw, *Landscape and Settlement in Romanov Russia, 1613–1917* (New York, 1990), p. 219.

[5]A. M. Bol'shakov, *Derevnia, 1917–1927* (Moscow, 1927), pp. 74, 117–118; *Moskovskaia promyshlennaia kooperatsiia* 1931 no. 11, p. 1; S. V. Shol'ts, *Klassovaia struktura krest'ianstva Moskovskoi gubernii* (Moscow, 1929), pp. 22–24.

[6]*Moskovskii kraeved* 1930 no. 5 (13), pp. 70–73. One district (uezd) alone in Moscow province already had 46 rural brick factories in 1787 and 52 rural textile mills by 1853; by 1900, rural mills and factories totaled 290 in this district.

[7]Robert E. Johnson, *Peasant and Proletarian: The Working Class of Moscow in the Late Nineteenth Century* (New Brunswick, N.J., 1979), pp. 12–13.

quite tenuous before emancipation, for they could be recalled to the village at any time by their lords.

Even emancipation in 1861 did not free peasants from ties to their villages. As part of the emancipation settlement, peasants were made collectively responsible for taxes and land-redemption payments through the peasant commune. This arrangement continued to bind peasants to the land, because separation from the commune, though theoretically possible, proved very difficult in practice. Peasants who traveled to Moscow to perform wage labor were required to obtain passports from their commune and local officials. Passports would be renewed only if their holders returned regularly to contribute their share to the commune's tax and redemption payments.[8]

The prerevolutionary working class was therefore distinguished by its large proportion of members who were temporary migrants (*otkhodniki*)—peasants who worked in the city for several months or years but who maintained a family in the village, owned land there, and eventually returned there to retire. Temporary migrants also maintained village ties for nonjuridical reasons. Landownership provided a form of insurance for them. In case of unemployment or illness, they could always return to their native village. Many Moscow factory workers who had lived in the city over fifteen years continued to maintain a household in the village and ultimately retired there.[9]

The Stolypin land reform after the Revolution of 1905 provided a means for workers of peasant origin to break their ties to the village. As of 1917, however, 38 percent of Moscow industrial workers still preserved ties to the land.[10] The skill and wage levels of workers of peasant origin often determined the extent and character of their connections to the village. Those who earned high wages could afford to move their families to Moscow, but unskilled workers, less financially secure, generally held on to their land and left their families behind in the village.[11]

[8]Ibid., pp. 30–31.

[9]Ibid., pp. 40–42, citing studies of P. A. Peskov and E. M. Dement'ev.

[10]A. Ia. Grunt, *Pobeda oktiabr'skoi revoliutsii v Moskve* (Moscow, 1961), p. 16. See also A. G. Rashin, *Formirovanie rabochego klassa Rossii: Istoriko-ekonomicheskie ocherki* (Moscow, 1958).

[11]Victoria E. Bonnell, *Roots of Rebellion: Workers' Politics and Organizations in St. Petersburg and Moscow, 1900–1914* (Berkeley, 1983), pp. 54–55.

The overwhelming majority of peasants who joined the Moscow workforce traveled relatively short distances, and a large proportion of them came from Moscow province itself.[12] Statistics from the 1902 Moscow census indicate that even peasants who migrated from outside Moscow province tended to come from a very short distance beyond its border.[13] The regions from which they came generally had no rural factories to offer them opportunities for nonagricultural wage labor closer to home.[14]

In some villages, traditions of temporary migration (*otkhodnichestvo*) became so strong that virtually all young peasants went to Moscow to earn money. One peasant in the prerevolutionary period recalled:

> All the strong, healthy, and able fled the village to Moscow and got jobs wherever they could—some at the factory, others as domestics. Others turned into real entrepreneurs—the carrying trades, street vending, and so forth. All left—men, women, boys. . . . We eagerly awaited the time when we would be old enough to be fit for something in Moscow and when we could leave our native village and move there.[15]

During the 1890s, 14 percent of the rural population (over one-third of all adult male peasants) in the Central Industrial Region left their villages for temporary labor elsewhere.[16]

The peasants of a village or a district tended to cluster in a specific trade or factory in Moscow. One study revealed that over half of the workers in one Moscow mill in 1899 came from a single province, over one-fifth from a single district of that province. Other research showed that nine out of ten workers from one village became dye printers while five out of six from another became carpenters.[17]

[12]Joseph Bradley, *Muzhik and Muscovite: Urbanization in Late Imperial Russia* (Berkeley, 1985), p. 105.

[13]*Perepis' Moskvy, 1902 goda*, ch. I, vyp. 2 (Moscow, 1906), pp. 24–29.

[14]Johnson, *Peasant and Proletarian*, pp. 33–34.

[15]S. T. Semenov, *Dvadtsat' piat' let v derevne* (Petrograd, 1915), pp. 5–6, as quoted in Bradley, p. 130.

[16]Jeffrey Burds, "The Social Control of Peasant Labor in Russia: The Response of Village Communities to Labor Migration in the Central Industrial Region, 1861–1906," in *Peasant Economy, Culture, and Politics of European Russia*, Esther Kingston-Mann and Timothy Mixter, eds. (Princeton, 1991), p. 55.

[17]Johnson, *Peasant and Proletarian*, p. 69.

These clusterings resulted both from craft specializations, passed down from one generation to the next, and from village networks (*zemliachestvo*) that guided peasants to work sites in Moscow. Relatives and fellow villagers helped new arrivals find work in Moscow, often in the same trade or enterprise in which they were already working. These migration traditions and village networks, established over generations, continued to exert an important influence on peasant in-migration during the 1930s.

Industrialization (and consequently peasant in-migration) in the prerevolutionary period was most rapid during the 1890s. Moscow's population increased by 30 percent between 1890 and 1900. The size of Moscow's workforce grew by 50 percent in the course of the decade, and former peasants accounted for most of this growth. By 1902 the Moscow workforce numbered 429,000 workers, of whom 260,000 were employed in the manufacturing sector (in either factory or artisanal production).[18]

Unlike industrial expansion in St. Petersburg and the Donbass region, Moscow's economic growth was not primarily the result of state and foreign investment. Native Russian capital and management continued to predominate in Moscow, and light industry remained more important than heavy industry to the city's economy. One consequence of this pattern of development was a slower pace of technological innovation and more traditional styles of management. Another consequence was the continued presence of small-scale factories and workshops, which had characterized Moscow's economy since the early nineteenth century. Even as larger factories were built at the end of the century, these handicraft and semiartisanal operations continued to function alongside them. A sizable majority of Moscow's industrial workers in 1900 were employed in enterprises with fewer than 500 workers, and many of these enterprises were nonmechanized workshops.[19]

The most important sector of Moscow's prerevolutionary economy was the textile industry. Textile mills were the largest factories in the city and employed over 50,000 workers in 1902. A large percentage of textile workers were unskilled or semiskilled, and nearly half of all Moscow textile workers were women, who remained concen-

[18]Laura Engelstein, *Moscow, 1905: Working-Class Organization and Political Conflict* (Stanford, 1982), pp. 21–40.
[19]Johnson, *Peasant and Proletarian*, pp. 22–24.

trated in low-paying jobs.[20] The diversification of Moscow industry in the early twentieth century did not reduce the predominance of textile production. Even after the armaments industry expanded during World War I, textiles were still the largest branch of Moscow's industry, employing 37 percent of the industrial workforce, followed by metalwork and food processing.[21]

In contrast to textile manufacturing, the metal industry remained semiartisanal in its production process. Accordingly, its workers achieved much higher levels of skill than did textile workers, and most worked in small workshops. Only ten machine-building plants in Moscow employed more than 500 workers; 400 shops employing fewer than 100 workers formed the core of the metal industry. The printing industry, too, was concentrated in small shops and involved a variety of production tasks, most of which required high levels of skill.[22] Both metalworkers and printers usually acquired their skills through apprenticeships. The artisanal nature of production and the skill levels of the workforce in this period were in sharp contrast to the assembly-line production and low skill of workers in the 1930s.

Over half of Moscow's manual workers were employed in nonindustrial occupations. Tailors, furriers, cobblers, woodworkers, and so forth numbered as many as 55,000 by 1905. Moscow also had nearly 40,000 transportation workers (it was the major railroad hub of the country), as well as many workers in construction—a sector with a particularly large proportion of workers with ties to the village. Peasant women who migrated to Moscow in the prerevolutionary period often found jobs in domestic service. In 1912 some 100,000 domestic servants worked in Moscow, the great majority of them women of peasant origin. The service sector offered other employment opportunities as cooks, waiters, doorkeepers, and janitors, though the bulk of these jobs went to men.[23]

Moscow offered people an array of opportunities for wage income, but life there was hard. Workers often lived in slumlike housing, eight or more people crowded into one room. Conditions in factories and workshops were dismal and presented health hazards.[24] The low

[20]Engelstein, pp. 27–31; Bonnell, p. 30.
[21]Grunt, pp. 12–16.
[22]Engelstein, pp. 27–28, 35–36.
[23]Diane Koenker, *Moscow Workers and the 1917 Revolution* (Princeton, 1981), pp. 21–24, 41; Engelstein, pp. 20–22; Bonnell, pp. 40–43.
[24]Koenker, pp. 54–56, 69–70.

living standard and arduous employment conditions of workers in this period fueled considerable labor unrest in Moscow. Trade unions eventually helped to organize strikes and other forms of protest, but independent trade unions were legalized only during the 1905 Revolution. Before that time workers had to rely on informal modes of organization, which included the same village networks that guided peasants to Moscow. In some cases clusters of fellow villagers formed the nucleus of a strike movement, and in other cases village networks disseminated information about working conditions and protests.[25]

Major strike waves occurred in 1885–87, 1895–98, 1905–7, 1912–14, and 1916–17. Workers' grievances before 1905 focused primarily on wages and working conditions, but later strikes were increasingly called for political reasons (for example, to protest the Lena goldfields massacre).[26] The working class thus came to serve as a center not only of economic discontent but of political protest as well.

Before 1917 the legal category "worker" did not exist. Even people who had worked for years in Moscow factories remained part of the peasant estate (*soslovie*) and had to get their passports renewed annually in the village. Tsarist officials insisted that Russia had no working class, and that the people employed in urban factories remained peasants, as both their mentality and their ties to the village attested. Workers consequently had no legal place in urban society, and no right to participate in urban public life.[27]

The working class ultimately came to stand as a symbol of opposition to the tsarist regime. Revolutionary parties—in particular the Social Democrats—championed the working class and defined it as the class of political consciousness and revolutionary aspirations. Cooperation between the revolutionary intelligentsia and the working class was embodied in the councils (*sovety*) of workers' deputies that emerged in 1905 and were to assume great significance in the 1917 Revolution. Workers elected representatives to serve on district and citywide councils, and thereby gained the public voice denied them by the tsarist autocracy. These councils also served as important political forums where the revolutionary parties could debate and articulate their ideas.

In 1905 the Moscow working class, in alliance with a broad spectrum of other classes in urban society, participated in widespread

[25]Johnson, *Peasant and Proletarian*, p. 159.
[26]Ibid., pp. 124–141; Koenker, pp. 76–78.
[27]Engelstein, p. 7.

strikes and demonstrations. These actions, on the heels of the tsarist military's embarrassing defeat in the Russo-Japanese War, became
part of an "all-nation movement against autocracy." When protests
culminated in a general strike, Tsar Nicholas II was forced to issue the
October Manifesto, which conceded the freedoms of speech and assembly and provided for the creation of a national elected body. Police
repression continued, however, and undermined workers' political
participation and genuine democratic reform. The Revolution of 1905
culminated in an armed insurrection of Moscow workers and its brutal suppression by the tsarist army, which shelled workers' quarters
and barricades. The carnage and bitterness of this confrontation left
a legacy of extreme mistrust and antagonism between the working
class and the autocratic establishment.[28]

Several years of harsh political repression severely inhibited revolutionary activity after 1905. Yet the working class remained a symbol
of resistance to the autocracy, and revolutionary agitators and organizers focused most of their attention on urban workers. When the
autocracy again came under attack in 1917, the working class played
a leading role in the revolution that not only overthrew the old tsarist
political and social order but led to the establishment of Soviet power
and a "dictatorship of the proletariat" under the leadership of the Bolsheviks.[29] With the Bolshevik Revolution, workers no longer lacked
a legal place in urban society. On the contrary, they were enshrined
as its leading class—a privilege that they would be called upon to
defend during the bloody civil war that followed.

The Civil War and Deurbanization

The Civil War devastated Moscow's economy and with it the working class. Moscow's population dropped by almost one million between 1917 and 1920, and the number of workers in large Moscow
factories fell by half.[30] Thousands of workers volunteered for or were

[28]For more on the 1905 Revolution in Moscow, see Engelstein.

[29]For more on the 1917 Revolution in Moscow, see Koenker.

[30]Diane Koenker, "Urbanization and Deurbanization in the Russian Revolution and
Civil War," in *Party, State, and Society in the Russian Civil War*, Koenker et al., eds.
(Bloomington, Ind., 1989), p. 90; *Istoriia rabochikh Moskvy, 1917–1945 gg.*, A. M.
Sinitsyn, ed. (Moscow, 1983), pp. 88–90.

conscripted into the Red Army, and many others starved to death or died in epidemics. In addition to the workers lost to military service, starvation, and disease, a great number of workers with ties to the village, and even some who had broken their ties but still had relatives in the village, returned there during the Civil War in order to survive.

Enterprise closings and unemployment provided one reason for workers to return home. With the loss of territory and the deterioration of the transport system during the Civil War, Moscow factories could not obtain the raw materials or fuel they needed to continue production. Over one-third of all Moscow enterprises closed, and many others laid off workers and curtailed production. By 1920 factory production had declined to 15 percent of its 1913 level. Food shortages also forced workers to abandon Moscow. In 1919 the average daily bread ration dropped to only 80 grams. The Soviet government opened public and factory dining halls to ensure that scarce food supplies went to workers. But the priority workers received in food distribution and rationing was only relative in this period of extreme deprivation, and thousands of workers either fled the city or remained and starved.[31]

Economic collapse and food shortages led some 8 million temporary migrants throughout the country to return to their native villages. By 1920, when Moscow had lost over 40 percent of its 1917 population, the populations of some villages of the Central Industrial Region had doubled.[32] Deurbanization proved as disruptive to the countryside as to the city. When temporary migrants returned home, they brought with them a new outlook and new modes of behavior, and they proved less willing to accept traditional village ways and hierarchies.[33] They also commanded a degree of respect; their urban clothing in itself gave them prestige.

Millions of veterans, too, came back to the countryside after the Revolution. Fifteen million men, most of peasant origin, had served in the Russian army during World War I. As the army disintegrated in the course of 1917, these peasant veterans returned home, bringing new ideas with them. Service at the front and in cities had substantially

[31]William J. Chase, *Workers, Society, and the Soviet State: Labor and Life in Moscow, 1918–1929* (Urbana, Ill., 1987), pp. 17–20, 25.

[32]V. V. Kabanov, *Krest'ianskoe khoziaistvo v usloviiakh "voennogo kommunizma"* (Moscow, 1988), p. 214; Kulischer, p. 81.

[33]Danilov, "Krest'ianskii otkhod," p. 102; Bol'shakov, p. 421.

broadened their outlook. New sights, experiences, responsibilities, and power relationships all contributed to their new worldview. Upon their return to the village, many of these veterans, graced with some prestige and independence, scorned traditional deference to village elders and assumed leadership roles.

Conscription of young men during the Civil War and throughout the 1920s continued this process of temporarily placing peasants in the world outside their villages and then returning them there. At the height of the Civil War, the Red Army numbered 5 million soldiers, and throughout the 1920s it took in over half a million conscripts a year. Red Army studies indicated that though soldiers of peasant origin were at first guarded or hostile toward official institutions and the city in general, they also were intensely curious about urban life and proved eager to visit libraries, clubs, and especially stores. As early as 1923 the Red Army began warning soldiers that unemployment would prohibit them from settling in a city at the end of their military service—a clear indication that a good number wished to do so.[34] The warnings proved correct, and the mass of these veterans returned to their native villages, bringing their interest in new ideas with them.

The return of millions of temporary migrants and veterans accelerated the forces of change in the village and heightened the level of peasant discontent, even as interference by outside authorities there diminished. The majority of these returnees, having become accustomed to a degree of independence, rebelled against the traditional patriarchal authority of their elders.[35] Tensions stemming from patriarchal authority were not new to the village. The subordination of the younger generation to their elders and the resentments aroused by it had been part of the village order for centuries.[36] Nor did the Revolution precipitate a collapse of patriarchal authority. Throughout the 1920s male heads of household continued to exercise control

[34]Mark von Hagen, *Soldiers in the Proletarian Dictatorship* (Ithaca, 1990), pp. 127, 175, 298–300.

[35]Studies of other societies also reveal the growing prestige and independence of young peasants who have earned wages in the city. See Frances Rothstein, "The New Proletarians: Third World Realities and First World Categories," *Comparative Studies in Society and History* 1986 no. 2, pp. 218–224.

[36]During the late nineteenth century, young peasants in regions where *otkhodnichestvo* was common already began to defy their fathers' authority in marital and financial matters. See M. Kubanin, *Klassovaia sushchnost' protsessa drobleniia krest'ianskikh khoziaistv* (Moscow, 1929), pp. 42–46, 57.

over members of their family.[37] But with the sudden return of millions of veterans and temporary migrants, patriarchal authority came under challenge as never before. The social changes produced by this challenge foreshadowed the massive rural out-migration of the 1930s.

That most returnees refused to submit to traditional patriarchal control is demonstrated by changing household patterns. Russian peasants traditionally had lived in extended families, often three generations to a household. In the nineteenth and early twentieth centuries they began the transition to nuclear families, but so gradually that it had affected only a fraction of rural households by 1917.[38] The return of millions of veterans and temporary migrants greatly accelerated household divisions. A survey by the Central Statistical Administration in 1922 concluded that virtually every commune had allocated some land to returnees, and that two-thirds of these people set up their own households rather than move back with their parents.[39]

The breakup of the extended peasant family is reflected clearly in statistics on households. Peasant households in the Central Industrial Region numbered 2.6 million in 1916, 2.8 million in 1923. Divisions raised the number of households in one village from 65 in 1917 to 109 in 1923.[40] As the number of households increased, their average size decreased, a signal that household division (not population growth) caused this change. The average number of persons per peasant household dropped from 5.6 in 1916 to 5.3 in 1923.[41] The significance of this decrease assumes greater proportions when one considers the huge number of peasants away at the front in 1916. One would expect household size to increase upon their return, but it declined instead as households divided.

[37]Moshe Lewin, *Russian Peasants and Soviet Power* (New York, 1968), p. 25; V. P. Danilov, *Sovetskaia dokolkhoznaia derevnia: Naselenie, zemlepol'zovanie, khoziaistvo* (Moscow, 1977), p. 51.

[38]Lewin, pp. 83–84; Cathy A. Frierson, "Peasant Family Divisions and the Commune," in *Land Commune and Peasant Community in Russia*, Roger Bartlett, ed. (New York, 1990), pp. 309–311.

[39]Danilov, *Sovetskaia dokolkhoznaia derevnia* (1977), pp. 210–211; A. I. Khriashcheva, "Usloviia drobinosti krest'ianskikh khoziaistv," *Ekonomicheskoe obozrenie* 1928 no. 9, p. 98; *Moskovskaia derevnia v ee dostizheniiakh: Sbornik statei*, G. Lebedev, ed. (Moscow, 1927), p. 20.

[40]Kabanov, p. 224.

[41]Danilov, *Sovetskaia dokolkhoznaia derevnia* (1977), pp. 213–215.

Soviet law guaranteed every male peasant 18 years of age and older the right to a fair share of his family's property upon division of a household, even when the division was against the wishes of the family patriarch. Only in 1927, however, did a decree set down norms for the distribution of property in such cases. In practice this decree proved difficult to implement. Some patriarchs refused to relinquish any of their property, and some movable property (the household's only horse, for example) simply could not be divided.[42]

Even as returning veterans and temporary migrants obtained land through the seizure of noble land and communal repartition, their new households lacked basic tools and draft animals, a problem compounded by the loss of livestock during the recent wars.[43] In this sense, the leveling of the peasantry as a result of the redistribution of land during the Revolution turned out to be illusory. In 1926, one-third of peasant households in the Central Industrial Region had no livestock with which to work their fields.[44]

Large numbers of peasants, especially young couples who had just established new households, found it necessary to rent both draft animals and equipment in order to farm. Given the overall shortage of livestock and equipment, the rent could be quite high (up to one pood of grain per day for a horse), and the renters found themselves subjected to disdain and scorn by the peasants from whom they rented. Yet they dared not protest such treatment if they wished to rent again the next season. Some peasants found it necessary to trade their field land for a second garden plot, while others leased their land. Ultimately, many of the newly created households proved inviable.[45]

Both the influx of returnees and the division of households increased the number of peasants unable to support themselves through

---

[42]Ibid., pp. 253–259.

[43]*Istoriia krest'ianstva SSSR*, vol. 2, G. V. Sharapov and V. P. Danilov, eds. (Moscow, 1986), pp. 286, 328; Kabanov, p. 228.

[44]V. P. Danilov, *Sovetskaia dokolkhoznaia derevnia: Sotsial'naia struktura, sotsial'nye otnosheniia* (Moscow, 1979), p. 51; Lewin, *Russian Peasants*, p. 30. See also Ia. Dorofeev, *Derevnia Moskovskoi gubernii* (Moscow, 1923), p. 9.

[45]"Kollektivizatsiia: Istoki, sushchnost', posledstviia: Beseda za 'kruglym stolom,'" *Istoriia SSSR* 1989 no. 3, pp. 33–35; L. N. Kritsman, "O statisticheskom izuchenii klassovoi struktury sovetskoi derevni," *Na agrarnom fronte* 1926 no. 2, pp. 4–5; *Istoriia krest'ianstva SSSR*, vol. 1, p. 322, and vol. 2, p. 61; Orlando Figes, *Peasant Russia, Civil War: The Volga Countryside in Revolution* (New York, 1989), pp. 108, 136.

agriculture. A study of the central provinces of European Russia found severe overpopulation and estimated that 37.8 percent of peasant working hands there were superfluous to the needs of agriculture. Another study, conducted in 1925, concluded that 10 million surplus peasant working hands existed in the whole of the Soviet Union.[46] In a poll of temporary migrants conducted in 1928, an overwhelming percentage cited insufficient land and a lack of agricultural equipment as their motivation for seeking work in the city.[47]

Economic hardship provided a strong incentive for these peasants to leave the village. Former temporary migrants in particular regarded city life as a welcome alternative to rural poverty, and many of them wished to return to Moscow. But urban unemployment was so high in the 1920s that this was not always an option. Instead peasants of the young generation who returned from the army and the cities after the Revolution found themselves with no choice but to remain impoverished in the village, in the shadow of the older generation.

The City and the Village during NEP

Under the New Economic Policy (NEP), instituted in 1921, Moscow recovered rapidly from the devastation of the Civil War. By 1926 both its economy and its population had regained their prewar levels, with the population at just over 2 million.[48] Some temporary migrants who had spent the Civil War years in the countryside returned to their jobs in Moscow as enterprises resumed operation. Economic recovery, however, was somewhat uneven. Light industry, textiles in particular, recovered very quickly in the first half of the 1920s, while heavy industry lagged.[49]

Soviet officials strove to establish larger factories during the 1920s by combining some small enterprises and steering investment toward larger ones. These policies prefaced what became a massive trend in the 1930s, but a great many small enterprises still operated through-

[46]Danilov, "Krest'ianskii otkhod," p. 62.

[47]*Statisticheskoe obozrenie* 1928 no. 2, pp. 108–109.

[48]*Vsesoiuznaia perepis' naseleniia, 1926 goda* (Moscow, 1928–1933), vol. 8, pp. vi–x, 2–7.

[49]Chris Ward, *Russia's Cotton Workers and the New Economic Policy* (New York, 1990), pp. 11–12, 22–23.

out the 1920s. Before 1929, Moscow factories consisted primarily of small textile mills and a number of semiartisanal metal workshops. Only 10 percent of all Moscow workers were employed in enterprises with more than 3,000 workers.[50]

The types of industry in Moscow during NEP varied little from those of the prerevolutionary period. Up until the beginning of the First Five-Year Plan, textiles continued to be the leading branch of industry, though textile mills did not substantially increase the number of workers they employed in the late 1920s.[51] Metalwork stood as the other major branch of Moscow industry in the 1920s, and as before the Revolution, it was dominated by skilled male workers. Despite high skill levels, roughly a quarter of metalworkers owned farmland—a reflection of their peasant origins and ties to the village. In unskilled work such as construction and transport, the proportion of workers who retained ties to the land was even higher.[52]

The dimensions of Moscow industry in the entire course of the 1920s did not expand much beyond their prerevolutionary level. This lag in industrial growth led to severe urban unemployment and posed a serious barrier to peasant in-migration. In 1924 Soviet cities registered 1.3 million unemployed persons, of whom over one-quarter were temporary migrants from the countryside. Estimates of Soviet urban unemployment reached 2 million by 1927, and a majority of the unemployed were laborers of peasant origin.[53] Peasants who migrated to Moscow suffered disproportionately from unemployment, because they lacked the skills and trade union membership that helped established workers retain jobs even during periods of high unemployment. Compounding the problem was the fact that unemployment became particularly severe in the construction industry, a sector filled primarily by temporary migrants.[54] In growing numbers,

---

[50]*Ekonomiko-statisticheskii spravochnik po raionam Moskovskoi oblasti* (Moscow, 1934), vol. 2, pp. 12–13.

[51]*Istoriia Moskvy: Kratkii ocherk* (Moscow, 1974), p. 269.

[52]Chase, pp. 108–109.

[53]Danilov, "Krest'ianskii otkhod," pp. 104–105; *Na agrarnom fronte* 1927 no. 4, p. 38. See also Chase, pp. 86–88; A. I. Khriashcheva, "Drobinost' krest'ianskogo khoziaistva i differentsiia," *Ekonomicheskoe obozrenie* 1927 no. 6, p. 107.

[54]Pavel Maslov, *Perenaselenie russkoi derevni* (Moscow, 1930), p. 12. See also John B. Hatch, "Labor and Politics in NEP Russia: Workers, Trade Unions, and the Communist Party in Moscow, 1921–1926" (dissertation, University of California, Irvine, 1985), pp. 51–52.

peasants arriving in the city found no work and had to return to the village.[55]

Urban women and young men also suffered very high unemployment rates in Moscow, and even established male workers had little job security under NEP. Economic fluctuations and layoffs throughout the 1920s sparked considerable labor unrest, and all branches of industry and transport in Moscow experienced wildcat strikes.[56] Unemployment did not abate until 1929, with the launching of the First Five-Year Plan. Those peasants who did venture to Moscow in the 1920s followed the migration patterns of the prerevolutionary period. The overwhelming majority of construction workers in Moscow came from villages of the Central Industrial Region, with more from Moscow province than from any other.[57] Of those migrants lucky enough to find jobs, most worked in sectors that traditionally employed seasonal laborers—construction, logging, peat mining, water transport, carting, domestic service, food preparation, and miscellaneous unskilled work.[58]

Temporary migrants in Moscow during the 1920s worked varying fractions of the year. Those in construction and transport averaged six months, and those in domestic service averaged nine months. Twenty percent of temporary migrants who performed factory work were employed year round by 1925–26.[59] Furthermore, evidence suggests that some temporary migrants began breaking their ties to the village by the mid-1920s, and that increasing numbers of peasants moved with their entire families to Moscow.[60] At the end of the nineteenth century, men had outnumbered women in Moscow, and married men outnumbered married women. This population imbalance reflected the traditional pattern: the husband took a temporary job in the city

[55]*Statisticheskoe obozrenie* 1929 no. 2, pp. 97–100; I. Zhiga, *Novye rabochie* (Moscow, 1928), pp. 74–78.

[56]Chase, pp. 138–150; John B. Hatch, "The 'Lenin Levy' and the Social Origins of Stalinism: Workers and the Communist Party in Moscow, 1921–1928," *Slavic Review* 1989 no. 4, p. 561.

[57]L. E. Mints, *Agrarnoe pereselenie i rynok truda SSSR* (Moscow, 1929), pp. 328–334, 350–354; Danilov, "Krest'ianskii otkhod," p. 112.

[58]TsGAOR f. 5451, op. 12, d. 183, ll. 7–9; Mints, *Agrarnoe pereselenie*, pp. 342, 386–393.

[59]Mints, *Agrarnoe pereselenie*, pp. 320, 342.

[60]M. Krasil'nikov, "Sviaz' naseleniia g. Moskvy s nadel'noi zemlei," *Statisticheskoe obozrenie* 1928 no. 6, pp. 103–105; Chase, p. 123; Khriashcheva, "Usloviia drobimosti," pp. 97–98.

and the wife stayed in the village. But by 1926 the sex ratio was more even in both the city and the countryside, and the number of married persons living apart from their spouses declined.[61] Peasant couples had begun to move to Moscow with no intention of returning to the village.

Indeed, the number of peasants who wanted to make such a move was substantial. Not only did economic hardship in the village prod peasants to seek opportunities elsewhere, but the mass of temporary migrants forced to return to the village during the Civil War made up a large pool of peasants who had experienced the independence of urban life and longed to return to it. Yet severe unemployment in Moscow and other cities stood as an enormous obstacle to migration, and it worsened in the late 1920s. Many peasants who wished to leave their villages languished there throughout the decade.

The presence in the countryside of a large number of dissatisfied young people heightened rural tensions and fomented sentiment for change. The peasant commune, with its function of dividing land on an egalitarian basis, had played an important role in uniting peasants against the nobility during the Revolution, but after the nobility had fled the countryside, tensions once again surfaced.[62] Tensions within the commune mirrored those within peasant households: they arose between the generations and between peasants who had lived outside the village and those who had remained there. Traditionally, all decision-making authority for the commune was invested in the male elders, who alone participated in the commune assembly (*mirskii skhod*). Women and the younger men had no voice in village affairs.

During the 1920s, some peasants not traditionally eligible to participate attended the commune gathering anyway—a right guaranteed to everyone who worked the land by the Soviet Land Code of 1922. One woman, for example, attended the commune gathering, though no woman in her village had ever done so. Because she had learned what she termed "the proper political language" at Komsomol (Communist Youth League) meetings, she even dared to criticize and question the elders.[63] Many young men, too, having established their own house-

---

[61]Robert Johnson, "Family Life in Moscow during NEP," in *Russia in the Era of NEP*, Sheila Fitzpatrick et al., eds. (Bloomington, Ind., 1991), pp. 110–111.

[62]Figes, p. 59; Donald Male, *Russian Peasant Organization before Collectivization: A Study of Commune and Gathering, 1925–1930* (Cambridge, 1971), p. 20.

[63]*Rabotnitsa na sotsialisticheskoi stroike: Sbornik avtobiografii rabotnits*, O. N. Chaadaeva, ed. (Moscow, 1932), pp. 78–80.

holds, could now attend the commune gathering as heads of household. The village elders continued to hold sway, but the participation of others in the commune gathering challenged their authority.[64]

Groups of young peasants began to recognize certain common interests, such as those surrounding issues of land repartition and cultivation, that stood in opposition to the interests of commune elders.[65] This dissension and factionalism shattered the traditional belief that the commune was based on the essential unity and oneness of the peasantry. In operational terms, it also undermined the commune gathering's procedure for making decisions, which had always been reached through consensus. The rise of factions dispelled the notion that the commune gathering represented the interests and will of all peasants, and detracted from its legitimacy as the governing body.

Official Soviet institutions were established alongside the commune after the Revolution. Though rural councils (sel'sovety) remained weak throughout the 1920s, they did provide forums where malcontented peasants could challenge village elders. Returning veterans took the lead in establishing these councils in their villages and generally held the dominant positions in them.[66] Soviet authorities also encouraged participation by other groups traditionally excluded from the commune gathering, and the percentage of women and landless laborers who voted in elections to rural councils rose throughout the 1920s. Peasants who participated in Soviet rural councils did not necessarily support Party policies, but these institutions did offer them a new vehicle for political activity and a forum to articulate their dissatisfaction with the village order.[67]

Rural schools, despite their inadequate funding throughout the 1920s, were another important source of ferment in the village.[68] Whatever their shortcomings, schools at a minimum taught millions of peasant children to read and write. The growing number of literate peasants eroded village elders' authority of memory and parish

---

[64]Male, pp. 68–70.

[65]Sazonova, pp. 136–137.

[66]Figes, p. 145; Male, pp. 68–70.

[67]John Slatter, "Communes with Communists: The *Sel'sovety* in the 1920s," in *Land Commune and Peasant Community in Russia*, Roger Bartlett, ed. (New York, 1990), pp. 278–279. In 1923 only 11.2 percent of peasant women voted, but this figure rose to 28.0 percent in 1925–26 and 46.9 percent in 1929. See also Sazonova, pp. 70–76.

[68]Larry Gringlas, "Shkraby ne Kraby: Rural Teachers and Bolshevik Power in the Russian Countryside, 1921–1928" (master's thesis, Columbia University, 1987), pp. 7, 60–66.

priests' monopoly on written knowledge. As peasants learned to read
Soviet decrees and publications, elders and priests lost their exclu-
sive power to dictate laws and define the proper conduct of village
affairs. Peasants did not comprehend or believe everything they read,
but books and newspapers did bring them new ideas and information
about life outside the village.

Even young peasants who had not lived in the city absorbed the
feeling that rural life was somehow inferior. Peasant songs (*chastushki*) from the 1920s contained such lyrics as "Village things are not
in fashion" and "It has become cramped for me in my village." A
song about the undesirability of marrying into and living with a large
peasant family expressed a desire for independence:[69]

I won't join a family	Ne poidu v sem'iu takuiu
With twelve not counting me.	Gde dvenadtsat' bez menia.
I'll choose a family	Vyberu sem'iu takuiu
Where I'll be the boss!	Gde khoziaikoi budu ia!

New ideas and economic hardship combined to produce antivillage
sentiments among many young peasants. To them the city represented
an opportunity for escape, independence, cultural excitement, and
material wealth.

Of course, adulation of the city and disdain for the village were far
from universal. While some young peasants pined for the city, others
regarded urban life as hostile and decadent. Urban influence on the
countryside varied from one region or village to another. Villages on
railroad lines or with long traditions of sending inhabitants to the
city for seasonal labor naturally received a much stronger infusion
of urban culture than did villages more remotely located.[70] Because
the Central Industrial Region was more urbanized and industrialized
than other parts of the country, its peasants had more contact with
urban influences through temporary migration and the marketing of
produce in cities.

In sum, there was considerable ferment and stratification in Soviet

---

[69]*Chastushki*, L. A. Astaf'eva, comp. (Moscow, 1987), pp. 156, 162, 166. On young
peasants' desire to leave the village, see also Maurice Hindus, *Red Bread: Collectivization in a Russian Village*, Ronald G. Suny, ed. (Bloomington, Ind., 1988), pp.
159–160.

[70]Sazonova, pp. 38–44.

villages during the 1920s, though not necessarily along the class lines that Marxist scholars so eagerly portrayed at the time.[71] The split tended to come between generations, and between those peasants who had been away from the village (as soldiers or as temporary migrants) and those who had remained behind. The tensions this stratification produced could be severe; resentments resulting from economic hardship were compounded by feelings of rebellion among the younger peasants who had experienced the wider world.

Consequently, large numbers of peasants, particularly those with experience outside the village, eagerly awaited an opportunity to move permanently to the city. The severe urban unemployment that kept them at home in the 1920s, ended with the initiation of the First Five-Year Plan. When opportunities for urban employment burgeoned during the 1930s, 2 million peasants moved to Moscow, and they were well served by long traditions of temporary migration and extensive contact with urban life. Indeed, for those peasants who had spent time in Moscow doing seasonal labor, serving in the army, or marketing produce, the city was already part of their world. These experiences and traditions, especially prevalent among peasants of the Central Industrial Region, helped prepare them to become permanent residents of the city.

[71]See, for example, Kubanin; L. N. Kritsman, *Klassovoe rassloenie v sovetskoi derevne* (Moscow, 1926).

2

The Process
of In-migration

Evgenii Mikhailovich moved to Moscow in response to both deteriorating conditions in the countryside and job opportunities in the city.
After Soviet officials established a collective farm in his village, his
family's living standard declined sharply. Government grain procurements left them hungry and the virtual end of private farming left
them no opportunity to improve their situation. His uncle in Moscow wrote that factories there were hiring workers at high wages, and
within a year Evgenii Mikhailovich set off for a new life in the city.[1]
Ekaterina Evgenevna, another peasant who moved to Moscow in the
wake of collectivization, had little choice in the matter. During the
collectivization drive, Soviet officials deported her father and turned
the rest of her family out of their home. She and her mother took
the few belongings left to them and went to stay with relatives in
Moscow.[2]

The year 1929 brought sweeping changes to the Soviet Union. The
launching of the collectivization and industrialization drives fundamentally transformed the country's social and economic structures,
and precipitated permanent peasant migration to Soviet cities on a
massive scale. Several phenomena—dekulakization, official attempts
to control population movement, continuity of migration patterns, vil-

[1]Interview with Evgenii Mikhailovich Kostin at the Hammer and Sickle plant, Moscow, May 16, 1989.
[2]Interview with Ekaterina Evgenevna Semenova at Izmailovskii Park, Moscow,
July 25, 1992.

lage networks and artels—contributed to the migration experience as a whole and its influence on former peasants' thoughts and behavior as they settled permanently in Moscow.

Collectivization

In response to the grain crisis of 1927–28, the Soviet leadership ordered forcible requisitioning of grain from peasants, with the highest grain quotas and most severe taxes assigned to "kulak" households. Prosperous peasants responded by selling their equipment and livestock to avoid being labeled kulaks, and this process of self-dekulakization (*samoraskulachivanie*) greatly accelerated in the summer of 1929 as grain requisitions intensified. Many wealthy peasants sold everything and moved to the city, while others simply curtailed their agriculture and sent extra hands away for temporary employment in the city.[3] Rather than reestablish market incentives to grow grain, Soviet authorities viewed curtailment of agriculture as "kulak sabotage" and increased their coercive measures. At the November 1929 plenum of the Party's Central Committee, Viacheslav Molotov (then Central Committee secretary in charge of agriculture) announced the leadership's decision to launch all-out collectivization on a national scale.[4]

The all-out collectivization drive required a decision as to what should be done with the kulaks. Party leaders believed that kulaks would be sources of capitalist influence and hostility to Soviet power if they were allowed to join collective farms. Stalin resolved the matter in his speech to the conference of Marxist agronomists on December 27, 1929, when he announced the policy of "liquidation of the kulaks as a class."[5] On January 5, 1930, the Politburo adopted a resolution calling for the completion of collectivization in major grain-producing areas. The resolution offered no precise timetable

[3]"Kollektivizatsiia," p. 37; Danilov, "Krest'ianskii otkhod," pp. 192–193; Harvard Emigré Interview Project (Harvard University Russian Research Center, 1950) no. 643.

[4]R. W. Davies, *The Socialist Offensive: The Collectivization of Soviet Agriculture, 1929–1930* (Cambridge, Mass., 1980), pp. 399–408.

[5]Iosif V. Stalin, *Sochineniia* (Moscow, 1953), vol. 12, p. 170. Stalin declared, "Dekulakization represents a component part of the formation and development of collective farms. Therefore it is absurd and frivolous to expatiate now about dekulakization. When a head has been cut off, no one cries over the hairs."

or program for collectivization, leaving much to the discretion of local authorities, but in conjunction with Stalin's speech, it clearly established the basic goals and methods of the collectivization drive: dispossession of kulaks and the complete collectivization of agriculture.[6] The tempo adopted by local officials turned out to be extremely rapid; the proportion of all peasant households collectivized reached as high as 83 percent by March in some regions. Moscow province experienced one of the most rapid rates of collectivization despite the fact that it was not a major grain-producing region; there the share of households collectivized rose from a fraction at the beginning of the year to fully three-quarters by March 1.[7]

On January 30, 1930, the Politburo approved a resolution, "On Measures for the Elimination of Kulak Households in Districts of Complete Collectivization," which classified kulaks in the following three categories: (1) "counterrevolutionary activists," who were to be identified, fully dispossessed, and arrested by the secret police; (2) "remaining elements of kulak activists," who were to be dispossessed of all but personal items and deported to labor camps; (3) all remaining kulaks, who were to be dispossessed only of their means of production and allocated new land beyond the boundary of the collective farm.[8]

Statistics on the number of peasants who suffered dekulakization are not precise, but even rough figures give an idea of the multitude of victims. By the end of 1930, authorities had deported over half a million peasants and dispossessed without deporting another 1.5 million. These totals climbed to some 3.5 million in 1931, of whom at least 1.4 million were deported. A note from the secret police chief, Genrikh G. Iagoda, to Stalin in January 1932 stated that since 1929, 540,000 kulaks had been deported to the Urals, 375,000 to Siberia, over 190,000 to Kazakhstan, and over 130,000 to the far north.[9]

---

[6]This resolution specified that kulaks should not be admitted to collective farms, and that kulaks' means of production should be confiscated for use by the collective farms. Kulaks were to be allotted the worst and most distant land in the village, and "malicious kulak elements" were to be exiled from the districts entirely. See *Istochnikovedenie istorii sovetskogo obshchestva* (Moscow, 1964), pp. 285–287.

[7]Davies, *Socialist Offensive,* pp. 203–204. Other parts of the Central Industrial Region were not subjected to such an intense collectivization drive until a second wave of collectivization in 1931.

[8]Ibid., pp. 235–236.

[9]"Kollektivizatsiia," pp. 38, 44–45; Sheila Fitzpatrick, "The Great Departure: Rural-Urban Migration in the Soviet Union, 1929–1933," in *Social Dimensions of Soviet*

Dekulakization bred heinous excesses. Though collectivizers had authority to expropriate only the means of production of kulaks in the last two categories, they often took all belongings of everyone labeled a kulak, and dekulakization assumed the character of drunken looting. Food and alcohol found in the kulaks' homes were consumed on the spot. Collectivizers were reported to have ripped shirts off peasants' backs and "confiscated" hats off children's heads. Rather than transfer impounded property to the collective farm, many of them divided it among themselves.[10] Party reports further acknowledged that activists dispossessed some middle peasants along with those considered kulaks.[11]

Under such circumstances, huge numbers of peasants left the villages permanently in 1930 and 1931. The nearly 2 million peasants dispossessed but not deported had little choice but to seek work in cities. Some peasants slated for deportation managed to escape and also ended up in the city. A report from Smolensk province noted that officials sometimes allowed "tearful good-byes to be drawn out," and during the uproar many men slipped away. Wives and children of men arrested as first-category kulaks were to be deported later as second-category kulaks, but awareness of this danger gave them time to leave the village before they could be deported.[12]

Many other peasants escaped the village before collectivization brigades arrived. Between 200,000 and 250,000 peasant families (over a million people) fled before they were victimized, selling what they could and leaving the rest behind.[13] Such cases were particularly numerous in the Central Industrial Region, where (with the exception of Moscow province) the first wave of dekulakization in early 1930 claimed few victims but nonetheless served as a warning. Wealthy peasants had time to leave for the city before the next wave of dekulakization in 1931. Temporary migrants threatened by dekulakization

---

Industrialization, William Rosenberg and Lewis Siegelbaum, eds. (Bloomington, Ind., 1993), pp. 24–25. See also *Istoriia krest'ianstva*, vol. 2, p. 225; Davies, *Socialist Offensive*, pp. 412, 447.

[10]TsGAOR f. 5475, op. 13, d. 426, ll. 12–14; "Kollektivizatsiia," p. 43; Merle Fainsod, *Smolensk under Soviet Rule* (New York, 1958), pp. 245–246; *Ob''edinennaia IV Moskovskaia oblastnaia i III gorodskaia konferentsiia VKP (b)* (Moscow, 1934), p. 51.

[11]TsPA f. 17, op. 114, d. 314, l. 50.

[12]*Sudebnaia praktika RSFSR* 1931 no. 5, p. 8; Harvard Project nos. 449, 476; Fainsod, p. 248.

[13]*Pravda*, September 16, 1988 (V. P. Danilov and N. V. Teptsov), p. 3.

were particularly quick to liquidate their property in the village, because they already had jobs in the city.[14]

Soviet commentators noted in 1930 that many peasants who fled dekulakization joined the urban workforce.[15] Dispossessed peasants had few other options. Deprived of their livestock and agricultural equipment, and often of their personal belongings as well, they could not continue farming. As class enemies, they were not permitted to join the collective farms. A few such peasants trekked to other villages or to state collective farms to work, but almost invariably local officials identified and expelled them.[16] Especially for peasants of the Central Industrial Region, many of whom had urban experience, the best option was to move to Moscow, where labor-short managers hired them without questions about their class background.

Collectivization naturally affected peasants temporarily working in the city as well, because it threatened their families and property in the village. Although in the long term they found collectivization to be a reason to remain in the city, many temporary migrants rushed back to the village when they heard about the collectivization drive, apprehensive about their families' welfare and fearful of being left out of any property settlement.[17] The fantastic rumors that circulated at construction sites—war was imminent, emergency measures were going into effect, women and children were to be socialized—lent urgency to the temporary migrants' rush for home.[18]

A small number of returnees volunteered to stay and act as collective farm administrators.[19] The vast majority of them, however, went back to the city with confused or outright hostile feelings about collectivization. At meetings of Moscow construction workers in the spring of 1930, workers of peasant origin asked: What will living

[14]MPA f. 432, op. 1, d. 49, l. 107.

[15]TsPA f. 17, op. 114, d. 314, l. 58; MPA f. 468, op. 1, d. 155, l. 207; f. 634, op. 1, d. 207, l. 60; *Sputnik kul'trabotnika sredi sezonnikov* (Moscow, 1930), pp. 20–21; Gan, pp. 40–41, 43; TsGAMO f. 4867, op. 1, d. 156, l. 22.

[16]Harvard Project no. 148; Fainsod, pp. 302–303.

[17]*Puti industrializatsii* 1930 no. 15/16, p. 32. See also Nobuaki Shiokawa, "The Collectivization of Agriculture and *Otkhodnichestvo* in the USSR, 1930," *Annals of the Institute of Social Sciences* (University of Tokyo) 1982–83 no. 24.

[18]TsGAMO f. 4867, op. 1, d. 156, l. 10; V. D. Fedorov, "Formirovanie rabochikh kadrov na novostroikakh pervoi piatiletki" (dissertation, Gorky State University, 1966), p. 90.

[19]TsGAOR f. 5475, op. 13, d. 276, ll. 20–21; *Sputnik kul'trabotnika*, p. 21. See also TsGAOR f. 5475, op. 13, d. 276, l. 16; d. 426, l. 15; f. 5469, op. 14, d. 44, l. 56; op. 15, d. 10, l. 141.

conditions be like on the collective farm? What will happen to a Komsomol member if his parents refuse to join the collective farm? Where did the kulaks disappear to? How are workers who own land in the village regarded?[20] One temporary migrant proposed the following resolution at a Moscow construction workers' trade union meeting in March 1930: "All of us will hurry as one to join the collective farm when all urban workers convert to a socialist way of life—refusing individual apartments, building communal homes, showing us an example. Then we too will collectivize."[21]

Soviet officials launched a propaganda campaign to allay temporary migrants' fears of collectivization. A report of the Moscow transport workers' union in June 1930 noted with alarm temporary migrants' "great dissatisfaction" with the Party's policy on collectivization, and called for lectures and discussions to justify the liquidation of the kulaks and to explain laws concerning collective farms.[22] The Moscow Party organization also arranged numerous lectures and question-and-answer sessions for new workers (with ties to the village) which outlined the tasks of collectivization.[23] Party and union officials hoped that such propaganda would not only defuse animosity toward the Soviet government but win converts who might support collective farms upon their return home.

When rapidly mounting unrest in the countryside threatened to jeopardize the 1930 spring planting, Stalin published his article "Dizzy with Success: Problems of the Collective Farm Movement," calling for a return to the principle of voluntary collectivization and denouncing the immediate socialization of all livestock.[24] Peasants responded by quitting the collective farms in droves. As of March 1, 1930, 57.2 percent of all peasant households (74.2 percent in Moscow province) had been collectivized, and as of June 1, 1930, only 24.8 percent (7.4 percent in Moscow province) remained in collective farms.[25]

Only with time did the collectivization campaign recover to its level

[20]TsGAMO f. 4867, op. 1, d. 156, ll. 11–13.

[21]TsGAOR f. 5475, op. 13, d. 276, l. 53.

[22]TsGAMO f. 738, op. 1, d. 37, l. 81.

[23]N. S. Davydova and A. Ponomarev, *Velikii podvig: Bor'ba moskovskikh bol'shevikov za osushchestvlenie leninskogo plana sotsialisticheskoi industrializatsii* (Moscow, 1970), p. 239. See also TsGAOR f. 5469, op. 14, d. 44, ll. 35, 69; AMOvets, April 17, 1931, p. 4.

[24]Stalin, vol. 12, pp. 193–198.

[25]Davies, *Socialist Offensive*, pp. 442–443.

Table 1. Percentage of peasant households and sown land collectivized, 1929–1938

Year	Households	Sown land
1929	3.9%	4.9%
1930	23.6	33.6
1931	52.7	67.8
1932	61.5	77.7
1933	65.6	83.1
1934	71.4	87.4
1935	83.2	94.1
1936	90.5	98.2
1937	93.0	99.1
1938	93.5	99.3

Source: *Sotsialisticheskoe sel'skoe khoziaistvo SSSR* (Moscow, 1939), p. 42.

of March 1, and only over the course of the entire decade was collectivization completed (see Table 1).[26] It is significant that as collectivization spread, the percentage of land collectivized exceeded the percentage of collectivized households. Even as peasants quit the collective farms after Stalin's article appeared, collective farms retained much of the land they had gained during the collectivization drive, and in particular the most fertile land. The Central Collective Farm Administration gave instructions that peasants who quit collective farms were to be granted a portion of land outside the boundaries of the collective farm—much of it inferior for cultivation. Collective farms also retained most of the livestock and equipment needed for farming.[27]

Peasants outside of the collective farms faced other hardships as well. Grain collections targeted noncollectivized peasants in 1931 and 1932, as part of the campaign to get them to join (or rejoin) collective farms. Soviet officials also renewed pressure on noncollectivized peasants with waves of dekulakization at the beginning of 1931 and again at the end of 1932.[28] Because the Central Industrial Re-

[26]By 1939 Moscow oblast had 6,573 collective farms with 271,522 peasant households; only 2,541 peasant households remained outside the collective farm system. See *Moskovskaia oblast' v tsifrakh*, P. A. Pozdeev et al., eds. (Moscow, 1939), pp. 26–28.

[27]TsGANKh f. 7446, op. 1, d. 161, l. 97; *Sudebnaia praktika RSFSR* 1931 no. 1, p. 21; Davies, *Socialist Offensive*, pp. 296–297.

[28]*Izvestiia*, August 26, 1932; Davies, *Socialist Offensive*, p. 359; Lewin, *Russian Peasants*, p. 507. A secret Stalin-Molotov letter (May 8, 1933) to Soviet officials stated, "The Central Committee and Sovnarkom are informed that disorderly mass arrests in

gion apart from Moscow province remained largely uncollectivized in 1930, these new waves of collectivization were concentrated there, and they spurred further out-migration from the countryside. Peasants who had believed that Stalin had corrected a monstrous mistake with his "Dizzy with Success" article discovered that this was not the case. They found it increasingly difficult and even hazardous to remain in their villages as noncollectivized peasants. They therefore had to choose: join the collective farm or leave the village. As one peasant said bluntly, "Some of the peasants were dekulakized and deported; the rest, not wishing to join the collective farm, moved to the city and entered the ranks of workers."[29]

Peasants who did join collective farms soon discovered their chaos, inefficiency, and poverty. Reports and letters from collective farm members to the Central Collective Farm Administration complained of "complete anarchy," "irresponsibility," inept management, unfair and poorly coordinated payment systems, and severe food shortages.[30] As late as 1933 the government admitted that collective farms still did not function smoothly. It also noted that machine tractor stations were poorly organized and often failed to provide the basic equipment needed for agriculture.[31]

The situation soon deteriorated even further. Total grain requisitions had already doubled between 1928 and 1930. The 1931 harvest turned out to be 20 percent less than that of 1930, but despite the decrease in available grain, Party leaders called for substantial increases in requisitions. The requisitions of 1931 left many peasants without seed to plant in 1932. This fact, coupled with the overall disorder on collective farms, led to a very poor harvest in 1932 and famine in 1932–33. Several million people starved to death. The famine was most severe in Ukraine, in the North Caucasus, and on the lower and middle Volga, though it also struck parts of Siberia and Kazakhstan.[32]

---

the countryside are still a part of the practice of our officials. . . . The organs of the secret police and the local police lose all feeling of moderation and often make arrests without any basis, acting according to the rule: Arrest first, then investigate": Smolensk archive, WKP 178, pp. 134–135, as quoted in Fainsod, pp. 185–187.

[29]TsPA f. 78, op. 6, d. 526, l. 58.

[30]TsGANKh f. 7446, op. 1, d. 161, ll. 99–100; op. 8, d. 232, l. 94; d. 241, l. 176; d. 312, ll. 20–22.

[31]*Sobranie zakonov i rasporiazhenii SSSR* 1933 no. 41. See also TsGANKh f. 7446, op. 1, d. 161, l. 143.

[32]*Pravda,* September 16, 1988, p. 3 (V. P. Danilov).

Large numbers of peasants fled their villages during the famine. Most went to cities and industrial areas within their native regions rather than to Moscow. Ukrainian peasants, for example, migrated in large numbers to Dneprostroi.[33] A Canadian traveler in 1932 reported that hundreds of peasants begging for bread were to be seen in cities and train stations on the Volga, in the Urals, and in western Siberia, but that conditions in the Central Industrial Region were comparatively good, with no mass starvation or flight of peasants from the countryside.[34] Yet even without famine, dire poverty in the villages of the Central Industrial Region prompted peasants to move to Moscow. One peasant wrote in May 1933:

> What does the peasant, flying from the collective farm, think? Here on the collective farm I am living the life of a badly fed animal. I have been robbed of my grain and all my reserves. My cattle have also been taken. . . . Therefore, life here is impossible. I go into the town, get a job as a workman, and there will be fed.[35]

Other accounts concur that many peasants left the village not only to evade collectivization but also to escape economic hardship and a falling living standard.[36]

In 1931 collectivized peasants accounted for one-third of all temporary migrants and by 1932 this figure surpassed 40 percent.[37] One peasant who became a Moscow construction worker said that after two years on a collective farm, he realized that "nothing good would come of it," so he left.[38] Another peasant explained why he moved to the city in 1930 in these terms: "At that time a complete turnover of life began. The collectivization began. The agricultural industry was worse off. Furthermore, there was a drop in number of cattle and raw materials. Whoever could ran away to industry. There it was easier than agriculture."[39] Collectivization clearly provided motivation for

---

[33]Rassweiler, pp. 234–235.
[34]British Foreign Office records, 371/16329, pp. 10–11.
[35]Ibid., 371/17251, p. 63.
[36]Harvard Project no. 60; Busygin, *Moia zhizn'*, p. 8.
[37]*Izmeneniia sotsial'noi struktury*, p. 199.
[38]TsGAOR f. 5475, op. 13, d. 426, l. 34.
[39]Harvard Project no. 115.

out-migration, even among peasants not victimized by dekulakiza-tion.[40]

Collectivization was not the sole factor that impelled rural-to-urban migration. Less than half (38.2 percent) of peasant households in Moscow province were collectivized as of August 1, 1931, yet huge numbers of peasants continued to leave for the city (211,000 tabu-lated in 1931, up from 57,900 in 1928–29).[41] No absolute correla-tion between collectivization and out-migration can be established for regions within Moscow province. The areas immediately around Moscow did experience somewhat more rapid collectivization and out-migration, but these areas also traditionally sent more peasants to Moscow for temporary labor.[42] Collectivization, therefore, must be considered in conjunction with other factors. A combination of in-creasing opportunities in Moscow and deteriorating conditions in the village induced peasants to leave for the city.[43]

To gauge whether negative changes (push factors) in the village or positive opportunities (pull factors) in the city proved decisive in the calculations of peasant in-migrants is difficult, because motivations for migration varied from one individual to another. Of course de-kulakized peasants had little choice but to flee to the city. For most peasants, however, opportunities in the city figured prominently in the decision to migrate. Poverty and overpopulation in the village had provided ample impetus for out-migration long before the catastro-phe of collectivization. Especially during the 1920s a large number of young peasants would have moved to the city if they could have found work there. Only when the First Five-Year Plan created enormous op-portunities for urban employment did rural-to-urban migration occur

[40]In regions with the highest rates of collectivization (the lower Volga and the North Caucasus) out-migration swelled enormously in 1930 and 1931, though very few peas-ants from these regions made their way to Moscow: S. Klivanskii, "Otkhodnichestvo v SSSR v 1928/29–1931 gg.," *Voprosy truda* 1932 no. 10, p. 71.

[41]Ibid.

[42]*Statisticheskii spravochnik po raionam Moskovskoi oblasti* (Moscow, 1931), pp. 360–401; *Moskva i Moskovskaia oblast': Statistiko-ekonomicheskii spravochnik po okrugam, 1926/27–1928/29* (Moscow, 1930), pp. 200–201; *Kolkhozy Moskovskoi oblasti po materialam maiskogo sploshnogo ucheta kolkhozov* (Moscow, 1930), p. 24.

[43]Scholars of Western European history have stressed the combination of push and pull factors to explain rural-to-urban migration. See Leslie Page Moch, *Paths to the City* (Beverly Hills, Calif., 1983), pp. 25, 36, 193–200; Everett Lee, "A Theory of Migration," *Demography* 1966 no. 1, p. 53.

on a massive scale. The fact that collectivization and hunger in the village coincided with growing opportunities in the city gave peasants all the more reason to move to Moscow and stay there.

Profile of the Peasant In-migrant

Evgenii Mikhailovich was fairly typical of the 2 million peasants who moved to Moscow during the 1930s. He was young, he was literate, and he came from a province near Moscow. Though he had never worked in the city, he did have some technical skills as a result of seasonal employment in a rural mill. Most important, he had relatives and fellow villagers who already lived in the city, and they housed him and found him a job. Vera Dmitreevna also relied on the help of relatives in Moscow. For generations the young men in her family had gone off to work in the city, while their mothers, sisters, and wives remained behind in the village. Many of the men spent several years there, but invariably they came back. In 1930, at age 20, Vera Dmitreevna became the first woman in her family to leave for work in the city. And though she went home for visits from time to time, she chose to settle permanently in Moscow, and lives there to this day.[44]

In all societies migration is a young person's enterprise, and peasant migration to Moscow proved no exception.[45] Moscow's population between the ages of 20 and 30 jumped from 530,700 at the end of 1926 to 934,300 by mid-1933.[46] The magnitude of this increase becomes even more apparent when we examine the population of a given cohort over time. Moscow residents between the ages of 20 and 30 in mid-1933 were between the ages of 13.5 and 23.5 at the end of 1926. Of the 934,300 members of this cohort in Moscow in 1933, fewer than 421,800 had been there in 1926.[47] In other words, over half of Moscow's population aged 20 to 30 in 1933 had moved there within the past six years. By contrast, of the 370,300 people in the

[44]Interview with Vera Dmitreevna Ivanova at the Hammer and Sickle plant, Moscow, April 10, 1989.

[45]Henry Shryock and Jacob Siegel, *The Methods and Materials of Demography* (Washington, 1971), p. 665.

[46]*Moskva v tsifrakh* (Moscow, 1934), pp. 14–15.

[47]Some of the 421,800 had moved away or died by 1933.

cohort between the ages of 40 and 50 in 1933, approximately 322,500 were already there in 1926. The overwhelming majority of peasants who migrated to Moscow were young adults.[48]

The number of young women who moved to Moscow rose dramatically, particularly after 1931. In December 1926, 51 percent of Moscow's population was female. By April 1931 this figure had dipped to 50 percent, but by July 1933 it had risen to 52 percent. The influence of migration on these shifting percentages becomes clearer when we examine the young-adult age groups. At the end of 1926 there were 130,000 men and 130,500 women between the ages of 20 and 25 in Moscow. As of mid-1931, the number of men in this age group had jumped to 202,700, while the number of women stood at 179,400. But by mid-1933 the number of women in this age group, 248,200, surpassed the number of men, 238,500. And by January 1937 women constituted nearly 54 percent of Moscow's population.[49] The rising number of peasant women who migrated to Moscow reflected the increasing permanence of in-migration and the end of the old pattern, whereby male peasants worked several years in the city while female peasants remained in the village. Other factors that encouraged female in-migration included expanding job opportunities and shifting gender roles.[50]

Among the first peasants to leave the village were those who already had urban experience or connections in the city. A survey of temporary migrants in Moscow in the late 1920s showed that over 40 percent of them had been there at least five times before for seasonal labor.[51] When the demand for labor began to rise in 1929, thousands of peasants with urban experience moved permanently to the city.

Peasants who moved to Moscow had higher rates of literacy than the peasantry as a whole. In 1932 nearly half the population in rural areas remained illiterate (this figure was probably somewhat lower

---

[48]*Ekonomiko-statisticheskii spravochnik po raionam Moskovskoi oblasti* (Moscow, 1934), vol. 2, p. 62; *Moskva v tsifrakh*, pp. 14–15.

[49]*Moskva v tsifrakh*, pp. 14–15; *Ekonomiko-statisticheskii spravochnik*, vol. 2, p. 62; *Vsesoiuznaia perepis' naseleniia, 1937 g.*, pp. 42–43.

[50]See chap. 4.

[51]O. V. Khlevniuk, "Izmenenie kul'turnogo oblika gorodskikh rabochikh SSSR, 1926–1939" (dissertation, Institute of History, Moscow, 1986), p. 91. See also Iu. V. Arutiunian, "Kollektivizatsiia sel'skogo khoziaistva i vysvobozhdenie rabochei sily dlia promyshlennosti," in *Formirovanie i razvitie sovetskogo rabochego klassa (1917–1961 gg.)* (Moscow, 1964), p. 102.

for the Central Industrial Region), but most of the peasants who found work in Moscow industry that year were literate or semiliterate.[52] Literate peasants considered themselves better prepared for life in the city. Aleksandr Maksimovich, an 18-year-old peasant from Riazan province, heeded his brother-in-law from Moscow, who explained to him that his seven years of primary education and full literacy would allow him to advance rapidly in industrial work and make enough money to buy several cows. Once in Moscow, he got a job, secured admission to a technical school, gained some qualifications, and advanced to a high-paying factory job.[53]

Peasants with nonagricultural skills also proved especially eager to leave. A 1930 report from one collective farm in Moscow province stated that over half of all the skilled peasants in the district had already left for the city.[54] Peasants with experience as technicians or repairers of agricultural equipment easily found urban employment. They commonly became mechanics and workers in the machine-building industry.[55] One peasant who had learned stonemasonry from his father began doing construction work in the city in 1932 and quickly rose to become a brigade manager. Another peasant easily found urban employment as an accountant after she learned to do some bookkeeping for a collective farm.[56]

By the Second Five-Year Plan, most new arrivals in Moscow were peasants who had profited from Central Collective Farm Administration courses intended to train people for skilled jobs on collective farms. In 1931 over 330,000 peasants were studying tractor driving, mechanics, agronomy, accounting, construction, and electrical work.[57] As soon as they completed their training, however, most of them left to find jobs in the city. Turnover among drivers at machine tractor stations in the First Five-Year Plan was 50 percent, and of the thousands of tractor drivers trained on state collective farms from 1931 to 1933, the great majority had left by 1934. Not surprisingly, reports from collective farms constantly complained about their high turnover and shortages of skilled labor.[58]

[52]*Istoriia krest'ianstva*, vol. 2, p. 268.
[53]Interview with Aleksandr Maksimovich Korneev at the Hammer-and-Sickle metallurgical plant, Moscow, April 24, 1989.
[54]TsGANKh f. 7446, op. 8, d. 88, l. 5.
[55]Harvard Project nos. 492, 519.
[56]Harvard Project nos. 61, 355.
[57]TsGANKh f. 7446, op. 11, d. 40, ll. 88–89, 101.
[58]I. S. Borisov, *Podgotovka proizvodstvennykh kadrov sel'skogo khoziaistva SSSR*

Most peasants who received technical training were young. Of the 4.5 million peasants trained for various collective farm jobs during the First Five-Year Plan, nearly all were in their late teens or early twenties. The Komsomol organized special courses for young peasants, and a network called the Schools of Peasant Youth provided further training.[59] Some schools established to train both workers and peasants in collective farm administration were located in cities, and many peasants who attended them or any other urban school remained in the city permanently.[60] A number of peasants enrolled in urban institutes with the deliberate intention of escaping to the city.[61]

The characteristics of peasants who left the village would in turn influence their adjustment to urban life. While peasants who were dispossessed but not deported during dekulakization had little alternative but to move to the city, most peasants did have some choice in the matter. The first peasants to leave the village voluntarily were those with prior urban experience. They and others who followed them were young and literate, and many of them possessed marketable skills. By the Second Five-Year Plan, when in-migration decreased in magnitude, most peasants moving to Moscow had acquired skills through collective farm technical training. The transition to urban and industrial life represented a considerable challenge for any peasant. But literacy, technical skills, and prior urban experience prepared many peasant in-migrants to accomplish this transition as smoothly as possible.

Organized Recruitment and the Internal Passport System

Soviet leaders strove to mobilize all resources, including labor, for the industrialization drive. Mobilization of labor required control over population movement and the ability to channel peasants into

---

v rekonstruktivnyi period (Moscow, 1960), pp. 275–278; Istoriia krest'ianstva, vol. 2, p. 299; TsGAOR f. 5515, op. 1, d. 191, l. 37.

[59]Sheila Fitzpatrick, Education and Social Mobility in the Soviet Union, 1921–1934 (New York, 1979), pp. 178–179; V. V. Mel'nikov, Kul'turnaia revoliutsiia i Komsomol (Rostov, 1973), pp. 239–241; Ocherki istorii moskovskoi organizatsii VLKSM, E. V. Taranov, ed. (Moscow, 1976), pp. 252–253.

[60]TsGANKh f. 7446, op. 11, d. 122, ll. 36–37, 52, 103.

[61]See, for example, Harvard Project no. 142.

urban industrial employment. Collectivization and the establishment of administrative control over the countryside seemed to offer the opportunity to regulate the flow of migration. Party officials declared that contracts with collective farms would guarantee the supply of labor for construction projects and industry. Organized recruitment (*orgnabor*) of peasants through the collective farms would not only ensure adequate numbers but also prevent the hiring of "alien, kulak elements."[62] Yet despite authorities' efforts to control the labor pool, organized recruitment proved to be a failure.

Part of the blame for this failure lies with the Commissariat of Labor (Narkomtrud). With the shift from widespread unemployment in Soviet cities to an increasingly severe shortage of labor by 1930, Party leaders changed the orientation of the Commissariat of Labor from unemployment relief to the recruitment of workers, and in the process reshuffled and weakened its executive committee.[63] Labor organs never gained enough power to fulfill their new task of finding new workers and regulating the labor market. The Moscow oblast department of cadres lacked experienced and efficient administrators and in 1931 fired a large share of its recruiters for inactivity and drunkenness.[64] A Commissariat of Labor report dated January 7, 1930, frankly admitted that the complete lack of labor organs in rural areas made organized recruitment of peasants into the urban workforce nearly impossible. The money needed to establish such organs, it added, was lacking as well.[65]

As recruiting efforts faltered, peasants continued to arrive on their own. In 1930 the construction trade union reported:

> In Moscow and Moscow oblast there are about 400,000 temporary migrants from the villages, and all winter the Commissariat of Labor

[62]*Sputnik kommunista* 1930 no. 6, p. 46.

[63]*KPSS v resoliutsiiakh i resheniiakh s"ezdov, konferentsii i plenumov TsK* (Moscow, 1984), vol. 5, p. 53; Nobuaki Shiokawa, "The Soviet Working Class under the Stalinist System, 1929–1933" (unpublished summary of a book in Japanese of the same title), pp. 6–7.

[64]A. M. Panfilova, *Formirovanie rabochego klassa SSSR v gody pervoi piatiletki (1928–1932)* (Moscow, 1964), p. 92.

[65]TsGAOR f. 5515, op. 1, d. 191, l. 191; MPA f. 635, op. 1, d. 41, l. 33. As recruiting efforts foundered, the Commissariat of Labor continued to issue ever more urgent calls for planned and systematic recruitment of new workers. See *Izvestiia: Ofitsial'noe izdanie Narkomata truda* 1930 no. 19, pp. 418–420 (circular, June 9, 1930, and decree, July 21, 1930).

asserted that in the current year no migrants would arrive on their own. In reality in the month of May we have an enormous influx of migrants arriving on their own [*samotechnye otkhodniki*] and overflowing at all the train stations.[66]

The frustration of industrial managers and trade union officials stemmed from the Commissariat of Labor's inability to control peasant in-migration and guarantee a steady supply of labor during the industrialization drive.

Another explanation for the failure of organized recruitment lies in the collective farms' efforts to hinder the recruitment of peasants for work in the city. A 1930 Commissariat of Labor report complained that collective farm officials did not welcome recruiters and sometimes even arrested them. Collective farm administrators who agreed to release peasant labor often reneged on their agreements, claiming, "We have our own work to do."[67] The drop in collective farm membership after Stalin's "Dizzy with Success" article made collective farm managers determined not to lose the peasants they had—if indeed they still had any; in some villages of Moscow oblast the only people who still belonged to collective farms were administrators.[68] With the decline in the rural living standard and the growth in opportunities for urban employment, managers realized that peasants who ostensibly were leaving only temporarily would probably not be back.[69]

Whether collective farm members left through organized recruitment or on their own, they faced penalties from the managers of their collective farms. Administrators garnisheed 30 to 50 percent (occasionally up to 80 percent) of the wages peasants earned from temporary urban employment and deprived their family members of a fair share of the harvest.[70] A decree drafted by the Central Collective Farm Administration (Kolkhoztsentr) and approved by the Politburo on February 25, 1930, legalized this practice, and required collectivized peasants to secure the permission of their administrators before they could leave for the city. At the urging of the Commissariat of

[66]TsGAOR f. 5475, op. 13, d. 194, l. 13.
[67]TsGANKh f. 7446, op. 8, d. 88, ll. 70–72.
[68]Ibid., ll. 2–3.
[69]MPA f. 634, op. 1, d. 207, ll. 60–61.
[70]TsGANKh f. 7446, op. 8, d. 101, l. 19; d. 232, l. 50.

Labor, however, the Council of People's Commissars (Sovnarkom) contradicted this decree on March 16, 1930 by granting collectivized peasants the right to leave for work in the city.[71]

In essence, a struggle over labor resources was taking place between collective farms and industrial enterprises, and between the Central Collective Farm Administration and the Commissariat of Labor. In the highly politicized atmosphere of the 1930s, Party leaders set unrealistically high production targets for factories and collective farms alike. Managers of these enterprises responded as best they could, struggling to obtain and retain as many laborers as possible. The Soviet state, far from monolithic, consisted of institutions that competed with one another for resources, and bureaucratic agencies that issued contradictory decrees.

Party leaders did not firmly take sides in this struggle until June 23, 1931, when Stalin outlined the prerequisites for the acceleration of industrial development. In his speech "New Conditions—New Tasks of Economic Construction," he stressed a need for the steady and orderly flow of peasant labor to factories and construction sites.[72] One week later the government forbade collective farms to expropriate a percentage of peasants' urban wages and guaranteed the families of peasants away in the city a fair share of the harvest.[73] On July 18, 1931, the Commissariat of Labor instructed industrial enterprises that contracts for peasant labor should offer collective farms technical assistance and agricultural equipment as an inducement for them to release their peasants.[74]

Such contracts multiplied after these measures went into effect, but they were often broken. Managers of industrial enterprises failed to honor their commitments to supply collective farms with technical assistance, and collective farm authorities persisted in penalizing peasants who left for the city or in trying to detain them altogether.[75] Also quite common was collective farm officials' outright refusal, in flagrant violation of the law, to sign contracts at all. Reports of the

[71]R. W. Davies, *The Soviet Collective Farm, 1929–1930* (Cambridge, Mass., 1980), pp. 163–164.

[72]Stalin, vol. 12, pp. 52–54.

[73]*Sobranie zakonov i rasporiazhanii SSSR* no. 42 (1931), art. 286.

[74]TsGANKh f. 7446, op. 8, d. 241, ll. 70–74; d. 232, ll. 1–5. See also TsGAOR f. 5451, op. 15, d. 751, l. 9.

[75]Dadykin, pp. 41–45; Panfilova, p. 106; *Voprosy truda* 1932 no. 7, pp. 11–16; TsGANKh f. 7446, op. 8, d. 240, ll. 7–9; d. 241, l. 85.

Central Collective Farm Administration, the Commissariat of Labor, and various periodicals throughout 1931 and 1932 stated that rural administrators balked at concluding labor contracts and unconditionally denied peasants permission to leave. Some collective farm managers apparently never received directives or decrees issued in Moscow; most simply ignored them.[76] Thus, even after Stalin clarified official policy to put recruitment on an expeditious contractual basis, collective farm managers blocked that policy's implementation.

Fortunately for labor-hungry industrial managers, while collective farm administrators could thwart organized recruitment, they could not control their own peasants. Those peasants who wished to work in the city found little difficulty in slipping away from their collective farms, as numerous reports throughout 1931 and 1932 confirm. Many collective farm managers confessed to having no idea where their peasants had gone and when or if they would be back. By 1932 every one of the thirty working male members of one collective farm had left (without permission) to work in the city. Officials of the Collective Farm Administration's sector of cadres reported in 1931 that 92 percent of collective farm members away doing seasonal work in the city had left on their own, rather than on the basis of a recruitment contract. They concluded that peasants who ostensibly left for temporary urban labor in reality had fled the collective farms permanently.[77]

With the failure of efforts to put recruitment of peasants on a contractual basis with collective farms, recruiters turned their attention to noncollectivized peasants. Because the percentage of peasants who belonged to collective farms dropped drastically in March 1930 and only gradually increased over the next several years, there was a large pool of noncollectivized peasants (*edinolichniki*) who represented potential recruits.[78] In 1930 and the first half of 1931, all new workers had to be recruited through organs of the Commissariat of Labor, but these organs provided, for example, only 13.4 percent of the 88,000

[76]TsGAOR f. 5515, op. 17, d. 212, l. 7; TsGANKh f. 7446, op. 8, d. 88, ll. 2–3; d. 232, l. 100; *Moskovskaia promyshlennaia kooperatsiia* 1931 no. 7 (August), p. 12; *Rabochaia Moskva*, October 7, 1931, p. 2; *Voprosy truda* 1932 no. 7, pp. 3–4.

[77]Panfilova, pp. 117–118; *Voprosy truda* 1932 no. 7, p. 5; TsGANKh f. 7446, op. 8, d. 232, l. 4.

[78]Throughout the First Five-Year Plan, a majority of peasants who obtained industrial employment were noncollectivized: *Izmeneniia sotsial'noi struktury*, p. 199. See also MPA f. 432, op. 1, d. 49, l. 107.

workers needed for important RSFSR construction projects during the first quarter of 1931.[79] On September 13, 1931, a government decree gave enterprises the right to recruit and hire workers directly, without going through the Commissariat of Labor.[80] Construction and factory managers, desperate to fulfill their plans, had been recruiting workers directly for some time, but legalization of the authority to do so sparked expanded efforts. This new drive resulted in a glut of recruiters from various enterprises, all competing for the same potential workers.[81]

The recruiting efforts of construction and factory managers proved little better than those of the Commissariat of Labor. Many recruiters enticed peasants with wage advances (they had their own quotas to meet) and often got drunkards as a result. The director of the Moscow ball-bearing factory construction site enlisted a group of gypsies for construction work in a desperate attempt to complete his plant on schedule. Some recruiters gave peasant women shawls in return for a promise to encourage their husbands to take jobs in the city. Others got peasants drunk in order to cajole them into signing labor contracts, and made false promises regarding wages and accommodations. These tactics generally backfired; peasants employed under false pretenses tended to slip off to other work sites or back to the village.[82]

By the spring of 1932, organized recruitment had clearly failed. Nearly a year after Stalin's "New Conditions" speech, Moscow construction and labor organs concluded that organized recruitment was still "very weakly developed," that the settling of labor contracts with collective farms was "exceptionally weak," and that the recruiting apparatus as a whole continued to be "unsatisfactory."[83] Party and trade union statistics offer further evidence that the vast majority of

[79]*Industrializatsiia SSSR: Dokumenty i materialy*, vol. 2 (Moscow, 1970), pp. 423–425.

[80]*Sobranie zakonov i rasporiazhenii SSSR* 1931 no. 60, art. 385.

[81]TsGAMO f. 6833, op. 1, d. 46, ll. 65–75.

[82]Solomon Schwarz, *Labor in the Soviet Union* (New York, 1951), p. 59; *Byli industrial'nye: Ocherki i vospominaniia* (Moscow, 1973), p. 168; M. T. Gol'tsman, "Sostav stroitel'nykh rabochikh SSSR v gody pervoi piatiletki," in *Izmeneniia v chislennosti i sostave sovetskogo rabochego klassa* (Moscow, 1961), p. 134; MPA f. 429, op. 1, d. 109, l. 209. Pirating of workers was a ploy used when recruitment efforts failed to meet labor demands; managers on visits to other factories, ostensibly on business, would attempt to lure workers away to work in their own plant: Schwarz, p. 88.

[83]TsGAOR f. 5515, op. 1, d. 441, l. 1.

peasants continued to migrate to Moscow on their own rather than through organized recruitment during the 1930s.[84]

Authorities' failure to control population movement led them to choose more coercive solutions to the problem of labor supply. The head of the Commissariat of Labor, Nikolai A. Uglanov, wrote in 1930 that with labor shortages in various timber-producing regions threatening nonfulfillment of the plan, "the need arose to attract the peasant population to timber cutting on the basis of labor conscription."[85] It is unclear whether Uglanov favored such measures or was simply reporting what Party leaders had ordered. Meetings of the Commissariat of Labor throughout 1930 showed its officials to be indecisive and unable to find solutions to problems. The Party leadership increasingly turned to other government institutions, including the secret police (OGPU), to meet labor demand.[86] In fact, with the arrest and deportation of over a million peasants during collectivization, a supply of conscripted workers was not only available but in the process of being sent to labor camps. Government directives on dekulakization even specified that only families with able-bodied men should be deported to labor camps.[87]

Soviet officials employed forced labor primarily in northern and Siberian timber camps and in new industrial areas such as the Urals and the Kuzbass, which faced extreme difficulty in obtaining workers by other means.[88] Authorities deported a very few "kulaks" to Moscow. Forced labor was used outside the city to dig the Moscow-Volga

[84]See MPA f. 69, op. 1, d. 947, l. 12; f. 468, op. 1, d. 155, l. 207; TsGANKh f. 7622, op. 1, d. 251, l. 2; TsGAMO f. 4867, op. 1, d. 156, ll. 21–22; Panfilova, pp. 30, 160. Enterprise officials occasionally tallied all new workers under the category of organized recruitment, including peasants who had arrived on their own and were hired at the factory gate (see *Voprosy truda* 1932 no. 7, p. 6). Thus organized recruitment statistics are inflated, if anything, yet they still account for well under half of all peasants newly hired in the city.

[85]N. A. Uglanov, ed., *Trud v SSSR: Sbornik statei* (Moscow, 1930), p. 14.

[86]Fitzpatrick, "Great Departure," pp. 19–21. The Commissariat of Labor was finally abolished in 1933, and it was never replaced by any bureaucratic organization charged with coordinating labor.

[87]*Neizvestnaia Rossiia*, V. A. Kozlov, ed. (Moscow, 1992), p. 190. On the horrors of deportation, see pp. 194–228.

[88]See ibid., pp. 237–257; John Scott, *Behind the Urals* (Bloomington, Ind., 1973), pp. 17–19, 85. Other late-industrializing countries (such as Kenya and Peru) have on a much smaller scale used physical coercion in labor recruitment. See Michael Hanagan and Charles Stephenson, eds., *Proletarians and Protest: The Roots of Class Formation in an Industrializing World* (New York, 1986), pp. 10–12.

Canal, and small numbers of prisoners worked on construction of the Moscow metro and the never-completed Palace of Soviets.[89]

Soviet leaders also instituted an internal passport system to control population movement. At the end of 1932 the Soviet economy was nearing a crisis. The threat of famine loomed over large parts of the countryside, construction projects had fallen behind schedule, industrial output failed to meet unrealistic plans, and labor shortages continued. Passports offered a means to limit the urban population—an important consideration with food shortages imminent. Authorities justified the resumption of the passport system (the Bolsheviks had abolished it after the Revolution) as a means to expel "class alien elements," but undoubtedly it was also intended to prevent an influx of starving peasants from famine areas into the cities.[90]

The passport decree (December 27, 1932) required that all citizens over age 16 living in cities be issued passports by the local police. The passports, valid for three years, contained the following information: name, age, nationality, social position, permanent place of residence, place of work, and acknowledgment of military service. "Persons not occupied in socially useful labor," "hidden kulaks," "criminals," and "other antisocietal elements" were not to receive passports. Persons who lived outside of urban areas were not to receive them either. Residence in any large city required a permit (*propiska*) stamped in one's passport. Any person who arrived in a large city without a passport bearing a permit was to be turned back.[91]

Implementation of the passport system in Moscow in January 1933 caused a small-scale exodus of people denied passports. Apparently some residents who were initially refused passports stayed anyway, however, and went from one district police office to another in the hope of wangling one.[92] This fact in itself indicates that authorities

[89]Nobuo Shimotomai, *Moscow under Stalinist Rule* (New York, 1991), p. 111; Harvard Project no. 118; TsGAORgM f. 150, op. 5, d. 24b. For more on forced labor, see O. V. Khlevniuk, "Prinuditel'nyi trud v ekonomike SSSR, 1929–1941 gody," *Svobodnaia mysl'* 1992 no. 13.

[90]*Sobranie zakonov* 1932 no. 84, art. 516; *Martenovka*, January 11, 1933, p. 3.

[91]*Sobranie zakonov* 1932 no. 84, arts. 516, 517; *Izvestiia*, December 28, 1932. Restrictions on the number of permits issued for residence in Moscow had no apparent effect, as the population continued to rise rapidly. See Robert A. Lewis, "Soviet Demographic Policy: How Comprehensive, How Effective?" in *Soviet Geography Studies in Our Time*, Lutz Holzner and Jeane M. Knapp, eds. (Milwaukee, 1987), pp. 28–29.

[92]British Foreign Office records, 371/17250, p. 269 (confidential report, February 3, 1933).

did not succeed immediately in enforcing the new system. Indeed, throughout the mid-1930s reports persisted of people without passports or residence permits working in Moscow factories and living in workers' barracks.[93]

Moscow's population declined slightly in 1933, though this dip is attributable to economic contraction more than to the passport system. Once industrial expansion began again in 1934, the city's population rose rapidly in spite of internal passports. The overriding economic consideration remained the great demand for labor, so legislation provided peasants living within a 100-kilometer zone around Moscow with passports and granted other peasants certificates for temporary labor in the city.[94] Even peasants who lacked such documents were routinely hired and issued passports by labor-hungry industrial managers.[95] The availability of forged documents also aided peasants who wished to move to Moscow; numerous reports attest to the ease with which they acquired and used false passports.[96]

Some evidence suggests that the passport system became more effective in the late 1930s (perhaps after the introduction of photographs on passports in 1938), for the number of people expelled for lack of a passport increased.[97] No doubt local police offices gradually established more complete registration records as time passed and as migration declined. Despite the expulsions, Moscow's population continued to climb as more peasants moved in. The passport and residence permit system did not control population movement in the 1930s and did not prevent peasants from moving to Moscow.[98] The Soviet government's lack of control resulted from both the weakness of its administrative apparatus on the local level and its own cross-purposes. It could not limit the flow of labor into cities and simultaneously expect labor-starved urban enterprises to meet the extravagant goals of the industrialization drive.

[93]TsGAORgM f. 214, op. 1, d. 284, l. 10; *Vecherniaia Moskva*, May 8, 1934, p. 3; V. Nikol'skii and I. Vanshtein, "Rabota s otstalymi gruppami rabochikh," *Voprosy profdvizheniia* 1933 no. 9, p. 47.

[94]*Sobranie zakonov i rasporiazhenii SSSR* 1932 no. 84, arts. 516, 517; 1933 no. 28, art. 168.

[95]Harvard Project no. 476; Kotkin, p. 194; Rassweiler, p. 94.

[96]Harvard Project nos. 46, 483; Kotkin, p. 190; Janucy K. Zawodny, "Twenty-six Interviews with Former Soviet Factory Workers," Hoover Institution Archives, I/12.

[97]Harvard Project nos. 417, 640.

[98]For more on the passport system, see Fitzpatrick, "Great Departure," pp. 28–32.

Traditional Migration Patterns

If migration to Moscow was not an orderly process regulated by
Soviet officials, then was it a chaotic flight from the countryside?
Certainly it seemed so to observers, foreign and Soviet alike. Contemporaries wrote of masses of peasants crowded in train stations, fleeing
the villages with all their belongings, apparently wandering aimlessly
from one city to another seeking work or begging for bread.[99] The
Commissar of Heavy Industry, Grigorii (Sergo) Ordzhonikidze, ex-
claimed in despair that drifting peasant-workers had made the Soviet
factory "a nomadic gypsy camp."[100] Leading scholars have characterized this period in similar terms, referring to "a country of vagrants,"
"quicksand society," and "uprooted" migrants "swamping" the city.[101]

Some peasants did flee their native villages to search haphazardly
for food and shelter, especially in Ukraine during the famine of 1933.
Accounts tell of starvation and death along the roads to Kharkov
and Kiev. Homeless children (*besprizorniki*), orphaned and starving, boarded trains for the nearest city and lived at the train station
there. Some of these orphans eventually made their way to Moscow,
where they begged for food, engaged in petty theft, and impelled the
city council in 1935 to create a special commission to place all such
children in orphanages.[102] But these cases, though numerous, were
exceptions to the overall process by which hundreds of thousands of
peasants migrated to Moscow every year. The overwhelming majority
of peasants who left their villages had a clear plan of action: they
knew where they were going, where they would live, and often even
where they would work in the city.

---

[99] Allan Monkhouse, *Moscow, 1911–1933: Being the Memoirs of Allan Monkhouse*
(London, 1933), p. 212; George Burrell, *An American Engineer Looks at Russia* (Boston,
1932), p. 64; Nadezhda Mandelstam, *Hope against Hope*, Max Hayward, trans. (New
York, 1970), p. 97; Ilia Ehrenburg, *A Street in Moscow*, Sonia Volochova, trans. (New
York, 1932), pp. 6–7.

[100] G. K. Ordzhonikidze, *Stat'i i rechi*, vol. 2 (Moscow, 1957), pp. 411–412.

[101] "Osnovnye etapy razvitiia sovetskogo obshchestva: 'Kruglyi stol,'" *Kommunist*
1987 no. 12, p. 72 (remarks by V. Z. Drobizhev); Igor' Kliamkin, "Pochemu trudno
govorit' pravdu," *Novyi mir* 1989 no. 2, p. 228; Moshe Lewin, *The Making of the Soviet
System: Essays in the Social History of Interwar Russia* (New York, 1985), p. 221.

[102] "Kollektivizatsiia," p. 52; Harvard Project no. 333; *Istoriia metro Moskvy: Rasskazy stroitelei metro*, A. Kosarev, ed. (Moscow, 1935), p. 163; *Nezabyvaemye 30-e:
Vospominaniia veteranov partii—moskvichei* (Moscow, 1986), pp. 68–69; TsGAORgM
f. 150, op. 5, d. 66, l. 94.

Demographic studies show that in all countries, migrants proceed along well-defined routes to highly specific destinations, and that the flow of knowledge back to the place of origin acts as a crucial determinant in the decision to move.[103] During the Soviet collectivization, of course, not all peasants had the time to plan their move. In case after case, however, even peasants whom Soviet authorities had dispossessed at gunpoint (or who had hurriedly decamped to avoid arrest and deportation) found their way safely and swiftly to the city. Village networks, family ties, and migration traditions guided them to their destinations.[104] What appeared to be anarchic flight to outside observers (who may have presumed the masses of dirty peasants they saw at train stations to be pitiful and obtuse in any case) was in fact a series of choices based on the resources peasants had for survival.

Statistics on migration for the periods before and after collectivization demonstrate that preexisting village networks and migration traditions continued to guide migrants to Moscow in the 1930s. Before the Revolution, during the 1920s, and during the 1930s too, almost all peasants who settled in Moscow came from European Russia. According to the 1902 Moscow census, the 1926 all-union census, and data compiled by the Central Statistical Administration during the 1930s, less than 5 percent of migrants to Moscow came from non-Russian areas or Siberia. In all these periods, virtually no peasants from Transcaucasia, Central Asia, or Siberia settled in Moscow, and few arrived from Belorussia and Ukraine.[105]

Table 2 provides Central Statistical Administration data on the number of people who arrived in Moscow from within the RSFSR in 1930. In 1929 and 1930 the provinces were consolidated into oblasts and Moscow oblast incorporated the provinces of Moscow, Tula, and Riazan and parts of Tver and Kaluga provinces.[106] Reordering the data of the 1926 census to establish comparable units reveals a remark-

[103]Lee, pp. 54–55; Bodnar, p. 57.

[104]Harvard Project nos. 107, 476, 640; Klivanskii, p. 68.

[105]*Perepis' Moskvy, 1902 g.*, ch. I, vol. 2 (Moscow, 1906), pp. 24–27; *Vsesoiuznaia perepis' naseleniia, 1926 g.*, vol. 39, pp. 216–221. In 1931, according to data compiled by the Central Statistical Administration, 2.3 million people came to large cities of the RSFSR from rural areas of the same republic and only 74,800 from other republics, of whom 40,300 came from Ukraine and 31,600 from Belorussia: TsGANKh f. 1562, op. 20, d. 25, l. 6. Proportions remained similar in 1934; see *Sotsialisticheskoe stroitel'stvo v SSSR: Statisticheskii ezhegodnik* (Moscow, 1936), p. 546.

[106]*Administrativno-territorial'noe delenie Soiuza SSR* (Moscow, 1929), p. 32.

Table 2. Number of people arriving in Moscow from within the RSFSR, 1930, by region

Region	Arrivals
Moscow oblast	341,600
Western oblast	92,300
Central Black Soil oblast	79,300
Ivanovo Industrial oblast	57,400
Middle Volga krai	33,500
Nizhnii Novgorod krai	23,600
Northern Caucasus krai	17,000
Leningrad oblast	4,900

Source: TsGANKh f. 1562, op. 20, d. 25, l. 10.

able constancy in migration patterns: in both 1926 and 1930, slightly over half (51 percent and 53 percent, respectively) of the people who migrated to Moscow came from Moscow oblast, while almost two-thirds (64 percent and 65 percent, respectively) came from the Central Industrial Region (Moscow, Tver, Iaroslavl, Kostroma, Ivanovo Voznesensk, Nizhnii Novgorod, Vladimir, Riazan, Tula, and Kaluga provinces).[107]

A comparison of smaller units within Moscow oblast and the Central Industrial Region again shows continuity in migration patterns. Before the Revolution and during the 1920s, most peasants who migrated to Moscow either permanently or on a temporary basis came from the three less industrialized provinces directly south of Moscow province (Riazan, Tula, and Kaluga), from Tver province, and especially from nonindustrial parts of Moscow province itself.[108] Moscow factories' data on newly arrived peasants employed during the First Five-Year Plan reveal that most of them continued to come from these same areas.[109] Furthermore, studies of out-migration show that during

[107]*Vsesoiuznaia perepis' naseleniia, 1926 g.*, vol. 36, pp. 216–221. The 1902 census showed slightly larger percentages arriving from the territory that was to become Moscow oblast (59 percent) and from the Central Industrial Region as a whole (75 percent): *Perepis' Moskvy, 1902 g.*, ch. I, vol. 2, pp. 24–27.

[108]Barbara A. Anderson, *Internal Migration during Modernization in Late Nineteenth-Century Russia* (Princeton, 1980), pp. 105–106; Bradley, pp. 105–106; Chase, p. 81.

[109]TsGAOR f. 5451, op. 13, d. 76, ll. 47–49; TsGAMO f. 4867, op. 1, d. 156, ll. 3–5; K. Strievskii, *Material'noe i kul'turnoe polozhenie moskovskikh rabochikh: Doklad na IV ob"edinennom plenume MK i MKK VKP(b)* (Moscow, 1929), p. 9. Systematic data below the oblast level do not exist for the post-1929 period, but the factory data cited here provide at least a general picture of migration trends.

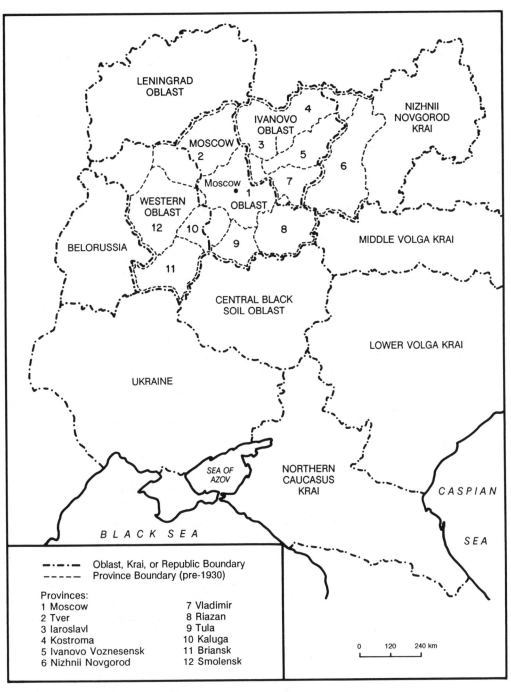

Oblasts of European USSR, 1930

the 1930s, rural areas immediately surrounding Moscow and those between Moscow and Leningrad experienced significant depopulation (15 to 20 percent decreases, despite a high fertility rate that would have led to population increases had massive out-migration not taken place), while rural areas farther from Moscow had population decreases of lesser magnitude.[110] Despite the upheavals of collectivization and industrialization, most migrants to Moscow continued to come from less industrialized areas of the Central Industrial Region and particularly from the rural areas closest to Moscow.

Definite reasons existed for the development and continuance of these migration patterns. Peasants naturally moved the shortest possible distance to escape rural poverty and to seek new economic opportunities.[111] Peasants in the more industrial provinces of the Central Industrial Region (Ivanovo Voznesensk, Vladimir, Iaroslavl, Kostroma, and Nizhnii Novgorod) sometimes found industrial employment opportunities close to home and had less need to journey to Moscow. Another pivotal factor in migration was prior experience in Moscow, which alerted peasants to opportunities there and eased their transition to urban life. Long traditions of trade and temporary labor in Moscow, particularly among peasants of Moscow, Kaluga, Tula, and Riazan provinces, acted to guide them to the city. Likewise, many generations of peasants from Tver province, situated between Moscow and Leningrad, had performed seasonal labor in the two cities, and they continued to arrive in large numbers in the 1930s.[112]

This continuity of in-migration patterns reflected the strength and vitality of migration traditions even in changing times. The traditions that dictated where peasants went and the type of work they found proved strong enough to frustrate recruiters' best efforts to get them to deviate from established patterns. In some villages of Tver province, migration to Leningrad had been traditional, and peasants refused even to consider Moscow. Peasants of other Tver villages had

[110]*Naselenie SSSR za 70 let,* L. L. Rybakovskii, ed. (Moscow, 1988), p. 51. Famine regions and rural areas immediately surrounding other industrial centers (especially the Donbass) also underwent significant depopulation.

[111]See Lee, p. 48. As a great urban center, Moscow did attract some peasants from a wider radius than other cities did, but even those people came almost entirely from the provinces immediately surrounding Moscow province. See Bradley, p. 120; TsGAOR f. 5475, op. 13, d. 426, l. 36; TsGANKh f. 1562, op. 20, d. 25, l. 15.

[112]Bradley, p. 168; TsGAMO f. 4867, op. 1, d. 156, ll. 3–5.

a tradition of doing work in Moscow, and they rebuffed recruiters from Leningrad, saying that the city was unfamiliar to them.[113] One survey of Moscow construction workers showed that some 82 percent found employment on the basis of previous seasonal work or information provided by fellow villagers.[114] It was natural that peasants relied on their own experiences and the experiences of fellow villagers in finding work—they correctly regarded this knowledge as more trustworthy than any information provided by recruiters.

Peasants from some villages developed skills, passed down from one generation to the next, that also determined the type of work they would find and where they would find it. Some districts (*uezdy*), counties (*volosti*), and even villages specialized in specific types of work. This specialization reflected the long historical development of crafts in particular areas. The large number of stoneworkers, carpenters, painters, and plasterers from Vladimir province, for example, resulted from the large number of stone churches built there over several centuries.[115] In the late 1920s, some counties (for example, Ovchinskaia county of Aleksandrovskii district, Vladimir province; and Dmitrievskaia county of Egorevskii district, Moscow province) sent over 10 percent of the entire population (perhaps up to half of all young men) to do seasonal construction work in Moscow.[116]

Reports during the First Five-Year Plan attest to the fact that these traditions and skills continued to channel peasants into urban jobs. Carpenters and joiners from a part of Riazan province with traditions of temporary migration to the city supplied Moscow construction sites with the skilled builders needed there. A 1930 Moscow construction union report remarked upon workshops in one village that taught peasants the fundamentals of carpentry—skills that virtually guaranteed urban employment during the 1930s.[117] Even in the wake of collectivization and industrialization, when peasant migration in-

---

[113]TsGAMO f. 6833, op. 1, d. 46, l. 65; *Sputnik kul'trabotnika sredi sezonnikov*, p. 13.

[114]*Rabochii klass—vedushchaia sila v stroitel'stve sotsialisticheskogo obshchestva, 1921–1937 gg.*, L. S. Rogachevskaia and A. M. Sivolobov, eds. (Moscow, 1984), p. 202.

[115]Danilov, "Krest'ianskii otkhod," pp. 90, 97.

[116]*Otkhod sel'skogo naseleniia na zarabotki v SSSR v 1926/27 g.* (Moscow, 1929), pp. 48ff.

[117]TsGANKh f. 7446, op. 8, d. 88, l. 134; TsGAOR f. 5475, op. 13, d. 276, l. 14; *Sovetskoe kraevedenie* 1932 no. 4, pp. 35–36.

creasingly came to mean a permanent move to Moscow rather than a temporary stay, village traditions and skills established over several generations continued to guide peasants to the city.

Village Networks and Artels

To understand how patterns of migration remained so constant even as the numbers of in-migrants grew so precipitously, it is important to consider the role of village networks. Those peasants who arrived in Moscow for the first time could conform to traditional patterns through chain migration—joining a relative or fellow villager who already lived there. Relatives provided newcomers with the information, work contacts, and shelter they needed. One peasant from Riazan province had a relative in Moscow who promised him a job in the same factory shop where he himself was working. Another peasant followed her husband to the city after he had found a job, and she soon began work in the same factory. A 16-year-old peasant planning to study in the city moved in with his uncle there and soon joined him in transportation work.[118]

A whole series of large factories in Moscow—the Tri-Mountain textile mill, the Frunze aviation motor plant, the Red Hercules rubber factory, the Hammer and Sickle metallurgical plant—relied on relatives of workers as a major source of new workers, and actively encouraged workers to persuade their relatives to join them. Several reports indicate that this method proved far more effective than official efforts at organized recruitment.[119]

The peasants' preference for chain migration over official recruitment is understandable. Moving to a big city involved a substantial

[118]Interview with Aleksandr Maksimovich Korneev at the Hammer and Sickle plant, Moscow, April 24, 1989; Harvard Project no. 107; *Molodaia gvardiia transporta* (Moscow, 1936), pp. 187–193. Studies have shown that kinship networks actually strengthened with urbanization, because peasants who migrated to cities needed help with jobs and housing. See Tamara K. Hareven, *Family Time and Industrial Time: The Relationship between Family and Work in a New England Industrial Community* (New York, 1982), pp. 86–102; Martin Katzman, "Urbanization since 1945," in *Social Change in Brazil, 1945–1985*, Edmar L. Bacha and Herbert S. Klein, eds. (Albuquerque, 1989), p. 118; Rothstein, pp. 218–224.

[119]AAN f. 359, op. 2, d. 499, l. 2; d. 507, ll. 26–27; TsGAORgM f. 168, op. 3, d. 7, l. 29; *Rabochaia Moskva*, October 29, 1931, p. 3; TsGAOR f. 5515, op. 15, d. 410, l. 55.

risk. Peasants could trust relatives' information regarding the availability of jobs and housing, and in the event of illness or injury, they could rely on relatives' aid and support. Official recruiters were strangers, and proved quick to lie and exaggerate in order to fill their quotas. Peasants contemplating migration to the city naturally relied on relatives instead of official recruiters for both guidance and assistance.

Peasants who had no relatives in Moscow could nonetheless receive similar help from fellow villagers (*zemliaki*) who already lived in the city. Numerous accounts attest to the guidance provided by fellow villagers to newcomers. One peasant consulted his fellow villager in Moscow for advice on employment opportunities and job specializations. Another became intrigued when a fellow villager told him about the construction of the Moscow metro, and after he found out what a metro was, he followed his friend to work there.[120] Officials at the construction site of the Moscow ball-bearing plant resolved that every shock worker should recruit at least two fellow villagers into the workforce. Workers' letters home did coax a number of peasants to the site.[121] Several factories, frustrated by the failure of official recruiters, even sent workers of peasant origin back home to recruit. One such worker was credited with persuading seventy-two peasants from his village to join him at a Moscow construction site.[122] A 1931 Rabkrin report stated that most workers at one Moscow mill had acquired their jobs through village acquaintances.[123] Another study found that 82 percent of all new Soviet construction workers during the 1930s had moved to cities on the advice of fellow villagers.[124] Urban workers began to complain that many jobs went not to urban proletarians but to newly arrived peasants, "thanks to connections."[125]

Those peasants who had no connections in Moscow could turn to

[120]Gudov, *Sud'ba rabochego*, pp. 5, 35; *Istoriia metro Moskvy*, p. 231.

[121]Panfilova, p. 97.

[122]Fedorov, p. 80; M. I. Eliseeva, "O sposobakh privlecheniia rabochei sily v promyshlennost' i stroitel'stvo v period sotsialisticheskoi industrializatsii SSSR (1926–1937)," in *Izvestiia Voronezhskogo gosudarstvennogo pedigogicheskogo instituta*, vol. 63 (Voronezh, 1967), p. 53.

[123]TsGAORgM f. 1289, op. 1, d. 91, ll. 107–108.

[124]Andrei K. Sokolov, "From the Countryside to the Cities," *Historical Social Research* 1991 no. 2, p. 117.

[125]TsGAORgM f. 176, op. 6, d. 184, l. 1. See also *Komsomol'skaia pravda*, May 20, 1932.

another traditional mechanism for guiding peasants to the city—the artel, a communal group of peasant laborers who banded together for collective economic security. One peasant who had experience working in the city, the elder (*starosta*), would organize a group of fellow villagers into an artel. They then traveled, lived, and worked as a group, and divided all expenses and earnings among themselves. Though artels were communal, they were not necessarily egalitarian; the elder wielded considerable power over artel members and received a larger share of the earnings. Nevertheless, this arrangement facilitated the transition to urban work for peasants new to the city, since the elder would find them employment and housing. The elder's knowledge of bargaining techniques and wages also protected them from being cheated by employers.[126]

The pervasiveness of artels in such seasonal work as construction, peat mining, and logging is evidenced by frequent references to them throughout the 1930s.[127] A Party official wrote that workers at one construction site "came in heated wagons [*teplushki*] with their carts and horses, with their shovels . . . —thousands of peasant migrants [*otkhodniki*], navvies [*grabari*], carpenters, and bricklayers. They lived in artels with elders in charge, observing old-fashioned customs [*dedovskie obychai*]."[128] Though artels were far less prevalent in manufacturing than in construction, some did operate in factories, including the Stalin automobile plant.[129]

The dearth of concrete research on this topic has allowed the fiction of Andrei Platonov to color our mental picture of peasants in cities. His story "Makar the Doubtful," which tells of the hardship faced by a peasant in Moscow, is an extremely perceptive critique of the Soviet bureaucracy's inability to function and communicate with uneducated people.[130] In reality, however, peasants did not wander

---

[126]For more on artels, see Hiroaki Kuromiya, "Workers' Artels and Soviet Production Relations," in *Russia in the Era of NEP*, Sheila Fitzpatrick et al., eds. (Bloomington, Ind., 1991); Timothy Mixter, "The Hiring Market as Workers' Turf: Migrant Agricultural Laborers and Mobilization of Collective Action in the Steppe Grainbelt of European Russia, 1853–1913," in *Peasant Economy, Culture, and Politics of European Russia*, Esther Kingston-Mann and Mixter, eds. (Princeton, 1991), pp. 318–320.

[127]TsGAMO f. 4867, op. 1, d. 156, ll. 24–26; *Za novyi byt* 1929 no. 9/10, p. 4; *Moskovskaia promyshlennaia kooperatsiia* 1931 no. 7, p. 12.

[128]*Rabochii klass—vedushchaia sila*, p. 201.

[129]*Istoriia Moskovskogo avtozavoda imeni I. A. Likhacheva* (Moscow, 1966), pp. 171–172; *AMOvets*, April 1, 1931, p. 1.

[130]Andrei Platonov, "Usomnivshiisia Makar," in *Gosudarstvennyi zhitel': Proza, rannie sochineniia, pis'ma*, M. A. Platonova, comp. (Moscow, 1988).

about the city in search of a comprehensible bureaucrat who would give them a job. Village networks and artels served this function, permitting peasants to accomplish what was admittedly a very difficult and even frightening transition with a minimum of adversity and trauma.

The Permanence of Migration

For generations the vast majority of peasants who had done temporary work in Moscow ultimately returned to the village. Many peasant in-migrants in the 1930s also sustained ties to the village, but virtually all of them were destined to remain in Moscow permanently, whether they realized it at the time or not. Among the factors that determined the permanence of migration were collectivization and the breaking of rural ties, expanding economic opportunities in the city, and notions of the superiority of life in Moscow over life in the village.

Peasants victimized by dekulakization had little choice but to settle in the city permanently. "Kulaks" who did return to their villages risked arrest and deportation. Some ventured back to reclaim their land in 1936, after the new constitution restored equal rights to all citizens, but authorities still often denied them permission to resettle there, so the city was their only option.[131]

Some peasants who had not been dispossessed also broke completely from the village when they moved to the city. One peasant decided in 1934 to leave his village and begin a new life in Moscow. Apparently ambitious, he had heard of the opportunities there and felt that the village held little future for him.[132] Most peasants, however, left open the option of returning. Seasonal laborers planned to spend part of the year in the village anyway; others looked on their village home as a type of insurance, should their health fail or should employment opportunities in the city dry up. Even a man who planned to stay in Moscow permanently typically left his wife and children behind until he was earning enough to support them and could arrange living space for them.[133]

[131]Harvard Project no. 107.

[132]Gudov, *Sud'ba rabochego*, pp. 3–5.

[133]One peasant woman moved to Moscow with her father in 1930 while her mother and younger sister stayed behind on a collective farm because they considered Moscow too big and dangerous: *Moskovskie stakhanovtsy* (Moscow, 1936), p. 100.

Most peasants who moved to Moscow only gradually decided to settle there permanently. Relatives kept them informed of negative events and trends in the village which dissuaded them from returning. As the rates of collectivization continued to rise throughout the 1930s, it became clear that collective farms were not about to disappear. Continued grain requisitions and a catastrophic decline in the rural living standard gave former peasants further reason to stay where they were.[134]

Also important were the changes going on in the city, particularly the growing number of year-round jobs. With the First Five-Year Plan, peasants suddenly received far greater opportunities for urban employment, especially in the construction industry. A major goal of construction managers at that time was to extend the construction season throughout the year. Seasonal laborers had traditionally arrived at construction sites in March or April, went home in August to help with the harvest, and then resumed construction work until October 14 (the Russian Orthodox holiday *Pokrov*), when they returned to the village.[135] With the sudden upsurge in demand for construction workers to reach the First Five-Year Plan's overambitious goals, managers encouraged workers to remain at construction sites throughout the year. A construction journal reported that the vast majority of construction workers in Moscow could be employed year round if only they could be persuaded to stay.[136]

Managers in Moscow and throughout the Soviet Union confronted situations like the one that arose at the Stalingrad tractor plant construction site. In the autumn of 1929 the site director, V. S. Ivanov, foresaw that he could not fulfill the plan if seasonal laborers returned home for the winter, so he tried to shame them into staying by announcing that permanent workers would lose their days off if seasonal laborers left. When this initiative failed, he called a meeting of all artel elders (de facto recognition that they controlled the labor force) and regaled them with a stirring speech about how desperately trac-

[134]A 1935 telegram signed by Stalin directed that industrial regions should continue to receive priority over rural regions in food distribution: TsPA f. 558, op. 1, d. 4979, ll. 3–6.

[135]*Moskovskii proletarii*, January 21, 1928; *Rabochii klass—vedushchaia sila*, p. 201; TsGAMO f. 6833, op. 1, d. 46, l. 103.

[136]*Stroitel'stvo Moskvy* 1930 no. 7, p. 4.

Construction workers secure transport rails at the Hammer and Sickle plant. Courtesy TsGAOR.

tors were needed to help the poor and backward Russian countryside. According to an account written by the local Party secretary, Ivanov concluded, " 'Now decide, either we work half years on construction, meaning that we don't produce the tractors so badly needed in the village, or we stay and get the job done. Whatever you decide, that will be it.' . . . Someone cried, 'We'll stay!' Others bawled, 'Let's go home to the village!' " When an influential elder announced that his artel would stay, the meeting as a whole finally voted to remain and work. Unfortunately for the director, many workers left for home just the same.[137]

Statistics on the number of construction workers in Moscow province in 1931 confirm that many continued to work only on a seasonal basis. Their numbers began to rise in April, peaked in July and again in September after a sharp dip during the August harvest, and then declined after mid-October.[138] There were indications, however, that by the end of the First Five-Year Plan, construction work had become a year-round occupation. The average number of construction workers in the USSR in 1928 was 723,000, but the figure varied from month to month, from a low of 390,000 in March to a high of over a million in September. By 1932 the yearly average had reached 3.13 million workers, and monthly figures stayed fairly constant, with a low of 2.95 million in March and a high of 3.38 million in July.[139] In other words, most construction workers were staying on the job year round.

A joint decree of the Moscow Party and Moscow city council in August 1933 stressed the need to establish permanent cadres in construction work, and mandated that the best construction workers have permanent residence permits for Moscow stamped in their passports. The decree went on to guarantee to construction workers living conditions equal to those of industrial workers, and also endorsed multiyear work contracts.[140] At one Moscow construction site where work was concluding, recruiters for metro construction approached peasant laborers who were preparing to return to their villages and persuaded them to stay by promising steady work and wages.[141] Year-round construction work appealed to peasants simply as a chance to

---

[137]*Govoriat stroiteli sotsializma: Vospominaniia uchastnikov sotsialisticheskogo stroitel'stva v SSSR* (Moscow, 1959), pp. 153–154. See also *Moskovskaia promyshlennaia kooperatsiia* 1931 no. 7, p. 12.

[138]TsGAMO f. 6833, op. 1, d. 46, l. 31; *Rabochaia Moskva*, September 19, 1931, p. 1. See also TsGAOR f. 5515, op. 15, d. 463, l. 5; *Postroika*, July 11, 1932, p. 1.

[139]Gol'tsman, "Sostav stroitel'nykh rabochikh," p. 148; Eliseeva, p. 68.

[140]V. E. Poletaev, *Na putiakh k novoi Moskve, 1917–1935* (Moscow, 1964), p. 57.

[141]*Pervyi Podshipnikovyi: Istoriia pervogo gosudarstvennogo podshipnikovogo zavoda, 1932–1972* (Moscow, 1973), p. 16; *Istoriia metro Moskvy*, p. 208. Construction union reports indicate that the superiority of labor and living conditions in Moscow over the horrendous conditions at other construction sites provided an incentive for peasants to relocate and remain there: TsGAMO f. 4867, op. 1, d. 156, l. 22.

Construction workers dig a tunnel for the Moscow metro, 1933. Metro construction workers faced some of the most arduous working conditions in Moscow. Courtesy Muzei Istorii Moskvy.

earn more money. Without making an irrevocable decision to leave the village for good, large numbers of them simply stayed on in Moscow.

One other set of figures demonstrates that during the First Five-Year Plan increasing numbers of temporary migrants already began to work year round, or at least returned to the village less often. According to Central Statistical Administration figures, in 1929 there were 610,772 "arrivals" to Moscow and 348,134 "departures." The corresponding data for 1931 were 1,056,244 arrivals and 320,802 departures. Though the precision of these numbers is quite dubious, they do convey the overall impression not only that more people arrived in Moscow in 1931, but also that a far smaller percentage of them left.[142] In fact, the total number of Soviet citizens employed in all sectors of industry was directly correlated with the number of people who stayed in cities (the surplus of arrivals over departures).[143]

[142] TsGANKh f. 1562, op. 20, d. 29, l. 5.
[143] Trud v SSSR (Moscow, 1936), pp. 7, 93.

Year-round employment was only one step in the transition to permanent residence. Throughout the First Five-Year Plan, most peasants who worked in the construction industry retained their ties to the
village. Though statistics from the 1932 Trade Union Census underrepresent the number of workers with a "connection to agriculture,"
they nonetheless show that over 70 percent of peasants who began
construction work in 1931 and 1932 maintained such ties. Furthermore, over two-thirds of the peasants who began construction work in
Moscow province in 1928–29 still had a connection with agriculture
when the census was conducted in 1932.[144]

Peasants who found industrial jobs broke their ties to the village
much more quickly than those in construction. Only 30 percent of the
people who began work at the Stalin automobile plant in 1932 had a
connection with agriculture, though over two-thirds of them were of
peasant origin. The percentage was slightly higher at the Hammer and
Sickle metallurgical plant, but within a few years most former peasants had sold their land or severed their connections with collective
farms. Former peasants employed in light industry also proved much
quicker than construction workers to break their ties to the village.[145]

Industrial employment clearly promoted permanent residence in
Moscow, and during the 1930s thousands of temporary migrants
switched from construction work to permanent factory jobs. Many
construction workers got jobs in the very factories they had built.
One prominent trade union official wrote in 1934 that "construction
was and still remains a transitional garden through which a seasonal
laborer who came from the village moves on to an operating factory."[146] Such an occurrence was logical, considering the vast scale of
industrial expansion and the tremendous labor demand of the period.
Directors of just-completed factories came under intense pressure to
begin production immediately, but they had no experienced workers
to hire. Naturally they offered jobs with attractive wages to peasant
construction workers, despite their lack of factory experience; the
absence of available skilled cadres left them no choice.

[144]*Profsoiuznaia perepis', 1932–1933 g.* (Moscow, 1934). Census takers defined "a
connection with agriculture" as landownership or membership in a collective farm.
These data are discussed in Appendix II.

[145]*Profsoiuznaia perepis'.* See Appendix II for data on other branches of industry.

[146]*Za industrializatsiiu,* June 30, 1934, p. 4. See also Vdovin and Drobizhev, pp.
222–223; Gol'tsman, "Sostav stroitel'nykh rabochikh," p. 159.

Evidence indicates that peasants from branches of seasonal industry other than construction began to take factory jobs as well. Virtually all peasants who worked as seasonal peat miners in Moscow province left to accept higher-paying employment in Moscow city factories by 1931.[147] Peasants who worked in rural textile mills and handicraft industry moved to the city for more lucrative employment.[148] A 1933 study of labor turnover concluded that young workers rapidly changed to jobs in industrial sectors that offered the highest wages.[149] The emphasis on heavy industry resulted in enormous demand for labor and high wages at metalworking plants. An entire series of huge new or expanded factories in Moscow hired thousands of peasant in-migrants every year to meet their labor needs.[150]

Once new arrivals had secured permanent jobs and steady incomes, they liquidated their property in the village. A 1930 report on Moscow factory workers stated that former peasants working in the city were sending letters back to their wives in the village telling them to sell all property and join them in Moscow.[151] With opportunities for economic advancement in the countryside eliminated, peasants turned to the city to fulfill their ambitions or simply to survive. Economic considerations, then, were paramount in peasants' decisions to accept full-time factory jobs, break ties to the village, and settle in Moscow for good.

Yet noneconomic factors must also be taken into consideration. Though prior urban experience and village networks eased their move to the city, peasants still faced a challenging transition. They left an environment where everyone and everything was familiar and found themselves in new physical surroundings, confronted by crowds of unfamiliar people, new modes of transportation, housing in barracks, and industrial labor. One Moscow factory's department of cadres described peasant youths who

---

[147]TsGAMO f. 6833, op. 1, d. 46, l. 33; *Materialy k otchetu Egor'evskogo raikoma VKP(b)* (Egor'evsk, 1932), pp. 26–27. Many seasonal workers in logging and rural food-processing operations also gradually found urban employment. See Arutiunian, p. 103.

[148]Eliseeva, p. 64.

[149]Vdovin and Drobizhev, p. 223; *Materialy . . . Egor'evskogo raikoma*, pp. 22–23.

[150]See Appendix II.

[151]MPA f. 634, op. 1, d. 207, l. 60. See also *Zavod sovetskogo khleba* (Moscow, 1932), p. 80; *Govoriat stroiteli sotsializma*, pp. 267–268.

could stand for hours on the hill by their residence with their heads back and mouths open, following airplanes in flight with greedy curiosity. Trams startled them, and they jumped aside to avoid automobiles. The factory staggered them—the impression made on them by its incomprehensible appearance was enormous.[152]

One former peasant recalled that she had never seen a building as large as the factory where she found work, and that at first she was afraid to enter it for fear it would collapse.[153] Such fright was natural for people in a new environment. The interesting question is: What led them to forsake the familiarity of their villages and choose to remain in Moscow, despite the difficulties they encountered there?[154]

Aside from the economic incentives, Moscow had a certain allure for peasants—the "bright lights" of the city, both figuratively and literally. Ivan Petrovich, who moved to Moscow in 1937, recalled his excitement on discovering that "electric lights shone in every building along the street. I had never seen such electric lights before—I liked them so much! . . . I liked Moscow so much that I think I would have sold my soul to stay in Moscow. Why? Because Moscow is a beauty. And when I went to Red Square, oh, I liked it, especially the Kremlin!"[155] Moscow offered stores, movie theaters, workers' clubs, organized sports, parades, parks. One group of peasants who arrived in Moscow to build the metro were so impressed by a performance at the Bolshoi Theater that the experience reportedly became a factor in their decision to remain permanently.[156] Other newcomers no doubt found themselves attracted by the less refined aspects of city life. Prostitutes, taverns, and clothing stores, while they did not exactly flourish in Moscow in the 1930s, provided scintillation that the village did not.

Peasant songs (*chastushki*) described in admiring terms the boule-

[152]AAN f. 359, op. 2, d. 507, ll. 27–28.

[153]Khlevniuk, "Izmenenie," p. 99.

[154]A sociological study of peasant migration in Serbia concluded that "the possible advantages of migration and optimistic images of the urban milieu must outweigh the strength of traditional social ties, the attachment to the predictable and familiar, and the often tenuous security of the land": Andrei Simic, *The Peasant Urbanites: A Study of Rural-Urban Mobility in Serbia* (New York, 1973), p. 75.

[155]Interview with Ivan Petrovich Gomozenkov for the documentary film *Piatachok* (Moscow, 1989).

[156]*Istoriia metro Moskvy*, pp. 208–209.

vards, buildings, and excitement of cities. They also expressed the desire of young peasant women to join their boyfriends in the city:

My sweetheart lives in the city	Milyi v gorode zhivet
While I'm miserable in the village.	A ia v derevne maiusia.
He doesn't think of me	On ne tuzhit obo mne
And I am worried.	A ia sumlevaiusia.[157]

Some young peasants were convinced that the city was culturally superior, and that the most attractive and urbane members of the opposite sex lived there.

Beyond the initial attractions and difficulties was the issue of social status. Newcomers normally engaged in unskilled labor, lived in barracks, dressed in peasant clothes, and consequently were looked down on by the Muscovites. When they returned to visit their villages, though, they were received with admiration and respect. They could tell stories about the city, they wore stylish urban clothes, and they had money "jingling in their pockets."[158] Polina Ivanovna, who moved to Moscow in 1935, recalled how very elegantly (*nariadnaia*) she dressed when she visited her native village, "putting on airs." Many young men there courted her and even proposed marriage, but she decided she would not "get married to the village."[159] This dual status—low standing in the urban hierarchy and prestige in the village—reinforced peasants' opinion that the city was somehow superior to the village.

A variety of considerations, psychological as well as economic, led peasants to settle permanently in Moscow. Collectivization and a drastic decline in the rural living standard certainly loomed quite large in their decision, but new opportunities and the excitement of the city figured prominently as well. In either case, village networks facilitated peasants' migration to Moscow, and continued to serve and influence them. The informal nature of these networks permitted a flexibility that ensured their perpetuation in changing times. As

[157]*Chastushki v zapisiakh sovetskogo vremeni*, B. N. Putilov, ed. (Moscow/Leningrad, 1965), pp. 42, 100–101. Another song spoke of the "many fine boys" in the city as a reason for moving there.

[158]*Moskovskie stakhanovtsy*, pp. 461–462.

[159]Interview with Polina Ivanovna Kazharina for the documentary film *Piatachok* (Moscow, 1989).

migration to Moscow changed from temporary to permanent, village networks guided peasants to permanent employment in the expanding sectors of the Moscow economy.

In a sense, migration traditions facilitated Soviet industrialization by guiding peasant labor to urban construction sites and factories. But as a consequence, village networks rather than official recruitment programs shaped the urban workforce. For Party leaders intent on fashioning peasants into a loyal proletariat, the failure to control migration amounted to a loss of influence over new workers. Nor did peasants' move to the city signal eagerness to advance Party leaders' plans for building socialism. Peasants who fled dekulakization and poverty in the village generally felt deep hostility toward the Soviet government, while those who sought employment opportunities in the city were attracted more to its material wealth and unofficial culture than to the task of constructing socialism. The fact that few newcomers shared Party leaders' goals and values would lead to protracted contestations between Soviet officials and former peasants in the formation of the urban workforce.

3

The Formation of
the Urban Workforce

When Mariia Aleksandrovna arrived in Moscow in 1929, though she had never worked in a factory before, she asked a friend to arrange a job for her at the Hammer and Sickle metallurgical plant. The plant needed so many new workers that her lack of experience proved to be no obstacle, and she was hired in the sheet-metal press shop. The actual work, which she undertook without any preparation or training, proved both taxing and dangerous. She and other workers used conveyors and levers to position red-hot ingots of molten steel under mechanized presses. Pointing to the scars on her hands, she explains that she was lucky—many workers lost fingers and even arms performing this work.[1]

Peasant in-migration dramatically altered both the composition and the character of Moscow's workforce. Former peasants filled the enormous demand for labor created by the Soviet industrialization drive, particularly in construction and heavy industry.[2] The number of construction workers in Moscow more than doubled during the First Five-Year Plan, from 62,000 to 146,000, and virtually all of them were of peasant origin.[3] Moscow's industrial workforce ballooned

[1]Interview with Mariia Aleksandrovna Filatova at the Hammer and Sickle plant, Moscow, April 17, 1989.

[2]This chapter focuses primarily on construction and heavy industry, the sectors of greatest concern to Soviet officials and the ones where most peasant in-migrants found employment. For a full discussion of the various jobs they obtained both in industry and in nonindustrial workplaces, see Appendix I.

[3]TsGAORgM f. 126, op. 2, d. 98b, l. 28; *Trud v SSSR: Ekonomiko-statisticheskii*

from 186,500 in 1928 to 433,900 in 1932 to 614,000 in 1937. Former peasants accounted for 68 percent of these new industrial employees during the First Five-Year Plan, and slightly over 50 percent during the remainder of the decade.[4]

Industrial managers faced the enormous task of training these thousands of new workers for factory labor. They also sought to impose on them a new work culture, with time-oriented labor and disciplined work habits. But newly urbanized workers resisted these attempts to enforce labor discipline. They drew upon their own work culture and preindustrial traditions to devise alternative work routines. And the village networks and artels that played such prominent roles in the migration process served to perpetuate this traditional work culture and reinforce their resistance to strict labor discipline. The failure to mold an efficient workforce resulted in Party campaigns and exhortations to raise productivity as well as police interventions in industry. It was the interactions and contestations between new workers, management, and the Party that formed the Moscow workforce. These contestations determined how much urban work changed former peasants and how much former peasants changed the Soviet workplace.

Training Former Peasants for Urban Labor

Though many peasants had held urban jobs before, few had worked in a large metalworking plant, so training them was an enormous task. Ivan Gudov, a peasant who arrived in Moscow during the First Five-Year Plan, described the fright he felt when he entered a machine-building plant for his first day of work.

> The ground shook from the rumble of machinery. On the equipment I was walking past there poured an unending stream of water and

spravochnik (Moscow, 1932), pp. 82–83. "Workers" is employed here as a generic term that encompasses four identifiable sociological groups within the workforce: peasant in-migrants, established (usually hereditary male) workers, urban male youth, and urban women.

[4]Tverdokhleb, "Chislennost'," p. 24; Vdovin and Drobizhev, pp. 115–116; Dadykin, pp. 46–49; M. Ia. Sonin, *Vosproizvodstvo rabochei sily v SSSR i balans truda* (Moscow, 1959), p. 143. During the First Five-Year Plan, 14 percent of new industrial employees were urban youth, 11 percent urban women, and 7 percent other urban groups.

milk (soon I learned it wasn't milk but emulsions). . . . I was trying
not to bother anyone, and not to catch on some sort of flywheel.
It seemed as if one careless movement and I'd be hurled into a
machine.[5]

Soviet officials recognized the desperate need for instructional programs. The Moscow oblast Party journal wrote of millions of young
peasants "pouring into production, never having worked before in a
mill or factory," and issued an urgent call for training.[6] But the training programs Soviet authorities organized failed to accommodate the
hundreds of thousands of peasants who joined the Moscow workforce
each year.

Moscow's system of higher and secondary technical education expanded considerably during the 1930s, but it did not offer the rudimentary instruction needed by people just beginning factory work.[7]
Traditionally new workers received basic training not in formal programs but through apprenticeships. The Commissariat of Education
(Narkompros), however, objected that this mode of training provided
exclusively practical instruction at the expense of any general education. Both the Commissariat of Education and the Komsomol pressed
for expansion of schooling for new workers, citing their need to develop "culture" and "social consciousness" as well as technical skills.
Officials hoped formal education would break former peasants of
their traditional work culture and instill in them a stricter sense of
time and discipline.

In June 1929 the National Economic Council (Vesenkha) endorsed
expansion of the system of factory apprenticeship schools (*fabrichno-
zavodskie uchenichestva*), which combined practical technical training with courses in the Russian language, mathematics, physics, military studies, and politics.[8] Factory apprentice schools throughout the

---

[5]Gudov, *Sud'ba rabochego*, p. 7.

[6]*Sputnik kommunista* 1930 no. 19/20, p. 54. See also *Za promyshlennye kadry* 1934 no. 21/22, p. 87.

[7]*Vo glave kul'turnogo stroitel'stva: Moskovskie kommunisty—organizatory i ruko-
voditeli kul'turnogo stroitel'stva v stolitse, 1917–1941: Sbornik dokumentov* (Moscow, 1983), pp. 181–182; *Za promyshlennye kadry* 1930 no. 2/3, p. 41; TsGAORgM f. 415, op. 7, d. 5, ll. 1–7. For more on higher technical education, see Kendall E. Bailes, *Technology and Society under Lenin and Stalin* (Princeton, 1978), pp. 218–229.

[8]Fitzpatrick, *Education and Social Mobility*, pp. 198–200; TsGAORgM f. 5301, op. 4, d. 66, l. 45; S. Filatov, *Partrabota na zavode "Serp i molot"* (Moscow/Leningrad, 1931), pp. 112–113; Mel'nikov, p. 225. The trade unions, in opposition to Narkompros, favored purely technical training programs.

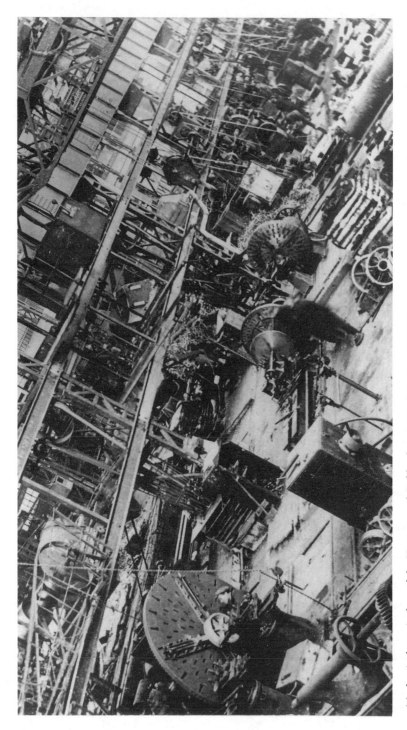

Mechanical repair shop of the Hammer and Sickle plant, 1932. Courtesy TsGAOR.

country enrolled over one million students by 1932, with branches at all major Moscow factories.[9]

During the First Five-Year Plan, most students in factory apprenticeship schools were of working-class origin.[10] The trade unions issued calls in 1932 for these schools to recruit more young peasants, and by 1935, half of all their students were peasants.[11] Despite these efforts, factory apprenticeship schools provided training to only a fraction of the peasants entering Soviet industry. Schools to train new workers for light industry were virtually nonexistent.[12] Even in heavy industry, where investment in education was far higher, factory apprenticeship schools faced a shortage of funds. At a metalworkers' trade union congress on training workers in 1930, one report after another assailed the inadequacy of cadre training, the lack of money to build or complete factory apprenticeship schools, and the insufficient number of students enrolled. Factory apprenticeship schools trained only 300,000 of the millions of new workers who entered Soviet industry during the First Five-Year Plan.[13]

The quality of institutionalized training also lagged. A Commissariat of Heavy Industry report in 1934 criticized the quality of institutionalized training and decried the shortage of equipment and teachers at factory apprenticeship schools.[14] With every competent engineer and foreman working in the factories, school administrators had to hire retired foremen to train the new workers, though they were not at all familiar with new technology.[15] Factory apprentice-

[9]Fitzpatrick, *Education and Social Mobility*, p. 100; B. Malinkin, "Shkola FZU na avtozavode im. Stalina," *Voprosy profdvizheniia* 1935 no. 10, p. 67; A. V. Kol'tsov, *Kul'turnoe stroitel'stvo v RSFSR v gody pervoi piatiletki* (Moscow, 1960), p. 162; *Istoriia Moskvy: Kratkii ocherk*, p. 281.

[10]F. Rakino, "Postanovka raboty s novymi sloiami rabochikh," *Partiinoe stroitel'stvo* 1931 no. 13, pp. 50–51; I. L. Kornakovskii, "Istoriia zavoda 'Serp i molot,' 1917–1932" (dissertation, Institute of History, Moscow, 1972), pp. 110–111, 388; TsGAOR f. 5475, op. 13, d. 160, l. 7; MPA f. 635, op. 1, d. 41, l. 14.

[11]*Voprosy truda* 1932 no. 1, p. 57; *Rabochii klass—vedushchaia sila*, p. 201.

[12]TsGAORgM f. 453, op. 1, d. 13, ll. 93–94; *Moskovskoe obshchestvennoe pitanie*, February 25, 1932, p. 11; *Moskovskaia promyshlennaia kooperatsiia* 1931 no. 13/14, p. 11.

[13]Fitzpatrick, *Education and Social Mobility*, p. 200.

[14]TsGAOR f. 5469, op. 14, d. 304, ll. 7–15; *Industrializatsiia SSSR*, vol. 3, pp. 397–399. See also MPA f. 432, op. 1, d. 75, l. 56; f. 635, op. 1, d. 41, l. 23; *Molodoi Bol'shevik* 1932 no. 17, p. 29.

[15]Iu. Kuz'minov, "Osvoenie novykh zavodov i novoi tekhniki i problema kadrov," *Problemy ekonomiki* 1935 no. 5, p. 40; *Za promyshlennye kadry* 1930 no. 2/3, p. 41; TsGAOR f. 5515, op. 17, d. 200, l. 130.

ship schools often faced a shortage of competent students as well, because managers could not afford to release unskilled workers even temporarily for fear of not fulfilling their plan. Schools could not be selective, and frequently got students who were unruly, lazy, or only semiliterate.[16]

A decree of the Commissariat of Heavy Industry in May 1933 emphasized the need for part-time study so that students would not have to stop work. The decree also recommended that two-year apprenticeship programs be shortened to ten months by reduction of the general education courses.[17] Several later reports stressed the weakness of nontechnical education in factory apprenticeship schools. As factories failed to fund their schools adequately, rudimentary technical training received priority and general education to instill new ideas and work discipline was neglected.[18]

Short training courses provided even less general education. The Central Institute of Labor, run by the trade unions and under the directorship of Aleksei Gastev, designed the short courses most widely used to train new workers. Held not in factories but at designated training sites, these courses taught new workers as quickly and simply as possible the basic steps required for construction work or for operation of machinery on an assembly line. Gastev's embrace of Frederick Taylor's "scientific management" and insistence on maximum efficiency in both training and labor left no time for general education and provided only a bare minimum of theoretical instruction for workers.[19]

The Central Institute of Labor programs enrolled primarily new arrivals from the countryside. Of the 101,000 students admitted at the beginning of 1931, two-thirds were former peasants or rural artisans. The Institute even established rural training sites (which proliferated

---

[16]TsGAOR f. 5469, op. 14, d. 312, l. 49; *Stroitel'naia promyshlennost'* 1929 no. 4. p. 379; archive of Hammer and Sickle metallurgical plant XXII (IV) 0001, l. 10.

[17]*Industrializatsiia SSSR*, vol. 3, p. 395. A study of factory apprenticeship schools in 1932–33 showed that theoretical study was superficial even before this decree. See Khlevniuk, "Izmenenie," p. 132. See also MPA f. 468, op. 1, d. 83, ll. 14–15.

[18]TsGAORgM f. 5301, op. 1, d. 68, l. 11; op. 4, d. 66, ll. 56–57; TsGAOR f. 5515, op. 17, d. 630, ll. 35–37.

[19]Fitzpatrick, *Education and Social Mobility*, p. 126; *Tsentral'nyi institut truda i ego metody NOT* (Moscow, 1970), pp. 70, 76; *Za kachestvo kadrov* 1931 no. 4, pp. 5–6. For more on Gastev, see Richard Stites, *Revolutionary Dreams* (New York, 1989), pp. 149–155.

from 720 in 1930 to 1,680 in 1931) to prepare peasants for urban construction work before they left the village.[20] With the growing demand for construction workers, the Moscow oblast department of labor resolved that these programs should train peasants in fifteen days, so that they could begin work almost immediately.[21]

Even the limited theoretical training prescribed by the Central Institute of Labor was often slighted. At one training site in Moscow, instructors devoted six hours a day to bricklaying and cement pouring and only one hour to the overall production process. Most of the instructors, themselves not engineers but workers, lacked any theoretical knowledge to convey to their students.[22] Numerous reports concluded that both theoretical training and political work among the students were deficient, and that even technical training suffered from insufficient funding, a shortage of equipment, and a scarcity of qualified instructors.[23]

Officials also organized short programs to prepare construction workers to fill industrial jobs once the factory they were building was finished.[24] Some construction managers held evening classes to retrain construction workers for the specific type of industrial work to be done in the factory.[25] In the weeks before the Kaganovich ball bearing plant opened, managers frantically tried to retrain construction workers to manufacture ball bearings. The short programs they organized, however, trained only around 750 of the more than 2,000 skilled cadres needed; the remaining new workers hired simply had to learn on the job. As a result, the plant operated with colossal inefficiency and waste, but the lack of skilled workers left the factory director no alternative.[26] Expanding factories such as the Stalin automobile plant, the Kirov Dinamo plant, and the Kuibyshev electronics factory also established programs to train former peasants, but the

[20]Fitzpatrick, *Education and Social Mobility*, pp. 178, 200; *Industrializatsiia SSSR*, vol. 2, pp. 411–412.

[21]TsGAMO f. 6833, op. 1, d. 46, l. 50.

[22]*Stroitel'naia promyshlennost'* 1929 no. 4, p. 378.

[23]TsPA f. 17, op. 114, d. 255, l. 30; TsGAORgM f. 5301, op. 4, d. 66, l. 39; TsGAOR f. 5475, op. 13, d. 160, l. 13; f. 5515, op. 1, d. 270, l. 18.

[24]TsGAOR f. 5515, op. 15, d. 210, l. 14.

[25]Fedorov, p. 216.

[26]*Za sovetskii podshipnik*, November 17, 1931, p. 1; December 3, 1931, pp. 1–4; December 15, 1931, p. 1; *Byli industrial'nye*, p. 172; *Pervyi podshipnikovyi*, pp. 22–23, 50.

influx of new workers was so great that teaching even fundamentals was almost more than they could manage.[27]

Instruction for transport workers, too, was criticized for its brevity and low standards. Most of the drivers, mechanics, and fuel attendants who received instruction were judged to be incompetent.[28] Training programs in nonindustrial work other than construction and transport were almost nonexistent. Former peasants who obtained jobs in the service sector or in state and cooperative trade simply learned their skills on the job.[29] The employment of untrained workers in industrial and nonindustrial sectors precipitated innumerable accidents, which resulted in damage to expensive equipment, the collapse of structures, and a profusion of injuries and fatalities.[30]

The shortcomings of training programs and in-migrants' continued ignorance of even basic principles of industrial production prompted the creation of technical-minimum examinations, designed to ensure basic technical knowledge among all industrial workers. The examinations, decreed on June 30, 1932, and administered directly in factory shops throughout the Second Five-Year Plan, tested knowledge of the most elementary industrial procedures—turning machines on and off, lubricating parts, handling equipment, and keeping the workplace clean and orderly.[31] The technical-minimum examinations represented a shortcut attempt to teach new workers rudimentary industrial tasks. By January 1934, 115,000 Moscow workers had passed

[27]Davydova, pp. 243–244; *Za promyshlennye kadry* 1930 no. 2/3, p. 42; *Istoriia Moskovskogo avtozavoda*, pp. 190–191; *Soveshchanie khoziaistvennikov, inzhenerov, tekhnikov, partiinykh i profsoiuznykh rabotnikov tiazheloi promyshlennosti: 20–22 sen. 1934* (Moscow/Leningrad, 1935), p. 162.

[28]TsGAOR f. 5515, op. 17, d. 200, l. 36; *Moskovskii transportnik*, February 4, 1940, p. 3.

[29]In contrast, rural women who obtained employment in urban department stores in the United States in the 1920s and 1930s received careful training, as retailers were determined to have knowledgeable and cheerful saleswomen. See Susan Porter Benson, *Counter Cultures: Saleswomen, Managers, and Customers in American Department Stores, 1890–1940* (Urbana, Ill., 1986), pp. 138–146.

[30]TsGAOR f. 5475, op. 13, d. 171, l. 96; op. 14, d. 67, l. 20; *Moskovskii mashinostroitel'nyi trest, Otchet* (Moscow, 1929), p. 25; *Dognat' i peregnat'*, December 15, 1935, p. 1; *AMOvets*, April 2, 1931, p. 4; *Stroitel'naia promyshlennost'* 1929 no. 3, p. 284.

[31]*Industrializatsiia SSSR*, vol. 3, pp. 434–435; T. S. Aleksandrova, "Rabochii klass Moskvy v bor'be za razvitie tiazheloi promyshlennosti v gody vtoroi piatiletki" (dissertation, Academy of Social Sciences of the Communist Party, Moscow, 1957), pp. 36–37; A. K. Gastev, *Kak nado rabotat'* (Moscow, 1966), pp. 322–327.

the examinations.[32] Of course the examinations did nothing to teach acceptance of managerial authority or time-oriented work routines.

Overall the technical-minimum examinations, in conjunction with all industrial training programs, raised the technical level of the workforce only slightly. In absolute terms the number of skilled workers increased quite dramatically, but the influx of unskilled in-migrants was so massive that the percentage of the Soviet workforce classified as skilled rose less than 1 percent from 1927 to 1934, and the percentage of workers classified as semiskilled increased only 6.5 percent. Even in the late 1930s the vast majority of Moscow workers remained at low skill levels.[33]

Because formal training programs failed to provide adequate instruction, most new workers simply learned on the job. A 1931 Commissariat of Labor report stated that the shortage of skilled workers was so severe in Moscow that new workers had to be put directly to work without any training at all.[34] Expansion of the Hammer and Sickle plant during the First Five-Year Plan required more skilled workers than the factory apprenticeship school could supply. Managers transferred some unskilled former peasants to skilled jobs and instructed them to observe other workers and do what they did. The factory's training bureau condemned the practice as "extremely detrimental," particularly because the reassigned workers were often chosen on the basis of connections rather than ability.[35]

The fact that peasants' connections and networks often determined their placement in factory jobs also influenced their acquisition of industrial skills. Village networks and artels played roles in conveying skills and knowledge about industrial work. In some factories, newly arrived workers were given jobs that normally required considerable training.[36] They were able to do the work only through the guidance of a fellow villager with industrial experience. The work

---

[32]*Delo chesti* (Moscow, 1934), pp. 22–25; *Nashe stroitel'stvo* 1936 no. 9, p. 61; *Biulleten' Narkomata kommunal'nogo khoziaistva* 1935 no. 5, pp. 79–83; *Nezabyvaemye 30-e*, pp. 66–67. Technical study circles, established to help workers pass the examination, experienced erratic attendance and limited success. See TsGAMO f. 214, op. 1, d. 147, ll. 30, 131; Aleksandrova, "Rabochii klass," p. 84.

[33]TsGAORgM f. 415, op. 3, d. 27, l. 1; TsGANKh f. 7622, op. 1, d. 251, l. 4. See also E. A. Anoshin, "Promyshlennye rabochie Moskvy v gody predvoennykh piatiletok" (dissertation, Moscow State University, 1979), p. 94.

[34]TsGAOR f. 5515, op. 1, d. 191, l. 127. See also Kuz'minov, pp. 41–42.

[35]Archive of Hammer and Sickle metallurgical plant XXII (IV) 0001, l. 4.

[36]MPA f. 429, op. 1, d. 109, l. 115.

routines they learned in this manner were not the strict and efficient ones prescribed by scientific management, but rather the permissive, task-oriented habits of their preindustrial work culture. In other words, fellow villagers taught first-generation workers not only to operate machinery but also to avert managerial discipline and circumvent norms.

The weakness of institutionalized technical education in the 1930s underscores a broader problem of the Soviet Union's rapid industrialization: the rush to begin production left no time for the preparation of a disciplined labor force. Had Soviet leaders chosen to industrialize the country over a span of several decades, they would have had time to train and discipline a limited number of new workers each year. Instead they mobilized all resources to construct hundreds of factories and bring them into production within ten years, and managers desperate to fulfill the plan hired as many peasant in-migrants as possible and put them immediately to work.

The low level of training among new workers forced managers to organize production accordingly. Building construction in Moscow during the First Five-Year Plan remained similar in both technology and tempo to construction done before the Revolution.[37] Foundations were dug manually by thousands of former peasants, and construction materials were hauled by horse-drawn carts.[38] As late as June 1935 the Moscow Party organization and Moscow city council derided the "low level of mechanization" in construction and insisted that "the primitive methods of constructing housing, embankments, roads, canals, and water pipes" must be improved.[39] Yet though the level of mechanization rose by the end of the Second Five-Year Plan, workers frequently did not know how to use the machinery effectively, and construction remained labor-intensive.[40]

As in the construction industry, the influx of new, unskilled workers in heavy industry required tasks to be subdivided and work simplified. Imported technology and Taylorist methods complemented this process by creating jobs that required little skill and experi-

[37]*Ekonomicheskoe stroitel'stvo* 1930 no. 6, p. 5. See also TsGAOR f. 5475, op. 13, d. 88, l. 81.

[38]*Stroitel'* 1934 no. 3, p. 8; *Pervyi podshipnikovyi*, p. 39.

[39]*General'nyi plan rekonstruktsii goroda Moskvy* (Moscow, 1936), pp. 23–25.

[40]*Nashe stroitel'stvo* 1936 no. 1, pp. 12–19; *Sbornik dokumentov po istorii SSSR*, vol. 3 (1933–1941), V. Z. Drobizhev, ed. (Moscow, 1980), p. 136.

Transport at a Moscow construction site. Note the unmechanized, labor-intensive nature of the work. Courtesy TsGAOR.

ence. Soviet industrialization in the 1930s, especially in the new or expanded heavy industry plants, saw the introduction of assembly-line production, in contrast to the semi-artisanal metalwork done earlier.[41] The Stalin automobile plant provides a prime example of this trend. On assembly-line equipment imported from the West, each low-skilled worker repeatedly performed one task in the assembly of automobiles.[42]

Other expanded and renovated Moscow factories and all newly constructed factories received similar equipment. The Kaganovich ball bearing plant operated with imported technology in an assembly-line system; none of the workers had any specialization and all were simply called machinists (*stanochniki*).[43] Though the new machinery caused problems for Soviet engineers (and indeed required Western engineers to put it in operation), it permitted the employment of unskilled workers.[44] Gudov recalled that on his first day on the job he was sent directly to the shop floor with no orientation, apprenticeship, or instruction whatever. When he expressed bewilderment, it was explained to him that in this new plant "the machines do everything themselves and a person only sits beside them, brings metal to them, and observes."[45]

The process of mechanizing old factories required a transitional period during which modern imported technology operated alongside unskilled manual labor. Paradoxically, then, a fair amount of labor-intensive production took place in Soviet industry even as equipment was modernized.[46] The mechanization of Soviet factories in this

[41]V. A. Kozlov and O. V. Khlevniuk, *Nachinaetsia s cheloveka: Chelovecheskii faktor v sotsialisticheskom stroitel'stve* (Moscow, 1988), p. 106. This aspect of Soviet industrialization resembled American industrialization in the early twentieth century, when Henry Ford set up assembly lines and hired unskilled immigrant workers.

[42]TsGANKh f. 7622, op. 1, d. 58, ll. 72–73; *Moskva: Sbornik statei po sotsialisticheskoi rekonstruktsii proletarskoi stolitsy*, Ia. Brezanovskii, ed. (Moscow, 1932), pp. 49–50.

[43]Gudov, *Sud'ba rabochego*, pp. 4–5.

[44]TsGAOR f. 7952, op. 3, d. 522, ll. 19–21; *Slavnye traditsii: K 100-letiiu zavoda "Krasnyi proletarii" im. A. I. Efremova, 1857–1957* (Moscow, 1957), p. 122.

[45]Gudov, *Sud'ba rabochego*, pp. 4–5. When Gudov asked a fellow villager in Moscow why workers no longer specialized, he replied, "Before there were lathe operators, drillers, and other specializations. But now everyone . . . is called a machinist or an operator. Any girl [*devchonka*] can master the complete 'science' of it in a day. . . . All our machinery is from Germany, America, Sweden, and Italy."

[46]Archive of Hammer and Sickle metallurgical plant IV (I-01), ll. 1–2; TsGAOR f. 7952, op. 3, d. 260, ll. 15, 43; Filatov, p. 37; V. A. Grudkov, *Peredovoi opyt—vsem*

Rolling shop of the Hammer and Sickle plant, 1930. Like most other factories, it substituted manual labor for a conveyor feed system. Courtesy TsGAOR.

period was not accompanied by automation (conveyer feed systems); most materials had to be manually transported and hand-hoisted into machines. As managers compensated for the lack of automation in their factories by hiring more labor, the ratio of workers to machines in the machine-building industry nearly tripled during the First Five-Year Plan.[47] The jobs of transporting and loading materials overwhelmingly went to newly urbanized workers, who carried out such work without any training.

Because of rapid peasant in-migration, insufficient training, and assembly-line production, the Moscow workforce as it formed in the 1930s consisted largely of former peasants who possessed low levels of skill, technical understanding, and labor discipline. Since they developed little sense of achieved status or pride in their work, industrial workers did not transform their sense of self-identity or social role. For these new workers, who did not measure their self-

stalevaram: Rasskaz starshego mastera Moskovskogo zavoda "Serp i molot" (Moscow, 1958), p. 6.

[47]David R. Shearer, "Rationalization and Reconstruction in the Soviet Machine Building Industry, 1926–1934" (dissertation, University of Pennsylvania, 1988), pp. 218–222, 277–279.

worth by their level of technical competence, this result posed no problem. But Soviet authorities expected the acquisition of technical skill and understanding to transform them into "conscious" proletarians. The absence of a highly skilled and politically loyal proletariat undermined Party leaders' ideological vision and basis of popular support.

Preindustrial Work Culture and Managerial Control

The village networks and artels that guided peasants to Moscow continued to function in the city. After their arrival, former peasants maintained informal networks not out of nostalgia for the past but rather because these traditional forms of organization continued to help them obtain desirable jobs, bargain collectively, and maintain cooperative security against drops in wages or shortages of food and housing. The survival of village networks and artels in turn reproduced their traditional work culture and labor organization in the urban workplace, and thus greatly hindered managerial control and industrial rationalization.

Artels provide the most vivid example of traditional forms of labor organization that contested managerial authority. Once in Moscow, former peasants continued to live and work collectively in their artels, under the guidance of their artels' elders. Elders retained complete command over their artel members, routinely overruling the orders of supervisory personnel. Elders not only decided where their artels would work but also made all work assignments and rotated members to various jobs.[48]

Because artels posed a challenge to managerial control, industrial managers fought to eliminate them. An official at one Moscow construction site complained that artels exerted an unhealthy influence on workers and had to be broken up. A Party journal claimed that a majority of the elders were "class alien elements." Propaganda officials even planned a film to show the "battle" between the old artels

---

[48]Kuromiya, "Workers' Artels," p. 75. Chinese foremen, too, had no direct control over workers and operated through group leaders: Andrew G. Walder, *Communist Neo-Traditionalism: Work and Authority in Chinese Industry* (Berkeley, 1986), p. 103.

(which worked poorly) and the new Soviet brigades (their members wholeheartedly devoted to building socialism). Top Party leaders also blamed artels for labor inefficiency and ordered their abolition.[49]

In actual fact, artels functioned efficiently, because elders disciplined lax members who jeopardized the productivity and income of the group as a whole. They did, however, thwart managerial control and industrial rationalization. Proponents of scientific management argued that artels hindered individual productivity and labor efficiency. Gastev, the leading Soviet adherent of Taylorism, wrote that artels and village networks had to be "either smashed or utilized cleverly."[50]

Managers created brigades (headed by foremen) to replace artels. Frequently, however, these new brigades in no way differed from artels; the former artel elder was simply elected brigade foreman by his workers.[51] Construction managers for the Moscow metro introduced a system of individual rather than collective payment in an effort to break the power of artels, but such efforts there and elsewhere proved futile.[52] Managers discovered that artels, brigades, and collective payment were not easy to eliminate. The amount produced by individual workers in a foundry, for example, could not be calculated, because the output of molten steel depended on a group of people working together.[53]

An even greater obstacle to individual work systems and industrial rationalization was opposition by workers of peasant origin. Especially in water transport and construction, where artels were particularly strong, attempts to enforce individual payment and progressive wages met great resistance.[54] Former peasants working in factories also objected to individual work systems. One complained, "In the

[49]*AMOvets*, April 1, 1931, p. 1; *Sputnik kommunista* 1930 no. 6, p. 48; *Amostroika*, April 11, 1931, p. 4; TsPA f. 17, op. 114, d. 255, l. 56.

[50]Kuromiya, "Workers' Artels," pp. 76–78.

[51]*Govoriat stroiteli sotsializma*, p. 150; *Amostroika*, June 18, 1931, p. 3; Nobuaki Shiokawa, "A 'Socialist State' and the Working Class: Labour Management in the Soviet Factory, 1929–1933" (unpublished summary of his book in Japanese of the same title), pp. 31–33.

[52]*Istoriia metro Moskvy*, p. 208; *Perestroika zarabotnoi platy rabochikh Moskovskoi promyshlennosti*, A. S. Putiatin, ed. (Moscow, 1932), pp. 36–37; TsGAMO f. 6833, op. 1, d. 46, l. 34.

[53]Archive of Hammer and Sickle metallurgical plant IV (I-01), l. 6. See also *Aviamotor*, September 10, 1931, p. 1.

[54]*Avral*, July 20, 1931, p. 1; December 25, 1931, p. 1; *Postroika*, January 4, 1932, p. 3; July 2, 1932, p. 1.

village you are driving peasants into collective farms, whereas here you divide us up into individuals." Another added, "We don't want to work individually. Many died in the Solovki [labor camps] because they wanted to work individually in the village."[55]

These remarks reflected not only the strong memory newly urbanized workers retained of the collectivization drive but also their recognition of contradictions between Soviet policies. Managers made no attempt to reconcile these contradictions or explain industrial rationalization. For them such measures were justified simply as means of raising labor productivity. But new workers opposed individual work systems and continued to belong to artels and receive payment collectively.[56] The campaign against artels in construction dragged on into the second half of the 1930s with little success.[57]

Given the shifting labor market and falling living standard of the 1930s, new workers had good reasons to cling to their artels. In bargaining with labor-short managers, they could always threaten to leave en masse if pay and conditions did not improve. When elders at one work site in Moscow province found the barracks and food supply unacceptable and led their artels elsewhere, they reduced the local workforce by some 20 percent.[58] Managers of the construction site of the Kaganovich ball bearing plant quickly granted new clothing, better food, and improved housing to the members of an artel that threatened to leave.[59]

Artels were less pervasive in factories than in construction, but the communal traditions of former peasants continued to influence industrial relations nonetheless. Fellow villagers who worked in factories often formed close-knit groups based on village networks or on previous artel experience. These groups naturally evolved over time as workers made new contacts and their informal associations assumed new functions. Cliques and "worker dynasties" developed within factories and operated in large part independently of management.[60]

[55]*Voprosy truda* 1932 no. 2, p. 3, as quoted in Kuromiya, "Workers' Artels," p. 80. See also *Sovetskoe gosudarstvo i pravo* 1933 no. 4, pp. 75–87.

[56]P. Ognev, "Zarabotnaia plata stroitel'nykh rabochikh," *Voprosy profdvizheniia* 1934 no. 3, p. 50.

[57]*Nashe stroitel'stvo* 1936 no. 3, p. 11.

[58]*Stroitel'naia promyshlennost'* 1929 no. 4, p. 380; Vdovin and Drobizhev, p. 217; *Moskovskaia promyshlennaia kooperatsiia* 1931 no. 7, p. 12.

[59]*Pervyi podshipnikovyi*, p. 35.

[60]Zawodny, "Twenty-six Interviews," Hoover Institution Archives, I/2, II/16; Kuromiya, "Workers' Artels," pp. 81–82.

Some groups of workers reconstituted themselves as self-cost-accounting (*khozrachet*) brigades—a form of labor organization tolerated by Soviet officials as a means to lower production costs and eliminate waste.[61] Self-cost-accounting brigades signed agreements with management regarding the amount they would produce in exchange for allocation of all necessary raw materials and equipment.[62] As this arrangement put the responsibility for reducing costs in the hands of the brigades and gave them complete authority to organize production, it undercut efforts to strengthen managerial authority. Despite guidelines to the contrary, the leaders of self-cost-accounting brigades were frequently elected by their members and exercised the same authority as artel elders.[63]

The survival of village networks and artel traditions not only perpetuated peasant in-migrants' forms of organization but also reproduced their traditional work culture in the factory. New workers brought with them from the village the task-oriented work culture characteristic of all preindustrial societies. Even those with previous experience in the city had as a rule performed work geared toward the completion of certain tasks rather than work that demanded efficient labor for a specified period of time. In nineteenth-century Western Europe and elsewhere, industrial managers imposed time discipline on workers over the course of several generations. Managers used bells and clocks to instill new work habits and a sense of time discipline, schoolteachers taught obedience and punctuality, the clergy preached against the evils of idleness.[64] Workers of peasant origin have been found to adapt to industrial labor more quickly than they were once thought to do, but only when labor is organized as a set of clearly defined operations, with monetary incentives to encourage the

[61]Lewis Siegelbaum, "Production Collectives and Communes and the 'Imperatives' of Soviet Industrialization, 1929–1931," *Slavic Review* 1986 no. 1, p. 82. Some Moscow factories reported that 30 to 40 percent of their output was waste: *Rabochaia Moskva*, January 26, 1931, p. 1.

[62]Ia. Z. Livshits, "Rabochie-metallisty Moskvy v bor'be za zavershenie pervoi piatiletki, 1931–1932 gg.," in *Trudy Moskovskogo gosudarstvennogo istoriko-arkhivnogo instituta*, vol. 14 (Moscow, 1960), pp. 261–262. Self-cost-accounting brigades encompassed 31 percent of all workers in the Moscow machine-building industry by the beginning of 1932. See also M. Krivitskii, ed., *Trud v pervoi piatiletke* (Moscow, 1934), pp. 60–61; S. Lapitskaia, *Byt rabochikh Trekhgornoi manufaktury* (Moscow, 1935), pp. 150–154.

[63]Siegelbaum, *Stakhanovism*, p. 49.

[64]E. P. Thompson, "Time, Work-Discipline, and Industrial Capitalism," *Past and Present* 1967 no. 38, pp. 60, 90; Cooper, p. 21.

acceptance of time-oriented labor.[65] Rather than provide these conditions, Soviet officials exhorted new workers to work more efficiently for the sake of building socialism—for a hazily defined future utopia. Not surprisingly, these former peasants did not develop a sense of time orientation or strict labor discipline.

New workers' resistance to labor discipline was strengthened by the desperate shortage of labor created by the industrialization drive. Managers generally tried their best to accommodate workers for fear that they would seek employment elsewhere. Both new and old workers routinely threatened to quit if their managers did not raise their skill ranks and wages, and despite rules to the contrary, they demanded and received full wages for defective production.[66]

Workers also frustrated managers' attempts to raise productivity through scientific determination of production quotas and work norms. Though managers continually raised norms, they invariably encountered resistance and failed to implement them effectively. Faced with the threat that workers would quit and find other jobs, managers let them circumvent norms. They would allow workers to work overtime one day, and thus qualify for bonuses for overfulfilling the norm, then skip work the next. Alternatively, they paid workers for fictitious piecework and awarded them bonuses that were unearned.[67]

The labor shortage also deterred managers from firing new workers for lax work discipline or absenteeism. A 1931 Party report concluded that 56.6 percent of all working hours at one construction site were wasted, and blamed the artels.[68] A study of the Kirov Dinamo plant in 1933 revealed that workers worked only four hours and seventeen minutes a day on average. Other Moscow factories reported that workers wasted hours each day loitering and taking smoking breaks, as well as searching for necessary equipment and materials, which were often in short supply.[69] One observer described laxness among workers at the Kuibyshev electronics factory:

[65]Vladimir Andrle, *Workers in Stalin's Russia: Industrialization and Social Change in a Planned Economy* (New York, 1988), pp. 114–115.

[66]*Voprosy truda* 1931 no. 7, p. 33. See also Andrle, p. 163.

[67]Filtzer, pp. 208–230.

[68]TsPA f. 17, op. 114, d. 255, l. 74.

[69]*Voprosy profdvizheniia* 1935 no. 2/3, p. 8; *Industrializatsiia SSSR*, vol. 3, p. 525.

Throughout the day an unending flow of people spills along the factory corridors, through the shops, along the stairwells. This is the best index of both the level of discipline and the organization of production. In the corridor of the electronics factory they trade books and sell ice cream. Sometimes it's a factory, sometimes it's a department store.[70]

A 1932 report on Moscow tram workers complained that discipline remained poor and tardiness and unexcused absences occurred regularly.[71] The 372 workers in one shop at a Moscow factory recorded 5,416 absences in 1929; one worker managed to miss 100 days in six months.[72]

In sum, efforts to discipline former peasants met with little success, and industrial rationalization suffered markedly.[73] That is not to say that first-generation workers could ignore a manager's authority. Once they entered the industrial workforce, they became dependent on management to hire them and pay their wages. But they did have resources with which to negotiate. Artel traditions and village allegiances remained strong precisely because of their utility and bargaining power. Some workers of peasant origin even demanded that trade union representatives be elected not by factory shop but by village.[74] In turn village networks perpetuated the preindustrial work culture and frustrated managerial attempts to fashion a disciplined workforce.

Campaigns to Raise Productivity

As the number of untrained and undisciplined workers employed in Moscow rose sharply throughout the First Five-Year Plan, the productivity of labor dropped precipitously. At the Hammer and Sickle plant, for example, productivity fell from 20.0 tons of steel per worker in 1928 to 10.6 tons in 1932.[75] In response Soviet leaders launched

---

[70]*Za industrializatsiiu*, August 2, 1937, as quoted in Filtzer, p. 166.
[71]TsGAORgM f. 1289, op. 1, d. 460, l. 2.
[72]N. Mikhailov, *The Fight for Steel* (Moscow, 1931), p. 3.
[73]TsPA f. 17, op. 114, d. 846, l. 11.
[74]Chaiko, pp. 15–16; Khlevniuk, "Izmenenie," p. 82.
[75]*Iz istorii razvitiia metallurgicheskoi promyshlennosti Moskvy, 1883–1932 gg.: Dokumenty i materialy*, I. L. Kornakovskii, ed. (Moscow, 1981), p. 186.

several campaigns to raise productivity and overall production, but these initiatives proved to be the very antithesis of efficient and routinized management. In 1929 a movement called socialist competition (*sotsialisticheskoe sorevnovanie*) spread across the Soviet Union. It consisted of workers' pledges to fulfill certain production goals and competitions between individual workers, brigades, and even factories to see which could most substantially increase production. Presumably spurred by socialist competition, brigades of shock workers (*udarniki*) began to exceed work norms and, in some highly publicized cases, set production records. Assuming the character of a mass campaign, the movement introduced "storming" and exhortations that were to become permanent features of the Soviet system.

Socialist competition had a task-oriented character in the sense that it set concrete work goals rather than requiring efficient labor over a period of time. It may even be seen as an attempt to appeal to former peasants and their task-oriented work culture. Yet socialist competition had other sources as well. Though shock work and socialist competition served the goals of Party leaders, these movements originated spontaneously at the initiative of young workers of urban origin who sought to raise their status by circumventing the shop-floor culture of established workers.[76]

Statistics on socialist competition reveal that former peasants did not participate in large numbers. As late as 1932, when socialist competition became ubiquitous, proportionately fewer former peasants than other workers joined in.[77] Young, urbanized workers with several years' work experience continued to dominate shock work and socialist competition. A 1930 Gosplan survey showed that 90 percent of workers who engaged in socialist competition had begun work at an early age before 1928, and that a majority were of working-class origin.[78] Data on shock workers show a similar predominance of young cadres of working-class origin.[79]

[76]For more on the origins of shock work, see Kuromiya, *Stalin's Industrial Revolution*, pp. 115–123.

[77]*Profsoiuznaia perepis'*, p. 7.

[78]S. A. Kheinman, "Sotsialisticheskoe sorevnovanie v promyshlennosti SSSR," in *Sotsialisticheskoe sorevnovanie v promyshlennosti SSSR: Sbornik statei*, Ia. M. Bineman, ed. (Moscow, 1930), pp. 13–14. On the youth of workers who took part in socialist competition, see TsGAMO f. 738, op. 1, d. 150, l. 3; *Voprosy truda* 1932 no. 2, pp. 89–93.

[79]O. V. Khlevniuk, *Udarniki pervoi piatiletki* (Moscow, 1989), pp. 31–32; Kuromiya,

Workers participated in shock work and socialist competition in large numbers only after managers introduced incentives and rewards to compensate them for their extra labor. Shock workers began to receive special meals (featuring beef Stroganov and apple torte at one factory).[80] The Stalin automobile plant rewarded the best shock workers with automobiles, while shock workers at the Hammer and Sickle plant received priority in access to housing, "deficit" goods, and discount theater tickets.[81] By 1931, 63 percent of all Moscow workers were in shock brigades and over 80 percent engaged in socialist competition.[82]

As shock work and socialist competition spread, the movements became subsumed in traditional shop-floor routines. Managers, eager to satisfy their workers, and themselves often impatient with the disruptions of shock work, cooperated with workers to set goals easily reachable within typical work routines.[83] Many workers began to sign socialist competition agreements or declare themselves shock workers without actually doing any more work than they had done before.[84] Trade union committees began to denounce the phenomenon of "false shock workers," who benefited from the rewards of shock work without actually fulfilling any of their goals. These reports concluded that by 1931 shock work and socialist competition had taken on a "completely formal character" and as such were ineffective.[85] Lazar Kaganovich, head of the Moscow Party organization, complained that in some factories everyone was called a shock worker, so that the term had lost all meaning.[86] Once again workers had managed to subvert official initiatives and rechannel them along lines that suited their own routines and interests.

During the years from 1931 to 1935, Soviet leaders endorsed a new wage policy designed to raise labor productivity through wage dif-

---

Stalin's Industrial Revolution, pp. 320–321; TsGAOR f. 5469, op. 14, d. 193, l. 243. See also American Engineers, Hoover Institution archives, account of J. P. Bendt, p. 10.

[80]TsGAOR f. 7952, op. 3, d. 96, ll. 92–93; f. 5469, op. 15, d. 10, l. 136; *Delo chesti*, p. 113.

[81]TsGANKh f. 7622, op. 1, d. 1948, l. 29; archive of Hammer and Sickle metallurgical plant, shock work booklet by E. E. Dorokhova, 1931. See also Filtzer, p. 98.

[82]*Moskva za 50 let Sovetskoi vlasti* (Moscow, 1968), pp. 100–101; *Istoriia Moskvy: Kratkii ocherk*, p. 276; Krivitskii, ed., p. 55.

[83]Andrle, pp. 173–175. See also Siegelbaum, *Stakhanovism*, p. 44.

[84]*Sputnik kommunista* 1929 no. 23, p. 23; S. I. Mirer and M. A. Mirer, *Delo chesti: Ustnye rasskazy rabochikh o sotssorevnovanii: Sbornik* (Moscow, 1931), pp. 17–19.

[85]TsGAMO f. 747, op. 1, d. 111, l. 14; f. 2534, op. 1, d. 217, ll. 5–6.

[86]L. M. Kaganovich, *Kontrol'nye tsifry tret'ego goda piatiletki i zadachi Moskovskoi*

ferentials. As early as the spring of 1930, trade union officials began to warn against wage leveling (*uravnilovka*). The equalization of the wages paid to skilled and unskilled workers, they argued, would eliminate any incentive for workers to improve their skill levels.[87] Wage leveling made no sense from a market point of view, either. In this period when skilled labor was in short supply, wage differentials should have increased as the only effective means to secure workers.[88] But no clear differentials or wage scales existed. Wages varied from one factory to another, sometimes from one shop to another within a factory, and these variations encouraged massive labor turnover.[89] Some unskilled workers earned more than skilled workers or even managers.[90]

On June 23, 1931, Stalin took a decisive stand against wage leveling in his "New Conditions" speech. Citing the intolerable level of labor turnover (at least 30 to 40 percent each half year, perhaps each quarter), he blamed wage leveling for a situation in which unskilled workers had no incentive to stay at one enterprise and raise their skill level, and skilled workers also moved around in a search for higher wages.[91]

Implementation of new wage rates proved difficult. As industry continued to expand and adopt new technology, flux in the workforce upset management's efforts to fix norms and eliminate wage leveling.[92] Despite problems in implementation, wage reform did increase differentials considerably. Differentials widened between skilled and unskilled workers in metalwork, construction, textiles, the automo-

---

organizatsii: *Rech' na V plenume MOK VKP (b), 19 fevralia 1931 g.* (Moscow, 1931), p. 34.

[87]TsGAOR f. 5451, op. 14, d. 305, l. 76; f. 5469, op. 14, d. 44, ll. 44–45.

[88]For further discussion of this point, see Kuromiya, *Stalin's Industrial Revolution*, pp. 246–247.

[89]Z. Mordukhovich, *Na bor'bu s tekuchest'iu rabochei sily* (Moscow/Leningrad, 1931), p. 61; archive of Hammer and Sickle metallurgical plant IV (I-01), l. 8; *Stroitel'stvo Moskvy* 1930 no. 7, p. 5; *Puti industrializatsii* 1930 no. 14, p. 28; no. 15/16, pp. 32–33.

[90]MPA f. 432, op. 1, d. 75, l. 85. For statistics on wage leveling, see A. A. Tverdokhleb, "Material'noe blagosostoianie rabochego klassa Moskvy v 1917–1937 gg." (dissertation, Moscow State University, 1970), pp. 326–328.

[91]Stalin, vol. 13, pp. 56–58. In an interview with the German writer Emil Ludwig on December 13, 1931, Stalin dismissed wage leveling as a phenomenon stemming from "an individual-peasant manner of thought": ibid., p. 119.

[92]MPA f. 432, op. 1, d. 79, l. 33; *Trud*, February 21 and 24, 1932; *Na trudovom fronte* 1932 no. 8/9, p. 13; *Vse dorogi vedut v Moskvu: O proshlom i nastoiaschem Moskovskoi zheleznoi dorogi* (Moscow, 1971), p. 129.

tive industry, and the food service industry.[93] Discrepancies in wages between branches of industry also grew, further increasing the pay of workers in heavy industry over that of workers in light industry.[94]

At the same time, managers expanded the use of piece rates, paying workers according to the amount they produced rather than the time they worked. Piece rates focused on the completed task and so represented another concession to peasant work culture. As a further incentive to raise productivity, managers applied progressive piece rates—rates that increased with the amount produced. Thus a worker received, for example, 103 percent of the standard rate for overfulfilling the norm by 5 percent and 110 percent for a 10 percent overfulfillment.[95] By the end of 1931, 70 percent of workers in Moscow industry were on some form of piece rates.[96]

Under the progressive piece-rate system, the setting of work norms assumed more importance. Throughout the 1930s norms lingered as a point of contention between workers and management, especially when changing technology prompted their upward revision. Managers attempted to set norms high enough to meet their production quotas but not so high that workers would quit. Methods of revising norms varied from shop surveys to laboratory experimentation, but new norms often proved unworkable and had to be adjusted.[97]

The large number of new workers with inadequate training made it particularly difficult to set norms. A norm that was impossibly high for first-generation workers might still be so low that experienced workers easily earned huge bonuses for overfulfillment. A 1934 Commissariat of Heavy Industry report noted that one-third of the workers

[93]TsGAOR f. 5515, op. 1, d. 443, l. 1; TsGANKh f. 7622, op. 1, d. 654, l. 8; f. 7676, op. 1, d. 610, l. 40; TsGAORgM f. 453, op. 1, d. 17, l. 14; Ognev, p. 48; Susan M. Kingsbury and Mildred Fairchild, *Factory, Family, and Woman in the Soviet Union* (New York, 1935), p. 50.

[94]From the first to the fourth quarter of 1931, average monthly wages in Moscow metallurgy and machine building rose from 110 to 130 rubles, and in the electrotechnical industry from 120 to 140 rubles, but in the cotton-processing industry only from 69 to 72 rubles: *Perestroika zarabotnoi platy*, pp. 29–30. See also TsGAORgM f. 176, op. 4, d. 4, l. 170; *Voprosy truda* 1932 no. 7, p. 5.

[95]TsGANKh f. 7604, op. 8, d. 113, l. 11; f. 7622, op. 1, d. 251, l. 81a; f. 7995, op. 1, d. 333, l. 6; TsGAORgM f. 453, op. 1, d. 13, l. 78. See also Schwarz, pp. 150–151.

[96]Livshits, p. 259. By 1935, 70 percent of all Soviet workers were on piece rates: Andrle, p. 147.

[97]Lewis H. Siegelbaum, "Soviet Norm Determination in Theory and Practice, 1917–1941," *Soviet Studies* 1984 no. 1, pp. 52–56.

at Moscow's Red Proletarian factory could not meet the revised norms, whereas 16 percent fulfilled them by over 150 percent.[98] Such problems were never adequately resolved and continued to cause friction not only between management and workers but between the Party and trade unions as well.[99]

Though workers contested the raising of norms, they did not oppose the progressive piece-rate system itself, because it gave them opportunities to earn bonuses. Some workers began to take home 100 to 150 rubles more each month than they had earned under time rates.[100] Worker productivity in Moscow rose in the second half of 1931, and so did the number of workers who fulfilled their norms.[101] Often they managed to do so only by working overtime. The seven-hour day officially remained in force, but workers regularly put in ten-hour days to overfulfill norms and earn bonuses. Legally overtime was restricted (it was prohibited entirely for workers under 18 years of age), but with the continued shortage of labor, managers ignored such strictures and let workers earn bonuses by working double or triple shifts.[102]

Because the juggling of norms continued, progressive piece rates did not boost productivity as much as Party leaders had hoped.[103] When a Donbass miner of peasant origin named Aleksei Stakhanov reportedly mined over a hundred tons of coal in a single shift in 1935, Party leaders initiated the Stakhanovite movement, another extrasystemic effort to raise labor productivity. Ordzhonikidze ordered widespread publicity designed to make a hero of Stakhanov. Stakhanov, he declared, had demonstrated that managers and engineers were lagging behind workers in the movement to use technology for maximum production.[104]

[98]TsGANKh f. 7995, op. 1, d. 91, ll. 1–2.

[99]For more on work norms, see Siegelbaum, "Soviet Norm Determination," and Andrle, pp. 149–154.

[100]TsGAOR f. 7952, op. 3, d. 260, l. 6; archive of Hammer and Sickle metallurgical plant IV (I-01), l. 6.

[101]*Perestroika zarabotnoi platy*, pp. 51–52.

[102]Andrew Smith, *I Was a Soviet Worker* (New York, 1936), p. 45; Schwarz, pp. 278–279. See also American Engineers, Hoover Institution archives, account of D. M. Forester.

[103]Party leaders were dissatisfied, for example, by the norm review campaign and managers' attempts to raise productivity in the spring of 1935: Andrle, p. 165.

[104]TsPA f. 85, op. 29, d. 640, ll. 3–7. For more on Stakhanov's record, see Siegelbaum, *Stakhanovism*, pp. 67–74.

Despite the spur Stakhanovism provided for productivity, managers often opposed it as disruptive to production and potentially damaging to equipment. A Moscow Party report in October 1935 condemned "conservative managers" who refused to aid or even hindered workers who were striving to become Stakhanovites.[105] As the opposite of routinized management, the Stakhanovite movement began to erode foremen's authority. Workers felt free to experiment with their equipment to raise production, disregarding warnings that such experimentation would damage machinery.[106]

Whereas the first shock workers were urban youth, the first Stakhanovites were new workers of peasant origin. A survey of the first 735 Stakhanovites indicated that around 60 percent were of peasant origin and under 28 years old.[107] In most branches of industry, the great majority of Stakhanovites had very few years of work experience, another indication of their newly urbanized status.[108] Even some peasants who had been dekulakized went on to become Stakhanovites.[109]

Stakhanovism also differed from shock work in its emphasis on material incentives. At a conference to publicize Stakhanovism, G. I. Likhoradov bragged that he earned over 1,000 rubles a month, "but I want to earn still more—2,000 rubles, 3,500 rubles, because our Soviet government gives us the opportunity to work well, to make good wages and to live in a cultured way. Why should I not wear a good serge suit, why should I not smoke good cigarettes?"[110] Articles in the press stressed the opportunity to earn high wages as a Stakhanovite.[111] With the abolition of rationing in 1935, wages in fact had assumed greater importance, and Stakhanovite bonuses permitted workers to raise their incomes substantially through intensive work.[112]

Stakhanovites received nonmonetary rewards, too—clothing,

[105]*Dokumenty trudovoi slavy Moskvichei, 1919–1965*, D. V. Diagilev, ed. (Moscow, 1967), pp. 145–147. See also TsGAORgM f. 415, op. 2, d. 397, l. 66; *Za udarnichestvo 1936* no. 2, p. 1.

[106]TsGAORgM f. 415, op. 2, d. 448, ll. 10–13.

[107]Khlevniuk, "Izmenenie," pp. 151–152, 173.

[108]Kozlov and Khlevniuk, *Nachinaetsia s cheloveka*, p. 154; TsGANKh f. 7622, op. 1, d. 653, ll. 3–11, 20; *Industrializatsiia SSSR*, vol. 3, pp. 580–581.

[109]Harvard Project no. 99.

[110]*Labour in the Land of the Soviets: Stakhanovites in Conference* (Moscow, 1936), p. 210.

[111]See, for example, *Ukhtomskii rabochii*, January 1, 1938, p. 2.

[112]MPA f. 80, op. 1, d. 526, l. 35; TsGAORgM f. 176, op. 4, d. 4, l. 178.

radios, automobiles, and preferential housing. These benefits came to
be well advertised in Stakhanovite autobiographies. One Stakhanovite moved from a makeshift wooden barracks to a "beautiful apartment . . . in a multi-story stone building, constructed according to the
latest word in technology," while another allegedly had an apartment
better than the one in which the factory director lived.[113] Stakhanovism, then, represented the Party's recognition that it could not
increase production merely through exhortation. At the same time,
former peasants' participation in the Stakhanovite movement marked
an accommodation from their side and a willingness to participate in
official campaigns when they were offered material incentives.

For workers the rewards of Stakhanovism did have a price. In the
spring of 1936, every branch of industry conducted a norm-review
procedure to set all workers' norms on the basis of the Stakhanovites' performance. Especially in heavy industry, where investment
continued at a rapid rate, incorporation of new technology had precipitated a need for norm revision anyway, but Stakhanovite record-
breaking acted as a catalyst for higher norms. In the words of one
former Soviet worker,

> The "Stakhanovites" used to prepare material and tools in advance
> and they also had the assistance of the Party and [factory] admin-
> istration. . . . After those fellows produced more than others, the
> trade union committee used to call a meeting and pointed out to
> the workers that we lagged in our efforts. Usually, the immediate
> motion was following, "Let's increase the quotas."[114]

The Commissariat of Heavy Industry, averaging Stakhanovite and
non-Stakhanovite production, in April 1936 raised its norms 30 to 40
percent, in some shops up to 60 percent.[115]

Shop-floor routines and traditional work culture, however, gradually subsumed Stakhanovism and rendered it less effective. To avoid
being accused of blocking Stakhanovism, foremen began to juggle fig-

---

[113]Siegelbaum, Stakhanovism, pp. 188, 227–231.

[114]Zawodny, "Twenty-six Interviews," Hoover Institution archives, II/22.

[115]Aleksandrova, pp. 45–46; TsGANKh f. 7995, op. 1, d. 344, ll. 116–120; TsGAORgM
f. 176, op. 4, d. 4, l. 181. Technological improvements had allowed worker productivity in Moscow heavy industry to grow substantially from 1932 to 1935. See Anoshin,
p. 159.

ures and assignments to help more workers become Stakhanovites—
a tactic that kept the workers content by allowing them to collect
bonuses without working any harder.[116] Whereas only 5 to 10 percent of workers at Moscow factories had qualified as Stakhanovites
in November 1935, the figure jumped to between 25 and 40 percent
by May 1936.[117] At several Moscow factories nearly half the workers
were classified as Stakhanovites. Party officials began to complain
that Stakhanovism existed only on paper.[118] By the spring of 1936 the
mania of Stakhanovism was coming under attack even in the press,
and aside from a brief campaign in early 1937, Stakhanovism became
deemphasized and shop routines were once again normalized.[119]

Exhortations, storming, and record setting succeeded in raising industrial output temporarily, but they did not inculcate new work
habits or create dedicated workers. Officially sponsored campaigns to
raise productivity proved effective only to the extent that they offered
concrete material benefits to shock workers and Stakhanovites—that
is, only to the extent that they paid workers for doing extra work. In
that sense the shop floor served as an arena of implicit negotiation
between workers and managers regarding wages and work norms.
Workers depended on managers' cooperation to meet their norms,
but managers could not impose productivity initiatives on a recalcitrant workforce without wage bonuses. Moreover, these initiatives—
socialist competition, progressive piece rates, and Stakhanovism—all
accommodated former peasants' task-oriented work culture. Soviet
industry never established an efficient and routinized system of production.

Party and Police Interventions

Workers and managers were not the only actors involved in the
formation of Moscow's industrial workforce. Throughout the 1930s
the Party and police regularly intervened in industry, both against

[116]MPA f. 635, op. 1, d. 135, l. 15; Siegelbaum, *Stakhanovism*, pp. 165–166. Even
as norms rose, they continued to be outpaced by the spread of mechanization, which
created more Stakhanovites.

[117]*Dokumenty trudovoi slavy Moskvichei*, p. 162; TsGANKh f. 7622, op. 1, d. 653,
l. 66; MPA f. 432, op. 1, d. 203, l. 18.

[118]MPA f. 69, op. 1, d. 942, l. 21; f. 429, op. 1, d. 429, l. 37; f. 262, op. 1, d. 114, l. 1.

[119]Andrle, pp. 190–198.

managers and against workers. Each enterprise had a Party committee and a "special [NKVD] department" that oversaw production as
well as matters of internal security. Party and police interventions
in several ways weakened managers and their attempts to discipline
new workers. Party and police officials criticized, harassed, and even
arrested "bourgeois specialists" (the prerevolutionary technical intelligentsia). A landmark in the escalation of class-war hostilities was
the Shakhty affair—the 1928 arrest and conviction of a group of "bourgeois engineers" at the Shakhty coal mines in the Donbass region
on the charge of counterrevolutionary treason.[120] The Shakhty affair
inflamed long-standing antagonisms between Russian management
and labor. After the Shakhty trial, workers regarded all nonproletar-
ian technical elites with suspicion, refused to heed their orders, and
even assaulted them.[121] Engineers and other managerial personnel,
realizing that any technical error or anything that aroused workers' resentment would be branded treason, tended to shun all responsibility,
and some of them quit work altogether.[122]

The Party furthermore intervened in managerial decisions—a practice only intensified by the politicization of industry during the First
Five-Year Plan.[123] The attacks on management, and indeed the entire
atmosphere of the First Five-Year Plan, diminished managerial control and undermined scientific management. The arrest of engineers,
workers' denunciations of bourgeois specialists, and the wholesale
purge of old technical elites from industrial enterprises and state
planning agencies militated against the consolidation of managerial
control.[124]

[120]For more on the Shakhty affair, see Bailes, pp. 73–94; Kuromiya, *Stalin's Industrial Revolution*, pp. 12–17.

[121]Davies, *Soviet Economy in Turmoil*, p. 113. One Moscow worker recalled that
"workers looked askance at the [factory] administration, saying to themselves that these
swine were the ones who [before the Revolution] used to oppress [*davit'*], squeeze
[*tesnit'*], and fine us": archive of the Hammer and Sickle metallurgical plant 0 (XVII,
II, IV), l. 63.

[122]TsGAOR f. 7952, op. 3, d. 522, ll. 45–47; TsGAORgM f. 1289, op. 1, d. 680, l. 18;
Monkhouse, p. 266; Khlevniuk, "Izmenenie," pp. 46–47.

[123]Filatov, p. 20. The Moscow Party Committee and even the Central Committee sent
commissions to check on problems at Moscow factories and occasionally overturned
the decisions of factory directors: Catherine Merridale, *Moscow Politics and the Rise of
Stalin: The Communist Party in the Capital, 1925–1932* (New York, 1990), pp. 171–178.
See also MPA f. 432, op. 1, d. 104, l. 203.

[124]The Industrial Party affair in 1930 led to further arrests and show trials of the old
technical intelligentsia. See Bailes, pp. 95–98. On police intervention in factories, see
also *Sudebnaia praktika RSFSR* 1931 no. 1, p. 9; Merridale, p. 186.

Interventions were not always to the detriment of managerial personnel. The Party also intervened frequently on the side of management against workers. The continued inability of managers to discipline and control new workers of peasant origin (exacerbated by Party attacks on management) led Party leaders to enact repressive labor legislation. Two decrees in 1929 permitted managers to fire workers without warning for breaches in factory discipline. Though these decrees theoretically increased managers' leverage over workers, in practice managers remained reluctant to use this authority for fear of reducing their labor force.[125]

In November 1932 the Soviet government issued a decree aimed at putting a stop to rampant absenteeism: for any unexcused absence, workers were to be fired, deprived of their ration cards, and evicted from enterprise housing.[126] At least one article justified these harsh measures as necessary to discipline the influx of "new workers from the countryside who have not developed a collectivist spirit of labor."[127] Workers' reaction to this law ranged from expressions of outrage and work stoppages to the looting of personnel offices and physical assaults on officials.[128] But as one American engineer employed in Moscow in 1932 later explained, managers acted quickly to appease and reassure workers.

> Word went around to obey the decree carefully for a few weeks. Afterwards, in the old Russian fashion, all would be as before. This was exactly what came to pass. Less than two months after the initiation of the decree, the reins had slackened. The former lackadaisical attitude was again in evidence.[129]

Realizing that rigorous enforcement would exacerbate the labor shortage they already faced, managers chose to reclassify unexcused absences as excused.[130] On paper the number of unexcused absences dropped from an average of 5.96 days in 1932 to 0.93 days in 1933, but in reality little changed.[131]

---

[125]Andrle, pp. 129–130.

[126]*Sbornik vazhneishikh postanovlenii po trudu* (Moscow, 1935), p. 99.

[127]*Bol'shevik* 1932 no. 21, p. 3.

[128]Andrle, p. 153.

[129]Zara Witkin, *An American Engineer in Stalin's Russia: The Memoirs of Zara Witkin, 1932–1934*, Michael Gelb, ed. (Berkeley, 1991), p. 126.

[130]MPA f. 432, op. 1, d. 80, l. 116.

[131]Schwarz, p. 99.

In the years from 1931 to 1934, Party policy generally strengthened the power of managers over workers. In June 1931 Stalin signaled a shift in emphasis from class war to strong management by defending bourgeois specialists.[132] In 1934 the Party initiated a campaign to give shop foremen greater power and accountability, in the hope that they could impose stricter labor discipline.[133] As the ineffectiveness of repressive labor legislation had already shown, however, managers proved unwilling or unable to exercise the power given to them.

The emergence of Stakhanovism in 1935 marked the Party's turn against management once again. Stalin cited Stakhanovite records as evidence that another leap forward in industrial production was possible, and he criticized the conservatism of managers and Party moderates.[134] Political pressure on managers and engineers mounted throughout the year, especially against those opposed to Stakhanovite record setting on the grounds that it disrupted production. Party and police officials castigated and overruled factory directors and engineers.[135] As they had done in the wake of the Shakhty affair, the police began to interrogate managerial personnel in factories. At first they denounced managers who opposed Stakhanovism for sabotage of the movement; by 1936 they had begun to arrest such managers on charges of general sabotage and "wrecking."[136]

The bloody purges from 1936 to 1938 further diminished managerial authority. On orders from the Central Committee, factory Party committees expelled a number of officials and managers, charging them with Trotskyism, wrecking, espionage, and sabotage.[137] A number of purged managers were also charged with aloofness toward workers, failure to visit the shop floor regularly, and mistreatment of workers.[138] Such charges were frequently connected with managers' failure to promote Stakhanovism and with their neglect or abuse of Stakhanov-

[132]Stalin, vol. 13, p. 72.

[133]Andrle, p. 162.

[134]TsPA f. 85, op. 29, d. 640, ll. 3–4.

[135]Victor Kravchenko, *I Chose Freedom* (New Brunswick, N.J., 1989), p. 192.

[136]On the progression from Stakhanovism to the purges, see Francesco Benvenuti, "Stakhanovism and Stalinism, 1934–1938," discussion paper, Centre for Russian and East European Studies, Birmingham, 1989, p. 53.

[137]The initial impetus for the purges came from the Central Committee in the form of a top-secret letter dated July 29, 1936, directing local Party committees to root out all Trotskyists. In turn the Moscow city and oblast Party committees sent a secret letter to all factory Party committees on August 16, 1936, advising them to do the same: MPA f. 432, op. 1, d. 165, ll. 125–126; f. 468, op. 1, d. 155, l. 207.

[138]MPA f. 432, op. 1, d. 176, ll. 138–139; d. 178, ll. 35, 71–76.

ites. Indeed, the language of charges brought against purge victims often echoed the antimanagerial tone of Stakhanovism, as purged managers were denounced for "conservatism and sluggishness" and for "sabotaging the Stakhanovite movement or ignoring it." [139]

Labor discipline deteriorated rapidly with the onset of the purges. Absenteeism and tardiness shot up and factory production slowed substantially.[140] Workers became emboldened to criticize their foremen, and managers were reluctant to discipline workers for fear of provoking denunciations. Party officials called the workers at the Kuibyshev electronics factory together to denounce the head of one shop who was notorious for rudely ordering workers about.[141] Of course some workers resisted purges of managerial personnel, particularly of those they had worked with and respected. But the extreme hardship of the 1930s exacerbated workers' frustration with high-handed officials and heightened their resentment of the privileges enjoyed by technical and Party elites. Given state control of the media and the dangers of opposing the purges, most people believed or pretended to believe that internal enemies were numerous and that the purges were justified.[142]

The purges did victimize some new workers of peasant origin. Former peasants who had been dispossessed as kulaks during collectivization were especially at risk. In August 1936, in response to a secret directive from the Moscow Party committee, factory Party cells began to take measures against "class alien elements" that had penetrated the factory. Numerous accounts confirm that peasants who had fled dekulakization were in danger of arrest.[143]

Overall the purges disrupted production and left a legacy of embitterment and fear extremely detrimental to normal industrial and societal function. Industrial growth fell from 28.8 percent in 1936 to

---

[139]MPA f. 69, op. 1, d. 947, ll. 10–12; f. 432, op. 1, d. 176, l. 23. One "Trotskyist" was accused of impeding a Stakhanovite ten-day campaign (*dekada*) by mistreating workers, and an engineer was purged for calling Stakhanovites "self-seekers" (*rvacha*); see MPA f. 432, op. 1, d. 165, l. 126; d. 180, l. 16.

[140]MPA f. 432, op. 1, d. 180, l. 9.

[141]MPA f. 468, op. 1, d. 157, ll. 30–31. See also Gabor Rittersporn, *Stalinist Simplifications and Soviet Complications* (Philadelphia, 1991), pp. 255–256.

[142]See O. V. Khlevniuk, *1937–i: Stalin, NKVD, i sovetskoe obshchestvo* (Moscow, 1992), pp. 190–209.

[143]Zawodny, "Twenty-six Interviews," Hoover Institution archives, II/24, 26; MPA f. 468, op. 1, d. 155, l. 207; Harvard Project no. 98, no. 483; *Materialy . . . konferentsiiam VLKSM*, p. 13.

11.8 percent in 1938, and contemporaries wrote of an "atmosphere of distrust" that poisoned initiative and cooperation.[144] In 1938 the annual call for norm revisions was skipped because the managerial ranks had been so badly depleted.[145] At the end of that year Party leaders launched a campaign to reestablish the authority of managers and engineers, crediting them with technical innovations that a short time earlier they would have attributed to Stakhanovites.[146] Despite these efforts, managers' prestige did not recover quickly, and labor discipline was still extremely low through 1939.[147] The Party initiatives and police interventions intended to raise productivity, then, generally disrupted industrial operation and eroded managers' authority.

The years from 1938 to 1941 saw even harsher measures to tighten labor discipline as international tensions rose.[148] In December 1938 a series of decrees required that any worker who was late three times in one month be fired, mandated that workers give a full month's notice before leaving a place of employment, and instituted new labor books that all workers had to present before they could be hired. In June 1940 the government went so far as to decree a mandatory prison term of two to four months for any worker who quit a job.[149] Yet these laws, too, could rarely be enforced and proved largely ineffective. Labor discipline and productivity continued to lag, while absences and tardiness among some workers even increased.[150]

The impotence of repressive labor legislation stemmed once again from Soviet industry's insatiable demand for labor. The lack of a disciplined and efficient workforce throughout the 1930s led Soviet managers to rely on large amounts of labor to compensate for low productivity. The military mobilization of 1938 (which increased the size of the standing army to 4 million troops) exacerbated the labor

[144]Khlevniuk, *1937-i*, pp. 239–241.

[145]Andrle, p. 200.

[146]Siegelbaum, *Stakhanovism*, pp. 265, 292–293. Stakhanovites continued to receive some publicity, but no longer as a challenge to managers. See *Moskovskii transportnik*, February 10, 1940, p. 1.

[147]MPA f. 432, op. 1, d. 180, l. 9; d. 205, t. 2, l. 58; d. 226, l. 47; f. 468, op. 1, d. 157, ll. 30–31.

[148]The fascist threat received constant attention in the Soviet press. See, for example, *Kirovets* May 1, 1938, p. 4.

[149]Schwarz, pp. 100–102; O. V. Khlevniuk, "26 Iiulia 1940 goda: Illiuzii i real'nosti administrirovaniia," *Kommunist* 1989 no. 9, pp. 87–89.

[150]MPA f. 429, op. 1, d. 429, l. 9; f. 432, op. 1, d. 205, t. 2, l. 58; d. 216, ll. 15–16; d. 218, ll. 4–6.

shortage that had existed continuously since 1929. In such conditions, factory managers were desperate to retain their workers. How could they enforce measures that required workers to be fired or imprisoned? Old and new workers alike continued to move from one factory to another, knowing they could easily be hired with or without their labor books.[151]

In October 1940 the Soviet government established the State Labor Reserve System, which provided for the conscription and militarization of labor. The system entailed the recruitment and conscription of up to one million youths aged 14 to 17 for labor training and work. The regimen established included military drills and uniforms, and the penalty for desertion was one year in prison (but desertion proved to be high anyway).[152] In the autumn of 1940, 600,000 youths were enlisted (reportedly 71 percent voluntarily); two-thirds of them were peasants and three-quarters were male.[153] The system represented a desperate attempt to mobilize and control labor, created in part because organized recruitment still failed to function. But the numbers of peasants who moved to Moscow on their own (with the help of village networks and artels) and shifted from one job to another vastly outweighed the number of workers in the labor reserves.[154]

In 1941 Aleksandr S. Shcherbakov, secretary of the Moscow Party organization, reported that production in several Moscow factories had actually declined in 1940.[155] Of course, not all factories worked poorly. In the second half of the 1930s, special priority was assigned to factories involved in military production. At these plants workers engaged in constant "storming," putting in twelve- and even thirty-hour shifts to increase production.[156] Few peasant in-migrants found work at military factories, for these plants strove to hire the most experienced workers. Ultimately the campaign character of the 1930s accomplished the tasks that Party leaders accorded priority while perpetuating inefficiency and a lack of labor discipline elsewhere.

More broadly the escalation in repressive labor legislation reflected

---

[151]Khlevniuk, "26 Iiulia 1940," pp. 87–88.

[152]Gregory M. Smith, "The Impact of World War II on Women, Family Life, and Mores in Moscow, 1941–1945" (dissertation, Stanford University, 1990), pp. 45–48.

[153]Mervyn Matthews, "The State Labor Reserves," *Slavonic and East European Review* 1983 no. 2, pp. 241–242.

[154]MPA f. 432, op. 1, d. 216, ll. 17–22; Matthews, pp. 238–242.

[155]Khlevniuk, "26 Iiulia 1940," p. 96. See also MPA f. 432, op. 1, d. 226, l. 47; d. 230, l. 11.

[156]MPA f. 69, op. 1, d. 942, ll. 25–26; f. 635, op. 1, d. 10, l. 8.

a lack of systematic control over the workforce. Had Soviet officials succeeded in molding an efficient and reliable proletariat through a program of fines and incentives, they would not have needed repressive legislation. Instead continued turnover and lax labor discipline led Party leaders, who already had displayed authoritarian tendencies, to pass ever-harsher labor laws. Rigorous enforcement of labor discipline nonetheless remained elusive. Repressive laws arbitrarily sent small numbers of workers to labor camps, but did nothing to transform the mass of former peasants into efficient and loyal workers.

The harsh labor laws decreed by Party leaders acted to undermine the idea that the Soviet Union was a working-class state. The government's arbitrary and severe punishment of workers established an antagonistic relationship between the two. While this antagonism was tempered by official paternalism, it nonetheless reinforced new workers' impression that their interests diverged sharply from those of Soviet officialdom. These former peasants, the memory of the brutal collectivization campaign still fresh in their minds, continued to regard Soviet authorities and Soviet policies with suspicion and hostility.

The Moscow workplace during the 1930s, then, was characterized by contestations between managers and newly urbanized workers, and by arbitrary and often coercive interventions by the Party and the police. The workforce that emerged from these contestations was neither highly skilled nor well disciplined. The village networks and artels that had guided the former peasants to Moscow continued to serve them as means both to resist managerial control and to perpetuate preindustrial forms of work organization and culture. Official policies intended to raise production, such as record-setting campaigns and police interventions, only further militated against systematic functioning in factories. The Soviet industrial system, with its undisciplined workforce, weakened management, and Party and police interference, never achieved rationalized and routinized production.

4

The Workplace
as Contested Space

Aleksandr Maksimovich moved from his native village to Moscow in 1935, and with the help of his brother-in-law he landed a job as a steelworker. With no experience or training, he had to rely on other workers to teach him the production process. As he soon discovered, however, established workers—workers of long standing who had been born in the city or had lived there for some time—were unwilling to help him. They guarded their knowledge and skills, aware that teaching new workers about metallurgy would only devalue their own expertise. Moreover, they ridiculed his ignorance about the factory, made fun of his shoes, and called him a peasant. It was only thanks to his brother-in-law and several other fellow villagers who worked alongside him that he learned to perform his job.[1]

The workplace was contested not only by management and workers but also by groups of workers competing against one another for control and influence. At stake was dominion over the most favorable factory positions, which determined working conditions, wages, and status. Particularly as the living standard plunged in the early 1930s, factory jobs that granted sizable rations and the opportunity to earn bonuses were greatly contested. Established workers customarily monopolized the best jobs. But the influx of peasants into the workforce, as well as technological innovations, disrupted established hierar-

[1] Interview with Aleksandr Maksimovich Korneev at the Hammer and Sickle plant, Moscow, April 24, 1989.

chies and work routines, and provoked multiple conflicts between established workers and new workers.[2] Conflicts also erupted between former peasants and young urban workers, between female and male workers, and between workers of differing nationalities.

The instruments in the struggle for control of the workplace were in part institutional, but were also rhetorical and definitional. Groups of workers tried to exclude other workers by defining themselves as the true workers ("cadre workers") and labeling all others as incompetent and illegitimate. The Soviet urban workforce as it emerged in the 1930s was the product not only of the struggle between rationalized management and traditional work culture but also of the multiple conflicts between groups of workers themselves.

Established Workers, Production Communes, and Skill Ranks

Peasants who found urban jobs in construction and transport generally interacted with few established workers, simply because the overwhelming majority of workers in these sectors were of peasant origin.[3] As former peasants entered industrial jobs and began to mingle with established workers in large numbers, the two groups remained sharply stratified and in conflict. One official summarized the situation this way:

> New workers [adopt] hostile attitudes toward the older, skilled proletarians, envy their better working conditions, or fawn upon them. The skilled workers in turn adopt scornful, haughty attitudes toward new workers, even beat them, and demand [of management] an exclusive right to occupy the best positions in production.[4]

The struggle for hegemony in the workplace extended beyond control of the best jobs. Established workers challenged new workers'

[2]Peasants who moved to Moscow during the First Five-Year Plan would themselves become established workers by the end of the decade. The categories used for analysis here (new workers, established workers) were neither static nor absolute. Indeed, attempts to label and categorize workers were a large part of the struggle for control in the factory.

[3]MPA f. 635, op. 1, d. 69, l. 16. See Appendix I for further discussion.

[4]*Sputnik agitatora dlia goroda* 1929 no. 8, p. 39, as quoted in Hiroaki Kuromiya, "The Crisis of Proletarian Identity in the Soviet Factory, 1928–1929," *Slavic Review* 1985 no. 2, pp. 285–287.

right to run in elections for local councils, claiming that only "cadre workers" were qualified. Physical fights between established workers and newcomers were not uncommon.[5]

Established workers called former peasants country bumpkins (*derevenshchiny*) and hicks (*lapotniki*).[6] Such labels denigrated first-generation workers and challenged their legitimacy. By designating themselves as the only true proletariat, established workers bolstered their claims to the best jobs and high status. "Cadre workers" by definition deserved more respect and better pay than "country bumpkins."

Established workers' animosity toward peasant in-migrants was fed by new workers' defiance of established shop-floor culture. Earning piece rates, some workers of peasant origin would work up to twelve hours a day to collect more pay, but by producing so much they often prompted management to raise the norms for all workers. Naturally this practice provoked resentment among established workers, who by tacit agreement did not overfulfill norms. New workers also violated customs and hierarchies, whereby they were to respect older workers and bring them gifts of food and drink.[7] Customary patronage systems began to disintegrate with the influx of thousands of former peasants, who relied on village networks to help them get settled in factory jobs.

Established workers retaliated with several tactics to exclude peasant in-migrants from their shops. Sometimes they complained about new workers' lack of ability and discipline, and refused to work with them.[8] In other instances they formed production collectives and communes as a formal means to exclude workers of peasant origin from certain factory shops. Workers who formed a collective or commune claimed the right to control its membership. In response, newly urbanized workers often formed their own production collectives and communes, many of them derived directly from artels.[9]

---

[5]TsGAOR f. 5451, op. 13, d. 76, ll. 36, 66; Nikol'skii and Vanshtein, p. 48.
[6]Kuromiya, "Crisis of Proletarian Identity," pp. 285–287.
[7]Ward, pp. 94–100.
[8]Khain and Khandros, p. 8.
[9]TsGAOR f. 5451, op. 14, d. 305, ll. 80, 96; d. 306, l. 16. Reports described artels as continuing "under the guise of being a commune": G. S. Polliak et al., "Proizvodstvennye kollektivy i kommuny," in *Sotsialisticheskoe sorevnovanie v promyshlennosti SSSR: Sbornik statei*, Ia. M. Bineman, ed. (Moscow, 1930), p. 54.

Production communes bore a striking resemblance to artels, and in fact workers and journalists often referred to them simply as artels. They consisted of groups of workers who assumed joint responsibility for work, pooled their wages, and elected an elder to act as their leader.[10] The elder represented commune members in negotiations with management and made all work assignments.[11] Production communes thrived among construction and transport workers as well as among workers in the textile, metal, tanning, food-processing, and paper industries.[12]

Production collectives and communes arose without the participation, encouragement, or even sanction of managerial, Party, or trade union officials. In many Moscow factories they operated unstudied and in some cases unnoticed.[13] Some officials lauded production communes for lowering workers' absences and raising productivity, but most regarded them with suspicion. Production communes encroached on the authority of managers and limited the ability of officials to conduct political work. At one construction site where many communes had formed, trade union officials found that workers of peasant origin who belonged to communes refused to engage in socialist competition. Managers' efforts to divide the communes into brigades had no effect. Commune members at one Moscow factory were judged to be "isolated" from political education; some workers there even quit the Komsomol after joining production communes.[14]

Despite managerial opposition, production communes thrived be-

[10]Kuromiya, *Stalin's Industrial Revolution*, p. 252; *Industrializatsiia SSSR*, vol. 2, pp. 511–513. Some contemporary commentators idealized production communes as a step toward communism. See S. Zarkhii, *Kommuna v tseke* (Moscow/Leningrad, 1930), pp. 12–14. These descriptions, however, were simply the rhetoric of outsiders, who did not understand the traditional basis of communes or the way they promoted or defended the interests of workers.

[11]*Moskovskii proletarii* 1930 no. 4, p. 18; Zarkhii, p. 50; TsGAOR f. 5451, op. 14, d. 305, l. 53.

[12]TsGAOR f. 5475, op. 13, d. 206, l. 3; op. 14, d. 62, l. 15; TsGAMO f. 738, op. 1, d. 37, l. 15; Iu. A. Kalistratov, *Za udarnyi proizvodstvennyi kollektiv* (Moscow, 1931), p. 55; Lewis H. Siegelbaum, "Production Collectives and Communes and the 'Imperatives' of Soviet Industrialization, 1929–1931," *Slavic Review* 1986 no. 1, p. 70.

[13]TsGAOR f. 5469, op. 14, d. 44, ll. 44–45; Polliak et al., p. 80. At the Kuibyshev electronics factory, production communes "took hold silently" and were discovered completely by chance: Khlevniuk, *Udarniki pervoi piatiletki*, p. 26.

[14]TsGAOR f. 5469, op. 14, d. 44, ll. 44–45, d. 193, l. 234; f. 5475, op. 14, d. 62, l. 15.

cause they offered workers economic benefits and control in the workplace. Since commune members' wages depended on the group's production, they helped one another and applied pressure to members who loafed on the job.[15] Communes also provided collective security. Workers paid piece rates normally lost wages if their equipment broke or if raw materials ran short, but membership in a production collective or commune guaranteed them a percentage of the group's earnings regardless of their individual production.[16]

The way production communes divided their wages varied. A few communes paid each member according to the number of dependents they had, so that workers with families received more than single workers. Most communes simply took into account the number of days and hours that each member worked and divided wages accordingly, so that regardless of the skill level or productivity of individual workers, they all received the same pay. Production collectives, by contrast, did apportion wages on the basis of skill. Members of collectives still pooled their wages, but the skilled received a larger percentage than the unskilled.[17]

Some semiskilled workers created production communes that excluded unskilled newcomers. Not only did they fear pooling their wages with lower-paid workers, they also wished to avoid working with people whose lack of experience could lower the overall output of a brigade. Some of these semiskilled workers themselves had migrated to the city only a few years before, but now they took pains to differentiate themselves from the "country bumpkins." They did not hesitate, however, to accept newly arrived fellow villagers into their communes as informal apprentices. For the first month these new arrivals worked without pay, and thereafter they received a reduced percentage of the commune's earnings. When their skill matched that of the other members, they began to receive equal pay.[18] Village networks, then, should not be idealized: they could be used to exploit as well as to help. Newcomers benefited from the guidance of their fellow villagers, but many of them had to pay for it.

Other workers of peasant origin formed production communes that

[15]Kalistratov, p. 23.
[16]Siegelbaum, "Production Collectives," pp. 74–75.
[17]Khlevniuk, *Udarniki pervoi piatiletki*, p. 29; Polliak et al., pp. 60, 63–64.
[18]TsGAOR f. 5451, op. 14, d. 306, l. 16.

enlisted skilled workers. It was unfair, they argued, for skilled workers to receive wages so much higher than their own.[19] Such arguments reflected not only the artel sensibilities of former peasants but their economic self-interest as well. By pressuring skilled workers to join production communes and share their high wages with all commune members, new workers could raise their own incomes substantially. Skilled workers naturally resisted joining communes with lower-paid workers, and some retaliated by forming their own communes.[20] Production communes and collectives were thus used by both established workers and former peasants in their struggle for higher wages and control in the workplace.

Apprenticeships became another arena of conflict between established workers and newcomers. The inadequacy of formal training programs led managers to arrange apprenticeships in some factories, but established workers generally did not wish to share their knowledge with new workers. One man declared, "Let them work as much as I worked, and then they'll be skilled workers too."[21] Established workers realized that every worker who acquired skill diminished the value of their own labor. Furthermore, under piece rates all workers were in a sense in competition with one another. Raising the skill level of recently arrived workers resulted in higher norms and lower wages for established workers.[22]

The lack of training programs forced reliance on the apprenticeship system, and the number of apprentices in large factories increased 4.4 times during the First Five-Year Plan, despite established workers' opposition. In Moscow alone there were 61,700 apprentices (12 percent of the industrial workforce) by 1932.[23] But in practice apprenticeships failed to live up to standards and expectations. Trade union reports in 1930 criticized apprenticeships for not providing the indi-

[19]Khain and Khandros, p. 7.

[20]Polliak et al., pp. 52–53, 72; Kalistratov, pp. 13–15, 39; Siegelbaum, "Production Collectives," p. 76.

[21]Khlevniuk, *Udarniki pervoi piatiletki*, p. 135.

[22]Michael Burawoy, *The Politics of Production: Factory Regimes under Capitalism and Socialism* (London, 1985), pp. 173–174. Some factory managers determined workers' food rations on the basis of their relative productivity. See E. A. Osokina, *Ierarkhiia potrebleniia: O zhizni liudei v usloviiakh stalinskogo snabzheniia, 1928–1935 gg.* (Moscow, 1993), p. 35.

[23]Khlevniuk, *Udarniki pervoi piatiletki*, pp. 69–70; Kingsbury and Fairchild, p. 63; Tverdokhleb, "Chislennost'," p. 31; TsGAORgM f. 415, op. 2, d. 397, l. 50.

vidual instruction they were supposed to give.[24] An apprentice at the Frunze aviation engine plant claimed that in his first ten days at the factory he received no instruction at all; then he was apprenticed to an inferior worker and not provided adequate tools.[25] No foreman or established worker at the Stalin automobile plant wanted to accept an apprentice, so in 1930 some 800 apprentices found themselves transferred endlessly from shop to shop, receiving training in none of them.[26] By denying newcomers access to training, established workers strengthened their own monopoly on specialized jobs.

Skill ranks served as another powerful instrument to exclude new workers from the most desirable jobs. Skill ranks in Soviet industry ranged from 1 (unskilled work) through 8 (highly skilled work). Some specializations (such as the semi-artisanal labor done on universal machines) in fact required years of training and experience, and could be performed only by workers with specialized skills.[27] But technological innovations permitted other tasks to be learned on the job despite their continued designation as "skilled."[28] Skill, then, must be understood not as an absolute measure of ability but as a socially constructed category—often a means used by established workers and foremen to exclude newcomers from prized positions.

New workers were often in effect segregated by factory shop from "skilled" workers. At the Hammer and Sickle metallurgical plant they worked predominantly in the foundry and the main rolling shops, in low-skilled, low-paying, and physically arduous jobs. Far fewer worked in the finishing shops, where higher-paying "skilled" jobs went to established workers, who also occupied the highly paid supervisory posts in the foundry.[29] Here again established workers touted their skill and proletarian background to gain the new managerial positions created by the industrialization drive.[30] Some young workers of urban origin, particularly those with technical education,

[24]TsGAOR f. 5469, op. 14, d. 313, l. 17; f. 5475, op. 13, d. 160, l. 62.

[25]*Aviamotor*, September 10, 1931, p. 4.

[26]*Za promyshlennye kadry* 1930 no. 2/3, p. 41.

[27]Shearer, "Rationalization and Reconstruction," pp. 232–233.

[28]Some cadre workers protested the introduction of new technology for fear of losing their positions and status: *Slavnye traditsii*, p. 123.

[29]TsGAOR f. 7952, op. 3, d. 214, l. 1.

[30]These promotees (*vydvizhentsy*) became the major basis of social support for the Soviet system in the 1930s. See Fitzpatrick, *Education and Social Mobility*.

Unskilled workers maneuver a huge vessel of molten steel in the foundry of the Hammer and
Sickle plant. Courtesy TsGAOR.

also received promotions. The number of former peasants promoted to supervisory positions remained negligible for most of the 1930s.[31]

Struggles among workers for control of the shop floor did not begin with the industrialization drive. During the era of high unemployment in the 1920s, established workers had largely excluded peasant in-migrants from factory jobs altogether. When the demand for labor skyrocketed in the 1930s, peasants did find many opportunities for industrial jobs, yet established workers continued to denigrate and exclude them in order to monopolize the jobs that offered the highest wages and status. Former peasants had to struggle against established workers' labels and barriers such as production communes and skill ranks. Their conflicts with established workers left them with a sense of differentiation and antagonism rather than common interest and solidarity.

Urban Youth and Shock Work

Young men and women of urban origin also entered the workplace in substantial numbers during the 1930s, and competed with both peasant in-migrants and established workers for the most desirable jobs. Like established workers, young urban workers characterized workers of peasant origin as "uncouth," "lazy," and "politically backward."[32] Though most of them had no industrial experience themselves, these young people trumpeted their working-class parentage as evidence of their proletarian character.

Shock work and socialist competition offered means approved by the Party for young urban workers to secure positions and exert power in factory shops. Some of these young people, declaring themselves shock workers, physically stormed factory shops, unfurled banners, and challenged other workers to match their norms or leave the shop. Control of shops allowed young urban workers to circumvent the industrial hierarchies in their drive to raise their stature and wages.[33] At the Kuibyshev electronics factory, young shock workers demanded

[31]AAN f. 359, op. 2, d. 351a, l. 11; MPA f. 432, op. 1, d. 178, l. 174.

[32]David Shearer, "The Language and Politics of Socialist Rationalization," paper presented at the conference "The Making of the Soviet Working Class," Michigan State University, November 1990, p. 39.

[33]Ibid., p. 38; Kuromiya, *Stalin's Industrial Revolution*, p. 115.

that they be looked upon "not as teenagers but as workers." Clearly they had seized upon shock work as a means of raising their status.[34]

Other workers did not passively accept shock work or the power it bestowed on young workers. Numerous reports attest to the opposition of former peasants to shock work and socialist competition— opposition that ranged from refusal to participate to violence against shock workers. At one factory an artel elder and his group "harassed" shock workers, and at another "kulak elements" hanged shock workers in effigy. Some former peasants in Moscow called shock workers "detachments of Antichrists."[35] The disruption of socialist competition projects, far from being "kulak sabotage," expressed newly urbanized workers' vigorous opposition to the privileged position that shock work gave urban youth.[36]

Established workers, too, found that shock work threatened to disrupt their shop-floor culture and raise their work norms. A mechanic in one Moscow factory later recalled, "This damned competition. They were not only competing among the workers but even between the gangs and the factories. The funny thing was, that really nobody cared about it, but when a young, stupid 'komsomolets' said publicly, 'Let's establish a socialist competition,' everybody was too scared to say 'No.' "[37] Some workers refused to participate in socialist competition, claiming they could produce no more than they did already; others agreed at first but later dissolved their shock brigades when managers raised their work norms.[38]

Opposition to shock work occasionally turned violent. At one construction site where a shock brigade was pouring concrete in a foundation pit 25 meters deep, workers of peasant origin started throwing boards down on them, shouting, "Hit the shock workers." One shock worker was killed and another injured.[39] Apparently such violence became widespread, as the Soviet government amended the criminal code to stipulate that violence against shock workers was punish-

---

[34]Khlevniuk, *Udarniki pervoi piatiletki*, pp. 12–14.

[35]*Vecherniaia Moskva*, February 11, 1930.

[36]Gan, p. 41; *Istoriia Moskovskogo avtozavoda*, p. 159; Rakino, p. 51; Khain and Khandros, p. 14.

[37]Zawodny, "Twenty-six Interviews," Hoover Institution archives, I/3.

[38]Filatov, p. 68; Davies, *Soviet Economy in Turmoil*, p. 270. See also Vdovin and Drobizhev, p. 228.

[39]*Govoriat stroiteli sotsializma*, pp. 128–129. *Rabochaia gazeta*, January 5, 1930, p. 6, tells of the murder of another shock worker.

able by five years in prison.[40] Physical violence against Stakhanovites was also widespread. At one Moscow textile mill, when Stakhanovite workers were away attending a Revolution Day banquet to honor them, "class enemy elements" slashed the warps of the best Stakhanovites.[41] Such instances of violence reflected the great tensions within the Moscow workforce during this period of flux.

Industrial managers generally frowned upon shock work and Stakhanovism because of the disruptions these extrasystemic initiatives caused. But Party officials' approval of these methods gave workers opportunities to raise their status and wages at the expense of other workers. Young Muscovites proved particularly willing to participate in shock work to this end. Though there was no shortage of employment opportunities in the 1930s, the huge numbers of people entering the workforce sparked competition for the best jobs and highest wages. Former peasants (the largest group of new workers) and urban youth (the most ambitious) naturally came into conflict. This conflict, expressed in disparaging labels and vandalism, left them sharply stratified throughout the period.

Female Workers and Gender Roles

The number of women in the Moscow workforce during the 1930s rapidly increased, especially in absolute terms, but also as a percentage of all industrial workers. On January 1, 1929, 82,500 women worked in Moscow industry (37.6 percent of the workforce), and this figure rose to 202,900 (40.8 percent) by the start of 1932, and to 317,600 (51.4 percent) by 1937.[42] In contrast to new male workers, however, the majority of new female industrial workers during the First Five-Year Plan (63 percent in 1931) were of urban origin, most of them daughters of workers (43 percent) or of white-collar employees (15 percent).[43]

[40]*Izvestiia*, March 2, 1932, p. 4. On violence between Komsomol members and non-Komsomol members in Moscow factories, see MPA f. 635, op. 1, d. 10, l. 36.

[41]*Legkaia industriia*, November 10, 1935, p. 2; Vdovin and Drobizhev, p. 232; Filtzer, pp. 201–202.

[42]TsGAORgM f. 2872, op. 2, d. 220, ll. 61–63; Tverdokhleb, "Chislennost'," p. 27. Nationally, the number of women in industry increased by over a million during the First Five-Year Plan alone: G. N. Serebrennikov, *Zhenskii trud v SSSR* (Moscow/Leningrad, 1934), p. 65.

[43]Serebrennikov, p. 82. See also M. Avdienko, "Sdvigi v strukture proletariata v

In expanding sectors such as construction and transport, where many male peasant in-migrants found work, the number of female workers grew slowly.[44] More women took jobs in heavy industry, though initially they tended to be of urban origin.[45] Female peasants who moved to Moscow generally did not take jobs in heavy industry until they had spent several years in the city. They more frequently found employment in light industry, where the percentage of women increased much more dramatically. Whereas 50 percent of all workers in light industry were women in 1929, this figure climbed to 62 percent by the beginning of 1933 and to 68 percent by mid-1936.[46] At the Tri-Mountain textile mill, women began to perform tasks once assigned only to men. A report on cadres explained that labor shortages in early 1931 required managers to employ women in positions of greater technical responsibility.[47]

Some peasant women who migrated to Moscow lived as homemakers at first and only later sought factory jobs.[48] Many single women first found employment in the service sector. Moscow city surveys in 1931 and again in 1933 found slightly over 50,000 women employed as domestic servants.[49] Numerous domestic servants eventually moved on to higher-paying industrial jobs and were replaced by more recent arrivals.[50] Typical of such women was a nineteen-year-old peasant who found work as a nanny in Moscow through the help of fellow villagers but left after six months to take a much higher-paying job as a textile worker.[51]

---

pervoi piatiletke," *Planovoe khoziaistvo* 1932 no. 6/7, p. 162; *Na trudovom fronte* 1932 no. 7, pp. 10–11; *Voprosy truda* 1932 no. 11/12, p. 23.

[44]Women accounted for 6.0 percent of all Soviet construction workers in 1928 and 12.8 percent by 1932. The proportion of transport workers who were women remained under 20 percent even in 1937: Serebrennikov, p. 68; *Statisticheskii spravochnik VTsSPS: Otdel statistiki* (Moscow, 1937).

[45]By mid-1936, 37 percent of workers in Moscow heavy industry were women: TsGAORgM f. 2872, op. 2, d. 220, ll. 61–63.

[46]*Ekonomiko-statisticheskii spravochnik*, vol. 2, pp. 10–11; TsGAORgM f. 2872, op. 2, d. 220, ll. 61–63.

[47]AAN f. 359, op. 2, d. 507, ll. 29–31.

[48]*Rabotnitsa na sotsialisticheskoi stroike*, p. 149.

[49]TsGAORgM f. 126, op. 10, d. 47, l. 18. These figures probably substantially underrepresent the number of domestic servants. Particularly peasant women from families that had been dekulakized had reason to withhold information or hide when a Soviet official came to the door.

[50]TsGAORgM f. 453, op. 1, d. 38, ll. 1–16; *Obshchestvennoe pitanie* 1935 no. 5, p. 12; *Rabochii narodnogo pitaniia* 1929 no. 1, p. 18.

[51]*Neizvedannymi putiami: Vospominaniia uchastnikov sotsialisticheskogo stroit-*

A few peasant women found jobs in heavy industry as soon as they arrived in the city. Vera Dmitreevna, hoping for good pay and a little prestige, ignored advice to become a domestic servant and went to the Moscow labor exchange. She was offered employment in a textile factory, but that job fell short of her expectations; she knew that workers in heavy industry received considerably better wages and rations than those in light industry. Vera Dmitreevna's father worked at the Hammer and Sickle metallurgical plant and had told her many fascinating stories about steel production. Though she suspected that her mother (who remained behind in the village) would not want her to work in a steel plant, she persuaded her father to arrange a job for her there. The plant manager, desperate for workers, hired her, and she became the first woman ever to work as a crane operator in the plant's rolling shop.[52]

Despite the increasing numbers of female peasants who found employment in urban industry, barriers for them remained, particularly in construction and heavy industry. Vera Dmitreevna's fellow steelworkers called her *kolkhoznitsa* (collective-farm woman), implicitly denigrating her as not only a peasant but a woman. Women who worked on Moscow metro construction had to endure male workers' taunts ("Show us your calluses") and their refusal to allow women to operate mechanized equipment.[53] Even as increasing numbers of women drove trams, male transport workers questioned their ability to handle the job.[54] Women in some Moscow factories had to create special female brigades because male workers refused to work with them.[55]

Male workers opposed female employment both because women in construction and heavy industry did not conform to their traditional notions of gender roles but also, more tacitly, because the entrance of women into these sectors increased competition for jobs and seemed to threaten their own positions. Just as established workers chal-

---

el'stva, V. A. Smyshliaev and V. F. Finogenov, eds. (Leningrad, 1967), pp. 309–310. See also M. T. Gol'tsman and L. M. Kogan, *Starye i novye kadry proletariata* (Moscow, 1934), p. 40.

[52]Interview with Vera Dmitreevna Ivanova at the Hammer and Sickle plant, Moscow, April 10, 1989.

[53]L. I. Kovalev, ed., *Metro: Sbornik posviashchennyi pusku moskovskogo metropolitena* (Moscow, 1935), p. 209; *Istoriia metro Moskvy*, pp. 107–108.

[54]*Moskovskii transportnik*, March 8, 1940, p. 1.

[55]*Govoriat stroiteli sotsializma*, pp. 234–235.

lenged former peasants' legitimacy as true members of the proletariat, male workers denigrated and harassed female workers.

Female workers also faced discrimination and hostility from male managerial personnel. Foremen did not always accept women assigned to their shops, even women who had studied at a technical school.[56] The few women promoted to lower-level management encountered even greater resistance. Male administrators at one Moscow factory assigned only menial tasks to a woman who had achieved the rank of forewoman.[57] A forewoman at the Kuibyshev electronics factory was assaulted by a male worker in the shop.[58]

Many female in-migrants still held to traditional gender roles themselves and simply declined to seek jobs considered to be "men's work."[59] Women who did take traditionally male jobs did not necessarily discard their notions of traditional gender roles or espouse the principle of equal rights for women. Falling living standards during the 1930s often forced women to seek industrial jobs simply to provide for themselves or to supplement their husbands' pay.

Practical considerations precluded many female peasant in-migrants from accepting employment in construction and industry. A Moscow construction trust reported that because of the housing shortage, unmarried men and women had to live in the same barracks—an arrangement that resulted in frequent cases of "tactless relations toward women." Some women construction workers in Moscow were subjected to so much sexual harassment that they quit their jobs.[60] Women with children faced substantial difficulties when they entered the workforce. Foremen routinely denied nursing mothers time to nurse their babies. The administration, the trade union, and the Party committee at one factory all refused to intervene on behalf of a worker who required three breaks a day to nurse her infant. Only when other women in her shop cornered the foreman and swore at him did he arrange for the woman to receive time off.[61] Public food services and child care, heralded by the Soviet press as institutions that would liberate women from domestic responsibilities, remained badly underfunded and underdeveloped in the 1930s.[62]

[56]*AMOvets*, April 4 and 16, 1931.
[57]*Iunyi kommunist* 1938 no. 5, p. 49.
[58]TsGAOR f. 7952, op. 3, d. 560, l. 13.
[59]See, for example, *Istoriia metro Moskvy*, pp. 107–108.
[60]TsGAORgM f. 5301, op. 1, d. 37, l. 8.
[61]Zawodny, "Twenty-six Interviews," Hoover Institution archives, II/16.
[62]TsPA f. 17, op. 114, d. 256, l. 70.

Despite the numerous obstacles, economic planners and Party leaders continued to recruit women into industrial jobs. A Central Committee resolution in 1930 called for the recruitment of wives of workers into production, and a subsequent Party directive specified concrete steps, including quotas, to raise the number of women employed in industry.[63] Official publications also encouraged the recruitment of women into construction and heavy industry, and decried barriers to female employment.[64] An article in the Stalin automobile plant's newspaper chastised male workers for discrimination against women, and declared it time to put aside their saying "Just as a chicken is not a bird, a woman [*baba*] is not a person."[65] A woman's committee was organized at the Hammer and Sickle plant to address the concerns of female workers. At a meeting in 1931 Nadezhda Krupskaia, Lenin's widow, addressed the women and complimented them on doing metallurgical jobs traditionally performed by men.[66]

Yet even as official recruitment efforts raised the number of female workers, equality of opportunity for women remained elusive, particularly in the high-paying, high-status jobs of heavy industry. Throughout the 1930s, female workers were concentrated largely in factories and shops where the work was considered to make few demands and where wages were correspondingly low. Gosplan statistics from 1933 show that most female heavy-industry workers were employed in electrotechnical factories, manufacturing lamps, stoves, and appliances. Even in rapidly expanding (and labor-short) machine-building plants, managers hired women only in certain capacities— as lathe operators and drillers, for example, but not as repairers, joiners, or other well-paid specialists.[67] At the Hammer and Sickle plant, women readily found work in the cable shop (they accounted for 40 percent of its workforce by 1931) but were rarely hired in the open-hearth shop or the rolling shop (there they represented only 1 and 2 percent of workers, respectively).[68]

Government policy contributed to women's continuing inequality

[63]Gail Warshofsky Lapidus, *Women in Soviet Society* (Berkeley, 1978), pp. 98–99.

[64]*Sputnik kul'trabotnika*, p. 14.

[65]*AMOvets*, April 16, 1931, p. 4.

[66]Interview with Mariia Aleksandrovna Filatova at the Hammer and Sickle plant, Moscow, April 17, 1989.

[67]TsGAMO f. 2534, op. 1, d. 485, l. 42; *Na trudovom fronte* 1932 no. 7, p. 9; *Profsoiuznaia perepis'*, pp. 22–23.

[68]TsGAOR f. 7952, op. 3, d. 214, l. 4.

Female workers transport materials in the yard of the Hammer and Sickle plant. Courtesy TsGAOR.

in the workplace. Protective legislation prohibited female workers from engaging in some strenuous industrial occupations.[69] Skill ranks also prevented them from moving into higher-paying jobs, just as they prevented new male workers from doing so. When the Commissariat of Labor, in its effort to recruit more female workers, issued lists of job openings to be filled primarily by women, it perpetuated the principle of the sexual division of labor even as it reordered this division.[70]

Propaganda also defined distinct gender roles for peasants who joined the urban workforce. The Stakhanovites who were publicized as models for male workers of peasant origin were miners and metal-workers, whereas most female Stakhanovites who received publicity were textile workers.[71] Literature of the 1930s presented female characters who performed some jobs traditionally done by men, but it did not portray them as innovators or highly skilled workers. These female characters gave their all to the industrialization drive, but they were always secondary in importance to men.[72] Soviet political

[69]Siegelbaum, *Stakhanovism*, p. 171.
[70]Lapidus, p. 99.
[71]See the workers featured at the First Congress of Stakhanovites: *Labour in the Land of the Soviets*.
[72]Xenia Gasiorowska, *Women in Soviet Fiction* (Madison, Wis., 1968), pp. 100–107.

posters, too, increasingly depicted women industrial workers, but as subordinate to men.[73]

The need that Soviet authorities felt to delineate gender roles stemmed in part from the state of flux of the workforce during the 1930s. The sudden entrance of thousands of urban and rural men and women into the workforce, combined with the mechanization and deskilling of industrial specializations during this period, disrupted traditional hierarchies in the workplace. With an increasing number of men and women working side by side in Soviet factories, the construction of gender—the designation of certain jobs as men's work and others as women's work—represented an effort, conscious or unconscious, to establish order in the workplace and a sense of identity among workers.[74]

In other words, the delineation of gender roles, invariably related to issues of domination and subordination, contributed to the establishment of new hierarchies among the disparate social groups that made up the urban workforce. Gender roles, like skill ranks and the derogatory labeling of former peasants, served to secure the status of established workers, who saw the influx of new workers as a threat. For the sake of the industrialization drive, the Soviet government required the labor of urban and peasant women in factories, but it made sure that managerial and skilled positions went to men.[75] Earlier the recruitment of women into the workforce had been regarded as a means to female economic independence and emancipation, but in the 1930s it became a policy to use women's labor while maintaining male superiority.

Women seized industrial employment opportunities despite their continued subordination. Factory work, even in low-status, low-paying jobs, offered substantially better wages and benefits than em-

[73]Elizabeth Waters, "The Female Form in Soviet Political Iconography, 1917–1932," in *Russia's Women: Accommodation, Resistance, Transformation*, Barbara Evans Clements et al., eds. (Berkeley, 1991), p. 238.

[74]A similar process occurred in nineteenth-century French factories, where mechanization and the entrance of women into the workforce led to regulation based on the construction of gender. See Joan Wallach Scott, *Gender and the Politics of History* (New York, 1988), pp. 148, 151–152.

[75]Nazi Germany had a similar policy in the late 1930s. See Annemarie Troger, "The Creation of a Female Assembly-Line Proletariat," in *When Biology Became Destiny: Women in Weimar and Nazi Germany*, Renate Bridenthal et al., eds. (New York, 1984).

ployment in the service sector. In this period of falling living standards, rationing, and distribution of goods through special factory stores, women who secured industrial jobs were able to support themselves and their families better than those who did not. And the low living standards of female peasants who became urban workers were nonetheless far higher than those of women who remained in the village.

National Minority Peasants in Moscow

Conflict between workers also erupted along ethnic lines. In some cities and construction sites, especially those in Ukraine, the Urals, and Siberia, national minority peasants joined the industrial workforce in large numbers during the 1930s. In Moscow, however, the number of national minority peasants remained limited. Moscow's population in 1933 was 87.5 percent Russian, 6.6 percent Jewish, 1.5 percent Ukrainian, 1.0 percent Tatar, 0.6 percent Belorussian, 0.6 percent Polish, 0.4 percent Latvian, 0.3 percent Armenian, 0.3 percent German, and 1.2 percent other nationalities.[76] Various Moscow work sites reported small numbers of Ukrainians, Tatars, Bashkirs, and Mordvinians.[77]

Few as they were, national minority workers came into open conflict with Russian workers. Strife was concentrated in construction and transport, where minority peasants most easily found work. A brawl broke out between Russian and Tatar construction workers at one Moscow site in 1930. Ethnic hostility clearly motivated the melee, as witnesses heard the combatants crying "Beat the Russians!" and "Beat the Tatars!" Large-scale police action proved necessary to separate the combatants, and many arrests followed.[78] At another construction site a prize awarded to a brigade of Bashkir and Tatar workers aroused such resentment among the Russian contingent that

[76]TsGAORgM f. 126, op. 10, d. 47, l. 19. These percentages remained virtually unchanged in 1937: *Vsesoiuznaia perepis' naseleniia, 1937*, p. 90.

[77]TsGAOR f. 7952, op. 3, d. 235, l. 31; TsGAMO f. 738, op. 1, d. 37, l. 81; *Istoriia rabochikh Moskvy*, p. 282; *Martenovka*, March 8, 1930, p. 2.

[78]TsGAOR f. 5475, op. 13, d. 426, l. 87.

they pelted the Bashkirs and Tatars with rocks.[79] Similarly, animosity among Russians, Tatars, and Mordvinians flared among transport workers on the Moscow River.[80]

The very few members of national minorities who worked in Moscow factories faced discrimination and even physical abuse. Russian workers periodically beat them at the barracks of the Moscow ball bearing factory. Officials blamed the assaults on "hooligans" and apparently took no specific action to prevent recurrences.[81] Anti-Semitism among Moscow factory workers was also common, though it usually was directed toward Jewish officials and engineers rather than toward fellow workers.[82]

Thus the workforce that formed in Moscow in the 1930s was far from harmonious. The enormous influx of new workers threatened hierarchies and disrupted work routines. Established workers strove to protect their privileged status by challenging new arrivals' legitimacy as workers. Young urbanites also denigrated workers of peasant origin and stressed their own working-class origins to define themselves as true proletarians. Russian male workers, established and newcomers alike, refused to accept women and national minorities as their equals. In this sense village networks were no more egalitarian than traditional shop-floor culture; both established gender roles and hierarchies that empowered some people while subordinating or excluding others.

The formation of the Moscow workforce must be understood as a series of exclusions as well as inclusions, and as a struggle for hegemony in the workplace. The extreme economic hardship of the 1930s only exacerbated competition between workers for factory jobs; a good wage or even a 5-ruble bonus could mean the difference between adequate food and hunger for workers and their families. Given the severity of this struggle, the disparate groups that made up the Moscow workforce found no basis for working-class solidarity. The former peasants who displayed strong collectivist tendencies among themselves did not cooperate with other groups of workers. The workforce as a whole did not generate a sense of common interests or collective

[79]TsPA f. 17, op. 114, d. 255, l. 68.
[80]TsGAMO f. 738, op. 1, d. 37, l. 81.
[81]TsGAORgM f. 214, op. 1, d. 284, l. 16.
[82]See, for example, TsGAOR f. 7952, op. 3, d. 235, l. 36.

identity, and differentiation among workers prevented the development of a cohesive working class. This lack of worker solidarity diminished the possibility of collective action to raise workers' living standard. Simultaneously it subverted the official myth of a strong working class united behind the Communist Party and undermined the concept of a working-class state.

5

The Urban Environment
and Living Standards

Nadezhda Andreevna, like most peasant in-migrants, felt bewildered by the novelty of her surroundings when she moved to Moscow in 1933 at the age of 16. It seemed that the city would transform every aspect of her life, and in fact it did fundamentally change the character of her work and the extent of her social interactions. Yet surprisingly some features of her life did not radically change. She still lived with relatives, if no longer with her parents. Their flimsy wooden house, like a peasant hut, had no electricity or plumbing. The neighborhood on the outskirts of Moscow was at best semiurban; the muddy streets and lack of urban services resembled conditions in her native village. She and other former peasants living there even cultivated gardens and grew much of their own food.[1]

Just as the factory was a point of engagement between Soviet managers and various groups of workers, the city became an arena for interaction between Soviet authorities and urban inhabitants, old and new. The degree of control exercised by Soviet authorities over peasants who settled in Moscow hinged in part on their control of the urban environment in which these newcomers lived. Municipal and enterprise officials took charge of housing and food supply in Moscow in accordance with the expansion of state control. Their efforts to house and feed people, however, fell far short of the grow-

[1]Interview with Nadezhda Andreevna Kuznetsova at Izmailovskii Park, Moscow, July 25, 1992.

ing population's needs. As the housing crisis worsened and living standards plunged, former peasants in Moscow came to rely on informal self-help associations and circles of illegal barter and exchange. Authorities' dominion over the urban environment, while expanded, therefore remained incomplete. New forms of self-help and resistance arose in response to new forms of state control over urban space and economic resources.

Moscow's Expansion and the Control of Urban Space

Soviet urban planners, such as Leonard Sabsovich and Konstantin Melnikov, conceived of the socialist city as a mechanism for directed political and social change. They believed their plans would not only redesign the urban environment but transform the people who lived there. Their highly idealized blueprints called for well-lit and orderly streets, wide squares and boulevards, and community-oriented housing complexes centered on schools, communal cafeterias, and cultural centers. Their model cities were to produce model citizens—cultured urbanites who would enthusiastically join forces to build socialism. In other words, Soviet officials and planners believed that the elimination of the old city would also eliminate the old ways; new socialist cities would instill in people new ideas and new modes of behavior.[2]

Moscow provided a special challenge to urban planners. Not only was it the largest Soviet city, but its thousand-year history left a complex legacy of development—an array of streets, buildings, churches, stores, markets, and neighborhoods—that could not be erased or easily altered. During the 1930s Moscow received the attention of national leaders as well as urban planners. In 1931 Kaganovich recommended a program of urban renewal for Moscow to eliminate the problems it shared with capitalist cities, such as crowding and slums. His stated goal was to convert Moscow from a "large village" into a

---

[2]S. Frederick Starr, "Visionary Town Planning during the Cultural Revolution," in Fitzpatrick, ed., *Cultural Revolution in Russia*, pp. 208–211. Sabsovich and other urbanists actually envisioned cities of very limited size as a means to eliminate urban problems.

capital of which the Soviet people could be proud. The Central Committee ordered a plan for reconstruction of the city to be drawn up, and, with Stalin reportedly overseeing architects and urban planners, the plan was completed by 1935. Even before the reconstruction plan was approved, Soviet authorities began to clear away vestiges of the central city's capitalist past. They bulldozed the market stalls and old wooden housing just north of the Kremlin and demolished churches, including the colossal Church of Christ the Redeemer. In their place they built expansive squares, wide streets, and monumental cement buildings.[3]

Beyond the city's center, however, Party leaders and urban planners proved less successful in realizing their visions of a new Moscow. Planners never worked out detailed budgets to show how newly designed cities could be paid for, nor did they confront the causes of the rapid urbanization that undermined their vision of "de-urbanized cities."[4] Moscow's reconstruction plan called for a population limit of 5 million and for a forest belt of parks to contain urban sprawl, but planners and even the Moscow city council exercised little control over the city's growth. Other Soviet bureaucrats did not share the planners' vision of model cities and ignored proposed limits on urban expansion. Industrial commissariats, for example, which wielded far greater power than municipal authorities, built new industrial enterprises in the designated forest zone.[5] As a result, regions of Moscow outside the city center expanded rapidly and in no way conformed to the planners' designs.[6]

Peasants who moved to Moscow during the 1930s settled not in the planned central districts of the city but rather in outlying districts or even beyond the city limits. The fastest-growing districts of Moscow in the 1930s were Stalinskii and Proletarskii, industrial regions that contained new and expanding metalworking plants.[7] Peasants who

[3]F. E. Ian Hamilton, *The Moscow City Region* (London, 1976), p. 39; I. S. Romanovskii, *Moskva sotsialisticheskaia* (Moscow, 1940), pp. 28–30; *Moskva rekonstruiuretsia: Al'bom diagramm* (Moscow, 1938).

[4]Starr, pp. 217, 232–237.

[5]TsPA f. 17, op. 116, d. 30, l. 25.

[6]Hamilton, p. 37. The city council had so little control over new construction in the Moscow suburb of Liubertsy that its members often learned of building projects only after they had been completed. See *Ukhtomskii rabochii*, January 9, 1938, p. 3.

[7]Other districts that grew rapidly included Pervomaiskii, Taganskii, Moskvoretskii, and Sokolnicheskii: *Moskva: Sbornik*, pp. 38–39. See also *Statisticheskii spravochnik po raionam Moskovskoi oblasti*, p. 73; TsGAORgM f. 126, op. 10, d. 47, l. 58.

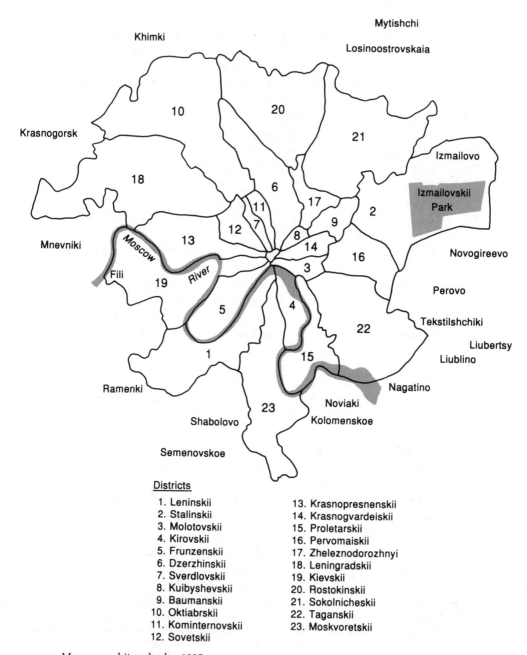

Khimki

Mytishchi

Losinoostrovskaia

Krasnogorsk

Izmailovo

10

20

21

Izmailovskii
Park

18

6

Mnevniki

Moscow

17

2

11

River

12

7

9

Fili

13

8

Novogireevo

19

14

3

16

Perovo

5

4

Tekstilshchiki

1

22

Liubertsy

Ramenki

15

Liublino

Nagatino

Noviaki

Shabolovo

23

Kolomenskoe

Semenovskoe

Districts

1. Leninskii
2. Stalinskii
3. Molotovskii
4. Kirovskii
5. Frunzenskii
6. Dzerzhinskii
7. Sverdlovskii
8. Kuibyshevskii
9. Baumanskii
10. Oktiabrskii
11. Kominternovskii
12. Sovetskii

13. Krasnopresnenskii
14. Krasnogvardeiskii
15. Proletarskii
16. Pervomaiskii
17. Zheleznodorozhnyi
18. Leningradskii
19. Kievskii
20. Rostokinskii
21. Sokolnicheskii
22. Taganskii
23. Moskvoretskii

Moscow and its suburbs, 1937

secured factory jobs settled in these regions on the east and southeast side of the city, where the greatest industrial expansion occurred. Stalinskii had more workers (77,000) than any other district by 1931, and the populations of Stalinskii and Proletarskii districts increased by almost 50 percent from 1933 to 1936.[8] Population at the center of the city remained about the same while the outlying industrial districts boomed.[9]

Equally striking was the growth of suburbs outside the city limits. The unincorporated suburbs of Perovo, Liublino, Liubertsy, Myti-shchi, Khimki, Tekstilshchiki, and Krasnogorsk—not to mention numerous workers' settlements (rabochie poselki) that did not even qualify as suburbs—all expanded tremendously.[10] Between 1926 and 1939 the population of Perovo went from 23,711 to 77,727, and the population of Liublino from 8,391 to 64,332. Liubertsy's population grew from virtually nil to over 45,000 by 1938.[11] Some 400,000 people lived in Moscow's suburbs by 1937.[12]

Peasant in-migrants accounted for this population explosion on the outskirts (okrainy) of Moscow. Chain migration led arriving peasants to settlements in outlying districts and suburbs, where they generally found lodging with relatives and fellow villagers.[13] As in prerevolutionary Moscow and in other Soviet cities in the 1930s, peasants' initial place of residence correlated with their village of origin. Moscow's suburbs developed as "urban villages"—clusters of fellow villagers, acquaintances, and relatives.[14]

Some newcomers who could not find housing in the suburbs lived even farther out, in the villages that dotted the countryside surround-

[8]*Moskva: Sbornik*, pp. 38–39; *Izvestiia Mosoblispolkoma, gorispolkoma i Moskovskogo soveta*, November 26, 1931, p. 3; *General'nyi plan rekonstruktsii*, p. 61. For the population of each district in 1936, see *Moskva v novykh raionakh* (Moscow, 1936).

[9]*Moskva rekonstruiuretsia*, pp. 59–60. For the population density of each district in 1936, see TsGAORgM f. 126, op. 10, d. 47, l. 15.

[10]Hamilton, p. 39; *Zhilishchno-kommunal'noe khoziaistvo gorodov i rabochikh poselkov Moskovskoi oblasti: Statisticheskii spravochnik* (Moscow, 1936), pp. 6–9.

[11]*Moskovskaia oblast' v tsifrakh*, p. 15; *Ukhtomskii rabochii*, April 17, 1938, p. 3.

[12]*Vsesoiuznaia perepis' naseleniia, 1937 g.*, pp. 70–71.

[13]TsGAORgM f. 1289, op. 1, d. 91, l. 104; John N. Hazard, *Soviet Housing Law* (New Haven, 1939), pp. 80–82.

[14]Bradley, pp. 134–140; Khlevniuk, "Izmenenie," pp. 123–124, 127. The area adjacent to the Cheliabinsk tractor factory was divided up into sections according to residents' village of origin; former peasants from Orel province lived in one area, those from Samara province in another, and so on.

ing the city. Ivan Gudov, having been advised by a fellow villager that it would be impossible to find housing in the center of the city, went to the village of Semenovskoe, just outside Moscow, and rented the corner of a peasant hut.[15] Many former peasants who worked in Moscow factories lived in the villages of Kolomenskoe, Nagatino, Novinki, and Losinoostrovskaia. Some commuted even greater distances. A few employees of the Kirov Dinamo plant lived 40 kilometers away, and a group of construction workers traveled 60 kilometers by train every day to build the Moscow metro.[16]

Life on the outskirts differed drastically from life in central Moscow. Remoteness from the city's center characterized these regions, for public transportation did not service them to any meaningful extent. The first line of the Moscow metro opened in 1935, but even by 1939 only three lines had been completed, none of which reached the outskirts or even to Proletarskii district.[17] The horse-drawn cart remained one of the primary modes of transportation in Moscow through much of the First Five-Year Plan.[18] Trolley-buses were introduced only in 1933, and trams remained limited to the central part of the city. Not before 1938 did authorities construct a tram line connecting the workers' settlement at Novogireevo with the city. As late as 1940, only one tram line linked the Stalin automobile plant's settlement on the outskirts of Moscow with the plant itself, so that during morning and evening rush hours, workers rode clinging to the outside of the trams.[19] A Moscow Party report in 1937 described settlements on the city's outskirts as isolated and completely lacking in municipal services.[20]

With no public transportation available, many new workers simply went on foot from their homes to Moscow proper. Gudov, for example, tried to hitch rides on passing carts or trucks in bad weather, and otherwise walked ten versts (slightly over six miles) to work and back. The ten-verst walk was not so far by peasant standards, and

[15]Gudov, *Sud'ba rabochego*, p. 7.

[16]TsGAORgM f. 1289, op. 1, d. 91, ll. 107–108; *AMOvets*, April 18, 1931, p. 4; MPA f. 432, op. 1, d. 190, l. 78; *Istoriia metro Moskvy*, p. 69.

[17]Archive of the Museum of the History of Moscow, d. 17, l. 4203/8.

[18]*Izvestiia Mosoblispolkoma*, November 26, 1931, p. 3.

[19]TsGAORgM f. 126, op. 10, d. 47, ll. 128–140; *Moskva: Razvitie khoziaistva i kul'tury goroda* (Moscow, 1958), pp. 76–77; *Martenovka*, January 30, 1938, p. 1; *Moskovskii transportnik*, March 8, 1940, p. 3. See also *Delo chesti*, p. 7.

[20]MPA f. 432, op. 1, d. 176, l. 137.

groups of former peasants would walk together, sometimes singing as they went to pass the time more pleasantly.[21]

The remoteness of the outskirts had important consequences for the people who lived there. Their distance from the city center separated them from established workers, who tended to live in more central districts. Even in the areas where newcomers lived close to established workers, they remained largely segregated by building. At one housing settlement of the Hammer and Sickle plant, for example, all established workers lived in one barracks and all newly arrived workers in another.[22] In the course of the decade, new and old workers alike moved about in search of better housing, so some degree of integration gradually took place. Initially, however, the de facto segregation of housing—which replicated the frequent segregation of old and new workers by factory shop—did not allow a single working-class community to develop, a situation that did not promote working-class unity.

The remoteness of the outskirts also insulated former peasants from the influences of urban culture. Many of them went directly home after work, the distances involved leaving no time to imbibe the cultural resources of Moscow. Some of them were unable to attend literacy classes because they lived too far from where the classes were held.[23] Women who worked at the Red Hercules factory reportedly absorbed no urban culture at all. "The life of these girls," a journalist noted, "consists of work, after work a stroll on the Sokolniki circle, and then home to sleep. One young female worker has not once been to a movie theater or seen the metro in the entire two years she has lived in Moscow."[24] Former peasants oriented their leisure activity around the particular culture that grew up on the outskirts of town, rather than around the urban culture of central Moscow. The lack of official influence in these regions permitted an alternative subculture, based on peasant culture and values, to flourish there.

The physical environment of settlements on the outskirts diverged quite sharply from the model communities envisioned by urban planners. One report denounced the anarchic building patterns that resulted as various commissariats, enterprises, and even individu-

[21]Gudov, *Sud'ba rabochego*, pp. 30–31.
[22]Trud, September 11, 1931, p. 3.
[23]MPA f. 468, op. 1, d. 157, l. 73.
[24]Komsomol'skaia pravda, October 11, 1936.

als constructed housing haphazardly, heedless of urban planning or infrastructure.[25] One settlement was described as "consisting of wooden houses, devoid of even elementary fire-prevention features. . . . With the onset of night the darkness envelops the settlement and the only light comes from flickering kerosene lamps in the windows of the houses. There are no telephone connections with the city."[26] Kozhukhovo, another settlement on the edge of Moscow, lacked any sewer system or water supply, and consisted of barracks and "wooden peasant-style houses . . . with thick, tall fences around them."[27] An American who walked through the suburbs of Moscow in 1931 remarked on the small wooden houses with chickens in their muddy yards and on the women washing clothes in the Moscow River.[28] In many ways the outskirts of Moscow closely resembled a series of villages.

Shantytowns sprang up as some new residents built their own housing.[29] Former peasants constructed makeshift dwellings or mud huts (*zemlianki*) by assembling scrap wood or by burrowing into the earth to form a dugout.[30] Newcomers cut down so many trees to build shanties that officials became concerned about the loss of foliage.[31] According to fiction of the period, people also lived in barns and haylofts.[32] The outskirts of Moscow thus became a hodgepodge of makeshift housing rather than a series of planned communities.

Urban services were all but nonexistent on the outskirts of the city. Most of the streets in workers' settlements, and even in Proletarskii district, remained unpaved.[33] In 1931 only 42 percent of inhabited buildings in Moscow had running water, and in some areas this figure

[25]*K probleme stroitel'stva sotsialisticheskogo goroda* (Moscow, 1930), p. 27.

[26]*Ukhtomskii rabochii*, May 12, 1938, p. 4.

[27]MPA f. 432, op. 1, d. 176, l. 137; *Pravda*, December 22, 1937, p. 2.

[28]Letter of Beatrice Kinkead, April 23, 1931, Kinkead Papers; Bancroft Library, University of California, Berkeley.

[29]Starr, p. 236. Some settlements consisted almost entirely of enterprise housing, but in others housing was private: *Zhilishchno-kommunal'noe khoziaistvo . . . poselkov*, pp. 16–17.

[30]Zawodny, "Twenty-six Interviews," Hoover Institution archives, I/7. In 1935 approximately 9 percent of the population of Magnitogorsk lived in mud huts: Kotkin, pp. 317–320.

[31]*Vecherniaia Moskva*, May 8, 1934, p. 3.

[32]Leonid Leonov, *Soviet River*, Ivor Montagu and Sergei Nolbandov, trans. (New York, 1932), p. 129. See also TsGAORgM f. 150, op. 5, d. 66, ll. 97–100.

[33]*Izvestiia Mosoblispolkoma*, November 26, 1931, p. 3.

was as low as 12 percent.[34] Workers' settlements generally lacked a sewage system, and electricity and central heating (universal throughout central Moscow in the 1930s) rarely reached settlements on the outskirts.[35] In many barracks the absence of electricity made reading impossible.[36]

The police presence on the outskirts was weak, and the unlit streets there were reputed to be unsafe. Officials attributed the rising crime rate, in particular the frequent incidence of "hooliganism," to young workers of peasant origin. A study conducted during the First Five-Year Plan found that 35 percent of the people convicted of hooliganism in the RSFSR were under 24 years old, and a large proportion consisted of former peasants.[37] Likewise, a 1933 survey showed that 60 percent of convicted hooligans were workers, two-thirds of whom had only recently begun work.[38] Of course many noncriminal activities could be interpreted as hooliganism; drunken carousing undoubtedly accounted for some of those arrests. Since officials regarded former peasants as barely civilized in any case, they found it easy to blame them for any criminal conduct in the working class.[39]

At the same time, some former peasants did indeed commit unlawful acts. Many young men on the outskirts formed gangs with their neighboring fellow villagers.[40] One gang dragged some visiting collective farm members from their carts and beat them. Police may have been correct in attributing such assaults to "dekulakized elements," as victims of dekulakization settled scores with peasants who had supported collectivization.[41] Another gang disrupted a Komsomol

[34]Starr, p. 228. See also H. Kent Geiger, *The Family in Soviet Russia* (Cambridge, Mass., 1968), p. 207.

[35]I. Kokshaiskii, "Obespechenie kommunal'nym blagoustroistvom otdel'nykh sotsial'nykh grupp naseleniia g. Moskvy," *Kommunal'noe khoziaistvo* 1931 no. 19/20, pp. 44–47; Poletaev, p. 39; *Ukhtomskii rabochii*, May 14, 1938, p. 1; Geiger, p. 207.

[36]TsGAMO f. 214, op. 1, d. 284, l. 4.

[37]S. Bulatov, "Khuliganstvo i mery bor'by s nim v rekonstruktivnom periode," *Sovetskoe gosudarstvo i pravo* 1933 no. 4, p. 70.

[38]A. Gertsenzon, "Klassovaia bor'ba i perezhitki starogo byta," *Sovetskaia iustitsiia* 1934 no. 2, p. 16.

[39]Bulatov (p. 68) pointed to the infiltration of kulaks into the working class as the source of the rising crime rate among workers.

[40]V. V. Ermilov, *Byt rabochei kazarmy* (Moscow/Leningrad, 1930), p. 15. On gangs in other parts of the country, see Gertsenzon, p. 17; *Sudebnaia praktika* 1931 no. 11, p. 14.

[41]Gertsenzon, p. 16.

conference and started a fight with Komsomol members.[42] In March 1935 the Soviet government promulgated a new decree specifying strong measures against hooliganism and "the manufacture, possession, sale, and carrying of side arms such as daggers and Swedish knives."[43] Press reports indicate that knife fights between youth gangs on the outskirts of the city were common, and that the police seldom intervened.[44]

Little information exists on the basis for gang membership, but given the clustering of fellow villagers in Moscow, these gangs probably formed around village networks. When former peasants held group fist fights for sport, they commonly organized gangs according to their village of origin.[45] Some gangs engaged in criminal activity, but more frequently peasant in-migrants banded together with fellow villagers to fight turf wars with rival gangs or simply to protect their homes and territory. Gangs had to patrol their neighborhoods, because they could not rely on the police to maintain order in their settlements.

The outskirts of Moscow, then, were not tightly controlled by municipal authorities and did not become agents for social change. The muddy roads and shantytowns not only failed to live up to planners' model communities, they did not even provide basic necessities. The absence of electricity, for example, inhibited the spread of literacy—something officials had assumed the urban environment would promote. Former peasants who settled on the outskirts were left to organize their own communities. These communities in turn perpetuated peasant culture, values, and forms of association, instead of promoting official values or allegiance to the Soviet government.

Housing and Household Patterns

Moscow's housing in the 1930s also fell far short of the clean, efficient, and commodious apartments envisioned by urban planners.

---

[42]*Sudebnaia praktika RSFSR* 1931 no. 5, pp. 8–9.

[43]*Izvestiia*, March 30, 1935. See also British Foreign Office records, 371/19469, pp. 174–181.

[44]Andrle, pp. 57–58; Gertsenzon, p. 16.

[45]During fistfights, Donbass miners formed teams with former peasants from their village or province of origin. See Hiroaki Kuromiya, "The Commander and the Rank and File: Managing the Soviet Coal-Mining Industry, 1928–1933," in *Social Dimensions*, Rosenberg and Siegelbaum, eds., p. 148.

Early in the First Five-Year Plan, when it became clear that Gosplan had substantially underestimated the number of peasants who would pour into Moscow, deputies to the city council began to call for a large-scale building program to alleviate the increasingly severe shortage of housing.[46] The city council's budget, however, included only 19 million rubles for housing renovation in 1931, and expenditures on housing did not rise substantially until after 1935. By that time the city was hopelessly overcrowded.[47]

The city council's lack of funding left the burden of housing construction largely to industrial enterprises, which had far vaster resources. Factory directors were concerned first of all with industrial production and plan fulfillment, but the lack of housing for their workers ultimately forced them to construct apartments and barracks. As labor turnover worsened throughout the First Five-Year Plan, enterprise managers recognized (far more quickly than Party functionaries) that inadequate housing often caused workers to seek work elsewhere.[48] Industrial commissariats and individual enterprises began to invest tens of millions of rubles in the construction of new housing, and their investments funded almost 70 percent of the housing constructed in Moscow in 1935.[49]

Enterprises constructed some housing for their workers on factory grounds or adjacent to transportation depots.[50] This housing accounted for the growth of population in districts within the city limits. Lacking ample space in the city, enterprises more frequently built housing on the far edges of Moscow's outer districts or beyond the city limits. The Hammer and Sickle plant established a workers'

[46]*Na planovom fronte* 1930 no. 6, pp. 25–30; TsGAOR f. 5475, op. 13, d. 276, l. 22. Moscow Party reports at this time warned of workers sleeping in factories and orphans living at train stations for lack of housing: MPA f. 432, op. 1, d. 73, l. 17; f. 635, op. 1, d. 41, l. 37.

[47]TsGAORgM f. 150, op. 5, d. 36, l. 57; *Materialy o rabote Moskovskogo Soveta rabochikh, krest'ianskikh i krasnoarmeiskikh deputatov za 1935–1936 gg.* (Moscow, 1936), pp. 18–19.

[48]TsGAORgM f. 5301, op. 1, d. 68, l. 2.

[49]*Rabochaia Moskva,* January 28, 1931, p. 4; TsGAORgM f. 176, op. 4, d. 4, ll. 15–16; Tverdokhleb, "Material'noe blagosostoianie," p. 479. On cooperative housing, which accounted for only 14 percent of housing constructed in Moscow in 1932, see Hazard, pp. 11–12.

[50]L. A. Anokhina and M. N. Shmeleva, *Byt gorodskogo naseleniia srednei polosy RSFSR v proshlom i nastoiashchem* (Moscow, 1977), pp. 193–194; *Moskovskii transportnik,* January 30, 1940, p. 3; *Plan g. Moskvy* (Moscow, 1935).

settlement in Novogireevo, and metro construction workers lived in barracks in the suburb of Fili.[51]

The influx of new workers was so huge, however, that it was impossible for enterprises to house all or even a majority of their employees. The Red Hercules factory hired 5,000 new workers in the summer of 1931 alone, and though it constructed several barracks, it still was unable to house most of them.[52] The Kuibyshev electronics factory hired 6,000 new workers in 1931 (and anticipated hiring another 13,000 in 1932) but had resources to construct housing for only 2,000. In October 1931 the Stalin automobile plant employed 13,800 workers and planned to expand to 27,000 in the course of 1932. It initiated five new housing projects, but each housed only a few hundred workers, leaving thousands without enterprise housing. Even in 1937 the plant housed less than 20 percent of its employees.[53] Some enterprises declared that they had enough apartments to accommodate only their best workers, and allocated housing accordingly.[54]

Complicating the situation was the fact that many enterprises could not maintain control over the housing they did own. The barracks of one metalworking factory in Proletarskii district remained filled with people who no longer worked at the factory. Most of them had found jobs elsewhere, but, lacking any new housing, they refused to move out.[55] The principle of eminent domain prevailed in much of Moscow's housing. A report in preparation for the Seventeenth Party Congress (1934) cited the urgent need for registration in enterprise barracks to evict the large number of unauthorized people living in them.[56]

In all, Moscow added 4 million square meters of housing from 1926 to 1936, but was still an estimated 46 million square meters short.[57] With the population burgeoning, the amount of housing per capita

[51]TsGAORgM f. 176, op. 4, d. 4, l. 206; *Metro v srok*, May 1, 1935, p. 4. See also *Istoriia Moskovskogo avtozavoda*, p. 192.

[52]*Rabochaia Moskva*, October 29, 1931, p. 3.

[53]MPA f. 468, op. 1, d. 102, ll. 58, 72; TsGANKh f. 7622, op. 1, d. 251, l. 2.

[54]Hazard, pp. 20–21.

[55]TsGAMO f. 214, op. 1, d. 122, ll. 1–3.

[56]TsGAORgM f. 214, op. 1, d. 284, l. 10. On evictions, see Hazard, pp. 83–84.

[57]Hazard, p. 16; *Statisticheskii spravochnik po zhilishchno-kommunal'nomu khoziaistvu g. Moskvy* (Moscow, 1939), pp. 9–10. For more on the institutional allocation of housing in Moscow, see Shimotomai, pp. 114–118.

fell from 5.9 square meters in 1928 to 4.9 in 1931 to 4.2 in 1935. Soviet authorities did give workers priority in housing, so that their average space per capita actually rose slightly, from 4.1 square meters in 1931 to 4.3 by 1935.[58] While most of what little housing was built went to workers, new arrivals received the lowest priority of all workers and generally lived in communal apartments or barracks.[59]

Soviet authorities had begun to require families to share apartments after the Revolution, and they continued this policy in the 1930s.[60] Communal apartments generally allotted one room to a family, with the kitchen and bathroom facilities for common use. Up to fifteen families might live in a single apartment—a situation that resulted in crowded and noisy hallways, lines of people to use the bathroom, and terrible filth in the kitchen. Sometimes more than one family had to live in the same room, partitioned by a curtain or blanket hung on a rope.[61] Basements also came to be occupied, despite their damp walls and lack of electricity.[62] For the Soviet urban population as a whole, the average number of persons per room rose from 2.71 in 1926 to 3.91 in 1940.[63]

Many peasants arriving in Moscow found housing in workers' residences or barracks. The layout of these structures did not differ in principle from that of communal apartments, though they generally lacked plumbing. The buildings were divided into rooms along a hallway with shared kitchen facilities and an adjacent outhouse. Many workers' residences were even more overcrowded than communal apartments—up to twenty people could inhabit a single room.[64] As artels from the countryside arrived almost daily at the construction site of the Kaganovich ball bearing plant in 1931, managers assigned them to already-occupied residences. Workers were forced to share beds, and finally to sleep on tables and benches. Many artels left after a few days to seek better accommodations at other work sites or in nonenterprise housing on the outskirts of the city.[65]

[58]E. D. Simon et al., *Moscow in the Making* (London, 1937), pp. 171–172; Tverdokhleb, "Material'noe blagosostoianie," pp. 454, 484.

[59]AAN f. 359, op. 2, d. 499, ll. 38–39.

[60]See Chase, p. 29.

[61]*Za novyi byt* 1929 no. 9/10, p. 13; Andrew Smith, pp. 48–49.

[62]Kingsbury and Fairchild, pp. 196–197; Harvard Project no. 541.

[63]Geiger, p. 206.

[64]TsPA f. 17, op. 114, d. 255, l. 77; Simon et al., p. 153.

[65]*Pervyi podshipnikovyi*, pp. 27–28. For statistics on the percentage of Moscow

Workers' residence no. 3, 1932. Many peasant in-migrants lived in such dwellings on the outskirts of Moscow. Courtesy Muzei Istorii Moskvy.

Workers' barracks offered still poorer accommodations. These hastily constructed shelters lacked any internal walls or amenities. An American worker who visited a Soviet friend at the barracks of the Kuibyshev electronics factory was appalled by what he found:

> Kuznetsov lived with about 550 others, men and women, in a wooden structure about 800 feet long and fifteen feet wide. The room contained approximately 500 narrow beds, covered with mattresses filled with straw or dried leaves. There were no pillows or blankets. Coats and other garments were being utilized for covering. Some of the residents had no beds and slept on the floor or in wooden boxes. In some cases beds were used by one shift during the day and by others at night. There were no screens or wall to give any privacy to the occupants of the barracks. . . . I could not stay in the barracks very long. I could not stand the stench of kerosene and unwashed bodies. The only washing facility was a pump outside. The toilet was a rickety, unheated shanty, without seats.[66]

---

workers in communal apartments and residences, see T. Sosnovy, *The Housing Problem in the Soviet Union* (New York, 1954), p. 271.

[66] Andrew Smith, pp. 47–48.

Soviet descriptions of workers' barracks are equally grim. A report on the barracks of a Moscow machine-building factory told of rats scurrying around, insufficient heat, and wind blowing through cracks in the walls.[67] The barracks for construction workers at the Stalin automobile plant were found to be just as unsanitary, filled with smoke and piles of trash.[68] Water transport workers slept outdoors on the ground in warm weather to escape the swarms of bedbugs and lice in their barracks.[69]

Regulations passed by the city council reveal the problems associated with extreme overcrowding. Henceforth no cooking was to be done outside the kitchen, wood was not to be chopped on the stairs, and no dirty linen or spoiled food was to be left in common rooms. Violation of any of these rules could lead to a fine or eviction. To enforce this code of behavior as well as to settle any disputes between tenants, authorities established "comradely courts" in all buildings with more than 100 residents. Judges elected by the tenants had authority in all noncriminal cases pertaining to housing.[70]

The list of negative consequences of overcrowding goes on. Cases of rape and wife beating were attributed to close quarters and drunkenness in workers' barracks.[71] Since privacy was impossible, tenants intruded into one another's personal affairs, and trivialities could assume dangerous proportions in the highly politicized environment of the 1930s. One memoirist recalled a fellow resident bursting into the room and demanding to see the identification papers of friends who were visiting.[72] Literature portrays the intelligentsia as the primary victims of such interference. In one story the tenants in a communal apartment, virtually all of them former peasants from the same village, are suspicious of anyone who does not display an icon, and team up against intellectuals who live in the building.[73] Yet newly urbanized workers, too, could become victims of neighbors' interference.

[67]TsGAMO f. 214, op. 1, d. 122, l. 9.

[68]*Amostroika*, March 31, 1931, p. 4.

[69]*Avral*, August 15, 1931, p. 3. Communal apartments and workers' residences were also plagued by filth and parasites. See *Biulleten' Narkomata kommunal'nogo khoziaistva* 1935 no. 6, p. 96; *Vecherniaia Moskva*, May 27, 1934, p. 3.

[70]Hazard, pp. 58–60, 113–114.

[71]Ermilov, *Byt rabochei kazarmy*, p. 13; *Sudebnaia praktika* 1931 no. 2, p. 7.

[72]Mandelstam, p. 130. Neighbors occasionally served as informants for the secret police, as close living quarters facilitated surveillance. See Kotkin, p. 378.

[73]Abram Tertz, "Tenants," in *Fantastic Stories* (New York, 1963), pp. 133–138.

Former peasants who had fled dekulakization risked denunciation if a neighbor discovered their past.

The housing shortage created particular hardships for families. Normally new arrivals left their families behind until they found a place for them to live. Often all they could arrange was a room shared with other families.[74] A survey at the Tri-Mountain textile mill showed that new workers and their families rarely had a separate room of their own, though the families of established workers did.[75] Some enterprises set aside housing for workers with families. One plant housed them in an old monastery; others reserved certain floors in residences for families, though these quarters were scarcely less crowded than the rest of the building.[76]

The struggle to obtain or retain housing became a matter of overarching importance for workers, and weighed heavily on decisions regarding family life. Many young married couples had no private room.[77] A number of court cases in the 1930s involved the rights of people to remain in a building after divorce. Divorced couples sometimes continued to live together, as both had a right to their housing and neither was able to move elsewhere.[78]

Overcrowded housing also had an impact on family size and household patterns. In most societies urbanization encourages both a transition from extended to nuclear families and a drop in fertility. The shift to nuclear families did not take place in Soviet cities, largely because of the housing shortage. Extended families who migrated to the city together also lived together simply because it was all they could do to find one room.[79] Soviet fertility, however, dipped quite sharply in the early 1930s, and the ratio of dependents to independents among the working class decreased from 1.72 in 1927 to 1.50 in 1931.[80] The drop in this ratio was caused in part by the huge number of young single peasants who joined the workforce, but other indices corrobo-

---

[74]*Krasnyi bogatyr'*, January 17, 1934, p. 1; American Engineers in Russia, Hoover Institution archives, account of F. R. Harris.

[75]AAN f. 359, op. 2, d. 499, ll. 38–39.

[76]Archive of the Hammer and Sickle metallurgical plant, VIII-07, XXII, l. 43; *Rabochii narodnogo pitaniia* 1929 no. 3, p. 12; *Ukhtomskii rabochii*, May 27, 1938, p. 3.

[77]Ermilov, p. 14.

[78]*Sudebnaia praktika* 1931 no. 8, pp. 3–4; Mandelstam, p. 130.

[79]Basile Kerblay, *Modern Soviet Society*, Rupert Swyer, trans. (New York, 1983), pp. 116–117.

[80]*Voprosy truda* 1932 no. 11/12, p. 19.

rate the decline in fertility. The average size of nuclear working-class families dropped from 4.0 in 1930 to 3.8 in 1935 and to 3.6 in 1939 (when rural families had an average of 4.3 members).[81] Furthermore, the number of infants and young children in Moscow actually decreased between 1926 and 1931, despite the overall marked increase in population.[82] These statistics indicate that former peasants in Moscow rapidly adopted levels of fertility more characteristic of urbanites than of villagers.

Alarmed by the decline in fertility, Soviet authorities outlawed abortion in 1936, and urban fertility duly rose.[83] At the same time they launched a campaign to celebrate the family and parenthood. A lead article in *Pravda* told readers that "a poor family member cannot possibly at the same time be a good Soviet citizen."[84] Subsequent articles in other publications also strove to dignify parenthood and encourage large families. One such article written by a Moscow woman with nine children claimed that "parents cannot possibly be unhappy over the birth of a child."[85] The jump in fertility was only temporary, though; Soviet urban society continued its overall trend toward a one-child family, in part because of insufficient housing space.[86]

Another factor that contributed to the decrease in fertility was the entrance of women into the urban workforce in record numbers. Even as average working-class family size decreased, the number of wage earners per family increased—from 1.32 in 1930 to 1.47 in 1935 in cities overall and in Moscow from 1.37 in 1929 to 1.63 by 1937. With the sharp decline in real wages, many working-class families could make ends meet only if all adult members worked. The wages of wives and adult children became as important to family income as the earnings of the head of household.[87]

[81]*Trud v SSSR* (1936), p. 342; Geiger, p. 174.

[82]TsGAORgM f. 126, op. 10, d. 47, l. 17.

[83]Wendy Goldman, "Women, Abortion, and the State, 1917–1936," in *Russia's Women: Accommodation, Resistance, Transformation*, Barbara Evans Clements et al., eds. (Berkeley, 1991), p. 265.

[84]*Pravda*, June 26, 1935, p. 1.

[85]*Martenovka*, May 1, 1936, p. 5.

[86]Genadii A. Bordiugov, "Nekotorye problemy kul'tury byta v kontse 20-kh–30-e gody," in *Dukhovnyi potentsial SSSR nakanune velikoi otechestvennoi voiny: Sbornik statei*, I. S. Borisov, ed. (Moscow, 1985), pp. 186–187.

[87]*Trud v SSSR* (1936), p. 342; Tverdokhleb, "Material'noe blagosostoianie," pp. 333–334; Lapitskaia, p. 173.

The emergence of women as wage earners implicitly challenged men's domination of their households. Once a woman began to earn factory wages, the husband's position as breadwinner and patriarch was undermined. Soviet authorities in the latter half of the 1930s reinforced husbands' traditional authority over their wives, in part because family order and cohesion seemed to serve the state's interest in social stability, a high birthrate, and maximal productivity of the labor force.[88] Soviet literature and propaganda invested all authority within the family in the husband. He had final say in all disputes and decisions, while the wife appeared as a dedicated but subservient homemaker.[89]

Because relations within the household were not restructured, women remained saddled with the majority of domestic chores. Time budget studies demonstrated that working women were still responsible for cleaning, shopping, food preparation, and the care of children.[90] One survey showed that Soviet urban women over age 25 averaged seven hours a day at work plus an additional four to six hours a day performing domestic chores. Men, who averaged only one hour a day on domestic duties, enjoyed far more time for education, social activities, leisure, and sleep.[91] The double burden of full-time employment and household maintenance served as a strong disincentive for women to have many children. Peasant in-migrants in Moscow, whose fertility rate had been slightly higher than that of urban-born women in the 1920s, abruptly limited the number of children they bore.[92]

Soviet propaganda and literature strove to counter this trend by portraying women as both dedicated workers and devoted wives and mothers. Socialist realism represented the building of socialism and fulfillment in one's personal life as inseparable. Romantic love, as depicted in Soviet novels, inspired people to work harder at the factory, and young couples spent their moments alone discussing how to become more productive workers.[93] In real life, women found little

---

[88]Lapidus, p. 237.
[89]Gasiorowska, p. 103; Gregory Smith, pp. 29–30.
[90]Serebrennikov, p. 96.
[91]Kingsbury and Fairchild, p. 249; *Trud v SSSR* (1932), p. 172.
[92]Chase, pp. 94–95.
[93]Gasiorowska, pp. 100–109.

in their domestic burden that inspired them to work harder in the factory.

Child-care facilities and communal dining halls theoretically were to relieve Soviet women of many of their housekeeping chores and establish a new socialist way of life. According to the planners' elaborate calculations, the employment of women would finance the development of these new services to a high level.[94] Communal dining halls also signaled an effort to expand the public domain to include functions that traditionally belonged in the private domain. Soviet planners saw housing complexes with communal child-care and dining facilities as a step toward a socialist lifestyle.

Despite elaborate plans, however, communal facilities proved woefully inadequate. Apartment complexes and barracks generally lacked any child-care facilities.[95] Like other urban services, child care fell to the enterprises, whose directors realized that they would have to establish nurseries and kindergartens if they expected to hire women with children. Even these services tended to be underfunded and understaffed, though most working-class families had little choice but to use them.[96] The basis of the Soviet industrialization drive was investment in heavy industry at the expense of light industry and the service sector. The quality of services from child care to retail stores to communal dining halls suffered as a result, just at the time when women entered the urban workforce and needed those services desperately.[97]

Though communal dining halls freed women from cooking, workers avoided them when they had an option.[98] One group of workers, protesting their barracks' communal cafeteria, said, "We don't need barracks socialism."[99] Workers of peasant origin were not against collectivism—many lived together in artels, after all—but they wished to form their own associations. They refused to share facilities with strangers, and they resisted urban planners' expansion of the public domain at the expense of their personal privacy.

[94]*Stroitel'stvo Moskvy* 1929 no. 5, pp. 3–5; no. 12, pp. 2–4.

[95]TsGAORgM f. 1289, op. 1, d. 174, ll. 3–4.

[96]TsGAMO f. 214, op. 1, d. 116, l. 24; Lapitskaia, p. 177.

[97]See Lapidus, p. 106.

[98]Simon et al., p. 147.

[99]*Rabochaia gazeta*, January 9, 1930, p. 6.

In organizing their lives, people drew upon their past sense of social and familial order. Communal dining halls offered few of the benefits touted by the Soviet press. Long lines, unhygienic conditions, and inferior food did not persuade workers to abandon the pleasure of dining with their families in private. Particularly in this period of economic hardship, people relied on habits and traditions they felt comfortable with. Wives' subordination to their husbands was another of those traditions—one that Soviet propaganda endeavored to reinforce. Young men who had rebelled against the patriarchal authority of village elders nonetheless perpetuated patriarchal authority in their own households. Women, too, preserved male dominance. In organizing their households they followed the models of their parents and accepted female subordination as part of the natural order.[100] The habitual and the traditional, particularly when no clear alternative was elucidated, continued to inform former peasants' behavior even after they moved to Moscow.

Food Supply, Rationing, and Real Wages

Party leaders in the 1930s set out to mobilize and control virtually all resources. Soviet authorities gained administrative control over agricultural produce through the collectivization of agriculture. Simultaneously they eliminated private trade and assumed control of food distribution. In 1929 authorities closed private shops, restaurants, and street bazaars, and consumers came to rely almost entirely on state stores for their food.[101] In theory the state supply network was to provide all necessary food products and manufactured goods to Soviet consumers; in practice the government channeled all available resources to the industrialization drive. With the abolition of private trade in 1929, food, clothing, dry goods, and heating fuel immediately became scarce and long lines formed at meagerly stocked state stores. No soap, tea, light bulbs, or cigarettes could be found in the city.

[100]Even the limited number of Soviet officials committed to women's equality offered working women no active part in debating and redefining their roles in society and in the household. See Elizabeth Wood, "Gender and Politics in Soviet Russia: Working Women under the New Economic Policy, 1918–1928" (dissertation, University of Michigan, 1991), pp. 616–620.

[101]Davies, *Socialist Offensive*, pp. 362–365.

Buildings went unheated and fell into disrepair. The drop in living standards reminded one observer of the Civil War, and in fact rumors began to circulate that war was imminent.[102]

The desperate poverty of the 1930s accounted in part for the extremely inhumane character of the decade. The Soviet government provided people with only the bare minimum of food necessary for survival. Clothing and basic household items became almost impossible to obtain. Some women turned to prostitution to acquire additional food and clothing.[103] Some children did not attend school because they had no clothes to wear. On cold days during the First Five-Year Plan people "dressed entirely in leather" could be seen "towing firewood on sleds" through the streets of Moscow, as during the Civil War.[104] Destitution led to rampant petty theft and corruption. Criminal gangs formed to steal and extort goods. People stole scrapwood to burn for warmth and filched industrial parts to barter for food. Twelve truckloads worth of bread were stolen from Moscow stores every day.[105] The police responded with extreme repression against even petty offenders. As Soviet authorities struggled to control all resources, the pilfering of basic supplies came to be considered a crime against the state. Because officials could not systematically prevent petty theft, law enforcement became arbitrary and penalties ever more severe.

Bread rationing was introduced in Moscow in March 1929, followed in April by the rationing of sugar, tea, butter, oil, macaroni, herring, and soap, and in September by the rationing of meat, eggs, potatoes, and clothing.[106] Workers received priority over other social groups in food rationing. They accounted for only 34 percent of Moscow's population in 1929, but collected 47 percent of the rationed food (including 52 percent of the bread and 50 percent of the meat).[107] Even

---

[102]I. I. Shitts, *Dnevnik "velikogo pereloma": Mart 1928–avgust 1931* (Paris, 1991), pp. 1, 77, 96, 181–183, 282. See also American Engineers, Hoover Institution archives, account of E. H. Collester.

[103]Ermilov, p. 16.

[104]V. Bogushevskii and A. Khavin, "God velikogo pereloma," in *God deviatnadtsatyi: Al'manakh deviatyi* (Moscow, 1936), pp. 329–331.

[105]TsGANKh f. 8043, op. 1, d. 72, l. 1, as cited in Osokina, p. 32.

[106]Schwarz, p. 136. By early 1930, rationing was in effect throughout the country. See Filtzer, pp. 92–94.

[107]*Spravochnik dlia vydachi zabornykh knizhek v Moskve s 1 oktiabria 1932 g.*

the largest rations, however, supplied only a minimum of food. A 1930 Commissariat of Trade (Narkomtorg) decree granted industrial and transport workers rations of 800 grams of bread a day; white-collar employees and dependents received only 400 grams.[108]

Implementation of the rationing system encountered serious difficulties, not the least of which proved to be illegal use of ration cards and corruption. Workers sought to augment their rations by acquiring extra cards. Some workers falsely professed to have lost their cards in order to get additional ones. Others claimed more dependents than they actually had. Some workers of peasant origin collected rations for relatives who actually lived in the village but visited Moscow in order to be claimed as dependents.[109] Ration cards remained valid for three months, so by changing jobs workers could obtain authorization for a new ration card while they continued to use their old one. In 1930 alone, officials reported the circulation of 300,000 unwarranted ration cards in Moscow, and throughout the First Five-Year Plan "dead souls" continued to vex the ration system.[110] Illegal sale of both ration cards and food products also vitiated the rationing system.[111]

By the end of 1930, a closed system of distribution took shape. Restricted state stores, generally located at enterprises and reserved exclusively for use by employees, began to distribute food and clothing.[112] In part this trend resulted naturally from the fact that enterprises controlled the greatest resources and wished to guarantee a reliable supply of food to their workers. Moscow stores not affiliated with an enterprise faced increasing difficulty keeping products on their shelves, and a number of them ceased operations entirely.[113] Workers began to receive virtually all items through the restricted

(Moscow, 1932), pp. 1–4; *Ekonomicheskoe stroitel'stvo* 1930 no. 7/8, pp. 17–19; Tverdokhleb, "Material'noe blagosostoianie," p. 281.

[108]Zawodny, "Twenty-six Interviews," Hoover Institution archives, I/1. For more on ration categories, see Davies, *Soviet Economy in Turmoil*, pp. 289–298; Osokina, pp. 15–24.

[109]TsGAORgM f. 214, op. 1, d. 284, l. 32; Aleksandr Salov, *Organizatsiia rabochego snabzheniia i opyt perestroiki rabochego snabzheniia na avtozavode im. Stalina* (Moscow, 1933), p. 9.

[110]Davies, *Soviet Economy in Turmoil*, p. 357; *Moskovskoe obshchestvennoe pitanie*, April 16, 1932, p. 3; *Sudebnaia praktika* 1931 no. 4, p. 11.

[111]TsGAMO f. 214, op. 1, d. 115, l. 1; *Rabochii narodnogo pitaniia* 1929 no. 3, p. 18.

[112]Tverdokhleb, "Material'noe blagosostoianie," pp. 283–286.

[113]*Nezabyvaemye 30-e*, pp. 7–8; *Vecherniaia Moskva*, May 15, 1934, p. 3.

stores and cafeterias at their factories.[114] Workers at well-supplied factories did not oppose this closed system of distribution. Given the shortages of food and supplies in Moscow, it was to their benefit to be guaranteed rations without waiting in line. One contemporary account stated that with the introduction of restricted stores, "even amidst the new strata of workers, the unhealthy disposition based on inadequate food for workers completely disappeared." [115]

In late 1932 the food supply deteriorated further still.[116] Famine loomed over the countryside and jeopardized the supply of food to cities, forcing the Soviet government to tighten the rationing system even more.[117] In addition to the passport law (to limit the urban population), the government issued decrees that put the directors of large enterprises directly in charge of ration distribution to their workers and gave them the power to issue ration cards (now valid for only one month and redeemable only at the restricted store of the enterprise). Restricted stores ceased to be called cooperatives and were renamed "departments of worker food supply." This widening of enterprise directors' authority and consolidation of the restricted-store system was justified as a means of eliminating illegal use of multiple ration cards. Factory administrations presumably kept accurate records of their employees and could invalidate the ration cards of workers who quit and went to work somewhere else.[118]

Factory directors, despite the extra effort involved, accepted the responsibility of providing for their workers. They recognized that labor productivity depended on adequate food and housing. Statistics on production showed that enterprises that better fulfilled the needs of workers functioned more efficiently than other factories.[119] In some large plants, shop administrators claimed control of food supply for their workers and even established separate cafeterias within the factory.[120] The failure of the municipal government to provide other services also led some enterprises to organize health care. But while

[114]*Kooperativnaia zhizn'*, January 4, 1931, p. 3; U.S. National Archives, Records of the Department of State, roll 37; *General'nyi plan*, p. 67.

[115]Filatov, pp. 107–109.

[116]Witkin, p. 114.

[117]*Sobranie zakonov* 1932 no. 80.

[118]*Izvestiia*, December 20, 1932; *Sobranie zakonov* 1932 no. 80, art. 489.

[119]MPA f. 69, op. 1, d. 84, l. 18.

[120]Shearer, "Rationalization," p. 331.

large enterprises wielded enormous resources, their first priority remained industrial production, and they extended to workers only the minimal services needed to retain their labor.

The state food supply network proved so inadequate that enterprise directors also began to conclude agreements directly with collective farms for food, and in some cases (illegally) offered manufactured goods to peasants in return for their produce.[121] Directors also established their own agricultural and livestock-raising operations. In late 1932 and early 1933, all large Moscow enterprises set up state collective farms (*sovkhozy*) to raise produce and livestock for their workers.[122] In 1933 the Stalin automobile plant administered no fewer than five state collective farms, as well as a fishing operation on the Caspian Sea. The Hammer and Sickle plant owned more than 2,500 cattle and 4,500 pigs, and the Kirov Dinamo plant and the Kaganovich ball bearing plant initiated large rabbit-breeding operations in 1935 to serve as an additional source of food. These operations unfortunately failed to meet workers' needs, for enterprises often lacked adequate labor, transportation, and storage capabilities.[123] Some factory directors became desperate enough to send detachments out on the roads leading to Moscow to intercept food transports and illegally barter for their food deliveries.[124]

Food supplies and distribution systems could not keep pace with the expanding workforce. The cafeteria at the Red Hercules factory was built to accommodate 2,600 workers, and by 1931 it had to serve 10,000.[125] Restricted cafeterias guaranteed food for workers, but the quality of meals steadily declined as supplies of meat and fresh vegetables dwindled.[126] Restricted stores in factories suffered similar supply problems, though they were still better stocked than other stores.[127] The average Moscow working-class family consumed less

---

[121]Salov, pp. 18–20.

[122]TsGANKh f. 7676, op. 1, d. 610, l. 33; Salov, pp. 11–16; *Pervyi podshipnikovyi*, p. 39.

[123]Tverdokhleb, "Material'noe blagosostoianie," pp. 293–296; TsGAORgM f. 1289, op. 1, d. 861, l. 3; f. 150, op. 5, d. 6, l. 51; d. 66, ll. 1–3, 371–373; TsGAOR f. 7952, op. 3, d. 560, l. 37.

[124]MPA f. 635, op. 1, d. 8, l. 6.

[125]*Rabochaia Moskva*, September 16, 1931, p. 3.

[126]Tverdokhleb, "Material'noe blagosostoianie," pp. 339–342; *Trud*, July 2, 1931, p. 1; *Izvestiia Mosoblispolkoma*, October 11, 1931, p. 1.

[127]TsGAMO f. 747, op. 1, d. 111, l. 37.

than half as much meat in 1932 as it had in 1929, and workers' diets came to rely much more heavily on fish and potatoes.[128]

Workers in nonindustrial jobs faced the worst living standards of all urban workers. Though the great majority of them had just arrived from villages where conditions were no better, they found many cafeterias and stores so unacceptable that they sought work elsewhere. At one construction site the food was unsanitary and the cafeteria lacked utensils, so that workers had to eat with their fingers.[129] In a cafeteria for water transport workers, salted fish was served as the main course every day and the soup frequently had flies in it.[130] Some restricted stores discriminated against seasonal workers, and refused to give them the food to which they were entitled.[131] When a water transport worker complained about the piece of meat he received after waiting in a long line, the clerk retorted, "Take what you're given, or you'll get nothing." When the worker continued to complain, the clerk seized the piece of meat and beat him over the head with it.[132]

The poor living conditions in Moscow did not drive people away only because they were still better than those in other parts of the country.[133] Memoirists recalled that in comparison with other Soviet cities, "Moscow seemed a haven of plenty," though such pronouncements reflected the destitution of other cities more than the prosperity of Moscow.[134] Conditions eased somewhat during the Second Five-Year Plan. Kaganovich, in addressing the priorities of the plan, stressed expansion of light industry to satisfy the population's need for food and clothing.[135] On September 25, 1935, the Central Committee decreed an end to rationing.[136] Bread and flour rationing had

[128]Tverdokhleb, "Material'noe blagosostoianie," pp. 347–351; S. R. Gershberg, *Rabota u nas takaia: Zapiski zhurnalista-pravdista 30-kh godov* (Moscow, 1971), p. 68; Osokina, p. 23.

[129]*Za novyi byt* 1929 no. 13/14, p. 11.

[130]*Avral*, August 15, 1931, p. 3.

[131]*Rabochaia Moskva*, September 16, 1931, p. 4.

[132]*Avral*, August 30, 1931, p. 3.

[133]TsPA f. 17, op. 114, d. 255, l. 33; d. 256, l. 68. On the priority assigned large industrial cities for food supply, see Osokina, p. 16.

[134]Kravchenko, p. 82. See also American Engineers, Hoover Institution archives, account of D. M. Forester, p. 1.

[135]*Chetvertaia Moskovskaia oblastnaia i III gorodskaia konferentsii VKP(b): Stenograficheskii otchet* (Moscow, 1934), p. 40.

[136]*Resheniia Partii i pravitel'stva po khoziaistvennym voprosam: Sbornik dokumentov za 50 let, 1917–1966 gg.* (Moscow, 1967–1985), vol. 2, p. 547.

already ended in Moscow on January 1, and by October 1 rationing on all other food products ceased.[137] Restricted stores at factories continued to operate without ration coupons, and they reserved the choicest products for the most productive workers.[138] By the end of the Second Five-Year Plan, the repeal of rationing, the improvement in the Soviet economy, and greater production of consumer goods had raised consumption above the subsistence level.[139]

Overall, however, the Soviet living standard dropped sharply during the 1930s, in tandem with the fall in real wages. Food accounted for the single largest expenditure of Soviet workers—more than all other expenditures combined for the average working-class family.[140] The average monthly budget per person for the families of Moscow construction workers in 1931 consisted of 61 rubles in wages, with 28 rubles spent on food, 14 rubles on clothing and toilet articles, and 3 rubles on rent.[141] The cost of food in restricted stores was contained somewhat by the state control of prices, but availability declined severely. The cost of one kilogram of meat in a state store rose from 87 kopeks in 1928 to 2.26 rubles in 1932. Availability improved after rationing was ended, but the price of meat reached 6 rubles per kilogram in 1936.[142]

The general price index in Moscow increased 5.2 times from 1928 to 1937.[143] As a result of rising costs and falling availability of clothing, the average number of clothing items acquired per person per month in Moscow fell from 2.5 in 1929 to 0.9 in 1932, and then rose to 1.3 in 1937. Wages of Moscow workers increased rapidly in the 1930s, but not so rapidly as prices. Between 1928 and 1937, wages of industrial workers in Moscow increased 3.3 times while prices increased 5.2 times. Thus the real wages of Moscow workers in 1937 were only 63.5 percent of their 1928 level—a drop of over one-third.[144] Data on

---

[137]Tverdokhleb, "Material'noe blagosostoianie," pp. 304–305. Rationing of some items of clothing continued until January 1936.

[138]*Elektrozavod*, January 16, 1935, p. 4.

[139]*Rabochii klass—vedushchaia sila*, pp. 239–243.

[140]*Trud v SSSR* (1936), p. 343. For statistics on the food consumption of Moscow workers, see Osokina, p. 39.

[141]*Trud v SSSR* (1932), pp. 151, 164.

[142]Tverdokhleb, "Material'noe blagosostoianie," pp. 307–308. See also *Istoriia rabochikh Moskvy*, p. 289.

[143]*Massovye istochniki po sotsial'no-ekonomicheskoi istorii sovetskogo obshchestva*, I. D. Koval'chenko, ed. (Moscow, 1979), p. 189.

[144]Tverdokhleb, "Material'noe blagosostoianie," pp. 331–332, 360–361.

the 1938–1941 period are not so complete, but they indicate a further catastrophic drop in living standards. The military mobilization and investment in the defense industry reversed the slight rise in living standards of the Second Five-Year Plan, and severe food shortages again became common.[145] Despite their relatively privileged status, then, Moscow workers suffered a steep decline in real wages and living standards during the industrialization drive.

The inability of authorities to provide more than minimal food and housing made village networks and collective security all the more important for newly arrived workers. The fact that they lived together in settlements on the outskirts of Moscow facilitated their cooperation. Some former peasants formed domestic communes (*bytovye kommuny*). Members lived together, pooled their wages, shared all living expenses, and divided various chores, from cleaning living quarters to washing clothes. They generally organized the distribution of living space within the barracks or workers' residence where they lived, and operated nurseries and dining halls. At one Moscow construction school with more than 1,000 students (almost all of peasant origin), 35 separate domestic communes formed. Students there preferred their own independent dining halls to the school cafeteria.[146] With the severe shortages of food and housing in the 1930s, domestic communes served important practical functions.

Domestic communes also provided emergency help to members and their families. A commune at the workers' residence of the Frunze aviation engine plant accepted special appeals if a member's relatives were in need, and decided as a group how much money should be granted. The commune collectively decided which members needed new coats, boots, or other clothing, and allotted money accordingly.[147] A number of domestic communes organized cultural activities and excursions for their members.[148] A commune at the Hammer and Sickle plant had its own dacha, and one at the Stalin automobile plant went on group vacations.[149]

[145]Nove, pp. 257–261.

[146]TsGAORgM f. 5301, op. 4, d. 66, ll. 14, 20, 69. See also MPA f. 635, op. 1, d. 10, l. 31; TsGAOR f. 5451, op. 14, d. 306, l. 5; *Aviamotor*, June 27, 1930, p. 3.

[147]*Aviamotor*, July 4, 1931, p. 3. Members of one domestic collective pooled only half of their wages for food and housing and retained the other half for their own use.

[148]TsGAOR f. 5451, op. 14, d. 305, ll. 1–8.

[149]*Molodoi mashinostroitel'* 1931 no. 4; Mirer, p. 66.

Domestic communes could also meet less tangible needs. They conveyed a sense of belonging to a group—certainly a help for newcomers
who were unaccustomed to the anonymity of life in a large city. In
this sense, domestic communes were an extension of village networks and artels, which guided peasants to Moscow in the first place.
Some provided moral guidance as well. One commune reportedly forbade drinking, discouraged smoking, and condemned "chance sexual
encounters," considering "the single correct resolution of sexual matters to be a long and stable marriage."[150] Most communes were less
virtuous; they could in fact serve to organize the drunken holiday
celebrations so central to peasant in-migrants' culture.

Workers' self-help efforts also involved the cultivation of gardens.
Some factories granted workers land for gardens, and trade unions
provided gardening implements.[151] More often former peasants on
their own initiative planted gardens as an additional source of food.
They cultivated hundreds of hectares on the outskirts of Moscow.[152]
Here again former peasants drew on their own traditions and initiative
to meet the challenges of surviving in Moscow.

Peasant markets emerged as another important source of food to
supplement the meager rations supplied by the state. Prohibited in
1929, markets where peasants could sell their produce at market
prices were allowed gradually to reopen in 1930. By 1931, twenty-
one markets existed in Moscow, and by the end of 1932 their number
reached forty-three, most of them in outlying districts.[153]

Soviet authorities tacitly admitted that markets distributed food
more efficiently than the state supply network when they eliminated
procurements on produce grown within a 50-verst radius of Moscow.[154] Because markets reduced government control over resources
and seemed to benefit entrepreneurs and other "class enemies," how-

[150]*Aviamotor*, July 4, 1931, p. 3. This commune was probably not typical; officials
publicized it because they hoped to propagate similar values.

[151]TsGAORgM f. 1289, op. 1, d. 861, l. 36; *Martenovka*, February 20, 1931, p. 2;
Profsoiuzy SSSR: Dokumenty i materialy, 1905–1963, 4 vols. (Moscow, 1963–1974),
vol. 2, pp. 752–753.

[152]*Statisticheskii spravochnik po zhilishchno-kommunal'nomu khoziaistvu*, p. 4;
Zhilishchno-kommunal'noe khoziaistvo, pp. 16–17; *Plan g. Moskvy*.

[153]Tverdokhleb, "Material'noe blagosostoianie," p. 292; *Vneshnee blagoustroistvo
g. Moskvy: Statisticheskii spravochnik po sostoianiiu na 1 ianvaria 1937 g.* (Moscow,
1937), pp. 188–189.

[154]Shimotomai, pp. 132–134.

Cobbler at the Sukharevka peasant market in Moscow, 1931. Courtesy Muzei Istorii Moskvy.

ever, inspectors and Party leaders criticized them as "chaotic," "unsanitary," lacking in adequate facilities for peasants and their horses, and conducive to "speculation."[155] At a 1932 Moscow city council meeting, Nikita S. Khrushchev, then a Moscow Party secretary, declared that "at our peasant markets and bazaars, production of collective farm members and laboring peasants falls into the hands of dealers [perekupshchiki] and speculators [spekulianty]."[156] The Sukharevka market, one of the largest in Moscow, was closed in November 1932 because of alleged profiteering. Given the shortage of food, many people naturally bought products for resale. Despite official disdain, these markets served an important function, and most of them remained open. In 1932 they supplied 15 percent of all potatoes and 60 percent of all milk and eggs consumed in Moscow.[157]

[155]MPA f. 69, op. 1, d. 804, l. 43; TsGAORgM f. 1289, op. 1, d. 493, l. 93; f. 150, op. 5, d. 6, l. 31; *Molodoi bol'shevik* 1932 no. 13, p. 23.
[156]TsGAORgM f. 150, op. 5, d. 6, l. 31.
[157]Shimotomai, pp. 132–134.

A black market also thrived in the 1930s as a vital mechanism for the exchange of scarce goods and food. Some black-market activity involved theft and sale of state supplies. Salespeople, distributors, transporters, and guards within the state supply system commonly purloined food to sell.[158] Peasants stole produce and livestock from collective farms and carted them to Moscow.[159] Even in 1939 such illegal activity was still widespread.[160]

Most black-market activity simply involved the sale or barter of belongings that people were eager to exchange for something unavailable in state stores. Workers routinely bought everything they were allowed to buy at their factory's restricted store, then bartered clothing or sugar they did not need for things they could not obtain—often chickens, eggs, or milk, which peasants were eager to exchange for manufactured and processed goods.[161] Workers of peasant origin had multiple contacts, both with their neighbors and with relatives and friends in the village, for such exchanges. Reports of the frequent illegal transportation of goods between Moscow and the countryside indicate that such transactions were widespread.[162]

Black-market dealings were not without substantial risk. A decree passed August 22, 1932, made speculators subject to five to ten years in a labor camp.[163] Because of the harsh penalties and high risk involved, people generally limited their black-market exchanges to a circle of trusted friends and acquaintances. For peasant in-migrants, fellow villagers made up these circles.[164] As former peasants made new acquaintances in the city, their circles widened and evolved. Informal connections and black-market exchanges persisted throughout the Soviet period and supplied vital goods and services that the command economy failed to offer.

With the falling living standards and desperate poverty of the 1930s, Soviet authorities provided no shining example of a new socialist lifestyle for new city dwellers to embrace. Peasants who moved to Mos-

---

[158]MPA f. 635, op. 1, d. 8, ll. 6, 42; TsGAOR f. 5469, op. 15, d. 10, l. 145; Zawodny, "Twenty-six Interviews," Hoover Institution archives, I/2.

[159]*Sudebnaia praktika* 1931 no. 2, p. 15.

[160]*Vecherniaia Moskva*, April 23, 1939, p. 3.

[161]American Engineers, Hoover Institution archives, account of Milo W. Krejci, p. 2; see also J. S. Ferguson, p. 3.

[162]TsGAORgM f. 1289, op. 1, d. 197, l. 21.

[163]Shimotomai, pp. 132–134.

[164]Zawodny, "Twenty-six Interviews," Hoover Institution archives, I/2, II/16, II/20.

cow lived not in the brightly lit, orderly neighborhoods envisioned by urban planners but in barracks and hodgepodge shantytowns on the outskirts of the city. Soviet authorities exercised little control over these regions, or over the lives of the people who lived there. This lack of official control did not mean that these neighborhoods were chaotic. Instead they were shaped by the former peasants who populated them. While newcomers to Moscow accepted the minimal rations and housing guaranteed to them by the government, they also built their own shanties, cultivated their own gardens, and formed self-help organizations and barter circles.

Rural-to-urban migrants in developing countries today grapple with the same problems that faced migrants to Moscow in the 1930s—an inhospitable urban environment, overcrowding, severe poverty. Observers commonly assume that the shantytowns on the peripheries of Rio de Janeiro, Cairo, Nairobi, and other burgeoning cities in Latin America, Asia, and Africa are centers of decadence, crime, and disease, but sociologists have discovered that they are actually characterized by strong families, village networks, and social cohesion. The former peasants there organize mutual aid societies, volunteer police patrols, informal clubs, systems of barter and commercial exchange, and day care for their children. Village ties in many ways strengthen in the urban environment and adapt to new tasks and needs.[165] For the former peasants on the periphery of Moscow in the 1930s the situation was much the same. And the resilience of their village ties diminished official control over their lives and perpetuated their own forms of social organization and culture.

[165]Janice E. Perlman, *The Myth of Marginality: Urban Poverty and Politics in Rio de Janeiro* (Berkeley, 1976), pp. 13, 133–135; Abu-Lughod, pp. 395, 402–403; Kenneth Little, *Urbanization as a Social Process: An Essay on Movement and Change in Contemporary Africa* (Boston, 1974), p. 91; Bryan Roberts, *Cities of Peasants: The Political Economy of Urbanization in the Third World* (London, 1978), p. 141. On informal self-help groups among turn-of-the-century migrants to American cities, see Joanne J. Meyerowitz, *Women Adrift: Independent Wage Earners in Chicago, 1880–1930* (Chicago, 1988), p. 93.

6

Official Culture
and Peasant Culture

Valentina Andreevna encountered an enormous range of new cultural activities and sources of information after she moved to Moscow. Soviet newspapers, pamphlets, radio broadcasts, films, and lectures conveyed ideas and perspectives quite new to her. With the exception of films, however, she eschewed these officially produced forms of culture. She preferred to spend her free days at Izmailovskii Park, where she would socialize with fellow villagers, sing peasant songs, and join in folk dances. These regular gatherings provided Valentina Andreevna with more than entertainment: they allowed her to keep up with friends, to gather information about events both back home and in Moscow, and to understand government policies as they affected her.[1]

People in all societies and at all strata in every society formulate an understanding of the world—a worldview that assigns some order to events in their lives and guides their interactions with other people. To the extent that members of a social group share a worldview, with collectively held ideas, beliefs, and values, they possess a culture. They express their culture by attributing meaning to symbolic forms—words, images, and behaviors—through which they represent themselves and the world around them. Culture in this broad sense consists not just of customs but also of socially established structures of meaning through which people give shape to their ex-

[1]Interview with Valentina Andreevna Melnikova at Izmailovskii Park, Moscow, July 25, 1992.

periences. Culture is an integral part of everyday life, an expression of self-identity, and a guide for social interaction and behavior.[2]

The mass of peasants who migrated to Soviet cities during the 1930s brought their culture with them when they left the village, and they used it to make sense of the urban world they confronted. The Soviet officials there possessed a quite different worldview and culture, which they hoped to instill in the newcomers. They assumed peasant culture to be nothing more than a collection of superstitions that could easily be supplanted or superseded by rational Soviet culture. This assumption reflected their ignorance of peasant culture and took no account of its resilience and adaptability.

Training the "New Soviet Person"

The Moscow Party journal in 1930 carried an article arguing that the training of new workers needed to encompass not only technical skills but also cultural education, to create a "New Person" on whom the socialist system could be based.[3] Countless official reports and directives echoed the same message, stressing the transformative power of cultural education in the training of former peasants.[4] Soviet authorities hoped to transform the newcomers into loyal citizens and workers. They strove to instill complete allegiance to the Soviet state. No other loyalty, even to one's family, was to come before a commitment to building socialism. In a slogan that set the tone for the decade to follow, Gleb M. Krzhizhanovskii, the head of Gosplan, said in 1929 that "whoever is not with us is against us."[5] These words served above all to inform "bourgeois specialists" that neutrality toward the Soviet government was no longer acceptable, but they also notified workers that indifference to official policies equaled opposition in the eyes of authorities.

Krzhizhanovskii's slogan reflected the class-war doctrine of official Soviet culture in the early 1930s. Class-war ideology was part of Party

[2]See Clifford Geertz, *The Interpretation of Cultures* (New York, 1973), pp. 312, 363, 405–406.

[3]*Sputnik kommunista* 1930 no. 2, pp. 38–39.

[4]See, for example, TsGAOR f. 5469, op. 14, d. 316, l. 66; TsGAORgM f. 176, op. 6, d. 200, l. 5.

[5]Davies, *Soviet Economy in Turmoil*, p. 114.

leaders' bipolar worldview—a mentality formed in the revolutionary underground and solidified during the Civil War. Official culture both reflected this worldview and promoted a class-war atmosphere. All characters in official literature of this period, for example, either enthusiastically supported the cause of socialism or maliciously sought to destroy it. Because progress toward socialism was considered to be the natural flow of history, official culture promoted myths about the country's bright future and inevitable success, denying that anything could go wrong under socialism and blaming any mishaps on sabotage by "wreckers" and foreign spies. Party leaders tolerated no dissent or questioning; they demanded unanimity to reaffirm the correctness of their interpretation of history and their own infallibility.

Soviet culture propagated official values and views in simplified terms for the benefit of "backward" workers. The enshrinement of socialist realism as the sole acceptable style in literature, film, and art was partly a response to what officials perceived to be the needs of the newly educated mass of workers. Filmmakers at a 1929 conference in Moscow resolved "to produce films about the everyday life of workers . . . , to portray on the screen issues of the five-year plan, socialist competition, and collective farm development."[6] Sergei Igonin's "We Are Building" was one of many poems intended to marshal enthusiasm for the great task of building socialism:

> Brigade of shock workers form platoons!
> Brigade of shock workers form ranks!
> Look! Around us rise factories
> And smoke is visible from new blast furnaces . . . .
> I hear with each blow of the hammer
> Catch up, catch up and . . . surpass![7]

As part of official culture, Soviet authorities had devised new holidays and rituals to propagate their ideals and goals. Processions and ceremonies glorified socialism on such political holidays as May Day and Revolution Day. Rituals and mass spectacles were expanded during the First Five-Year Plan to spread ardor for industrialization. One such ritual called upon workers to come forward before Party leaders to demonstrate their production processes, vow commitment

[6]Khlevniuk, "Izmenenie," pp. 119–120.
[7]*Aviamotor,* June 27, 1930, p. 3.

May Day posters at the Kirov Dinamo plant, 1932. Note the horse-drawn cart in front of the factory. Courtesy Muzei Istorii Moskvy.

to the industrialization drive, and promise to fulfill the plan.[8] The participatory nature of these rituals was intended to solidify workers' allegiance to the building of socialism.

Despite official faith in the power of cultural training to transform and "civilize" former peasants, directives on the teaching of official culture remained largely unfulfilled. Cultural education, like housing and urban services, remained secondary to the industrialization drive. Party members, trade union activists, and factory directors devoted almost all of their resources and energy to fulfilling monthly industrial output quotas. Little time or money was available for cultural education.[9]

Throughout the 1930s reports and articles accused enterprise direc-

[8]Christel Lane, *The Rites of Rulers* (New York, 1981), pp. 154–157, 174–175.
[9]TsPA f. 17, op. 114, d. 591, l. 38; d. 596, l. 6; *Spravochnik po partprosveshcheniiu na 1931–1932 uch. g.* (Noginsk, 1931), pp. 20–26.

tors, Party members, and trade union officials of failure to raise the cultural level of newly arrived workers.[10] Among construction workers, who were deemed most in need of cultural education, inspectors reported little or no instruction.[11] Political and cultural work among Moscow handicraft workers likewise proved weak and inadequate, and cultural education of water transport workers existed "only on paper."[12] Even at a residence for Stakhanovite metalworkers, no lectures were given, no radios were installed, and the lighting was too dim for reading.[13]

Party and trade union officials simply lacked the resources and personnel for cultural training. A metalworkers' trade union report noted that several good proposals for cultural work had been advanced, but that "not one kopek" was available to act upon them.[14] Officials installed radios in the barracks at the construction site of the Kaganovich ball bearing plant and set up a broadcasting center, but no one could be found to staff it. Instead, workers toyed with the transmitter, making "wild sounds and hooligan jokes."[15] Of 217 Moscow metalworking enterprises in 1929, only 22 had worker clubs.[16] Clubs at construction sites were even scarcer. The only cultural center for metro construction workers was a small shack that could hold no more than two people at a time.[17]

The Komsomol proved to be the one organization that at least partially fulfilled its commitment to cultural education. At enterprises that did establish a club, Komsomol cells organized lectures and activity circles to improve workers' cultural level.[18] Getting workers to attend lectures, however, was another matter. At the worker club of the Hammer and Sickle plant, only 200 workers attended lectures

[10]*Trud*, July 13, 1931, p. 4; *Za sovetskii podshipnik*, October 7, 1931, p. 4; TsGAORgM f. 1289, op. 1, d. 680, l. 43; *Martenovka*, January 30, 1938, p. 1.

[11]TsGAOR f. 5475, op. 13, d. 276, ll. 109, 114, 124; *Postroika*, January 3, 1932, p. 3.

[12]*Moskovskaia promyshlennaia kooperatsiia* 1931 no. 5/6, p. 13; *Ekonomicheskoe stroitel'stvo* 1930 no. 3, p. 69; *Avral*, October 18, 1931, p. 3.

[13]*Ukhtomskii rabochii*, February 20, 1938, p. 4.

[14]TsGAMO f. 214, op. 1, d. 125, l. 13.

[15]*Za sovetskii podshipnik*, April 11, 1931, p. 3. See also TsPA f. 17, op. 114, d. 559, l. 35.

[16]TsGAOR f. 5469, op. 13, d. 351, l. 73. See also TsGAMO f. 214, op. 1, d. 116, l. 15; TsGAOR f. 5469, op. 15, d. 165, l. 3.

[17]TsGAORgM f. 5301, op. 1, d. 68, l. 2; *Istoriia metro Moskvy*, p. 270.

[18]TsGAORgM f. 5301, op. 4, d. 66, l. 46; *Ocherki istorii Moskovskoi organizatsii VLKSM*, pp. 255–256.

titled "On Religion" and "Concerning the International Situation," in contrast to the 3,000 workers who regularly attended the club's soccer matches.[19] Lack of interest was one factor, but limited facilities and poor planning also reduced attendance. Women with children could not have attended lectures even if they had wanted to because worker clubs lacked child-care facilities.[20] A 1934 Party report acknowledged Komsomol campaigns for cultural education but criticized the bureaucratism, weak theoretical level, and lack of systematic work associated with Komsomol programs.[21]

Because workers would not stay after work, organizers resorted to holding lectures during lunch breaks or to enticing workers to the club with small gifts.[22] Even when workers attended lectures, they could not be made to listen. One inspector wrote, "The lectures completely fail to accomplish their goals. . . . Ask any worker what the lecturer talked about. 'Who knows, do you really remember everything?' is the usual answer."[23] Trade union officials at the Moscow clock factory frankly admitted in 1932 that long lectures would have to be held to a minimum if attendance at the club were to rise.[24]

Cultural organizers found that various activity circles were much more effective than lectures in drawing workers to the clubs. Komsomol-initiated singing groups and drama circles quickly enrolled workers.[25] At a bread factory where most workers were women who had recently arrived from the village, trade union activists organized first a sewing circle and then a choir and literary circle.[26] Clubs remained hampered by a lack of space and money but involved at least a limited number of workers in activity circles.[27]

Noting the popularity of musical and artistic circles, the Moscow metalworkers' trade union resolved that it should reorient these

[19]TsGAOR f. 7952, op. 3, d. 233, ll. 59–63. See also TsPA f. 17, op. 114, d. 315, l. 73.
[20]TsGAMO f. 214, op. 1, d. 124, ll. 1–4.
[21]TsPA f. 17, op. 114, d. 559, ll. 37–38.
[22]*Kul'turnaia revoliutsiia*, January 10, 1929, p. 25; *Nesushchii svet: Ocherk o delakh i liudiakh pervoi Moskovskoi gosudarstvennoi elektrostantsii* (Moscow, 1969), p. 100.
[23]*Kul'turnaia revoliutsiia* 1929 no. 1 (4), p. 24.
[24]TsGAMO f. 214, op. 1, d. 124, ll. 3–4.
[25]*Ocherki . . . VLKSM*, pp. 255–256.
[26]*Za udarnichestvo* 1936 no. 1, p. 16.
[27]Only 48 of the 5,000 workers at the Kauchuk factory participated in club circles, and this low turnout was attributed to a lack of funding and space. *Vo glave kul'turnogo stroitel'stva*, pp. 254–257.

circles toward the tasks of industrial production. This resolution, however, failed to produce any results.[28] Instead, former peasants reoriented the circles to match their own cultural tastes. Members of musical circles refused to substitute revolutionary songs for village folk songs.[29] Workers even dressed in peasant festival garb to perform village songs and dances at factory clubs.[30] Village culture in many instances supplanted organized cultural activity, and minimized the influence of official educational efforts.

The low level of literacy among former peasants posed a further obstacle to cultural education. The semiliterate simply could not absorb most written propaganda. More than half of Russian peasants were still illiterate in 1929. Though peasants who migrated to cities tended to be the younger and more literate ones, their ranks still included numerous semiliterate and illiterate people.[31] Particularly in construction, where a large portion of unskilled peasants found employment, the number of illiterate workers rose steeply from 1929 to 1932.[32] Illiteracy rates among food-processing workers, state trade workers, transport workers, and textile workers also rose during the First Five-Year Plan, and in every case officials attributed this rise to the proliferation of peasants in the workforce.[33]

The elimination of illiteracy received top priority among functionaries involved in cultural education. The Moscow Party organization, in conjunction with the trade unions and Komsomol, established dozens of evening literacy schools.[34] Enrollment in Moscow classes increased from 33,600 illiterate and 28,700 semiliterate workers in 1928–29 to 100,400 and 145,000, respectively, in 1930–31.[35] A report

---

[28]TsGAOR f. 5469, op. 14, d. 45, l. 34.

[29]*Za udarnichestvo* 1936 no. 1, p. 17; Chaiko, pp. 6–8.

[30]*Martenovka,* March 14, 1934, p. 3; interview with Vera Dmitreevna Ivanova at the Hammer and Sickle plant, April 10, 1989.

[31]Lewin, *Russian Peasants,* p. 25.

[32]TsGAOR f. 5475, op. 13, d. 206, l. 5; M. T. Gol'tsman, "Kharakteristika kul'turnogo urovnia i obshchestvenno-politicheskoi aktivnosti stroitel'nykh rabochikh SSSR v gody pervoi piatiletki," in *Metodologicheskie voprosy v statisticheskikh issledovaniiakh* (Moscow, 1968), p. 249.

[33]TsGAORgM f. 1289, op. 1, d. 185, l. 1; TsGAMO f. 747, op. 1, d. 165, l. 104; f. 738, op. 1, d. 94, ll. 3–4; E. S. Lapchenko, "Moskovskaia partiinaia organizatsiia v bor'be za likvidatsiiu negramotnosti sredi rabochikh-tekstil'shchikov v gody pervoi piatiletki," in *Partiia v period stroitel'stva sotsializma i kommunizma* (Moscow, 1977), p. 98.

[34]Davydova and Ponomarev, pp. 241–242; Aleksandrova, "Rabochii klass Moskvy," p. 54.

[35]Lapchenko, p. 95. The number of Soviet students in literacy schools rose from

at the end of 1931 boasted that as a result of these classes only 22,000 illiterate people remained in the entire city, whereas a year earlier every district had that many.[36] A conference on illiteracy in 1932 reported that of the limited number of workers who remained illiterate, 90 percent were learning to read and write.[37]

The high rates of participation in literacy classes reflected peasant in-migrants' awareness that they had to be literate if they were to function in Moscow. In contrast to other cultural education programs, literacy courses offered them a valuable skill. Organizers did encounter occasional problems when temporary migrants abandoned classes to return to their villages for the harvest in August.[38] But peasant in-migrants who had decided to reside permanently in Moscow understood the value of literacy—the need to read factory notices, recruiting posters, and newspaper listings. Literacy was also essential to anyone who aspired to study at a technical school and advance in the industrial hierarchy.

Though literacy programs achieved large enrollments, their quality was hampered by the same financial limitations that plagued other cultural work. The system of evening literacy schools appeared extensive on paper, but in reality many lacked such basic necessities as blackboards and books.[39] Many factory directors, afraid that study would distract workers from the tasks of production, refused to provide space or funding for instruction.[40] A trade union report complained that courses at Moscow construction sites were poorly organized, in part because even the Komsomol was too preoccupied with production tasks to devote time and resources to them.[41]

The inadequacy of resources limited literacy courses to basic reading and writing. Initial plans called for short segments of political education interwoven with literacy instruction, but reports indicate that even this minimal political work was not done.[42] The quality of liter-

---

2 million in 1929 to over 14 million in 1932. See *Izmeneniia sotsial'noi struktury*, p. 206.

[36]TsGAORgM f. 1289, op. 1, d. 185, l. 2.

[37]TsGAORgM f. 2617, op. 1, d. 130, l. 15.

[38]TsGAMO f. 738, op. 1, d. 37, l. 81.

[39]TsGAMO f. 747, op. 1, d. 165, l. 7; *Za sovetskii podshipnik*, April 5, 1931, p. 3.

[40]TsGAMO f. 747, op. 1, d. 165, l. 3.

[41]TsGAOR f. 5475, op. 14, d. 68, ll. 1–2.

[42]Ibid., l. 2; TsGAORgM f. 1289, op. 1, d. 185, l. 2.

acy instruction itself remained very low. Former peasants achieved rudimentary literacy but often little more. One director of technical courses in Moscow complained in 1936 that workers lacked even the most basic skills needed for study.[43] Even peasants who arrived in Moscow already literate (as well as workers born in Moscow) tended to have low levels of literacy and education. A 1931 survey showed that over 80 percent of all workers at the Hammer and Sickle plant and two-thirds at the Stalin automobile plant had less than four and a half years of schooling.[44]

Soviet authorities had assumed that along with literacy would come an interest in reading official publications and a rise in political consciousness. Yet because courses taught only the rudiments of reading and because peasant in-migrants simply found little reason to read official publications, the average time that city residents spent reading books and periodicals fell from 2.1 hours a week in 1923–24 to 1.0 hour in 1939.[45] New workers of peasant origin were four times less likely to subscribe to newspapers than were established workers, and inspectors rarely found books in their barracks.[46]

Many words used in publications simply lay outside the vocabularies of newly literate workers. At one political discussion circle, new workers of peasant origin experienced difficulty reading a passage that explained the difference between proletarian and capitalist countries. One new worker understood the passage to mean that "they [capitalist countries] have few or no workers, while we have workers." Others agreed with her: "They have no workers—there the bourgeoisie work." When competition (*sorevnovanie*) came up for discussion, another member of the circle declared, "The Soviet authorities are having a competition with the kulaks." Former peasants in a literacy class encountered similar problems when they tried to read a book titled *Lenin in the Underground*. They did not know the meaning of *underground*, *Mensheviks*, or *Provisional Government*.[47] One Komsomol cell decreed minimum cultural standards that required new

[43]TsGANKh f. 7622, op. 1, d. 56, ll. 87–88.

[44]*Trud v SSSR* (1932), pp. 86–88.

[45]L. A. Gordon et al., *Cherty sotsialisticheskogo obraza zhizni: Byt gorodskikh rabochikh vchera, segodnia, zavtra* (Moscow, 1977), pp. 49–57.

[46]Khlevniuk, "Izmenenie," pp. 83–84; Ermilov, p. 12.

[47]V. Vasilevskaia, "Kak chitaiut knigu malogramotnye," *Krasnyi bibliotekar'* 1931 no. 5/6, pp. 90–92, 94, 96.

members to read Tolstoi's *War and Peace,* but the novel proved far too long and difficult for newly literate workers.[48]

Similar problems arose with newspapers. The number of newspapers (including factory newspapers) published in Moscow increased from 65 in 1927 to 252 in 1933, but many of them proved incomprehensible to new workers, and special simplified editions had to be prepared for them.[49] One newspaper, *The New Proletariat,* was published exclusively for newly literate workers of peasant origin, with simplified slogans and articles of no more than fifty words printed in large type. An article explaining the importance of coal mining was headed "Coal—the Bread of Industry," and articles on the international situation succinctly spelled out the hostility of bourgeois countries and the need for the Soviet Union to prepare defenses.[50]

Surveys revealed that despite efforts to make such topics accessible, political issues had little appeal to new workers. They wanted sensational stories or practical everyday information *(bytovye fakty).*[51] Nor did most wish to read political books. Libraries at Moscow factories reported that only 10 percent of all workers requesting books wanted political literature; 70 percent wanted fiction.[52] Even socialist realist literature often proved too difficult or simply uninteresting to workers.[53] Surveys indicated that workers of peasant origin enjoyed only adventure novels and focused more on the action than on the values portrayed.[54] Official publications, then, even as they tailored their style to fit new workers' low level of literacy, failed to attract a wide readership. Rather than respond to readers' interests, Soviet presses published books and articles that authorities believed people should read. Actually getting them to read these publications lay beyond the scope of Soviet power.

[48]MPA f. 635, op. 1, d. 135, l. 29.

[49]M. D. Slanskaia, *Pechat' delo partiinoe: Iz opyta partiinogo rukovodstva mnogotirazhnymi gazetami Moskvy* (Moscow, 1978), p. 14; O. Rubtsov, *Stengazetu kazhdyi den'* (Moscow, 1931), pp. 8–9; TsPA f. 17, op. 114, d. 558, l. 5; Lapchenko, p. 92.

[50]*Novyi proletarii,* January 3, 1931, pp. 1–4.

[51]Khlevniuk, "Izmenenie," p. 84.

[52]D. Lekarenko and V. A. Nevskii, "Chitatel'skii spros rabochei molodezhi," *Krasnyi bibliotekar'* 1935 no. 6, p. 23.

[53]I. A. Shomrakova, "Massovyi chitatel' pervoi poloviny 30-kh godov XX veka," in *Istoriia russkogo chitatelia* (Leningrad, 1982), p. 77.

[54]Khlevniuk, "Izmenenie," p. 84.

Failing to transform former peasants' worldview and behavior through cultural education, Party and trade union functionaries often abandoned general training and focused on rudimentary hygiene and safety. Campaigns to raise the cultural level in workers' barracks amounted to nothing more than cleansing, whitewashing, and disinfecting, with no educational activities at all.[55] Because they viewed former peasants as gauche and callow, officials did not hesitate to intervene in their personal lives to teach cleanliness and a rigorous work ethic. Inspectors at one workers' residence busied themselves counting the number of toothbrushes on the premises. Finding only five rooms where workers had their own toothbrushes (in the remaining 135 rooms workers shared toothbrushes or owned none at all), they launched a campaign to improve dental hygiene.[56] City council regulations admonished occupants of Moscow housing to scrub and dust daily, to air the premises twice daily, to clean the bathtub after each use, to take out the garbage, and to notify a clinic of any outbreak of a contagious disease.[57] Factory newspapers even warned readers to cross streets only at crosswalks, to cross only on the green light, and to look both ways before crossing.[58]

Soviet authorities harbored ambitious goals in their aspiration to create the "New Soviet Person." They planned to transform former peasants into efficient workers who shared their worldview and their commitment to building socialism. Failing that, officials sought to mobilize the productive capacity of the population by prescribing new habits of cleanliness, discipline, sobriety, and physical fitness. They tried to dictate in petty detail the proper behavior they had expected would come naturally to former peasants who had been enlightened by Soviet culture. Government control over people's bodily health and everyday routines was intended to ensure efficient labor.[59] Indeed, the transformation of millions of peasants into industrial workers, however undisciplined and inefficient, represented an enormous mobilization of human labor for state goals.

[55]Ehrenburg, *Out of Chaos*, p. 104.
[56]*Klub* 1929 no. 10, pp. 39–40.
[57]Hazard, pp. 58–60.
[58]*Kirovets*, May 13, 1938, p. 4.
[59]Governments' efforts to mobilize their populations as a resource in this way dated from the rise of the modern state in seventeenth- and eighteenth-century Western Europe. See Michel Foucault, "Truth and Power," in *Power/Knowledge* (New York, 1977).

Soviet authorities' readiness to intervene in people's lives also stemmed from their condescending assumption that peasant in-migrants lacked culture and needed to be civilized. This condescension toward peasants was not unique to Soviet ideology—it was an attitude the Bolshevik leaders shared with other members of the (non-populist) Russian intelligentsia. During the prerevolutionary period, peasant in-migration had provoked similar concerns among tsarist officials and educated society that Moscow was "becoming more and more a peasant city," and that the "dark masses" arriving from the village were intemperate, lazy, and in need of discipline and a rational value system.[60] But both Soviet authorities and tsarist officials before them were wrong to assume that peasants lacked culture and could be easily reeducated and remolded. The thousands of peasants who moved to the city had their own values and their own culture, and this culture was not something they abandoned or outgrew. New workers continued to draw upon peasant culture as they organized their lives in Moscow.

The Survival of Peasant Culture in the City

Early experiences and conditions of life color people's perception and comprehension of subsequent experiences.[61] People who migrate from one place to another use those elements of their previous culture that provide a useful framework for understanding their new environment. The perpetuation of past culture was especially pronounced among peasants who migrated to Moscow during the 1930s. Had they arrived gradually and lived among established urbanites, peasant in-migrants would have received more exposure to urban culture and perhaps adopted it to a greater degree. But hundreds of thousands of them moved to Moscow every year during the 1930s and settled with fellow villagers in communities on the outskirts of town. These communities, largely isolated from the central city, helped perpetuate peasant beliefs, values, and modes of behavior.

Religion was one important aspect of peasant culture that the new arrivals perpetuated in the city, and throughout the 1930s Soviet offi-

[60]Bradley, pp. 352–356.
[61]See Bourdieu, p. 78.

cials called for antireligious propaganda to eradicate its influence.[62] Authorities also found religious sectarianism to be common among new workers.[63] Countless reports alerted authorities to religious services conducted by priests in barracks.[64] Monks led the residents of one workers' settlement in prayers, while at the barracks of Tatar construction workers in Moscow a mullah frequently held Islamic services.[65] Workers of peasant origin contested the closing of churches and contributed money for their restoration.[66]

Priests not only organized religious services, they also criticized Soviet policies. They vehemently condemned the continuous work-week, which required work on Sundays, as "the idea of the Antichrist."[67] Absenteeism among workers of peasant origin was extremely high on Sundays and religious holidays. At one construction site, all peasant in-migrants refused to work on Sundays.[68] At another, elders spoke out and aroused the hostility of their artel members against the continuous workweek.[69] Industrial managers gradually abandoned the system until it was abolished altogether in 1940.

Religious mementos and icons remained popular among former peasants throughout the 1930s. Mementos with drawings of saints and angels were crafted by hand and sold in Moscow.[70] Many workers of peasant origin displayed icons on the walls of their residences or barracks, though they denied to inspectors that the icons held any religious meaning for them.[71] When the plaster cracked on the wall of a barracks of Moscow construction workers, a number of icons crashed to the floor. The residents interpreted the event as a bad omen and moved out.[72]

---

[62]TsGAOR f. 5451, op. 13, d. 78, l. 12; f. 5469, op. 13, d. 48, l. 41; f. 5475, op. 13, d. 194, ll. 2–7.

[63]*Iunyi kommunist* 1937 no. 5, p. 19; TsGAOR f. 5451, op. 13, d. 76, l. 51.

[64]AAN f. 359, op. 2, d. 499, ll. 24–25; Ermilov, p. 17; TsGAMO f. 4867, op. 1, d. 156, ll. 9–10.

[65]Ermilov, p. 25; TsGAORgM f. 1289, op. 1, d. 173, l. 1.

[66]Gan, pp. 42–43; *Voprosy profdvizhenia* 1937 no. 11, pp. 11–13.

[67]Ermilov, pp. 25–26. See also *Rabochii narodnogo pitaniia* 1929 no. 23/24, pp. 4–5.

[68]*Govoriat stroiteli sotsializma*, p. 150; Kuromiya, *Stalin's Industrial Revolution*, p. 239.

[69]Eliseeva, p. 47.

[70]*Rabochaia Moskva*, September 23, 1931, p. 4.

[71]*Klub* 1929 no. 10, p. 42.

[72]*Istoriia metro Moskvy*, p. 220.

Former peasants continued to observe Orthodox baptism and marriage rituals. Many newly arrived workers at the Kuibyshev electronics factory had their children baptized, and at the Frunze aviation engine plant even some Komsomol members baptized their children and regularly attended Sunday services.[73] Former peasants' marriage patterns also corresponded to village religious traditions. As during the 1920s, wedding dates conformed to the Orthodox church calendar, as the number of marriages dwindled during Lent, Advent, and the Christmas season.[74]

Antireligious campaigns had little effect. In lectures at "red corners" and worker clubs, authorities assured workers that religion was a deception perpetrated by priests.[75] The Moscow planetarium chimed in with such programs as "The Creation of the Earth According to the Teachings of Science versus Those of Religion."[76] Officials also initiated atheist discussion circles, but these attracted little interest among former peasants. Many antireligious groups simply ceased activity for lack of members.[77] Religious believers occasionally even disrupted antireligious lectures held at Moscow factories.[78]

Antireligious propagandists concentrated their efforts on religious holidays. Several worker clubs in Moscow held parties on Christmas at which they sang antireligious songs.[79] Other clubs held special concerts and plays on religious holidays, to divert new workers from religious ceremonies or drunken celebrations.[80] Factory newspapers conducted vigorous antireligious campaigns before Easter, urging everyone to come to work. Newspaper headlines proclaimed: "Whoever abandons work during the days of the kulak holiday betrays the interests of socialist construction" and "Shame to the deserters who forsake construction to celebrate Easter."[81] Yet Moscow Party re-

[73]TsGAOR f. 7952, op. 3, d. 522, ll. 1–4; *Nezabyvaemye 30-e*, p. 108.

[74]Chase, pp. 93–94; Anokhina and Shmeleva, p. 47. Peasant newcomers to cities in other societies have similarly continued to observe the baptism, marriage, and funeral rituals they learned in the village: Rothstein, p. 227.

[75]*Rabochii narodnogo pitaniia* 1929 no. 23/24, p. 5.

[76]TsGAORgM f. 176, op. 6, d. 200, l. 8.

[77]MPA f. 432, op. 1, d. 178, l. 15; TsGAMO f. 738, op. 1, d. 37, l. 81; *Kirovets*, May 13, 1938, p. 3.

[78]*Moskovskii proletarii* 1930 no. 1, pp. 26–27.

[79]*Rabochaia gazeta*, January 5, 1930, p. 6.

[80]*Dinamo v gody stroitel'stva sotsializma*, p. 185.

[81]*Za sovetskii podshipnik*, April 11, 1931, p. 1; *AMOvets*, April 12, 1931, p. 1.

ports in 1930 and again in 1940 concluded that such campaign-style antireligious propaganda had little impact, partly because activists conducted it only during religious holidays and failed to provide systematic antireligious education the rest of the year.[82] Workers of peasant origin continued to stay away from work in droves on religious holidays.[83]

The persistence of peasant culture among new workers manifested itself in other ways as well. When former peasants constructed shanties, mud huts, and other makeshift housing, they imitated the distinctive styles of peasant huts in their native villages. The interior layout, external architecture, and decoration patterns of these dwellings were therefore characteristic of the occupants' region or village.[84] This duplication of village architecture contributed to an environment that fostered the preservation of peasant culture on the outskirts of Moscow.

Given the concentration of former peasants on the outskirts of Moscow, village culture served as the basis for their leisure activity as well. The village tradition of strolling (*gulian'e*) continued to be a major pastime. One observer described the evening strolls in a new workers' settlement as follows:

> Around the housing, back and forth stroll young men and women . . . . [V]illage songs fill the air. Not far from where the accordion is playing a Red Army soldier passionately tries to convince a young peasant woman of something, while she sits on a curbstone . . . naively and happily smiling. By the walls of the housing, on the steps, sit middle-aged and elderly women. Watching over the youth—here are strolling their sons and daughters—they appraise first one couple and then another.[85]

Village culture centered on such strolling and socializing, and former peasants continued these ways instead of participating in officially sponsored activities or in leisure activities common among city

[82]V. F. Starodubtsev, "Deiatel'nost' moskovskoi partiinoi organizatsii po razvitiiu obshchestvenno-politicheskoi aktivnosti rabochego klassa v gody pervoi piatiletki, 1928–1932 gg." (dissertation, Moscow Oblast Pedagogical Institute, Moscow, 1972), p. 116; MPA f. 432, op. 1, d. 220, ll. 25–26.

[83]*Rabochaia Moskva*, September 23, 1931, p. 4.

[84]*Sovetskoe kraevedenie* 1931 no. 10, p. 11.

[85]Zhiga, pp. 49–50.

people. New workers in one barracks seldom went to the movie theater, preferring to congregate in the corridor to talk, play cards and dominoes, or sing along to an accordion.[86] Some first-generation workers at the ball bearing plant site organized evening dances and games around their barracks, while others played cards and gambled late into the night.[87] Unmarried women of peasant origin in one barracks played cards and told fortunes in the evenings.[88] At other settlements, strolling, dances, and card playing were accompanied by drunken fights.[89]

Alcohol played an important role in leisure activity. The pub served as a male social center—usually the only social center in the settlement. Peasant in-migrants at the Kozhukhovo settlement spent a great deal of time at the pub and often engaged in acts the authorities labeled "hooliganism."[90] At another pub called the Stenka Razin, known for its tumultuousness, some workers of peasant origin drank so heavily on their days off that they were unable to report for work in the morning; others showed up hung over and took turns drinking on the sly from a bottle in the corner.[91]

Some new workers brewed their own alcohol (*samogon*) in their barracks, and drunken singing was a common pastime among them.[92] Rural holidays and saints' days continued to be celebrated in Moscow much as they had been in the village, with gatherings and widespread drinking.[93] Such activity clearly hindered industrial production, not only because new workers skipped work to celebrate but also because drunkenness impaired their work the following day. The Soviet government conducted vigorous campaigns against drinking in the 1930s. Officials declared drunkenness to be deviant behavior and hooliganism, and sought to deny alcohol a legitimate place in workers' culture. In spite of these efforts, alcohol remained an integral part of new workers' leisure activity.[94]

[86]*Molodoi bol'shevik* 1932 no. 21/22, pp. 11–14.
[87]*Za sovetskii podshipnik*, May 14, 1931, p. 3.
[88]Ermilov, p. 14.
[89]TsGAORgM f. 1289, op. 1, d. 173, l. 1; *Molodoi bol'shevik* 1932 no. 23/24, p. 16; *Iunyi kommunist* 1937 no. 8, pp. 14–16.
[90]*Pravda*, December 22, 1937, p. 2.
[91]*Moskovskii proletarii*, February 28, 1928, pp. 14–15. See also Zhiga, p. 50.
[92]Ehrenburg, p. 292; *Amostroika*, January 25, 1931, p. 4; Ermilov, p. 14.
[93]*Martenovka*, January 12, 1929, p. 3; *Klub* 1929 no. 10, p. 41.
[94]TsPA f. 17, op. 114, d. 255, l. 66.

On holidays, peasant in-migrants continued the village tradition of strolling in groups, singing along to the music of an accordion.[95] This tradition preserved village folk songs and prevented official and unofficial urban musical culture from supplanting them. Ethnographers studying village folk songs among workers of peasant origin found residents at one barracks suspicious of their motives. When the ethnographers explained that they only wanted to hear them sing, the workers agreed, adding, "But we'll sing our own songs, not yours." Once the workers had overcome their initial distrust, they all joined in, and singing and folk dancing engulfed the entire barracks.[96]

Songs and dances also accompanied the rituals of peasant culture. New city dwellers included village songs and dances at weddings. They also put on plays consisting of songs and pantomime, in accordance with village tradition. Typically a small group of former peasants would change into assorted costumes to portray gypsies, soldiers, bears, and various village characters. These plays took place not only at wedding parties but at other gatherings as well.[97]

On weekends and holidays peasant in-migrants regularly gathered in the park to sing and dance; they called this gathering a *piatachok* after the round, open area where they had congregated in the village. Folk gatherings were regular features of religious holidays in Moscow since the nineteenth century. In the 1840s the tsarist authorities banned such activities in the center of the city, so participants moved to Sokolniki, Novinki, and the Izmailovskii forest.[98] With the influx of peasants during the First Five-Year Plan, folk gatherings grew in popularity. Foreign observers testified to the large number of former peasants who joined in folk songs and dances in Moscow's parks.[99] Former peasants continued to congregate in several Moscow parks up until the mid-1970s, and they still do so in Izmailovskii park today.[100]

---

[95]Natalia Degteva, "Fenomen bytovoi kul'tury sovremennogo goroda—parkovyi piatachok: Izmailovskii park v Moskve," in *Traditsionnyi fol'klor v sovremennoi khudozhestvennoi zhizni: Sbornik nauchnykh trudov* (Leningrad, 1984), p. 54.

[96]Lev Ostroumov, "Kul'turno-bytovye usloviia truda na torforazrabotkakh," *Sovetskoe kraevedenie* 1932 no. 4, p. 40.

[97]Degteva, "Fenomen bytovoi kul'tury," pp. 54, 60.

[98]Natalia Degteva, "Piatachok" (unpublished manuscript), p. 78.

[99]Arthur Newsholme and John A. Kingsbury, *Red Medicine: Socialized Health in Soviet Russia* (Garden City, N.Y., 1933), p. 141.

[100]Iu. Boiko, "Leningradskii udel'nyi park," in *Traditsionnyi fol'klor*, pp. 61–62; G. G. Shapovalova, "Derevenskaia chastushka v gorode," in *Etnograficheskie issledo-*

Participants in the gatherings assembled in groups according to their village or province of origin, singing and dancing with fellow villagers.[101] The most popular kind of songs—four-line rhymed ditties (*chastushki*) accompanied by an accordion—often referred to specific villages or provinces:

We are Riazan peasant women	My riazanskie babenki
Talented in all matters.	Khoroshi po vsem stat'iam.
Singing songs we will not yield	Po chastushkam ne ustupim
Even to Kursk nightingales.	Dazhe kurskim solov'iam.[102]

Several songs referred to collectivization and the ensuing famine. One mentioned the narrow escape of the survivors:[103]

My dear friend,	Moia podruzhka dorogaia,
Let us dance and sing.	Davai spliashem i spoem.
There was a time we did not die	Bylo vremia—ne propali,
And now we will survive.	I teper' ne propadem.

Another song denounced the new hierarchy on collective farms and perhaps reassured former peasants that they were better off in the city.

The chairman goes by car,	Predsedatel' na mashine,
The accountant goes by tractor,	Svetovod—na traktore,
While the peasants go on foot	A kolkhozniki peshkom
Carrying sacks and swearing.	Materiatsia pod meshkom.

Because most peasant songs were composed by women, many reflected their particular concerns. One song ridiculed the fact that women did most of the work on collective farms while men held the positions of authority.

---

vaniia Severo-Zapada SSSR (Leningrad, 1977), pp. 83–85; Degteva, "Piatachok," p. 54. Such gatherings still occur during warm weather at Filevskii and Kuz'minkii parks and all year round at Izmailovskii Park.

[101]This pattern continued until the mid-1970s. A general integration of former peasants from various regions took place over time. See Degteva, "Fenomen bytovoi kul'tury," p. 58.

[102]Ibid., pp. 56–58.

[103]All of the following songs were taught me by Valentina Andreevna Melnikova in an interview at Izmailovskii Park, Moscow, July 25, 1992.

On March eighth our collective farm	Nash kolkhoz vosmogo marta
Honors women's labor.[104]	Uvazhaet zhenskii trud.
Women sow, women plow,	Baby seiut, baby pashut,
While men take inventory.	Muzhiki uchet vedut.

Another song complained about drunkenness among male in-migrants and about its detrimental affect on male-female relationships.

My sweetheart seldom visits me,	Redko milyi naveshchaet,
He says his parents don't let him.	Ne veliat roditeli.
It's not his parents stopping him—	Ne roditeli meshaiut—
It's the sobering-up tanks.	Bol'she vytrezviteli.

The themes of the songs ranged widely, but all pertained to the lives of peasants in the village and in the city. Old songs were sung, but new ones about life in Moscow were also generated.

Also manifest at these gatherings were traditional values—respect for one's elders, formality between men and women, and a division of function between men and women—men always played the accordion and women composed and sang the verses, though exclusively male singing groups existed as well. Many young men and women met their future spouses at these gatherings, a trend that further perpetuated peasant culture in the city. These gatherings resembled village life in that the participants all knew one another, in contrast to the impersonality of urban industrial life. Contemporary interviews with former peasants who migrated to Moscow in the 1930s (and still gather in Izmailovskii Park today) revealed a nostalgia for the intimacy of village life. One said, "In the village it's merry! There everybody knows everybody else and they all have a good time together. As soon as the accordion is picked up . . . people begin to sing and play and go on playing all day." An old woman explained that she and her fellow villagers gathered in Izmailovskii Park "to relax as we did in our youth in the village, to talk a bit with our girlfriends."[105] Such conversation allowed them to exchange information and ideas about city life, as well as to keep up with news from home.

New city dwellers trusted the advice of relatives and fellow villagers more than the cultural education of Soviet officials. Elders instructed

[104]March 8 is International Women's Day.
[105]Degteva, "Piatachok," pp. 40, 20.

artel members, for example, whether to follow cultural measures pre-scribed by Party and trade union functionaries.[106] One slightly older woman assumed the role of "educator" (*vospitatel'nitsa*) to young workers at her barracks, offering them advice on everything from everyday concerns to such large matters as marriage and raising chil-dren.[107] These informal contacts also provided vital information on job possibilities and living conditions, and with this information the newcomers could form opinions and make decisions. The Communist Party maintained strict censorship over the media and other ideologi-cal resources, but it could not control ideas spread through informal social networks. And because official news accounts were not to be trusted, the Soviet population came to depend on the advice of friends and even on rumors as alternative sources of information.

In a broader sense, rejection of official culture in favor of informal networks and peasant culture amounted to an act of self-definition for new city residents. When they sang with their friends instead of attending trade union lectures they were rejecting the official model of proper behavior for workers. Such activity not only reflected their culture, it also served to reaffirm and consolidate their sense of social identity. Singing peasant songs in the park or drinking with fellow villagers in the neighborhood built up allegiances and solidarities, as well as shared understandings of the world. These solidarities stood as an alternative to acceptance of official ideology and allegiance to the state.

The Retreat from Revolutionary Values

The failure of Soviet leaders to instill new ways of thinking, new allegiances, and new values in the mass of the population ultimately impelled them to retreat from revolutionary culture. In a sharp shift from the revolutionary values they had espoused up until the mid-1930s, Soviet leaders either manipulatively or resignedly or even unconsciously began to invoke traditional values and symbols in an attempt to create cultural unity between government and people.

[106]*Istoriia Moskovskogo avtozavoda*, pp. 171–172.
[107]Interview with Maria Aleksandrovna Filatova at the Hammer and Sickle plant, April 17, 1989.

Such unity appeared especially urgent after the extensive government coercion and extreme social disruption of collectivization and industrialization.[108]

A turn away from revolutionary asceticism accompanied this realignment, and materialism and the aesthetic of kitsch came to permeate much of official culture. Pretentious, colossal architecture, blatant materialism, and a bourgeois mode of dress and decoration were encouraged. Hailing this shift, Stalin proclaimed, "Life has become better! Life has become more joyous!" Because the turn toward materialism coincided with efforts to raise living standards during the Second Five-Year Plan, Soviet citizens could in fact aspire to a slightly improved material existence. Reinforcing this shift toward pretentious materialism was a sociological change within Soviet officialdom. The promotion of thousands of established workers into managerial and bureaucratic positions during the early 1930s created a new elite that leaned toward traditional values and grasped at bourgeois status symbols.[109]

Fine clothing received special attention as a symbol of cultural maturity. Workers were encouraged to dress well and to cultivate a well-groomed appearance. The Stakhanovite movement provided models not only of efficient laborers but also of "cultured" workers for new workers to emulate. A photograph of one Stakhanovite showed her in a fur coat and feathered hat. Another Stakhanovite wrote in her factory's newspaper that before leaving for work she always cleaned her shoes and carefully arranged her dress, adding that she had given up cursing, because "it does not befit us Stakhanovites." [110] These standards signaled a marked change from the stiff leather jackets, black tobacco, bobbed hair, and austere dwellings that had expressed the official asceticism throughout the 1920s and early 1930s.

Model worker apartments were described in glowing terms: "In a worker's apartment at the Tri-Mountain textile mill, it is not unusual

---

[108]Nicholas S. Timasheff, *The Great Retreat: The Growth and Decline of Communism in Russia* (New York, 1945), pp. 132–133. Timasheff asserts that in 1934 Party leaders "foresaw war with a formidable enemy and simultaneously realized the dissatisfaction of the population with the existing social and economic order."

[109]Geoffrey Hosking, *The First Socialist Society* (Cambridge, Mass., 1985), pp. 212–216. Vera S. Dunham, *In Stalin's Time: Middleclass Values in Soviet Fiction* (New York, 1976), explains the *embourgeoisement* of Soviet culture in terms of an implicit deal between the Soviet regime and the bureaucratic middle class in the postwar period.

[110]Siegelbaum, *Stakhanovism*, p. 231.

to find a piano; almost every apartment has a radio, flowers, books, newspapers. On the walls are portraits of influential people—Lenin, Stalin, Voroshilov, Kaganovich." The new furniture that adorns the apartment, we are told, is beautiful. Workers also allegedly demanded flower gardens about their apartments: "Flowers and beauty in general—this is not petty bourgeois [*meshchanstvo*]. Flowers must be accessible to the mass of all workers." [111]

To sum up this shift from revolutionary asceticism to blatant materialism, one Soviet commentator declared, "The transition from socialism to communism does not at all mean the gradual (or even any) liquidation of articles of personal consumption. . . . Yesterday's peasant, sleeping on sackcloth draped over the planking above the stove, now acquires a bed with springs, good furniture, sheets, tulle blankets, curtains, and so on." [112] Whereas the struggle to build socialism had been associated with sacrifice, it now came to include aspirations for material betterment. Teaching "yesterday's peasant" to dress well and live in decent conditions seemed to represent progress toward a more civilized existence. The fact that the qualities associated with socialism could be reoriented so completely reflected the concept's abstractness. Soviet leaders had no blueprint for building socialism. When put into practice, Soviet socialism came to be equated with very concrete and simplified notions of progress—the construction of steel mills and teaching newly urbanized workers to dress well.

Also abandoned in the retreat from revolutionary values was the attempt to create a genuine proletarian culture to replace bourgeois art forms and folk music. A revival of popular songs, dances, and musical shows began in 1935. To accommodate the continued popularity of peasant culture, an olympiad of peasant folk songs was held in Moscow that year, and performances of peasant songs and dances became common in theaters throughout the city, even at the Bolshoi Theater. [113] The traditional accompaniment to peasant folk songs, the accordion, achieved enormous popularity in Moscow. An accordion-

[111]Lapitskaia, pp. 161–163. Postwar fiction described living quarters with embroidered doilies and colored vases on the tables, and postcards of movie stars on the walls: Dunham, p. 42.

[112]*Leningradskaia pravda*, June 6, 1936, as quoted in Siegelbaum, *Stakhanovism*, p. 229.

[113]Timasheff, pp. 270–271.

playing contest in 1930 attracted 30,000 contestants.[114] Appropriating traditional genres (epic songs, laments for the dead, lyric songs, and folktales) for their own purposes, Soviet officials recruited folk performers to compose folkloric panegyrics to Stalin.[115]

As revolutionary values waned, Russian nationalism revived. In 1934 the Komsomol declared that young people should love their motherland and consider it an honor to die for their country.[116] Soviet propaganda began to glorify Russian national heroes of the past. Among the most widely shown films in Moscow in 1937 was *Peter I*, followed the next year by *Alexander Nevsky*.[117] These films diverged sharply from previous Soviet depictions of prerevolutionary history, which had found little to praise in this period or in its leaders. Nationalist propaganda strove to establish among former peasants a new allegiance to their country based on traditional appeals. Parades and mass demonstrations on national holidays served this function. The Komsomol and trade unions mobilized workers to don uniforms and march in Red Square—an exercise to promote collectivism and patriotism.[118]

The cults of Lenin and Stalin played large roles in the promotion of national consciousness. Lenin, his body displayed in the mausoleum much the way the relics of saints were traditionally enshrined in Russian Orthodox churches, was honored as the founding father of the Soviet Union.[119] Parallel to the Lenin cult arose the cult of Stalin, with such slogans as "Stalin is Lenin today!"[120] On December 21, 1929, Stalin's fiftieth birthday, praise was heaped upon him as a wise and omnipotent leader, and his portraits were everywhere.[121]

The cults of Lenin and Stalin provided accessible symbols that the Soviet government relied on to promote national unity. Some people genuinely believed that Stalin was a benevolent patriarch, just as they had believed in the tsar as the "little father." Occasionally people re-

[114]*Nezabyvaemye 30-e*, p. 241.

[115]See Frank J. Miller, *Folklore for Stalin: Russian Folklore and Pseudofolklore of the Stalin Era* (Armonk, N.Y., 1990).

[116]*Komsomol'skaia pravda*, October 18, 1934.

[117]*Vo glave kul'turnogo stroitel'stva*, p. 312.

[118]*AMOvets*, April 29, 1931, p. 1.

[119]See Nina Tumarkin, *Lenin Lives: The Lenin Cult in Soviet Russia* (Cambridge, Mass., 1983).

[120]*Martenovka*, April 22, 1936, p. 2.

[121]Davies, *Soviet Economy in Turmoil*, pp. 470–471.

ferred to "grandfather Stalin" and sent him telegrams asking him to intercede to right some personal injustice they had suffered.[122] In a sense, the personality cults of Lenin and Stalin substituted for a real understanding of Marxism-Leninism, Soviet history, and the ideals underlying the Soviet system. The campaign to inculcate revolutionary values by cultural education having failed, the authorities turned to patriotic films and veneration of Lenin and Stalin to win people's loyalty.

The strengthening of the family as an institution in the late 1930s also played a role in attempts to build national loyalty. In addition to championing family values to arrest the decline in fertility, Party leaders invoked the unifying image of the family (under the father's patriarchal control) to promote national unity. The family offered a valuable model of cohesion and order, with parental authority as the model for all political authority.[123] Thus Stalin was hailed as the "father of all Soviet peoples," and the country was increasingly referred to as the motherland (*rodina*).

A concern for national defense played a role in Party leaders' turn away from revolutionary culture. With the rise of Nazism in Germany, they sought national unity and military preparedness. Trade union committees organized discussion groups to teach workers about the threat posed by capitalist encirclement, and the Komsomol composed an examination to test its members' knowledge on this subject.[124] With the outbreak of the Spanish Civil War, increased attention was given to international events both in the press and at workers' meetings. A Spanish delegation visited the Tri-Mountain textile mill in 1936, for example, to tell workers about the conflict in Spain and the struggle of the Spanish people against fascism.[125]

Military training of civilians increased substantially. The Komsomol organized war games and military exercises in which tens of thousands of Moscow workers participated. It also promoted physi-

---

[122]E.g., interview with Ivan Petrovich Gomozenkov for the documentary film *Piatachok*, 1989; TsGANKh f. 7446, op. 1, d. 161, ll. 70–71.

[123]The use of parental authority as a model for social and political authority was not unique to the Soviet Union. See Mary McIntosh, "The Family, Regulation, and the Public Sphere," in *State and Society in Contemporary Britain: A Critical Introduction*, Gregor McLennan et al., eds. (Cambridge, 1984), p. 237.

[124]TsGAORgM f. 176, op. 2, d. 190, l. 2; TsGANKh f. 7622, op. 1, d. 1948, l. 30.

[125]*Raduga trekh gor: Iz biografii odnogo rabochego kollektiva*, P. Podliashuk, ed. (Moscow, 1967), pp. 250–257.

cal culture and sports as part of an expanding program to keep youth physically fit and prepared.[126] A Moscow winter festival in 1934 included a parade of cavalry troops, parachute jumping, a sharpshooting exhibition, and a mock battle.[127] Parachuting clubs were organized at the Kuibyshev electronics factory and other enterprises in the mid-1930s, at a time when efforts by Soviet pilots to set aviation records received enormous publicity.[128]

The patriotism inspired by military parades, appeals to Russian nationalism, and the Stalin cult during the 1930s should not be overestimated. The allegiance of the Soviet people to their country and to Stalin was secured only during World War II, when they were fighting for national survival. Indeed, victory in World War II became the keystone of the Soviet government's political legitimacy in the postwar era. It would be a mistake to project Stalin's unchallenged postwar popularity back onto the prewar period. Though the Soviet government's campaign to promote national unity and win the allegiance of the newly urbanized masses was more effective than its efforts to instill revolutionary values, its success was still limited in the second half of the 1930s.

The Evolution of Peasant Culture

Peasant culture did not remain static in an urban setting. Though new city dwellers did not adopt official culture, at the very least they had to come to terms with it and with unofficial urban popular culture, which held enormous appeal for some of them. Of course notions of rural and urban culture should not be reified. The collection of beliefs, values, and symbols that made up those cultures evolved in accordance with external surroundings, social interaction, and the influence of other cultures. Urban popular culture and rural culture were not entirely distinct, for they had been intermixing and influencing each other for centuries. Songs based on urban literary works, for example, were quickly adopted or imitated in the village

---

[126]*Ocherki . . . VLKSM,* pp. 268–269, 313–316; *Kirovets,* April 8, 1938, p. 3.
[127]*Moscow Daily News,* January 29, 1934.
[128]*Elektrozavod,* January 20, 1935, p. 3; Aleksandrova, p. 51.

in the nineteenth century, just as peasant songs were popularized by recordings in the 1930s.[129]

The urban environment exerted influence on in-migrants' culture. Peasant culture had developed in tandem with subsistence agriculture, and centered on holidays (initially pagan holidays, subsequently syncretized with Christianity) that corresponded to the agricultural calendar and on the needs of agriculture. Many beliefs and folk legends lived on among former peasants in Moscow.[130] But some peasant beliefs and holiday rituals had no place in an urban environment. Spirits that lived in the forest and saints who protected livestock had no role to play in a large city. Former peasants focused instead on folk beliefs and tales that retained importance or could be seen to have some allegorical meaning in the city. Sometimes, as in the case of folk songs, they used traditional village forms to generate new tales concerning their lives in the city.

Other village rituals survived but took on new meanings. Peasant songs and dances performed in a theater no longer constituted a village ritual of celebration or a means of social bonding. This form of village culture became instead a statement of social identity for its performers, or simply a form of entertainment for observers. Songs sung at gatherings of fellow villagers in Moscow parks, with no official audience in attendance, retained more of their original meanings, yet even this aspect of peasant culture underwent some evolution over time. Participants remembered the distinctive singing styles of their villages, but they tried as much as possible to sing village songs in an urban style. Harmonizing, customary in the village, came to be considered "incorrect" and "uncultured"; the correct way to sing was in unison, "as songs are performed on the radio."[131]

Peasant culture in Moscow incorporated new elements drawn from official and unofficial urban culture, but rearranged to fit forms and

---

[129]A. F. Nekrylova, "Ob izuchenii russkogo iarmarochnogo fol'klora," in *Aktual'nye problemy sovremennoi fol'kloristiki: Sbornik statei i materialov* (Leningrad, 1980), p. 131. Elements of trade fairs, of the carnivalesque, and of rural holiday celebrations all fused together in nineteenth-century urban holidays—another instance of the intermixing of rural and urban popular culture.

[130]Khlevniuk, "Izmenenie," p. 129. On the superstitions, folktales, and village customs of English and Irish peasants in nineteenth-century London, see Thompson, *Making of the English Working Class*, pp. 404–408; Lees, pp. 170–191.

[131]Degteva, "Piatachok," pp. 6–9.

meanings inherent in peasant culture. A number of new city dwellers, for example, hung portraits of Lenin alongside icons in their barracks.[132] This practice ostensibly indicated an acceptance of official culture and support for the Lenin cult, but Lenin's significance for former peasants had little to do with his role as founder of the Soviet state. Rather they venerated his quasi-religious status as a deified figure, and hung his portrait to conjure its arcane powers. In other words, they took a new symbol from official culture and invested it with traditional meanings.

The religiosity of peasant culture also evolved in Moscow. Especially apparent was the weakening of its hold over the children. Antireligious education in schools, kindergartens, and the Young Pioneer organization proved to be, in the judgment of one observer, "stronger than the influence of the family."[133] The elementary school system in Moscow, in contrast to other urban services, expanded rapidly enough to keep pace with the multiplying population, and atheism was one of the official cultural values it strove to instill.[134] Even children whose parents took them to church ridiculed icons and cursed the church after a few years in Moscow schools.[135]

Generational tensions between new city dwellers and their children arose over other issues as well. Some children regularly read books and newspapers, whereas their parents remained barely literate. This situation promoted not only differences of leisure activity but differences of opinion as well.[136] Schoolteachers encouraged children to denounce their parents' habits—failure to read regularly, alcohol consumption, and corporal punishment of children.[137] Children of former peasants also rejected their parents' practice of gathering with fellow villagers in the parks. Ironically, just as many peasants had chosen city life over the village, many of their children chose urban popular culture over their parents' peasant-based culture.

[132]Ermilov, p. 38.

[133]Lapitskaia, p. 193.

[134]*Moskva: Razvitie khoziaistva i kul'tury goroda* pp. 86–88; TsGAORgM f. 126, op. 10, d. 47, ll. 200–210.

[135]Bordiugov, pp. 173–179.

[136]Lapitskaia, p. 185.

[137]Bordiugov, pp. 173–174. A 1929 study at one Moscow orphanage claimed that 28.4 percent of the children there were not orphans at all but had simply run away from home.

For their part, parents expressed doubts about their ability to raise children according to traditional morals and norms of behavior, given the competing culture taught in the schools.[138] Of course the majority of peasant in-migrants did not face these problems during the 1930s, because they did not yet have school-age children. But as during all periods of rapid social change, especially among immigrant families, generational conflicts flared.

Both former peasants and their children had to confront urban social hierarchies. Measures of social status emerged as a major difference between rural and urban cultures. Status in the village depended on personal evaluations of individuals and their families—their character, their reputation, their influence in the village. In the city occupation and educational level became measures of both achievement and social standing.[139] Furthermore, in the more impersonal environment of the city, outward symbols of wealth—clothes, jewelry, trinkets—assumed greater prominence.

To some extent, peasant in-migrants were insulated from the urban social hierarchy by their close-knit communities on the outskirts of the city. In these communities everyone was poor, so there was no one to envy or resent. But Moscow's social hierarchy could not be ignored. In their jobs and in their daily lives, former peasants had to confront the condescension and scorn of officials and established workers. Urbanites ridiculed their accents, haircuts, and clothes, called them "dirty," made fun of their shoes.[140] As newcomers struggling for acceptance, many former peasants found such scorn painful and pined for the symbols of urban status.

Material goods, which had attracted many peasants to urban life in the first place, were among the most apparent status symbols. The new arrivals often emulated the kitschy aspects of popular urban culture. They dressed in the latest urban fashions and decorated their rooms with figurines and paper lanterns.[141] The ostentatious elements of urban culture most readily attracted their attention. Ownership

[138]Ibid., pp. 181–184.

[139]See V. N. P. Sinha and Md. Ataullah, *Migration: An Interdisciplinary Approach* (Delhi, 1987), pp. 148–149.

[140]Interview with Polina Ivanovna Kazharina for the documentary film *Piatachok*, 1989.

[141]Khlevniuk, "Izmenenie," p. 128.

of urban wares allowed them to claim membership in urban society even while they retained their traditional allegiances and values.[142]

Urban clothing served as perhaps the most important symbol of membership in urban society. Even as former peasants snatched at city fashions (a difficult task given the clothing shortage), peasant culture continued to influence their dress habits. When they gathered with fellow villagers in Moscow parks, some women wore peasant-style skirts and white kerchiefs on their heads—traditional holiday garb in the village. Other women wore urban dresses—brightly colored ones that echoed the colors customarily worn at festive gatherings in the village. Men generally wore urban clothing, though they too often appeared in the embroidered shirts and belts distinctive to their native villages.[143]

Urban and rural elements were so thoroughly intermixed in the subculture of former peasants that it would be impossible to disentangle them entirely. New cultural symbols (such as Lenin portraits) were imbued with traditional meanings, while traditional cultural forms received new contents and assessed new urban phenomena. The new arrivals composed traditional peasant songs about urban life and factory work. Some songs spoke of taverns in Moscow, dealings with factory foremen, and the tragedy of industrial accidents.[144] Other songs articulated peasant in-migrants' dissatisfaction with the low living standards of the 1930s. One song in the traditional peasant form (*chastushka*) complained about food shortages:[145]

Scientists came to us	Priezzhali k nam uchenye
To make us false teeth,	Chtoby zuby nam vstavliat',
But why have false teeth made	A zachem nam ikh vstavliat'
If there is nothing to eat?	Esli nechego zhevat'?

---

[142]"Lacking more deeply rooted social integration, the city dwellers seek to conform to their neighbors' way of life by possessing certain articles or adopting certain patterns of behavior as outward signs of their membership of urban society": Kerblay, p. 61.

[143]Degteva, "Fenomen bytovoi kul'tury," p. 59.

[144]Iurii M. Sokolov, *Russian Folklore*, Catherine Ruth Smith, trans. (New York, 1950), pp. 578, 593, 598. Peasant songs composed by first-generation workers before the Revolution were still sung in the Soviet period.

[145]The following songs were taught me by Valentina Andreevna Melnikova in an interview at Izmailovskii Park, Moscow, July 25, 1992.

A worker in the wire shop of the Hammer and Sickle plant wears a traditional embroidered peasant shirt. Courtesy TsGAOR.

Another song ridiculed both Soviet bureaucrats' penchant for meetings and the lack of clothing in stores:

They've met at high levels	Na verkhakh oni zasedali
And they've continued to meet.	I prozasedalisia.
Meanwhile the stores became empty	Magaziny opusteli
And we were left without pants.	Bez shtanov ostalisia.

A great many songs complained about city life.[146] Thus songs served more than an aesthetic function: they permitted former peasants to articulate their views of urban life, to assess conditions in Moscow by their own belief system, and to reaffirm their values among fellow villagers who shared their worldview.

Because all experience is construed experience, the cultural forms and symbols used to understand and order human interaction assume enormous importance.[147] Had new city dwellers relied solely on official Soviet language and ideology to make sense of their new surroundings, they might have accepted their low living standard as "the heroic sacrifice of the Soviet working class." Instead they used peasant cultural forms to question and ridicule government policies, and to secure their own sense of identity and self-interest in the urban world they confronted.

Former peasants demonstrated considerable flexibility as they incorporated new elements into their traditional worldview and cultural practices.[148] The new symbols they adopted tended to be the more superficial and ostentatious features of urban culture. At the same time they continued to rely on village culture and networks to organize their lives in the city. Peasants brought their traditional social norms and values with them to Moscow, and they conceptualized, categorized, and attributed meaning to their new environment through their preexisting belief system.

The peasant culture that survived in the city was not static or tied to the past. All cultures evolve. The elements that change are

[146]Degteva, "Piatachok," p. 22.

[147]See Geertz, p. 405.

[148]Historical and sociological studies of peasant migrants to cities in other countries have found a similar adaptability of culture and behavior. See Emilio Willems, "Peasantry and City: Cultural Persistence and Change in European Perspective," *American Anthropologist* 72 (1970), pp. 522–539; Perlman, pp. 142–145.

those that are no longer useful or that yield to new influences and challenges. The peasants who settled in Moscow kept those cultural traditions that served their economic, social, and psychological needs and discarded those that did not. Unfortunately for Soviet officials, the impersonality and arduousness of life in Moscow during the 1930s only reinforced former peasants' village and kinship bonds, and did little to replace those allegiances with loyalty to the Soviet state.

7

Social Identity
and Labor Politics

When Aleksandr Maksimovich began work in a Moscow factory, he still looked and felt like a peasant from Riazan province—a fact that established workers were not about to let him forget. Fifty-four years later (after a forty-year career in a steel factory), he does not hesitate to call himself a (retired) worker. He cannot recall a point at which he ceased to think of himself as a peasant and began to identify himself as a worker. Throughout his life he continued to visit relatives in his native village, but at the same time he grew accustomed to life in Moscow and work at the factory. When he is asked if he felt like a worker in a working-class state during the 1930s, he shrugs. "The Party elite [nomenklatura] controlled everything. We workers just worked."[1]

According to official ideology, the Soviet Union was a working-class state, ruled by the Communist Party in the name and interests of the country's workers. The millions of peasants who joined the industrial workforce during the 1930s had to come to terms with this state and with their place in it. Their political behavior, and the social identity underlying that behavior, hinged upon their acceptance of the Soviet state as one ruled in their name. In an effort to gain new workers' support, Soviet authorities recruited them into political organizations and inundated them with political propaganda. The

[1] Interview with Aleksandr Maksimovich Korneev at the Hammer and Sickle plant, Moscow, April 24, 1989. Aleksandr Maksimovich's remark echoes the antiestablishment criticism prevalent in the late 1980s, reminding us that memory is always colored by intervening events and ideas.

effectiveness of these efforts, however, was questionable. Though Soviet workers rarely engaged in collective protest, their behavior must be considered in connection with material incentives offered quiescent workers and repression of any labor unrest.

Party, Komsomol, and Trade Union Membership

Because political and administrative power in the Soviet Union was concentrated in the Communist Party, membership stood as a prerequisite for effective input into the political system. During the 1920s, Soviet leaders became concerned about the large number of white-collar people in the Party. Since this was presumably a working-class state, they set out to recruit more workers into the Party—a policy continued during the 1930s. It is important to examine whether peasant in-migrants were among those workers who joined the Party (and other official organizations), and whether their participation translated into political support for the Soviet system.

By October 1930, 53.8 percent of Moscow Party members were workers.[2] Statistics on social origin, however, reveal that workers who entered the Party during the First Five-Year Plan were overwhelmingly of working-class origin.[3] Even if these statistics are somewhat inflated (working-class origin counted as an asset for Party membership, and some people may have misrepresented their origin to gain entry), such indices as skill level and the number of years worked confirm that very few new workers of peasant origin joined the Party from 1929 to 1932.[4] Party recruiters gave preference to hereditary workers, whom they considered more proletarian, and hence more politically conscious.[5]

Heavy recruitment into the Moscow Party organization ceased in 1933 and resumed from 1936 to 1939, as the Party sought to replace the thousands of members expelled, arrested, or executed during the purges.[6] The majority of workers recruited at Moscow factories dur-

---

[2]Merridale, p. 130. More than half of all Party members at some Moscow factories in 1934 had joined during the First Five-Year Plan: Lapitskaia, pp. 145–146.

[3]*Sputnik kommunista* 1930 no. 1, p. 12; Kornakovskii, p. 295.

[4]Starodubtsev, pp. 78–79; Filatov, p. 31; *Rabochii klass—vedushchaia sila*, p. 207.

[5]TsPA f. 17, op. 114, d. 846, l. 15.

[6]Merridale, pp. 124–130.

ing the late 1930s once again were of working-class origin, though a meaningful fraction were of peasant origin. The Party favored Stakhanovites and other former peasants who had distinguished themselves both at work and in technical studies.[7] The great majority of workers of peasant origin, however, were not readily accepted into the Party. Nor is it clear that many of them wished to join it. Party membership entailed considerable extra work and responsibility, and benefited only those who hoped to advance in the Party apparatus.

Komsomol membership, while it did not encompass the power or privilege of Party membership, was a means to participate in an official political organization. The Komsomol attempted to recruit all youth, regardless of social origin, and it served as a vehicle for the political education of young workers. Early in the First Five-Year Plan, Komsomol recruiters experienced little success. Of the several hundred young workers who started work at the Stalin automobile plant in January 1931, for example, only twelve joined the Komsomol.[8] In the second half of 1931 a recruiting drive spurred a sharp rise in Komsomol membership.[9] By the end of 1932, 70 percent of all young workers were members, and at many large Moscow factories this figure exceeded 90 percent.[10]

Initially the drive to expand Komsomol membership succeeded primarily among young workers of urban origin. But Komsomol recruiters gradually persuaded young workers of peasant origin to join, and these were the people who accounted for the growth in Komsomol membership by the end of the First Five-Year Plan.[11] Did this rise in membership signal former peasants' enthusiasm and support

[7]MPA f. 432, op. 1, d. 151, ll. 72–77; d. 178, l. 174; d. 191, ll. 96–97; d. 191a, l. 33; d. 216, l. 2.

[8]*Istoriia Moskovskogo avtozavoda*, p. 188. Of the several thousand construction workers at the site of the future ball bearing factory in May 1931, only seventy-eight belonged to the Komsomol: *Ocherki istorii . . . VLKSM*, p. 239.

[9]*Martenovka*, July 18, 1931, p. 1. See also *Trud*, July 1, 1931, p. 2.

[10]T. Osipova, "Komsomol Moskvy v gody pervoi piatiletki," *Molodoi kommunist* 1958 no. 4, p. 91. Despite low recruitment totals in the early months of 1931, some 5,000 young workers joined the Komsomol at the Stalin automobile plant in the course of the year: *Istoriia Moskovskogo avtozavoda*, p. 188.

[11]MPA f. 635, op. 1, d. 10, ll. 27, 31. Membership continued to rise during the Second Five-Year Plan and surpassed 150,000 in Moscow alone by the beginning of 1936, an increase of almost 60,000 over the 1932 figure: *Materialy k otchetu Moskovskogo oblastnogo i gorodskogo komitetov VLKSM 4-i oblastnoi i 3-i gorodskoi konferentsiiam VLKSM* (Moscow, 1936), pp. 7–8, 87.

for official organizations? We must consider a range of factors that induced these new workers to join the Komsomol. Camaraderie with Komsomol members may have persuaded some of them to join. One Kuibyshev electronics factory worker recalled that "Komsomol members gave a friendly welcome to the young people who came to work at the factory. This guaranteed the rapid growth of their ranks, since each new worker was eager to join the friendly Komsomol family." [12] Another recruit recalled that Komsomol members at his construction site befriended him and took him to their meetings, and yet another, an orphan, claimed that the Komsomol became his "new family." [13]

The Komsomol, however, was but one of several options for young newcomers who sought a peer group. Fellow villagers, artels, and production communes all provided them with unofficial support networks. A journalist complained that new workers' tendency to congregate with their fellow villagers hindered the Komsomol's efforts to win their membership. [14] At the Hammer and Sickle plant, even at the height of the recruiting drive in the summer of 1931, former peasants in shops with high concentrations of fellow villagers refused to join the Komsomol. [15]

Of the young workers who did join the Komsomol, a sizable majority felt no strong allegiance to it. Many found it easier to join than to resist the recruiters simply because, as one former worker put it, they "kept pestering" nonmembers. [16] Others joined to receive the priority Komsomol members enjoyed in admission to educational institutions. That young workers eventually joined the Komsomol reveals more about their socialization into the Soviet system—a process whereby they learned new rules of political conduct that allowed them to function and pursue personal gain—than about their commitment to Komsomol ideals.

Trade union membership provides a third measure of participation in official organizations. In theory the trade unions represented the workers' interests. With the defeat of independent trade union-

[12]N. K. Laman and Ku. I. Krechetnikova, *Istoriia zavoda "Elektrozavod"* (Moscow, 1967), pp. 200–201.

[13]*Govoriat stroiteli sotsializma*, p. 53; *Ocherki istorii . . . VLKSM*, pp. 240–241. See also TsGAOR f. 5475, op. 14, d. 62, l. 15.

[14]*Komsomol'skaia Pravda*, May 20, 1932, p. 3.

[15]*Martenovka*, July 18, 1931, p. 1.

[16]Harvard Project no. 20.

ism and workers' control in 1921, however, unions lost most of their autonomy.[17] For a time they exercised some authority by reserving factory jobs for their members.[18] But after the defeat of the Right Opposition and the removal of Mikhail Tomskii as head of the national trade union council in 1929, unions became completely subordinate to the tasks of production and ceased to defend workers' interests. With no function to fulfill, trade unions plunged into a state of crisis. By 1933 they had even lost their input into the determination of wages and norms, as complete authority in this sphere came to rest with management.[19]

The number of trade union members as a percentage of all workers declined substantially during the First Five-Year Plan, from 84.8 percent in 1929 to 72.6 percent in 1931.[20] Reports on the decline singled out the refusal of recently arrived workers to join the unions.[21] Workers of peasant origin saw no need for membership in a union that offered no benefits or bargaining leverage. Wages were negotiated individually or, more advantageously, through artel elders. Even established workers ceased to pay much heed to union activities after 1929. Fewer than 200 of the 1,500 workers at one Moscow textile mill attended union meetings called in 1931.[22]

Trade unions eventually boosted their membership and regained a role among Soviet workers only by finding a new function to fulfill: the dispensing of social services and perks, ranging from complimentary theater tickets to visits to rest homes (*sanatorii*). In April 1932 the trade union congress resolved that union organs were to pay attention to workers' needs and demands, including those related to everyday life.[23] When the Commissariat of Labor ceased to exist in June 1933, the trade unions inherited its social security functions and

---

[17]Hatch, "Labor and Politics," pp. 151–153.

[18]Sheila Fitzpatrick, "Klassy i problemy klassovoi prinadlezhnosti v Sovetskoi Rossii 20-kh godov," *Voprosy istorii* 1990 no. 8, p. 21.

[19]Kuromiya, *Stalin's Industrial Revolution,* pp. 46, 300–301.

[20]TsGAOR f. 5451, op. 15, d. 56, l. 1. The percentage of Moscow construction workers who belonged to the union fell to 55.8 by 1932: Poletaev, *Na Putiakh,* p. 54; TsPA f. 17, op. 114, d. 255, l. 22.

[21]The ninth national trade union congress, in April 1932, resolved that recruiting efforts be focused on "young workers from the village" in particular: Filatov, p. 39; Nikol'skii and Vanshtein, p. 48.

[22]*Rabochaia Moskva,* October 27, 1931, p. 2.

[23]*Profsoiuzy SSSR,* vol. 2, p. 671.

also assumed responsibility for industrial safety regulations and free health care.[24]

As long as trade union services in no way impeded production, union functionaries were free to grant workers' requests. They found places for workers in technical institutes and allotted them vacations. They provided emergency financial assistance when a worker was hospitalized or was unable to pay for the funeral of a family member. Workers who lost a ration card or found themselves without housing could appeal to the trade union office and expect officials to intercede on their behalf.[25] Once trade unions began to provide incentives for membership, most new workers quickly joined. By July 1, 1936, 83.5 percent of all Soviet workers (87.9 percent in Moscow oblast) belonged to a trade union.[26]

The social service role of trade unions still left workers without an institutional basis to organize, bargain collectively, or articulate their interests. According to one former Soviet worker, established workers "felt that they had been cheated" by the weakening of the trade unions.

> You know, after the Revolution, the old workers could fight even the Party and management through their trade unions. Later on, the power of the trade union was taken away from them. It was obvious they felt deeply hurt and they still tried to strengthen the trade union. We younger workers, we saw there was no use in it, so we jumped into *blat* [unofficial influence] deals.[27]

Newly arrived workers, having no experience of union bargaining power, joined only for the social welfare benefits. Union membership did not signify their conviction that trade unions represented or articulated their interests.

The character of trade unions reflected more broadly Soviet authorities' paternalism toward workers. Especially because so many workers had recently arrived from the village, Party leaders viewed

[24]*Istoriia Moskovskogo avtozavoda*, p. 192; *Istoriia Moskvy: Kratkii*, p. 284.

[25]Zawodny, "Twenty-six Interviews," Hoover Institution archives, I/2, I/9, II/13, II/18; Tverdokhleb, "Material'noe blagosostoianie," p. 484; TsGAMO f. 747, op. 1, d. 111, l. 37.

[26]*Statisticheskii spravochnik VTsSPS*, pp. 3, 22.

[27]Zawodny, "Twenty-six Interviews," Hoover Institution archives, I/3.

them as unprepared to participate in politics. (The Bolsheviks' distrust of popular initiative, especially among peasants, dated from at least the Civil War.) To Party leaders, steeped in Marxism's teleology and more generally in the Russian intelligentsia's condescension toward the peasant masses, peasants who had just joined the workforce lacked political consciousness. In the words of one Komsomol official, the peasants who migrated to Soviet cities were "rather backward people who thought first of all about higher wages."[28] Authorities refused to acknowledge higher wages as a legitimate interest and claimed to know the workers' interests better than they did themselves. This mentality, in conjunction with the extreme authoritarian tendencies already exhibited by Party leaders, led to rigid bureaucratic control of trade unions and a ban on workers' independent political organizations.

While the paternalism of Soviet officialdom denied workers a political voice, it did offer them many benefits: full employment, free education and health care, meager but inexpensive rations, and a guaranteed minimum level of existence. The same paternalism that led Soviet authorities to deny workers a voice led them to care for the welfare of workers, particularly because they viewed most of them as ill prepared for urban life and in need of state assistance.

Actually officials' condescension toward newly urbanized workers was inappropriate. Peasant in-migrants were capable of identifying and pursuing their interests, which often did not correspond to state goals. Officials' misplaced paternalism nevertheless served as a basis for government policies. Aside from the relatively small percentage recruited into the Communist Party, workers were denied any institutionalized role in politics. At the same time they received priority for government benefits over other social groups. Even as they maintained their own informal aid networks, new workers readily accepted state assistance, and over time came to expect it.[29]

[28]*Govoriat stroiteli sotsializma*, p. 193.

[29]Former Soviet workers interviewed in emigration despised the Soviet government but favored its social welfare policies. See Alex Inkeles and Raymond A. Bauer, *The Soviet Citizen* (New York, 1968), pp. 234–238.

Political Socialization

It would be wrong to assume that the influx of peasants somehow depoliticized the working class. Just as former peasants did not become uprooted or atomized, they were not apolitical or powerless. They proved particularly vocal in their protests against collectivization. In the spring of 1930, workers of peasant origin at trade union meetings at several Moscow construction sites asked such questions as "What has become of the kulaks?" and "Who made mistakes in collectivization—Comrade Stalin or the Party?"[30] At one site a group of new workers from the village of L'govo complained about abuses connected with collectivization, and one asked, "Do peasants join collective farms voluntarily or forcibly?" (For asking the question he was arrested.)[31] As late as 1932 former peasants enrolled at a Moscow construction school complained that "in the collective farm they forcibly work people to death." Officials held a special hearing to determine their punishment and expelled two of them.[32]

An anonymous poem written in 1931 condemned Soviet leaders for the arrest and deportation of peasants during collectivization:

You have shot many people,	Vy mnogo liudei rasstreliali,
You have let many rot in prison,	Vy mnogo sgnoili v tiur'me,
You have sent many into exile	Vy mnogikh na ssylku soslali
To certain death in the forest.	Na vernuiu gibel' v taige.[33]

The government's attempts to ban criticism of its policies, then, did not totally stifle expression of the enormous resentment aroused by collectivization.

Workers of peasant origin demonstrated their political awareness of other issues as well. One challenged the legitimacy of the industrialization drive: "Did Lenin know about the Five-Year Plan, and did he approve of this course?"[34] Another complained that "German construction workers earn twenty-five rubles a day but our workers earn

---

[30]TsGAMO f. 4867, op. 1, d. 156, ll. 11–13; TsGAOR f. 5475, op. 13, d. 426, ll. 53–54.
[31]TsGAOR f. 5475, op. 13, d. 276, l. 53.
[32]TsGAORgM f. 5301, op. 4, d. 66, l. 70.
[33]*Neizvestnaia Rossiia*, p. 225.
[34]TsGAMO f. 4867, op. 1, d. 156, ll. 11–13.

only three to four rubles."[35] Another worker wrote a letter to Stalin in which she criticized both local officials and Party leaders ("who live in palaces") for neglecting the needs of workers.[36] Some new workers complained in more explicitly political terms: "The Party and government have deceived the workers"; "The Central Committee and Stalin do not keep their word and will lead the country to ruin." One worker called for the murder of Stalin, and when Sergei Kirov was assassinated, several workers publicly wished that Stalin had been killed as well.[37]

Over time, however, new workers learned not to make such overtly political statements. By the Second and Third Five-Year plans, they continued to voice their complaints at factory and trade union meetings, but only in apolitical terms. When asked to join the Izotovite (exemplary worker) movement in 1933, several Moscow workers responded, "It's possible to work better, but for this we need to eat well. Our rations are poor. Give us more bread and meat . . . and we will work like Izotovites."[38] When officials conducting an atheist propaganda campaign questioned construction workers about religion, one former peasant replied, "Improve conditions on the construction site . . . and then we'll stop believing in God." Another answered, "I haven't forgotten God, because I'm paid two and a half rubles a day. If I were paid five rubles a day, then I'd forget God."[39] An American observer of a workers' meeting at a Moscow plant noticed that workers did not hesitate to make suggestions about the production process and even criticized the plant director, but when it came to general Party directives and foreign policy, they unanimously passed previously prepared resolutions without discussion. "The Soviet workers had learned what was their business and what was not."[40]

Through political socialization, new workers learned which matters could be criticized (and the terms suitable for criticism) and which were not to be discussed. Three components of the socialization process—political propaganda, material incentives, and shame

[35]TsGAOR f. 5475, op. 13, d. 426, ll. 53–54.

[36]TsPA f. 85, op. 29, d. 755, l. 3.

[37]TsGAORgM f. 5301, op. 4, d. 66, ll. 75–76; TsGAOR f. 5475, op. 13, d. 426, l. 114; Khlevniuk, *1937-i*, pp. 52–53. See also *Sokol'niki*, V. Boborykin, comp. (Moscow, 1967), p. 160; *Ogonek* 1989 no. 23, pp. 10–11.

[38]Gudov, *Sud'ba rabochego*, p. 18.

[39]*Kul'turnaia revoliutsiia*, November 30, 1929, pp. 26–27.

[40]John Scott, p. 264.

—schooled them in behavior acceptable to Soviet authorities and determined whether their quiescence reflected genuine acceptance of Soviet ideals or merely necessity and expediency.

Party and trade union officials considered political propaganda to be of the utmost importance for new workers. They assumed that political enlightenment of "backward" workers would lead them to become both more efficient in the factory and more loyal to the Soviet government. The rapid influx of former peasants into the workforce incited ever more urgent calls for political work among "the mass of politically undeveloped youth who just arrived from the village."[41] The Party cell at one Moscow factory declared the greatest task of the Party and the trade union to be "the reeducation of newly arrived workers in the spirit of those who will fulfill the tasks of the proletariat."[42]

Throughout the 1930s, in factories, on construction sites, and among transport workers, a proliferation of newspapers, political agitators, and discussion circles strove to indoctrinate new workers and secure their political support.[43] Political propaganda, however, was no more effective than cultural education. Countless Party reports throughout the 1930s complained that political work was inadequate or existed only on paper.[44] At one factory many workers signed up for a political education circle but half of them never attended it.[45] Reports cited a paucity of political work especially among transport and handicraft workers, but among factory workers as well.[46] In other cases, political education continued but at "a very low level."[47] Political propaganda materials proved too difficult for newly literate workers, so theoretical readings were jettisoned for more dogmatic texts.[48] Nor is it clear that Party propagandists really wished to stimulate genuine political consciousness and debate among workers.

[41]MPA f. 635, op. 1, d. 69, l. 16.
[42]MPA f. 432, op. 1, d. 50, l. 169.
[43]*Istoriia Moskovskogo avtozavoda*, p. 197; Poletaev, *Na putiakh*, p. 59; *Govoriat stroiteli sotsializma*, p. 280; *Vse dorogi*, p. 135.
[44]MPA f. 3, op. 17, d. 7, l. 64; f. 429, op. 1, d. 109, l. 66; f. 432, op. 1, d. 104, l. 211; f. 433, op. 1, d. 43, l. 1.
[45]MPA f. 667, op. 1, d. 4, l. 44.
[46]TsGAORgM f. 1289, op. 1, d. 91, l. 111; d. 493, l. 13; *Za Bol'shevistskie tempy*, September 14, 1931, p. 2.
[47]*Materialy k otchetu . . . VLKSM*, pp. 117–120.
[48]Merridale, p. 150.

Foundry workers in a political education circle at the Hammer and Sickle plant, 1932. Courtesy TsGAOR.

Political discussions were pre-scripted and catechism-like. Participants memorized and echoed politically acceptable answers without contemplating or internalizing their meanings.[49]

Because workers would not attend political meetings after work, Party propagandists held sessions during the workday, and tension inevitably arose between propagandists and factory directors. Political discussions took workers out of the shops for several hours every week, to the consternation of plan-conscious managers. One article complained that Komsomol meetings to educate young workers were held virtually every day and greatly interfered with factory production.[50]

Yet even regular political meetings did not necessarily result in an informed and politically loyal working class. The same article went on to note that in spite of the daily Komsomol meetings, workers knew little about politics. They could not even answer basic questions about topics just discussed at a meeting and thoroughly covered by the press. A report at the Moscow Party conference in 1934 confirmed that political work in factories had proved largely unsuccessful. Agitators who addressed brigades often saw workers reading during meetings rather than listening. Some workers heckled Party agitators: "We've listened to you enough already." To gain the audience's attention, agitators had to begin meetings by answering questions, and thereby allowed workers to set the agenda for discussion.[51]

More significant than propaganda in the process of political socialization were the material rewards held out to politically acquiescent workers. The designation of the Soviet Union as a working-class state held more than simply rhetorical significance. In the 1930s, workers in the Soviet Union received larger rations than any other social group.[52] They had priority in housing, extensive educational opportunities, and ample prospects for promotion. New workers who never challenged the Party's hegemony or questioned its policies became entitled to all of these benefits.

[49]See Wood, pp. 616–620.

[50]*Komsomol'skaia pravda*, May 20, 1932, p. 3. Propagandists, for their part, complained that storming to meet production targets prevented them from conducting political work: MPA f. 432, op. 1, d. 101, l. 107.

[51]*Ob''edinennaia . . . konferentsiia VKP(b)*, p. 109.

[52]Party and bureaucratic elites were also in the highest ration category, and through special stores they actually received a far better selection of food than did workers; see Osokina, pp. 63–64.

New workers also discovered that they could use Soviet ideology to their advantage. They could, for example, appeal for better food or housing in the name of the working class. One group of workers wrote to Mikhail I. Kalinin, chair of the National Executive Committee, and vowed to fulfill the Second Five-Year Plan, but added that they would be able to do so only if their living standard was improved.[53] Another strategy was to declare oneself a shock worker or Stakhanovite and collect bonuses. If a foreman raised the norm excessively, workers could denounce him as interfering with shock work or Stakhanovism. In other conflicts with management, workers could appeal to the Workers' Control Commission (composed of representatives of the factory administration, trade union, and workforce) for retribution.[54] Once new workers learned the terms of official Soviet discourse, ideology became a weapon they could use against management.

Another benefit offered to politically acquiescent workers was the opportunity for education and promotion into the ranks of management. Promotions during the First Five-Year Plan went primarily to workers with several years' experience. Large numbers of young urban workers enrolled in factory training schools and technical institutes, and later became engineers and bureaucrats. Many established workers received promotions to lower-level managerial posts even without additional education.[55] By the Second Five-Year Plan a limited number of former peasants who had accumulated some experience (and had learned to speak and act like "politically conscious" workers) also began to rise in the industrial hierarchy. A few reached the rank of foreman.[56]

Even workers who did not advance in the industrial hierarchy benefited from Soviet employment policies. The industrialization drive and planned economy ensured a job to all manual workers. Workers who were fired could appeal to the Party or the union, and in most cases were reinstated.[57] Reinstatement of indolent workers detracted from industrial efficiency, but this was the price Soviet leaders paid

[53]TsPA f. 78, op. 6, d. 526, l. 40.

[54]MPA f. 432, op. 1, d. 50, l. 33; Zawodny, "Twenty-six Interviews," Hoover Institution archives, II/16, II/17.

[55]TsGANKh f. 7622, op. 1, d. 251, ll. 3–5; Aleksandrova, "Rabochii klass Moskvy," pp. 103–104; *Industrializatsiia SSSR*, vol. 2, p. 530. See also Andrle, pp. 34–35.

[56]TsGANKh f. 7622, op. 1, d. 1948, l. 38.

[57]TsPA f. 17, op. 114, d. 348, ll. 1–11; TsGAMO f. 747, op. 1, d. 111, l. 37.

to win workers' support. For their part, workers found less need for overt protest or antagonistic relations with authorities when they could obtain concessions simply by asking for them. In essence, they traded political acquiescence for job security and material benefits.

If concrete benefits did not win the professed allegiance of new workers, then penalties and shame obliged them to conform, at least outwardly. Particularly because the Soviet Union was a "working-class state," any worker who did not actively contribute to the five-year plans could be denounced, deprived of privileges, and even sentenced to a labor camp. A slogan of the 1930s proclaimed, "Whoever does not work does not eat."[58] Work became not only a right but an obligation—everyone had the right to a job but no one was allowed not to work. Failure to do "socially useful work" could lead to arrest and forced labor.[59]

As part of the campaign to ensure workers' commitment to the industrialization drive, officials began to shame workers who did not fulfill their quotas. Enterprises established "red bulletin boards" to honor the best workers and "black bulletin boards" where the names of delinquent workers were displayed. Workers guilty of violating labor discipline had their names announced at workers' meetings.[60] At the Kirov Dinamo plant, "lazy workers" who failed to fulfill their norms received their pay at a special window, where their photographs were taken for publication under a derogatory heading in the factory newspaper.[61] Parades held to encourage industrial achievement displayed the names of enterprises that failed to fulfill the plan.[62]

Another means of punishing poor workers consisted of "comradely courts" in the factories. Workers accused of absenteeism, lax labor discipline, hooliganism, or theft had to appear before a judge (an elected peer) to answer questions about their activities. Workers found guilty of some violation could have their rations reduced, be expelled from the union, or be fired altogether.[63] Comradely courts virtually never fired anyone, but the sharp reduction of rations and public

---

[58]See, for example, *Martenovka*, November 14, 1932, p. 3.
[59]Kotkin, pp. 531–532.
[60]TsGAOR f. 5469, op. 15, d. 10, l. 144; *Delo chesti*, p. 105; *Nezabyvaemye*, p. 92.
[61]*Dinamo v gody stroitel'stva sotsializma*, p. 185.
[62]Lane, p. 176.
[63]TsGAOR f. 5469, op. 15, d. 10, l. 155; Livshits, p. 260; Records of the Department of State, National Archives, roll 37; Newsholme and Kingsbury, pp. 104–105.

chastisement in themselves were severe punishment for delinquent workers.[64] Shame and penalties, then, acted alongside incentives to induce workers' outward compliance with Party policies.

The Soviet government did have the power to forge outward acquiescence among new workers; both the coercion and incentives behind this power were considerable. The government both wielded unlimited authority to punish anyone who openly opposed it and determined the paths and behavior people had to follow to achieve wealth and status in the Soviet system. But outward compliance with official norms should not be interpreted as belief and commitment. Evidence does not indicate that workers internalized official slogans or dedicated their lives to building socialism. Party and union functionaries had to orchestrate "mass worker enthusiasm" for production drives by pressuring workers to sign declarations of their "spontaneous support."[65] It was largely the incentives and coercion that enabled Soviet authorities to impose official language and standards of public behavior. Propaganda did little to establish genuine belief in Soviet ideology among first-generation workers, in part because peasant in-migrants had means to resist it.

New workers privately mocked Soviet institutions and subverted the meanings of official discourse. To ridicule the highest government body (Sovnarkom), a group of workers formed a "Small Council of People's Commissars" (Malyi Sovnarkom), whose purpose was to supply its members with vodka. Some other workers of peasant origin formed the "Youth Society for the Criticism of Soviet Power" (mimicking the numerous official societies for criticism of bureaucratism, industrial inefficiency, and so forth) as an unofficial means to denounce collectivization. An underground organization called Black Half-Moon (Chernyi Polumesiats) conducted political agitation against Party policies.[66] Other workers jointly criticized the privileges of Party members and complained about inequality.[67] Because mem-

---

[64]*Industrializatsiia SSSR*, vol. 3, pp. 522–523. For more on comradely courts, see I. S. Dvornikov, *Tovarishcheskie sudy i ikh rol' v bor'be za ukreplenie trudovoi distsipliny* (Moscow, 1956).

[65]Shitts, p. 311.

[66]MPA f. 635, op. 1, d. 41, ll. 16–17.

[67]B. Ratner, ed., *Istoriia Moskovskogo instrumental'nogo zavoda* (Moscow, 1934), pp. 160–161.

bers of illegal organizations risked arrest, the number of people who joined them undoubtedly was small.

Much more common was informal criticism of the government. Some peasant in-migrants composed peasant-style songs that ridiculed Party leaders by describing them without their clothes on.[68] Anti-Soviet jokes and anecdotes circulated, despite the risk of imprisonment if one were caught telling them. In one such anecdote, a person about to be deported to the far-north labor camp of Solovki asks what country rules this distant region. When told that Soviet power reaches even there, the deportee inquires, "Would it be possible to be sent somewhere even farther?"[69] While Soviet authorities sought to impose an official discourse, in which "conscious workers" were self-sacrificing and anyone opposed to Soviet policies was a "class enemy," former peasants parodied and subverted this discourse. Official language never became incontestable; its meanings were never absolute.[70]

Soviet authorities could restrict workers' actions in public, but they could not control workers' words or thoughts. Political socialization consisted not in making workers believe in the Party's goals but rather in securing their outward compliance—in creating the appearance of a politically supportive proletariat. Party leaders demanded public unanimity behind their policies; any open dissent they regarded as treason and dealt with accordingly. But beneath the surface and outside the public arena, workers continued to contest official discourse, subvert intended meanings, and pursue their own interests.

Strikes, Repression, and Labor Turnover

Despite official attempts at political socialization, some peasant in-migrants did engage in strike activity, at least during the early 1930s. Construction workers in particular held wildcat strikes, in part because their living standard was generally lower than industrial workers'. A number of strikes, some involving several hundred

---

[68]*Chastushki*, F. M. Selivanova, comp. (Moscow, 1990), p. 153.
[69]*Desiat' tysiach anekdotov*, vyp. 1 (Moscow, 1991), p. 6.
[70]See Mikhail M. Bakhtin, *The Dialogic Imagination*, Caryl Emerson and Michael Holquist, trans. (Austin, 1981), p. 273.

workers, occurred in Moscow's Krasno-Presnenskii district in 1930. Strikers' demands there focused almost entirely on wages. Construction workers in other parts of the city struck to demand reductions of work norms as well.[71] Factory workers in several Moscow plants also protested work norms by both strikes and petitions.[72] Disputes over wages and norms occasionally led to violence. One worker of peasant origin organized a work stoppage, and when the dispute escalated, he beat and killed his foreman.[73]

Food shortages also precipitated unrest and strikes. When authorities failed to provide basic necessities, workers (whose personal stockpiles were limited or nonexistent) proved quick to protest. During the First Five-Year Plan, workers wrote asking that Party leaders "save us from starvation."[74] In 1932 and 1933, when food shortages were particularly severe, strikes broke out across the country.[75] Soviet officials arrested strikers, but in most cases they simultaneously improved the food supply for the remaining workers. Strike activity, never as extensive as it had been in the 1920s, diminished during the Second Five-Year Plan.[76]

In view of the sharply falling living standards of the 1930s, more strikes might have been expected. Yet the readiness of authorities to suppress any unrest left workers with a sense that overt protest was futile and dangerous. Party leaders in the 1930s found discord intolerable and were particularly sensitive to labor protest, since it directly threatened their legitimacy as leaders of a "working-class state." Workers who did engage in strike activity met with swift retribution. In virtually all cases of overt labor protest, authorities arrested the organizers and participants and sentenced them to a labor camp.[77]

In the face of coercive measures, workers of peasant origin naturally avoided confrontation with Soviet officials. They had brought with them from the countryside an attitude of suspicion and circumspection in dealings with authorities. For centuries Russian peasants had defered to authorities while passively resisting their demands,

[71]TsGAOR f. 5475, op. 13, d. 276, l. 9; d. 426, ll. 76, 96.
[72]MPA f. 635, op. 1, d. 10, l. 33.
[73]*Sudebnaia praktika RSFSR* 1931 no. 3, p. 19.
[74]Osokina, p. 42.
[75]Khlevniuk, *1937-i*, pp. 10–13.
[76]For more on strike activity, see Filtzer, pp. 81–85.
[77]TsGAOR f. 5475, op. 13, d. 276, ll. 36, 105; d. 426, l. 76; Kravchenko, p. 80.

and the experience of collectivization reinforced such caution. Open political activity being unwise, peasant in-migrants followed their age-old strategy of low-profile resistance—foot-dragging and evasion, taught by fellow villagers and reinforced by peasant popular culture.[78] Indeed, in the politically charged atmosphere of the 1930s, first-generation workers were well served by peasant traditions of nonconfrontational resistance and cagey pursuit of their own interests.

The most direct and least dangerous means of pursuing better wages and living conditions was simply to leave one place of employment for another—a practice that resulted in enormous labor turnover. Before the beginning of the First Five-Year Plan, turnover at most major Moscow enterprises registered under 20 percent annually, but in 1929 this figure jumped to over 50 percent.[79] Nationwide turnover continued to climb, surpassing 150 percent in 1930, and remained high for the rest of the decade (approximately 100 percent in 1934 and 90 percent in 1936).[80] Construction, in part because the work was seasonal and transient, experienced labor turnover of up to 300 percent in the early 1930s and of 80 percent as late as 1939.[81]

One fact somewhat mitigated the detrimental effect of high turnover on production. Gosplan statistics showed that three-quarters of industrial workers were relatively stable; most of the turnover was attributable to the other quarter, who changed jobs up to four times in a year.[82] Party leaders and officials singled out former peasants as the ones who could not settle into permanent jobs. Lazar Kaganovich explained that turnover was caused by "the mass of new workers entering the ranks of the proletariat who frequently bring petty-bourgeois attitudes to enterprises."[83] An official commenting on the twenty to thirty jobs that turned over every day at the Hammer and Sickle plant

[78]See James Scott, *Weapons of the Weak: Everyday Forms of Peasant Resistance* (New Haven, 1985), pp. xv–xvii.

[79]TsGAORgM f. 415, op. 3, d. 26, l. 1; *Ekonomicheskoe stroitel'stvo* 1930 no. 9/10, p. 45; Anoshin, pp. 97–98.

[80]Ia. Kats, "Tekuchest' rabochei sily v krupnoi promyshlennosti," *Plan* 1937 no. 9, p. 21; *Industrializatsiia SSSR*, vol. 3, p. 421. Turnover rates in Moscow approximated the national average. See TsGAORgM f. 126, op. 10, d. 47, l. 78.

[81]TsPA f. 17, op. 116, d. 30, l. 82; *Stroitel'stvo Moskvy* 1930 no. 7, p. 5; *Industrializatsiia SSSR*, vol. 3, p. 421.

[82]*Industrializatsiia SSSR*, vol. 3, p. 491; *Voprosy truda* 1930 no. 9, p. 17.

[83]*Voprosy profdvizheniia* 1933 no. 1/2, pp. 26–27.

blamed the "gray mass of peasants" and insufficient political work to instill in them the proper consciousness.[84]

Statistics demonstrated that new workers did account for a substantial portion of the turnover.[85] But they changed jobs out of necessity and self-interest, not out of an inability to adjust to factory work or a lack of "consciousness." New workers quartered in overcrowded, disease-ridden barracks sought jobs at enterprises that offered better housing. Some official reports frankly admitted that new workers left jobs because they lacked adequate housing.[86] Furthermore, because government repression prevented strikes, the best alternative for low-wage workers was to seek employment elsewhere. Given the severe shortage of labor throughout the 1930s, they encountered little difficulty finding new jobs at higher pay.

Facilitating the search for better wages and living conditions were the same village networks and artels that had guided peasants to the city. Artel members continued their tradition of leaving as a group to seek work elsewhere when they were dissatisfied with their pay and working conditions.[87] Over time informal networks expanded and provided workers with new connections to pursue better jobs and wages. Soviet émigrés confirmed that though workers could not overtly protest conditions, they could improve their lot through unofficial influence (*blat*) and with the help of "very cohesive" groups of acquaintances.[88] These methods of implicit bargaining proved not only safer than organized protest but more effective too.

Contrary to the Soviet ideal (workers giving freely of their labor in pursuit of the state's goals), the relationship between officials and workers was fundamentally exploitative. As under industrial capitalism, Soviet officials and managers tried to extract as much labor

[84]Filatov, p. 37.

[85]*Sovetskoe gosudarstvo i pravo* 1933 no. 5, p. 55; TsGANKh f. 7622, op. 1, d. 251, l. 11. See also Vdovin and Drobizhev, p. 219.

[86]Schwarz, pp. 92–93; TsGANKh f. 7622, op. 1, d. 251, l. 50; *Pervyi podshipnikovyi*, p. 38; Kats, pp. 25–26; TsGAMO f. 214, op. 1, d. 182, l. 5.

[87]*Sputnik kommunista* 1930 no. 6, p. 49. Some artels, acting on information gathered by their elders regarding wages and the availability of goods, moved all around the country: Vdovin and Drobizhev, pp. 217–219; *Stroitel'naia promyshlennost'* 1929 no. 4, p. 380.

[88]Zawodny, "Twenty-six Interviews," Hoover Institution archives, I/2, I/3, I/9, II/16. On the similar importance of personal connections among Chinese workers, see Walder, pp. 179–186.

from workers as possible at the lowest cost. Yet other features of Soviet socialism created labor relations much different from those in capitalist countries. As workers in a "working-class state," peasant in-migrants could expect preferred rations, priority in housing, educational opportunities, and other benefits. The other side of the state's paternalism was a prohibition on strikes and public criticism of the government, foreclosing options enjoyed by workers in most capitalist countries. New arrivals in Moscow had to pursue their interests within these parameters by dragging their feet, changing jobs, and relying on *blat* or other forms of implicit labor negotiation.

Working-Class Identity in the Soviet Context

If we are to determine the significance and staying power of working-class identity and the extent to which it informed workers' behavior, we need to understand how and when disparate groups of workers came to identify themselves as members of a working class. Studies of working-class formation in Western Europe have emphasized various factors. According to E. P. Thompson, common experiences—both inherited traditions and the shared experience of economic exploitation—provided the basis for workers to identify collective interests and adopt a collective identity.[89] Politics and ideology also played roles in this process. Only a particular linguistic ordering of workers' experiences gave these experiences meaning.[90] This linguistic ordering—these terms of political discourse—defined working-class identity in a way that silenced alternative constructions of social identity.[91]

Like Western workers, Soviet workers had traditions that were sub-

[89]Thompson, *Making of the English Working Class*, pp. 9–10. See also William H. Sewell, Jr., "How Classes Are Made: Critical Reflections on E. P. Thompson's Theory of Working-Class Formation," in *E. P. Thompson: Critical Perspectives*, Harvey J. Kaye and Keith McClelland, eds. (Philadelphia, 1990), p. 69.

[90]Gareth Stedman Jones, *Languages of Class: Studies in English Working Class History, 1832–1982* (New York, 1983), p. 101.

[91]Jacques Rancière, *The Nights of Labor: The Workers' Dream in Nineteenth-Century France*, John Drury, trans. (Philadelphia, 1989), p. xxiii. See also Joan Wallach Scott, "The Evidence of Experience," *Critical Inquiry* 1991 no. 4. Scott argues that experience cannot be regarded as foundationalist, because it is political discourse that positions subjects and produces their experiences.

jected to exploitation during industrialization. But did exploitation result in common experiences on which workers could build a collective identity? And what effect did class discourse have in the Soviet context? As we have seen, the extremely rapid expansion of the Moscow workforce during the 1930s led to strife between new and old workers. Furthermore, the de facto segregation of new workers prevented a sense of working-class community from developing and provided few common experiences to promote worker solidarity.

Of course disparate groups and social conflict were not unique to the Soviet workforce. Friction between established workers and new workers of peasant origin was common before the Revolution.[92] Class has never provided a sufficient rubric to encompass all the competing allegiances and identifications that workers feel, nor has it ever fully described all the divisions and tensions in society. Working-class cultures naturally include tendencies toward class fragmentation as well as toward class solidarity.[93] The question then becomes: How have workers in some historical situations overcome their differences and assumed the collective self-representation "working class"? And did working-class identity come to overshadow the competing allegiances of Soviet workers and to guide their behavior?

The construction of working-class identity in prerevolutionary Moscow offers a useful basis of comparison. Under the tsarist autocracy the very concept "working class" entailed opposition to the establishment. Workers were not recognized juridically under the imperial order, and to identify oneself as a member of the working class was to attach oneself to the very symbol of revolutionary opposition. That so many disparate workers were willing to adopt this revolutionary self-representation reflected the bitterness they felt toward their common enemies—factory owners and tsarist police officials. In this sense, the working-class identity of prerevolutionary workers was constructed oppositionally; it defined workers as opponents of industrial capitalism and the tsarist autocracy.

Prerevolutionary workers played at least some role in defining their own social identity. It is true that members of the radical intelligentsia put forward competing definitions of the working class and

---

[92]AAN f. 359, op. 2, d. 231, ll. 26–27.

[93]Richard Oestreicher, "Working-Class Political Behavior and Theories of American Politics," *Journal of American History* 1988 no. 4, p. 1286.

of working-class consciousness, but these definitions remained contested and open to redefinition by workers themselves. The fact that workers played an active role in defining working-class identity encouraged the internalization of this identity and increased its significance as a basis for collective action. Working-class identity united workers in the pursuit of common interests, and in turn workers' collective action (in strikes, demonstrations, and the revolutionary battles of 1905 and 1917) served to secure this identity. The 1905 Revolution brought the hostility between workers and employers into focus and resulted in the creation of separate working-class organizations.[94] And despite considerable differentiation of Moscow workers by social origin and branch of industry, the radicalizing struggle of the 1917 Revolution acted to unite them.[95]

The meaning of "working class" in the Soviet period sharply differed from its earlier meaning. In contrast to the West and prerevolutionary Russia, the Soviet Union industrialized without private property or a bourgeois class against which workers could unite. In place of a bourgeoisie, Party officials oversaw industrialization, and they had co-opted the very image "working class," claiming to rule in the interests of workers. Soviet industrialization provided no clear class enemy, and Party officials prevented the voicing of any antiestablishment ideology that might have created a sense of common interests and class solidarity among workers. Not only did authorities maintain tight control over the media and other ideological resources, they appropriated the language of class and of revolution to serve as the language of the Soviet establishment. Even if workers did not believe that the Soviet Union was a working-class state, they could not use the language of class to stir rebellion when Party leaders had co-opted it as a means of political legitimation.

Furthermore, no institutional basis existed to create worker solidarity. Under state control, trade unions did not articulate the common interests of workers. Had independent trade unions been allowed, they might have united all workers behind demands for better wages and working conditions; as it was, workers were left to compete against one another. Soviet workers strove to better their

---

[94]Mark Steinberg, *Moral Communities: The Culture of Class Relations in the Russian Printing Industry, 1867–1907* (Berkeley, 1992), p. 183.
[95]Koenker, *Moscow Workers*, p. 364.

own situation and did not object if management favored them at the expense of other workers.[96]

Soviet workers did not constitute a class in the sense of a group united by shared experiences and common interests. Nor did the dominant (and officially controlled) political discourse of class place any emphasis on class solidarity or collective action. Rather than articulate an understanding of workers' relations with one another or with other groups in society, "working class" in Soviet ideology defined workers' position vis-à-vis the state. To Party leaders, *class* was a label that identified a social group as either supporters or enemies. In establishing a new social and political order after the Revolution, the Bolsheviks institutionalized class categories. Voting rights, taxation, rationing, distribution of housing, the legal system, and admission to the Party, Komsomol, Red Army, and universities all depended on one's class.[97]

Soviet authorities also defined the working class through models and symbols. Posters, novels, and films all conveyed the images of clean, efficient, and loyal workers.[98] Stakhanovites and other "hero workers" were held up for new workers to emulate. These model workers possessed the qualities Soviet officials wished to instill: literacy, punctuality, mastery of industrial equipment, Komsomol and trade union membership, and enthusiasm for the Soviet industrialization drive. The Stakhanovite Ivan Gudov described his prize for shock work in terms of the patriotic pride that Soviet authorities wished to inspire in all workers: "Perhaps for the first time in my life I felt myself to be a worthwhile person. For me it was not the prize but the recognition that I too participate in the great work of the rebuilding of our country. How could I not be proud of this?!"[99] Stakhanovite memoirs thus ordered workers' experiences in a way that tied personal advancement to the building of socialism.

The factory history project similarly employed narrative to order

[96]Burawoy, p. 188.

[97]Sheila Fitzpatrick, "L'Usage bolshévique de la 'classe': Marxisme et construction de l'identité individuelle," *Actes de la Recherche en Sciences Sociales* no. 85 (November 1990), p. 71.

[98]MPA f. 635, op. 1, d. 135, l. 21.

[99]Gudov, *Sud'ba rabochego*, p. 13. Other Soviet accounts also link workers' achievements with a new sense of pride and self-identity. See Busygin, *Moia zhizn'*, pp. 7–9; *Govoriat stroiteli sotsializma*, p. 131; Vdovin and Drobizhev, p. 215.

workers' experiences, attach certain meanings to those experiences, and inform workers' identities.[100] At special gatherings workers were called upon to explain their past and present roles in the factory, casting their accounts in official language and using the official categories. Their stories were then compiled with other information to form the history of their factory.[101] By creating a usable past through official narratives, authorities sought to solidify workers' allegiance to their factory and to instill in them working-class identity as officially defined. Other government projects that purported to depict the working class also acted to define what it should be. The 1932 trade union census, for example, categorized the workforce in terms that reflected officials' definition of a "conscious" worker: social origin, level of education, literacy, participation in socialist competition.[102]

In this way, Soviet authorities delineated the "working class" and created a standard of behavior that became part of each worker's public persona. To claim the concrete benefits offered to loyal workers, former peasants had to conform at least superficially to the official model. A publicly maintained peasant identity could become a liability in the industrial labor force. Any worker who appeared, spoke, or acted like a peasant (wore a beard or peasant clothing, spoke with a provincial accent, neglected to use Soviet terminology or profess a commitment to building socialism) could be denied a high-paying job, educational opportunities, and Party membership.[103]

But to what degree did new workers internalize the official characterization of the working class and how much did it inform their behavior? Here it is noteworthy that workers had no active part in the construction of the Soviet working class. Party leaders and functionaries defined working-class identity, and most workers outwardly conformed to the definition. Passive conformity did not lead them to internalize this identity or adopt it as a guide for their actions. Most workers publicly behaved in accordance with the authorities' expec-

---

[100]On the importance of narrative in the establishment of identity, see Jerome Bruner, *Acts of Meaning* (Cambridge, Mass., 1990).

[101]*Gor'kii i sozdanie istorii fabrik i zavodov: Sbornik dokumentov*, L. M. Zak and S. S. Zimina, eds. (Moscow, 1959).

[102]See Appendix II.

[103]On the mimicry of official slogans, see Jeffrey Brooks, "Revolutionary Lives: Public Identities in *Pravda* during the 1920s," in *New Directions in Soviet History*, Stephen White, ed. (New York, 1992), pp. 31–32.

tations but few lived up to the Soviet model of hardworking, self-sacrificing laborers. Productivity actually declined during the First Five-Year Plan, and labor turnover throughout the 1930s remained at extremely high levels.[104]

We all consciously assume roles in response to the expectations of the people with whom we are dealing; role enactment makes behavior predictable and facilitates social interaction.[105] Particularly in dealings with people in positions of authority, subaltern groups (and especially peasants) calculatingly follow routines of deference, compliance, and political conformity.[106] New workers assumed the roles required of them when they dealt with Soviet officials, but they had no trouble adopting other roles with other people. One new worker in Moscow who returned regularly to the countryside said, "At the factory I call myself a worker, but in the village—at the village assembly—I call myself a peasant."[107] When peasant in-migrants left the factory and returned to their neighborhoods on the outskirts of Moscow, they reverted to the language, cultural expressions, and modes of behavior expected by the fellow villagers who lived there.

The cultural forms that flourished among former peasants promoted alternative understandings and allegiances. The autobiographical narratives composed by these new city dwellers, for example, ordered experiences and prescribed meanings in ways very different from official narratives recited at Soviet factory meetings. When Nadezhda Andreevna told the story of her life, she did not mention her contribution to the building of socialism or employ teleologies describing her progression from peasant to worker. Instead she recalled the poverty of her village after collectivization, the way she circumvented the passport system to move to Moscow, the help of fellow villagers in finding a factory job, her marriage, and her children. Her sense of accomplishment was connected not with the industrializa-

[104]MPA f. 429, op. 1, d. 429, l. 9; Anoshin, pp. 97–98; *Iz istorii razvitiia metallurgicheskoi promyshlennosti Moskvy,* p. 186; *Za promyshlennye kadry* 1934 no. 21/22, p. 87.

[105]Louis A. Zurcher, *Social Roles: Conformity, Conflict, and Creativity* (Beverly Hills, Calif., 1983), pp. 12–14; Gregory Stone, "Appearance and the Self," in *Human Behavior and Social Processes,* Arnold M. Rose, ed. (Boston, 1962), pp. 93–95.

[106]James Scott, p. 278.

[107]*Molodaia gvardiia* 1929 no. 14, p. 60. See also Sam Sieber, "Toward a Theory of Role Accumulation," *American Sociological Review* 39 (August 1974), p. 571.

tion drive but with having survived and raised a family during very difficult times.[108]

The Party's power to define the working class did not include the power to dictate workers' thoughts and behavior; officials failed to remold peasant in-migrants into the "New Soviet Person." The Soviet working class remained a political construct that determined workers' position in relation to the state; it did not become a collective self-representation that informed the behavior of workers toward one another or toward other groups. Interviews with Soviet émigrés in 1950 revealed that while they identified themselves in terms of class labels, they felt no class hostility and had no class consciousness.[109] Class held no sense of collectivity for Soviet workers and provided no basis for collective action. Workers' appeals in the 1930s were not to fellow workers but to a higher authority—to Soviet officials or the Soviet state for better living and working conditions.

In the Soviet context, "working class" symbolized neither collectivity nor revolutionary opposition to the established order. It defined all members of the industrial workforce—themselves in sharp conflict with one another—as supporters of the Soviet government, and it delineated their privileged place in Soviet society. Workers accepted the self-representation "working class" as part of their public persona, but they did not internalize it as a guide for their behavior or allow it to deter their pursuit of individual interests. Far from becoming a galvanizing symbol that roused workers to collective action or support for Party policies, the representation "working class" remained a sterile fixture of Soviet ideology.

[108]Interview with Nadezhda Andreevna Kuznetsova, Izmailovskii Park, Moscow, July 25, 1992. She also expressed her regret that she had not visited America in her lifetime—another reminder that narratives are influenced not just by their tellers but also by their audience.
[109]Inkeles and Bauer, pp. 318–319.

Conclusion

Reflecting upon his life, Evgenii Mikhailovich recalls moving to Moscow, the arduous working conditions at the factory, the overcrowded apartment he shared with relatives, and his camaraderie with the many men and women who, like himself, left their native villages during the 1930s to begin new lives in the city. They had all been part of Communist Party leaders' tumultuous attempt at industrialization, social transformation, and working-class creation, but Evgenii Mikhailovich does not conceptualize his life in those terms. Instead he sees himself as a former peasant who overcame many hardships to make a successful career as a steelworker and amateur actor and folk singer. The 1930s were a pivotal period in his life, not because of the building of socialism but because it was then that he met and married his wife (also then new to Moscow). He looks back on the decade with nostalgia. Despite the dire poverty, it was a time of youthful excitement and possibility.[1]

A historian looking at Evgenii Mikhailovich's life might see it in broader terms. He was one of 23 million Soviet peasants who moved permanently to cities during the 1930s—a rate of rural-to-urban migration unprecedented in world history. When he and millions of peasants like him took factory jobs, they doubled the size of the Soviet industrial workforce, seeming to offer Party leaders a large proletariat

---

[1]Interview with Evgenii Mikhailovich Kostin at the Hammer and Sickle plant, Moscow, May 16, 1989.

and hence a broadened base of social support. But at this point the historian would need to consider the sense that Evgenii Mikhailovich had about his life and his place in the Soviet system. For if he was no longer the wide-eyed peasant lad who stepped off a train in Moscow years ago, neither had he become the New Soviet Person who was to build the socialist order. He and other new arrivals drew upon peasant culture and village networks to formulate conceptions of social identity very different from the self-sacrificing proletariat envisioned by Soviet officials.

Party leaders, as Marxists, assumed that once peasants changed their relation to the means of production by becoming factory workers, they would develop proletarian consciousness and identify the interests of the working-class state as their own. Though a combination of incentives and coercion did ultimately secure the quiescence of new workers, most former peasants never internalized the role of loyal proletarian, nor did they develop allegiance to the Soviet government. Those workers who were promoted into positions of authority and privilege (the "Brezhnev generation") acquired a stake in the Soviet system and a belief that it represented their interests; but for the vast majority of newly urbanized workers, the myths and ideals of Soviet ideology held little currency. The low-status jobs, incessant exhortations to fulfill the plan, incomprehensible cultural education, overcrowded barracks, and low living standard that made up their world did not correspond to official promises of a workers' utopia. In fact, the designation "working-class state" rang hollow for old and new workers alike. Party leaders presumed to know the interests of workers and established a "working-class state" with no meaningful input or political participation of rank-and-file workers. It is true that special benefits accrued to workers under the Soviet system, but state policies in the 1930s often violated their interests and lowered their living standard.

Despite resistance to official ideology, for much of the decade Soviet authorities persisted in trying to mold former peasants into model proletarians. They proved incapable of doing so not only because of the inadequacies of political and cultural education but also because they presumed to instill a consciousness that was alien to peasants. Soviet authorities did not understand that peasants had their own culture and own way to conceptualize the world. The urban environment did not instantly transform new arrivals, in part because the city itself was changing as a result of their presence, but also because former peasants drew upon useful elements of their past to guide their behavior. The subculture of these new city dwellers maintained those aspects of village culture that helped them respond to the new tasks and power relationships they confronted in Moscow.

In particular, migration traditions and village networks guided peasants to the city and helped them find work and housing. Peasant traditions in this sense contributed enormously to the industrialization drive by channeling labor to the city. Unfortunately for Party leaders, migration networks and artels also resulted in clusters of fellow villagers in certain factories and neighborhoods—clusters that perpetuated village forms of organization and community, task-oriented work habits, peasant modes of cultural expression, and circumspection toward authority. Fellow villagers in Moscow formed self-help associations, relied on one another for information and camaraderie, organized drunken celebrations on traditional peasant and religious holidays, and resisted authorities' attempts to impose upon them official definitions of working-class identity and behavior.

But if newcomers to Moscow were not model workers, neither were they simply peasants in the city, or even peasant-workers gradually shedding rural traits on their way to becoming archetypal proletarians. The complex world of peasant in-migrants encompassed the village, the semirural outskirts of Moscow, and the factory, and the roles they assumed were accordingly varied. Moreover, they defined themselves not only by their environment but also in relation to other people. In comparison with established workers, former peasants in the factory were the newcomers from the village, the country bumpkins. When they returned to visit their villages, they were looked upon not as peasants but as the ones who had moved away to the city. Peasant in-migrants experienced shifting subject positions and consequently developed a complex sense of social identity, formed in opposition to the people they encountered and in relation to the ways those people tried to define them.

Soviet authorities were in the forefront of people eager to define the new workers. Their control over the media and other ideological resources allowed them to establish the dominant political discourse— a discourse in which "conscious proletarians" supported the Soviet state while "class enemies" opposed it. Peasants who moved to the city had to come to terms with Soviet authorities and official discourse. Those who aspired to advance in the system had to play by its rules and even those who merely sought material benefits from the Soviet state had to speak its language. Though official discourse did not change the consciousness or identity of former peasants, it did set boundaries for them. The village-based subculture of peasant in-migrants could subvert official discourse but could not erase it.

Authorities' control over official discourse enabled them to co-opt the language of class and revolution, and to use it as a means of political legitimation. In contrast to workers' traditions under capitalist industrialization, the traditions of Soviet workers subjected to exploitation could not be transformed by political agitation into working-class solidarity against the establishment. Instead new workers fell back on the nonconfrontational forms of resistance characteristic of peasant culture. The result was falling worker productivity and enormous turnover, but little overt labor protest.

Even passive resistance among former peasants had far-reaching implications for what Soviet leaders could accomplish. New workers' unwillingness to subscribe to the tenets of Soviet ideology deprived the Party leadership of the large, politically supportive proletariat that was to build the socialist order. Party leaders consequently remained distrustful of societal initiative, retained authoritarian control over political and economic institutions, continued their extensive use of coercion, and mixed authoritarianism with paternalism—in effect granting economic security in exchange for political quiescence. Eventually they also resorted to more traditional, non-Marxist appeals (such as Russian nationalism and the Stalin cult) to foster at least a minimal link between the government and the populace. The contradictions that resulted from the intertwining of Marxist ideology with non-Marxist appeals, as well as the contradictions inherent in a working-class state that lacked the active support of its workers, undermined the long-term stability of the Soviet system.

More generally the failure of Soviet authorities to fashion a self-sacrificing proletariat reflects the limitations of revolutionary vanguardism. Even as collectivization and industrialization transformed the population, the millions of peasants who became workers rejected the identity of New Soviet Person that officials sought to impose upon them. The great Russian thinker Mikhail Bakhtin defined the measure of human freedom as people's resistance to all attempts to finalize them, all attempts to regulate their actions with reference to eternal norms. Ideology and ruling truth, he held, can never penetrate "to the core of the people's soul."[2] Communist Party leaders sought to monologize existence in an authoritarian discourse that set forth one interpretation of history, one all-encompassing ideology and world-view, and one correct social identity for manual laborers. But the millions of peasants who filled the ranks of the Soviet workforce pas-sively resisted these attempts to define them, and ultimately forced Party leaders to seek ideological retreats and accommodations.

[2]M. M. Bakhtin, "Zametki," in *Literaturno-kriticheskie stat'i* (Moscow, 1986), p. 514.

Workers in Moscow's Economic Sectors

Because all data on the composition of the Soviet workforce were gathered by various Soviet bureaucracies, it is impossible to analyze them without discussing official efforts to define, categorize, and shape the workforce. Soviet authorities regarded the industrial proletariat and skilled metalworkers in particular as the most politically conscious members of the urban workforce, and the information they collected focused heavily, in some cases exclusively, on workers in large heavy-industry factories. Workers in light-industry workshops, in construction, in transportation, and especially in the service sector received far less attention. Thus the available information about the workforce was determined in part by Soviet officials' definition of workers.

As Table I.1 shows, the workforce expanded most rapidly during the First Five-Year Plan, particularly from 1930 to 1932. By 1932 over half of all workers had begun urban industrial work within the past three years. These years also corresponded to the greatest influx of peasants.[1] Sixty-eight percent of all new industrial personnel hired in the USSR during the First Five-Year Plan were peasants; 14 percent consisted of urban youth, 11 percent urban women, and 7 percent other urban groups.[2] The Second Five-Year Plan witnessed a decrease not only in the number of new workers but also in the percentage of new workers from the countryside. In this period, 54 percent of new industrial employees were of peasant origin.[3] During

Table I.1. Number of workers in Moscow industry, 1928–1937

Year	Workers	Year	Workers
1928	186,500	1933	443,500
1929	208,300	1934	474,400
1930	241,600	1935	490,300
1931	339,000	1936	558,900
1932	433,900	1937	614,000

Source: A. A. Tverdokhleb, "Chislennost' i sostav rabochego klassa Moskvy v 1917–1939 gg.," *Vestnik Moskovskogo universiteta* ser. 9, 1970 no. 1, p. 24.

the Third Five-Year Plan the size of the industrial workforce hardly changed, though military mobilizations led to the drafting of some workers out of factories and necessitated recruitment of new workers to replace them.[4]

The age of the workforce shifted as rapidly as its social composition, partly because many urban young people were hired but primarily because the majority of peasant in-migrants in the 1930s were young. From 1926 to 1929 only 30 percent of all new Soviet workers were under 23 years old, but this figure jumped to 70 percent for the 1929–1932 period.[5] By 1933 over 40 percent of all industrial workers were under age 23, and in 1936 the proportion of Moscow workers in this age group was still roughly 36 percent.[6]

Construction and Transport

A large number of peasants who moved to Moscow in the 1930s found their first jobs in construction, a sector that traditionally employed many unskilled seasonal workers. The First Five-Year Plan

[1]These figures include both workers and white-collar employees (*sluzhashchie*) hired in industry. As few in-migrants obtained white-collar posts, the percentage of new blue-collar workers of peasant origin must have been higher still.

[2]Vdovin and Drobizhev, pp. 115–116.

[3]Dadykin, pp. 46–49.

[4]Lewin, *Making of the Soviet System*, p. 249; Vdovin and Drobizhev, p. 97.

[5]M. V. Abrosimova, "Rukovodstvo moskovskoi partiinoi organizatsii podgotovkoi molodykh rabochikh kadrov v gody stroitel'stva fundamenta sotsializma (1926–1932 gg.)" (dissertation, Lenin State Pedagogical Institute, Moscow, 1975), p. 9.

[6]A. G. Rashin, "Dinamika promyshlennykh kadrov SSSR za 1917–1958 gg.," in *Izmeneniia v chislennosti i sostav sovetskogo rabochego klassa* (Moscow, 1961), p. 18; *General'nyi plan*, p. 61.

entailed over a thousand construction projects, many of them factories in Moscow.[7] The number of construction workers in Moscow expanded from roughly 62,000 in 1929 to over 146,000 by July 1932.[8] Construction workers climbed from 6.5 percent of all Soviet workers in 1928 to 9.5 percent in 1932. During the Second and Third Five-Year plans, when planners concentrated on bringing recently constructed plants into operation, the proportion of the national workforce accounted for by construction workers fell to 5.6 percent.[9]

The overwhelming majority of construction workers in Moscow were of peasant origin, and some two-thirds of them retained ties to agriculture during the First Five-Year Plan.[10] This fact, in conjunction with the low pay and low status of their work, accounted for the continued high turnover of construction workers (around 300 percent in 1932) despite the transition to year-round construction during the First Five-Year Plan.[11] Nearly all construction workers were transients. They returned to the village more regularly than other new workers, they traveled in artels from one construction site to another to obtain better wages, and the more ambitious of them found higher-paying jobs in industry and left construction work altogether.[12] Not surprisingly, a very large percentage of construction workers were young (almost half under the age of 24 in 1932) and had worked less than two years (40 percent).[13]

Of all construction workers in Moscow in 1932, some 130,000 worked on buildings; another 10,000 paved streets, laid railroads, and dug canals.[14] The latter figure jumped suddenly in 1933 as work on the Moscow metro forged ahead. The number of people employed on metro construction rose from 2,500 in 1932 to 27,700 in 1933 and to 75,000 (including engineers) by May 1934.[15] The tunneling required

[7]Arvind Vyas, *Consumption in a Socialist Economy: The Soviet Industrialization Experience, 1929–1937* (New Delhi, 1978), pp. 75–76; Livshits, pp. 263–265.

[8]*Trud v SSSR* (1932), pp. 82–83; TsGAORgM f. 126, op. 2, d. 98b, l. 28

[9]*Rabochii klass—vedushchaia sila*, p. 197; Vyas, pp. 82–83.

[10]A. S. Strigin, "Deiatel'nost' Moskovskoi partiinoi organizatsii po razvitiiu trudovoi aktivnosti molodezhi na stroikakh pervoi piatiletki," *Uchenye zapiski Moskovskogo pedagogicheskogo instituta* 1969 no. 357, p. 167; *Istoriia metro Moskvy*, p. 70.

[11]*Industrializatsiia SSSR*, vol. 3, p. 512.

[12]Ognev, p. 47.

[13]I. Berlin and Ia. Mebel', "Strukturnye svidgi v naselenii proletariata," *Voprosy truda* 1932 no. 11/12, p. 23.

[14]TsGAORgM f. 126, op. 2, d. 98b, l. 28; *Rabochaia Moskva* October 15, 1931, p. 4.

[15]Anoshin, p. 84; Shimotomai, p. 124.

the assistance of some miners recruited from various parts of the country. Except when thousands of Komsomol members were mobilized to complete the first metro line, the great majority of construction workers were of peasant origin.[16]

Because construction work was still largely unmechanized, almost all of it could be done by new workers without training. Procedures more complex than digging and hauling were subdivided and simplified to accommodate the large number of unskilled new workers. A new system of bricklaying, for example, divided brigades into three groups: one to move the scaffolding, another to haul and prepare materials, and a third to lay the bricks. This system enabled workers with experience in laying bricks to do the job with maximum efficiency, and those who were completely unskilled could work without any training.[17] Unskilled laborers (chernorabochie and zemlekopy) accounted for 40 percent of all construction workers in Moscow province, carpenters 20 percent, bricklayers 7 percent, plasterers 4 percent, concrete pourers 4 percent, and a variety of other specializations the remainder.[18]

Transport work resembled construction in several ways. It too expanded rapidly during the First Five-Year Plan, required no training for many of its tasks, and employed large numbers of former peasants. The number of transport jobs soared as people were hired to load and haul industrial materials and other supplies, to drive trams in the expanding public transportation system, and to load and pilot barges on the Moscow River.[19] Rail transport workers alone numbered over 60,000 in Moscow by the beginning of 1932, and other city transport workers added another 80,000 to the workforce.[20]

Workers of peasant origin filled almost all of the demand for transport labor. Some of them arrived in Moscow with some experience in transporting goods by water or land in the countryside; those with no experience could still perform most loading tasks.[21] Even jobs that required some skill, such as driving a truck, increasingly were given to unskilled new workers. A protocol of the Moscow transport workers'

[16]Istoriia metro Moskvy, p. 70.

[17]Poletaev, Na putiakh, pp. 52–53; Govoriat stroiteli sotsializma, p. 149.

[18]TsGAMO f. 6833, op. 1, d. 46, l. 25.

[19]Rabochaia Moskva, September 16, 1931, p. 1; Poletaev, p. 87; Avral, July 29, 1931, p. 1.

[20]TsGAORgM f. 126, op. 2, d. 98b, ll. 32–33.

[21]Anoshin, p. 50; Molodaia gvardiia transporta, pp. 173–177.

union reported at the end of 1929 that the demand for truck drivers had greatly exceeded the number of experienced drivers available, and that young, unqualified workers were to be hired and hastily trained to keep the transport system in operation.[22] Three-quarters of Moscow tram drivers in 1929 not only were of peasant origin but maintained close ties to the village.[23]

Like construction workers, transport workers tended to be young, uneducated, and, as one article concluded, "given to drunkenness."[24] Though driving jobs paid somewhat better, most transport jobs brought both low pay and low status. Because more qualified workers eschewed transport and construction work, peasants who moved to Moscow could easily get jobs in these sectors. These jobs also provided seasonal work for temporary migrants who planned to return to the village. As migrants gradually decided to settle permanently in the city, they generally sought jobs with higher pay and higher status in industry.

Heavy Industry

The greatest expansion in industry in the 1930s—indeed, the focus of the Soviet industrialization drive—came in branches of heavy industry: metallurgy, machine building, automotive production (automobiles, tractors, and airplanes), and the electrotechnical industry. During the First Five-Year Plan overall industrial output increased 2.5 times in Moscow, while the output of heavy industry alone rose 4.3 times.[25] The number of Moscow workers in heavy industry jumped from 72,900 in 1929 to 233,200 in 1932 to 306,700 in 1936 (rising as a proportion of all workers in Moscow industry from around one-quarter to over half within the First Five-Year Plan).[26]

The construction of huge new plants and the expansion of existing factories during the First Five-Year Plan transformed Moscow's economy and accounted for the predominance of heavy industry. Until 1929, Moscow factories consisted primarily of small textile mills

[22]TsGAMO f. 738, op. 1, d. 33, l. 29.
[23]*Sputnik kommunista* 1929 no. 23, pp. 29–30.
[24]*Krasnyi bogatyr'*, October 10, 1934, p. 2; TsGAORgM f. 726, op. 1, d. 414, l. 1.
[25]*Istoriia Moskvy: Kratkii ocherk*, p. 283.
[26]TsGAORgM f. 126, op. 10, d. 47, l. 72.

and a number of semi-artisanal metal workshops; only 10 percent of all Moscow workers were employed in enterprises with over 3,000 workers. By the beginning of the Second Five-Year Plan, 37 percent of Moscow industrial workers were in enterprises with over 3,000 workers, including 17 percent (over 100,000 workers) in enterprises employing more than 10,000 workers.[27]

Peasant in-migrants who entered Moscow industry found employment precisely in these huge new plants. In fact, a large part of the workforce in these plants consisted of the construction workers who had built them.[28] Accordingly, workers' average age and number of years in industrial employment were much lower at new or expanded plants than at older factories. At new Moscow machine-building enterprises (such as the Ordzhonikidze electromechanical factory and the Kalinin cutting-tools factory), some 70 percent of the workforce were under 24 years of age. Old artisanal-style metalworking factories (such as the Moscow instrument factory, the Red Torch factory, the Compressor factory) hired so few young workers that youth made up only around 30 percent of their workforces.[29]

These employment patterns led to de facto segregation of new workers from established workers. Old machine-building factories did not employ unskilled new workers because the unmechanized, semi-artisanal modes of production in these enterprises required specialized skills. New and reconstructed plants, by contrast, could employ unskilled workers on mechanized assembly lines, and amassed their workforces by hiring peasant in-migrants.

The Stalin automobile plant, the centerpiece of Moscow's automotive industry, became the largest automobile factory in the world in the 1930s. It underwent reconstruction and expansion twice in this period, employing 2,600 workers in 1928, 13,900 in 1932, and 28,100 by 1938.[30] During the Second Five-Year Plan about half of the workers were under 24 years old, and most of them were of peasant origin.[31]

[27]*Ekonomiko-statisticheskii spravochnik*, vol. 2, pp. 12–13; Aleksandrova, p. 6. The concentration of workers in huge industrial plants was a nationwide trend. See V. M. Selunskaia, *Sotsial'naia struktura sovetskogo obshchestva: Istoriia i sovremennost'* (Moscow, 1987), p. 99.

[28]Dadykin, p. 49; Tverdokhleb, "Chislennost'," p. 25.

[29]*Ocherki istorii Moskovskoi organizatsii VLKSM*, p. 282; Aleksandrova, p. 6; TsGANKh f. 7995, op. 1, d. 391, l. 17.

[30]Anoshin, p. 82.

[31]*Istoriia rabochikh Moskvy*, pp. 282–283.

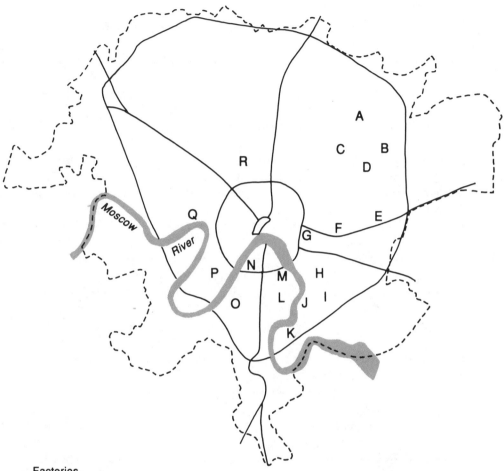

Factories

A. Red Hercules rubber factory
B. Factory #4
C. Storm Petrel leather factory
D. Kuibyshev electronics factory
E. Frunze aviation engine plant
F. Hammer–and–Sickle metallurgical plant
G. Klara Zetkin textile mill
H. Moscow meat–processing plant
I. Kaganovich ball–bearing plant

J. Kirov Dinamo engine plant
K. Stalin automobile plant
L. Ordzhonikidze electro–mechanical factory
M. Paris Commune shoe factory
N. Red October candy factory
O. Red Proletarian machine–tools factory
P. Red Rosa textile mill
Q. Tri–Mountain textile mill
R. Factory #2

Large factories in Moscow, 1932

The largest machine-building factory in Moscow, the Kirov Dinamo plant, specializing in the production of heavy-duty motors and cranes, expanded its workforce from around 1,500 in 1928 to 5,330 by 1932. Most of its workers were of peasant origin and had less than one year of industrial work experience in 1932.[32] The average age of workers at the factory in 1932–33 was 25 years, only slightly less than the average age (26 years) for all Moscow metalworkers at the time.[33] The machine-building and automotive plants offered higher wages (at least for some specializations) than any other employer of blue-collar workers in Moscow. Reports indicate that a large number of dispossessed "kulaks" found work in machine-building plants. Because their ties to the village had been severed, seasonal work in transport or construction held no advantages for them, so they sought jobs in branches of metalwork with constant employment and the potential for higher wages.[34]

The Kaganovich ball bearing factory was built during the First Five-Year Plan and went into operation in 1932. Intended to free the Soviet Union from dependence on imported ball bearings, it supplied virtually all the ball bearings used throughout the country. When it opened it employed only 2,400 workers, but by 1934 it boasted 11,300 workers, and 23,600 by 1937.[35] Of these workers, almost 60 percent (14,000) were of peasant origin. Early in the Second Five-Year Plan, over half of all workers were under 24 years old, and even in 1937 around one-third were under this age.[36]

The Kuibyshev electronics factory, a small manufacturer of transformers and electric lamps, expanded from 500 workers in 1928 to 7,000 in 1930 and over 15,000 by 1932.[37] In 1931 workers under the age of 24 accounted for some 70 percent of the factory's workforce, and over half had less than three years' industrial work experience and were of peasant origin (including many who still maintained ties to the village in 1930).[38]

[32]*Dinamo v gody stroitel'stva sotsializma*, pp. 172–173.

[33]Tverdokhleb, "Chislennost'," p. 29.

[34]TsGAOR f. 5469, op. 14, d. 45, ll. 12–13.

[35]TsGAORgM f. 2872, op. 2, d. 220, ll. 6–9; Anoshin, p. 82.

[36]TsGAMO f. 2534, op. 1, d. 485, l. 53; *Pervyi podshipnikovyi*, pp. 79–80.

[37]Aleksandrova, p. 45; TsGAORgM f. 2872, op. 2, d. 220, ll. 6–9. Figures on the number of workers at this factory vary from one source to another because of administrative reorganizations, but all are within these general dimensions.

[38]*Nezabyvaemye 30-e*, p. 88; TsGAOR f. 5469, op. 14, d. 45, l. 4.

New, moderate-sized metalworking factories also helped to account for the growing numbers of workers in Moscow heavy industry. The Moscow bicycle factory, the Ordzhonikidze electromechanical factory, the Gauge factory (which manufactured measuring instruments), the Kalinin cutting-tools factory, and the Central foundry (which made metal castings) all were built during the First Five-Year Plan and by 1934 employed between 1,000 and 3,000 workers each. The Lepse engine factory and the Red Proletarian machine-tools factory were moderate-sized metalworking plants that were expanded during the 1930s.[39] Trade union reports attributed weak labor discipline in some of these plants to the fact that so many of the workers were young and of peasant origin.[40]

A number of Moscow factories were involved in military-related production. The Frunze aviation-engine plant (Factory no. 24), for example, produced engines for military airplanes as well as for other aircraft, as did Aviation Works no. 22. Factories engaged exclusively in military production, such as Factory no. 2 and Factory no. 4, as a rule employed few peasant in-migrants. Because of the priority given to these enterprises and the high wages they offered, they recruited more experienced workers.[41]

As Moscow became the country's leading machine-building center, the need for steel rose sharply. Until the building of the Tula metallurgical plant and the reconstruction of the Kosogorskii plant during the Second Five-Year Plan, the Hammer and Sickle plant supplied the only steel produced in the Moscow area.[42] Expansion during the First Five-Year Plan raised the total number of its workers to 8,700 by 1932, but introduction of more efficient technology reduced that number to 7,300 by 1936.[43] Most Hammer and Sickle workers in 1929 were older than 25 and had several years' experience. The hiring of almost 2,000 new workers during the next two years sharply swung the balance in favor of young workers of peasant origin with less than two years of industrial experience.[44]

[39]Rashin, "Dinamika promyshlennykh kadrov," pp. 38–39; *Moskva: Sbornik statei*, pp. 47–54.

[40]See, for example, TsGAOR f. 5469, op. 14, d. 24, l. 16.

[41]Little information is available on military factories. On the number of workers in military plants, see MPA f. 4, op. 2, d. 10, l. 141; *Moskva v novykh raionakh*.

[42]Aleksandrova, p. 27.

[43]TsGAORgM f. 2872, op. 2, d. 220, ll. 6–9.

[44]AAN f. 359, op. 2, d. 529, ll. 6–10; Kornakovskii, p. 317.

Metallurgy required at least a hundred people per blast furnace to smelt the iron into steel. The founder (*stalevar*) in charge of adding the metals and chemicals to produce steel had to be highly skilled, but most of the other workers in the foundry shop did nothing more exacting than stoking the blast furnace, prodding clumps of coal to maintain the fire, and transporting ore to the founder.[45] Workers of peasant origin filled these jobs, because the work, arduous though it was in the heat of the foundry, required little skill and paid well. Once the steel had been smelted and poured into five-ton blocks, it was transported to the main rolling shop, where it was cut into ingots and then transported on to various specialty rolling shops that shaped the metal into sheets, bands, cable, and wire. Unskilled workers transported the molded steel down the conveyer, poured oil on it to prevent cracking, positioned it under presses for sheet metal, and so forth. They also sorted finished nuts, bolts, and other metal goods to be sent out.

Workers of peasant origin were predominant in the foundry and the rolling shops, but not so numerous in the shops requiring more precise skilled work, such as the calibrating shop.[46] Established workers and young urban adults who had received specialized training filled most positions in shops requiring more than rudimentary skills. Peasant in-migrants were in effect segregated from the skilled urban workers by shop as well as by factory, so the two groups shared few experiences and had little basis for cooperation.

Heavy industry provided more jobs for new workers than any other branch of the economy, because of both its extremely rapid expansion and the multitude of unskilled tasks it required. With little or no training, newly arrived workers could perform one repetitious job on an assembly line or serve as manual laborers, carting materials and products around the factory.

Light Industry

Though the bulk of investment and expansion in Moscow industry occurred in heavy industry during the 1930s, light industry also ex-

[45]TsGAOR f. 7952, op. 3, d. 260, l. 31.
[46]Ibid., d. 214, l. 1.

Table I.2. Number of workers in light industry, Moscow, 1929–1935

Industry	1929	1932	1935
Textiles	37,800	42,600	41,900
Shoes and clothing	44,900	80,100	88,500
Food processing	28,400	42,300	48,500

Source: TsGAORgM f. 126, op. 10, d. 47, 1. 72.

perienced some growth (see Table I-2). In no textile mills, however, did half of the labor force consist of former peasants who had begun work within the previous two years, as was the case in new heavy-industry plants. In 1932 just over half of the workers at the Tri-Mountain textile mill were of peasant origin, but most of them had worked in industry over five years (and many over fifteen years), an indication that they had moved to Moscow in the 1920s or before the Revolution.[47]

The percentage of young workers also was lower in light industry than in heavy industry. Evidence indicates that a number of young peasants did initially find work in light industry but soon left for higher-paying jobs in heavy industry.[48] The proportion of workers who were of peasant origin and who had worked less than one year was higher in food processing than in other light industries. Many food-processing enterprises in effect offered only seasonal labor—the canning of fruits and vegetables at harvesttime. Peasant in-migrants may have found temporary employment in these enterprises at first but sought better pay and year-round work in heavy industry once they resolved to settle in Moscow permanently.

Light-industry enterprises varied widely in size; some were very large. In 1932 the Red Hercules rubber factory, which produced shoes and galoshes, employed just over 10,000 workers and the Paris Commune shoe factory had over 5,000 workers. By 1936 the Red Rosa, Tri-Mountain, and Klara Zetkin textile mills each had around 5,000 workers. The Freedom soap factory employed 1,800 workers in 1932 and 2,700 by 1936. Food-processing enterprises tended to be smaller, though the Moscow meat-processing plant had over 1,000 workers

[47]Statistics not otherwise attributed are from the trade union census conducted in 1932, which is discussed in detail in Appendix II.
[48]AAN f. 359, op. 2, d. 499, l. 14; TsGAOR f. 5451, op. 13, d. 76, ll. 47–49.

in 1932 and over 6,500 by 1936, and the Red October candy factory employed around 5,000 workers throughout the 1930s.[49]

Alongside these huge factories were many small workshops, especially prevalent in shoe and clothing production as well as in food processing. Moscow registered 466 factories with a total of 203,300 workers in light industry in 1930. These enterprises included 213 food-processing enterprises with a total of 37,200 workers and 81 clothing factories with a total of 78,200 workers.[50] These figures represent only industries covered by government industrial surveys; the many enterprises of workshop dimensions were not tallied.

Food processing was often a small-scale operation—canning vegetables, producing cooking oil, baking bread. Lack of investment in these enterprises caused production to lag behind the city's needs, especially as the population rose so quickly in the 1930s.[51] Twelve new bread factories constructed in the course of the decade and equipped with imported technology employed up to 400 workers, most of whom had recently arrived from the village, and many of whom were women.[52] The majority of Moscow bakeries, however, remained small-scale operations with little or no mechanization.

Some enterprises—sewing, weaving, woodworking shops—were more accurately called handicraft operations than light industries. Such workshops were quite numerous in Moscow before the Revolution and in the 1920s. With the First Five-Year Plan, private ownership of the means of production became illegal and these enterprises converted to a cooperative basis or closed altogether.[53] Workshops that remained open as cooperatives faced severe shortages of labor and materials throughout the 1930s. Handicraft cooperatives fulfilled only 26.2 percent of the production called for by government planners during the first half of 1931.[54] Worsening shortages of furniture, clothing, blankets, and other handicraft items were attributed to the difficulty cooperative workshops faced attracting and keeping workers with the

[49]TsGAORgM f. 2872, op. 2, d. 220, ll. 6–9.

[50]*Statisticheskii spravochnik po raionam Moskovskoi oblasti,* p. 73.

[51]*Pishchevik,* September 4, 1930, p. 2.

[52]*Zavod sovetskogo khleba,* pp. 19–21; Romanovskii, pp. 21–22; *Za udarnichestvo* 1936 no. 1, p. 16. One Jewish bakery manager trusted dekulakized peasants and gave them priority in hiring: Harvard Project nos. 20, 380.

[53]*Ekonomicheskoe stroitel'stvo* 1930 no. 3, pp. 64–65.

[54]*Moskovskaia promyshlennaia kooperatsiia* 1931 no. 7, p. 1.

low wages they offered.[55] With investment in heavy industry a priority throughout the 1930s, handicraft production lacked the resources needed to sustain itself. Traditionally many peasants who arrived in Moscow had found work in handicraft shops because they had experience doing this type of work in the countryside. With shrinking opportunities in this area and higher wages in other sectors, however, even the few who initially took such work soon left for other employment.

The Service Sector

Historians and even Soviet officials have tended to ignore the service sector when they have discussed the working class. Such jobs as cafeteria employee, street cleaner, domestic servant, nursery attendant, night watchman, and doorkeeper generally required little or no skill and therefore attracted a large number of former peasants. Though the status and wages of such jobs remained low, the growing population increased the demand for such workers throughout the 1930s. The recruitment of women into the workforce added further reason to expand such services as cafeterias and nurseries. This expansion in turn created new jobs, largely filled by women.

The number of cafeterias in Moscow grew to 2,400 by mid-1932, with over 47,000 employees (some 65 percent of them women). By 1939, 59,000 employees worked in public cafeterias.[56] Cafeterias and restaurants employed workers as cashiers, waitresses, three categories of cooks, servers, carters, cleaners, and bread cutters. Buffets and kiosks that sold prepared foods also required attendants. Most of these employees were female in-migrants who lacked experience but could learn the basic skills involved very quickly. After some time in the city, many of them moved on to higher-paying jobs and were replaced by more recent arrivals.[57]

[55]TsGAORgM f. 1289, op. 1, d. 91, ll. 10, 20, 66.

[56]*Moskovskoe obshchestvennoe pitanie,* August 25, 1932, p. 2; TsGAORgM f. 126, op. 2, d. 98b, ll. 32–33; *Moskva v tsifrakh,* I. A. Grakin and T. A. Selivanov, eds. (Moscow, 1940), p. 82. This growth paralleled a nationwide increase in public catering workers, from 80,000 in 1929 to 554,000 (63 percent of them women) in 1935: *Trud v SSSR* (1936), p. 25.

[57]TsGAORgM f. 453, op. 1, d. 38, ll. 1–16; *Obshchestvennoe pitanie* 1935 no. 5, p. 12; *Rabochii narodnogo pitaniia* 1929 no. 1, p. 18.

Former peasants also filled the rising demand for maintenance workers. The growing number of apartments and barracks required some 60,000 cleaning people, doorkeepers, and attendants by 1940, and the low status of these jobs ensured that recently arrived peasants filled them.[58] Municipal authorities also hired new workers to sweep streets in the summer and plow snow in the winter.[59] Other service jobs—repairers, plumbers, window washers, and so forth—absorbed thousands of other workers of peasant origin.[60]

Trade and the Black Market

In late 1929 authorities closed all private shops and began to arrest petty traders for "speculating." Street vendors, most of them peasants selling food they brought from the countryside, virtually disappeared from Moscow in the winter of 1929–30. Officials at that time forbade peasants to carry sacks of food on trains, though frequent arrests of petty traders in Moscow indicate that some continued to do so. In an effort to alleviate food shortages, in March 1930 the Central Committee reopened peasant markets and proclaimed that peasants were not to be hindered in selling food they had grown. The buying and reselling of food ("speculation"), however, was still outlawed.

State and cooperative trade replaced private trade as the (albeit inadequate) supplier of goods and food in Moscow stores. During the First Five-Year Plan there were calls in the press to recruit more workers for the supply system and stores, and by 1935 nearly 100,000 people worked in this area.[61] In 1935 most store workers were young women, most warehouse workers young men, and in both cases a large portion had less than two years of work experience.[62] The Moscow trade census does not include data on social origin, but the unskilled nature of this work made it available to former peasants. Countless reports sounded the alarm that "alien elements," "kulaks," and "swindlers" had penetrated the system of state and cooperative trade.[63] In

[58]*Moskva v tsifrakh* (1940), p. 23; Harvard Project no. 324.
[59]TsGAORgM f. 126, op. 10, d. 47, l. 151; Romanovskii, p. 51.
[60]Harvard Project no. 92.
[61]*Rabochaia Moskva*, September 16, 1931, p. 2; *Trud v SSSR* (1936), pp. 34–35; TsGAORgM f. 126, op. 10, d. 47, l. 151.
[62]TsGAORgM f. 126, op. 10, d. 47, ll. 176–178.
[63]TsGAORgM f. 1289, op. 1, d. 839, l. 4; N. N. Evreinov, "Novye kadry i zadachi

part these reports reflected Soviet officials' vigilance against "class enemies" and their impulse to find a scapegoat for the ailing food-supply system, but undoubtedly some former NEPmen and trading peasants did obtain employment in state trade once private trade had been outlawed.

Official efforts to eliminate private trade did not succeed entirely. Throughout the 1930s a thriving second economy continued alongside state and cooperative trade. One report claimed that some cooperative stores were in fact run by private owners for their own profit. Another report revealed that black-market vodka was widely available on the streets, and these sales increased when a local liquor store was closed.[64] Particularly common was illegal sale of cigarettes by homeless children, who also made a living by begging, gambling, and stealing.[65]

Official attempts to eliminate the black market led to numerous arrests but ultimately failed. Crackdowns brought the dispersal of market activity but not its elimination. People continued to produce and sell things, now secretly in their homes rather than in stores. The need for exchange of goods grew as the availability and quality of items in state stores declined during the First Five-Year Plan.[66] Statistics on the total number of people engaged in illegal trade obviously do not exist. It was a full-time occupation for relatively few, but most people found it necessary to barter and trade illegally to obtain the goods they needed.

The numbers of workers employed in state and cooperative trade remained small in comparison with those in other sectors. The priorities of the industrialization drive determined where resources were invested, where jobs were created, and where wages were highest. Thousands of the peasant in-migrants who initially found employment in construction, transport, the service sector, and trade ultimately moved on to the assembly lines in Moscow's new and renovated heavy-industry plants.

---

profsoiuzov," *Voprosy profdvizheniia* 1933 no. 5, pp. 25–26; TsGAMO f. 747, op. 1, d. 165, l. 5; Salov, p. 46.

[64]TsGAORgM f. 1289, op. 1, d. 197, ll. 1–21; *Rabochii narodnogo pitaniia* 1929 no. 2, p. 19.

[65]British Foreign Office 371/19469, p. 200; TsGAORgM f. 150, op. 5, d. 66, l. 51.

[66]One woman found that even stores purchased her privately (and illegally) produced blouses because manufactured consumer goods were so scarce: Harvard Project no. 100. See also Kotkin, pp. 460–468.

The 1932 Trade Union Census

The most significant body of statistical data on workers in the 1930s is the 1932 trade union census. Trade union leaders commissioned the census out of concern over the social origins of new workers. The data they collected, then, are quite useful in an effort to gauge the impact of peasants who entered the workforce. All information is broken down by branch of industry and by territorial or productive units, with entries for many individual enterprises in Moscow. This presentation of data permits a factory-by-factory examination of the workforce.

One of the census indices is the social origin of workers (father's occupation), and it is cross-tabulated with the year workers began work. One may observe, for example, that at the Hammer and Sickle plant, 70.2 percent of the 570 workers polled who began work in 1932 were of peasant origin.[1] Though social origin is not cross-tabulated with other indices, one may glean some profile of new workers of peasant origin by checking the other cross-tabulations of the cohort that began work in 1932. Such indices include age, gender, nationality, Party membership, literacy, education, previous occupation, participation in socialist emulation, and ties with agriculture.

The questionnaire, the instructions to census takers, and our knowledge of the trade union leaders' motives in conducting the census enable us to clarify some of these indices. The fact that the trade union

[1]*Profsoiuznaia perepis'*, p. 94.

leadership commissioned the census out of concern that the massive influx of peasants might dilute the politically conscious proletariat influenced the census categories. Union leaders hoped to measure the political consciousness of workers. Census categories therefore reflect their preconceptions of a politically conscious worker (an educated, literate person who engaged in socialist emulation and had no ties with agriculture). The questions in turn implicitly informed workers' mental picture of a politically conscious worker, and may even have influenced their behavior.

Thus the census is not a dry body of objective data; it is a product of its time, and of the interaction between workers and trade union activists. The category "ties with agriculture," for example, is vague and would reveal little if it were taken at face value. But the question asked was "Do you (alone or jointly with your family) belong to a collective farm or engage in independent agriculture?" Instructions informed census takers that garden plots and cows in the suburbs did not qualify as agriculture.[2] One must imagine the dynamic between the urban-bred trade union activist who asked this question and the former peasant who answered. A young in-migrant who wanted to make a good impression on the activist questioning her might untruthfully deny ties to her family back in the village, especially if her family had refused to join a collective farm and were farming independently. Conversely, an in-migrant who felt allegiance only to his artel elder might not hesitate to answer affirmatively, and if he were bearded and wore peasant clothes, then the census taker probably would not hesitate to classify him as having ties with agriculture.

Census takers were instructed that Party candidacy qualified as Party membership, but membership in the Komsomol did not, and that self-education or home education did not count as years of education. They were to ask workers to classify themselves as "illiterate," "able to read," or "able to read and write." A separate study conducted in February 1933 showed much higher rates of literacy among workers than the trade union census did. Compilers noted that many workers counted as "semiliterate" in the separate study (a category absent from the census) must have called themselves "illiterate" in the trade union census.[3] The fact that the census takers were so quick

[2]Ibid., pp. 35, 70, 259.
[3]Ibid., pp. 41, 70, 259.

to recalculate the illiteracy rate indicates their sensitivity to the subject. The fact that a large number of workers could be reclassified simply by the addition of the category "semiliterate" also indicates the tenuousness of these classifications.

Before analyzing the data, we have to evaluate their accuracy by considering the scope of the census and how it was conducted. The 1932 census was indeed a full-scale census, in contrast to the trade union's selective surveys of workers in 1929 and 1931. A mass political campaign accompanied the census; newspapers, meetings, and radio broadcasts explained its importance to all workers. Census-taking brigades composed of the most literate volunteers were provided with special instruction before they undertook the survey.[4] All of these features inspire confidence in the results.

Some other aspects of the census are less inspiring. Each branch of industry was to conduct the census in five to fifteen days, but in reality the average time was two months. Not all branches began at once; the cement workers' union initiated its census in June 1932, the majority of unions conducted theirs in September and October, and the metallurgical workers' union surveyed its members in early 1933.[5] With the high rate of labor turnover in this period, census takers counted some workers twice and missed others entirely.

A mandatory exchange of trade union cards accompanied the census and was largely responsible for the delays. Officials required payment of all back dues as a prerequisite for exchanging cards and participating in the census. An article in the daily trade union newspaper scolded workers for neglecting to keep up their dues, indicating that such neglect was common.[6] The campaign waged to encourage participation in the census may have persuaded many delinquent union members to pay up, but those who did not were simply excluded from the census. Nor can this exclusion be regarded as random error, because workers who did not pay their dues may have been the least literate or the least educated.

The percentage of members polled varied from union to union. Over 80 percent of the transport machine builders' union participated, but only 55 percent of construction union members did so. Nonetheless,

[4]Ibid., pp. 63, 65.
[5]Ibid., p. 65.
[6]*Trud*, August 8, 1932, p. 4.

these figures are still much higher than those of the 1929 and 1931 surveys, both of which lacked funds to canvass workers in more than a few selected branches or enterprises. Moreover, the 1932 census results are much more complete for Moscow than for many other parts of the country. Non-Russian republics, where the questionnaire had to be translated, dragged down the national percentage of workers polled. (In 1934, when the census was published, many Central Asian trade unions were still compiling results.) In Moscow oblast, an average of 78.8 percent of members were polled in each union. Census takers canvassed 93.5 percent of railroad union members in Moscow oblast but only 67.8 percent in the nation as a whole.[7]

What of workers who did not belong to a union? Efforts to poll such people succeeded only marginally; less than 5 percent of the workers surveyed were not union members.[8] This fact is of particular concern, because peasants who recently began industrial work were less likely to have joined a union. Between January 1928 and October 1931 the number of Soviet workers increased by 10.6 million while the number of trade union members grew by only 4 million.[9] A selective survey of Moscow metalworkers in October 1931 showed that the union enrolled 95 percent of those who began work before 1928, but the figures for those who began work in 1930 and 1931 fell to 60 and 41 percent, respectively.[10]

A trade union plenum in 1931 called for a campaign to increase membership, and as a result over a million workers joined between October 1931 and January 1932. This increase brought membership in the metallurgy and machine-building unions to roughly 85 percent of workers, but membership in the construction and logging unions remained low, at 65 percent and 45 percent, respectively. The relevant figures are unavailable, but census compilers claimed that many more workers joined a union in the course of 1932 (partly in response to the campaign surrounding the census), and were therefore included in the census.[11]

One final calculation provides a clearer idea of the completeness of the census. Census tables list the total number of workers polled

[7]*Profsoiuznaia perepis'*, pp. 63, 65–67.
[8]Ibid., p. 66.
[9]*Materialy k otchetu VTsSPS IX s''ezdu profsoiuzov* (Moscow, 1932), p. 167.
[10]*Profsoiuznaia perepis'*, p. 172.
[11]Ibid., pp. 168, 172, 66.

Table II.1. Social origin and rural ties of workers in two Moscow factories, 1932 (percent)

Year began work	Number of workers	Social origin[a]		Connection with agriculture
		Worker	Peasant	
Hammer and Sickle plant				
To 1917	1,697	46.1%	52.2%	11.8%
1918–21	444	44.9	52.0	12.7
1922–25	1,008	40.2	57.2	14.9
1926–27	627	35.5	60.2	22.0
1928–29	885	42.3	51.8	20.2
1930	1,037	39.1	54.7	28.0
1931	893	28.1	67.0	31.5
1932	570	25.7	70.2	38.2
Stalin automobile plant				
To 1917	1,722	53.4	43.2	11.7
1918–21	600	50.6	43.8	11.3
1922–25	1,437	46.0	44.6	12.3
1926–27	1,251	44.0	48.0	13.4
1928–29	1,976	44.8	45.5	16.9
1930	1,917	43.2	43.9	16.2
1931	1,908	34.4	58.1	26.4
1932	822	27.8	67.9	30.3

[a] Father's occupation.

at each Moscow factory, and these figures may be compared with the total number of workers at each factory in 1932, as obtained from independent sources. The official history of the Stalin automobile plant, for example, states that the factory had 14,000 workers in 1932.[12] The trade union census polled 12,671 workers at this plant, or approximately 90 percent of all workers. The census data, then, are relatively good for large Moscow factories, but are less complete for the construction industry and the service sector.

Tables II.1 through II.9 present 1932 trade union data on industry in and around Moscow.[13] Tables II.1 and II.2 provide data on workers' social origin and connection with agriculture. These figures probably underrepresent the workers who maintained a connection with agriculture, but they do show that the percentage rose rapidly as peasants poured into the city. Construction work, because of its

[12]*Istoriia Moskovskogo avtozavoda*, p. 189.
[13]All tables in this appendix are based on tables in *Profsoiuznaia perepis'* (n.p.).

Table II.2. Social origin and rural ties of workers in four sectors of the Moscow oblast economy, 1932 (percent)

Year began work	Number of workers	Social origin[a]		Connection with agriculture
		Worker	Peasant	
Textile industry				
To 1917	12,943	60.3%	38.6%	9.3%
1918–21	1,340	63.8	34.2	8.9
1922–25	4,656	65.0	32.5	11.9
1926–27	1,582	61.1	36.5	15.6
1928–29	2,315	65.2	31.9	16.1
1930	1,598	57.7	39.1	19.7
1931	2,379	43.1	54.2	29.2
1932	2,064	43.0	54.4	28.4
Flour, bread, and candy industry				
To 1917	7,878	47.8	49.7	18.2
1918–21	1,428	48.5	48.3	14.6
1922–25	2,647	46.2	50.4	16.9
1926–27	1,910	43.0	53.7	20.7
1928–29	3,023	39.7	56.6	23.6
1930	2,946	33.2	63.1	29.4
1931	4,024	26.7	70.9	37.3
1932	3,264	22.2	76.0	43.2
Construction				
To 1917	16,004	32.3	66.3	44.7
1918–21	4,843	30.4	67.3	43.4
1922–25	10,315	27.8	70.6	46.6
1926–27	8,858	25.7	72.4	48.3
1928–29	14,911	22.3	75.5	51.2
1930	13,336	18.8	79.4	55.7
1931	13,716	15.7	82.9	59.9
1932	11,343	15.1	82.8	59.8
Municipal economy[b]				
To 1917	8,011	45.5	52.8	9.8
1918–21	2,007	44.2	52.6	9.5
1922–25	2,669	42.8	53.5	12.4
1926–27	1,818	44.0	52.8	15.9
1928–29	2,566	45.4	51.2	18.3
1930	2,641	41.5	55.2	20.9
1931	2,847	31.9	65.8	30.0
1932	1,888	33.2	64.8	30.0

[a] Father's occupation.
[b] Kommunal'noe khoziaistvo.

Table II.3. Workers of peasant origin in six economic sectors who maintained ties to agriculture in 1932, by year work begun (percent)

	1928–29	1930	1931	1932
Hammer and Sickle plant	39.0%	51.2%	47.0%	54.4%
Stalin automobile plant	37.1	36.9	45.4	44.6
Textile industry	50.5	50.4	53.9	52.2
Flour, bread, candy industry	41.7	46.6	52.6	56.8
Construction	67.8	70.2	72.2	72.2
Municipal economy	35.7	37.9	45.6	46.3

seasonal character, employed large numbers of temporary migrants who maintained a connection with agriculture. Even during the First Five-Year Plan, when managers attempted to continue construction work throughout the year, a large percentage of construction workers preserved their ties to the land.

A useful calculation indicates the percentage of workers of peasant origin who had a connection with agriculture.[14] If we divide the number of workers with a connection to agriculture by the number who were of peasant origin, we find roughly the extent to which workers of peasant origin were maintaining their ties to agriculture over several years. (See Table II.3.)

These figures demonstrate even more clearly the persistence of construction workers' ties to the village. Over two-thirds of peasants who began construction work in 1928–29 continued either alone or jointly with their families to engage in agriculture through 1932. Though the percentage of textile workers who had a connection with agriculture is smaller, these ties appear to have been equally tenacious, owing to the fact that many textile mills in Moscow oblast were located in rural areas. (Unfortunately, the census provides no separate statistics on textile workers in Moscow city as distinct from Moscow oblast.) Peasants from the surrounding countryside staffed these mills and simultaneously continued to farm with their families.

Peasant in-migrants with jobs in the municipal economy (including various service-sector jobs, from work in cafeterias and nurseries to driving trams) and in flour, bread, and candy manufacturing appear

[14]The trade union census may have underestimated the number of workers of peasant origin by classifying some who had grown up in the village as hereditary proletarians if their fathers had done some seasonal work in the city.

to have been more ready to break their ties with agriculture, perhaps because many of these workers were women. Female in-migrants who broke their ties with agriculture may have moved to Moscow in the wake of collectivization or joined husbands already working in the city. When the whole family was in Moscow, the reasons for sustaining ties to the village sharply declined. Alternatively, these women may have been orphans or widows who left the village permanently because they had no future there.

The Hammer and Sickle metallurgical plant and the Stalin automobile plant provide an interesting contrast. Metallurgy traditionally attracted more temporary migrants than other heavy industry because it employed more unskilled labor and also because the plant had to close periodically for repairs to the blast furnace, allowing migrants to return to the village frequently. Peasants who secured the more skilled jobs at the automobile plant worked year round and earned higher wages, so many of them turned their backs on agriculture altogether. Not more than 39 percent of workers of peasant origin who began work at the Hammer and Sickle plant in 1928–29 maintained (or admitted to having) ties to agriculture through 1932. Even in the absence of precise figures, the contrast here between peasant in-migrants in factories and those in construction is clear. Though workers' connections with agriculture did not disappear as quickly as trade union officials would have liked, those ties did weaken among workers in industry.

Table II.4 shows the previous occupations of workers who began work in 1932. A large percentage of workers in this cohort were peasant in-migrants (as Table II.1 indicates, over 70 percent at the Hammer and Sickle plant and over 80 percent in the Moscow oblast construction industry). One problem with the category "previous occupation" is that it recognizes only the primary previous occupation, not part-time nonagricultural work. The construction workers who said they had previously worked in agriculture, for example, may have been part-time stonemasons or carpenters before they ever left the village.

The previous occupations of new workers at the Hammer and Sickle plant were much more widely distributed. Because this cohort was overwhelmingly of peasant origin, most workers who listed domestic service as their previous occupation were undoubtedly women who had found jobs as servants when they arrived in Moscow and then switched to factory work when such higher-paying employment pre-

Table II.4. Previous occupations of people who started work in four industrial sectors in 1932 (percent)

	Hammer and Sickle plant	Construction	Flour, bread, industry	Municipal work
Agricultural wage laborer	4.2%	3.9%	2.8%	2.5%
Other wage laborer	8.3	12.3	4.4	9.3
Domestic servant	8.5	1.7	6.7	8.7
Agriculturist	48.3	75.1	68.1	44.2
Handicraft worker	,1.3	0.5	0.8	0.9
Homemaker	10.4	1.2	9.2	17.3
Student	9.1	3.8	4.8	7.5
Soldier	2.3	0.6	0.4	0.9
Unemployed or retired	7.6	0.8	2.8	8.6

sented itself. High-paying factory work apparently also attracted a sizable number of homemakers and students to the workforce (most of whom were of urban origin). The strikingly large percentage of workers in the flour, bread, and candy industry who named agriculture as their previous occupation does indicate that most came from the countryside, but it does not reveal the sizable number who may have been involved part-time in cottage industry or some other rural but nonagricultural occupation.

Previous occupation in private trade is one important category omitted from the trade union census. Again this omission reflects a Soviet bias; since private trade was now illegal, it was regarded as an inappropriate previous occupation for workers. (Indeed, beginning in 1929 a private trader could be arrested and sentenced to a labor camp, so even had the category been included, few workers would have admitted to having been one.) It is likely, however, that a number of municipal workers of peasant origin had been active in private trade (transporting produce and goods between the countryside and the city during NEP, for example). Once private trade became illegal, many of these people took jobs in cafeterias and restaurants.

Table II.5 shows the percentage of people who began work in 1932 who were illiterate. Because literacy is such a subjective concept, these figures are meaningful only as a basis for comparison. The differences among workers in the various sectors are not great. The particularly small percentage of illiterate municipal workers reflects the fact that some service-sector jobs required at least rudimentary literacy. The relatively high rates of literacy overall reinforce the point

Table II.5. Illiteracy among new workers in four industrial sectors, 1932 (percent)

	Percent illiterate
Hammer and Sickle plant	10.5%
Construction	12.8
Flour, bread, candy industry	16.5
Municipal economy	6.2

that the most literate and most prepared peasants were the first to migrate to Moscow.

Tables II.6 and II.7 characterize all workers polled in the factories and branches of industry we have been contemplating. Still largely male in 1932, the workforce at the Hammer and Sickle plant (Table II.6) included more workers of peasant than of proletarian origin (the balance consisted of workers of white-collar origin). The workers overall were quite young (the women overwhelmingly so) and roughly half of the men and 80 percent of the women had worked in metallurgy less than three years.

The workers at the Stalin automobile plant (Table II.6) were similar, though the men tended to be a bit older and more experienced. The women, though, were overwhelmingly young and inexperienced, a reflection of the fact that virtually no women had been hired in heavy industry before the First Five-Year Plan.

The textile industry traditionally had attracted a large number of female workers. Because light industry expanded very little during the First Five-Year Plan, the workforce at the Tri-Mountain mill (Table II.6) hardly changed despite the influx of peasants to the city. Even though the percentage of workers of peasant origin was quite large, the relatively small number of workers with under five years' experience indicates that these people had come to Moscow before the 1930s, many of them even before the Revolution.

The youth and peasant origin of the construction workforce (Table II.7) stands out most prominently. Also noteworthy is the small number of women involved, and the fact that those women who did work in construction were young and new to that type of employment. Male construction workers as a whole also had few years of experience; normally peasants who became construction workers found higher-paying and more prestigious work after a year or two in the city.

Table II.6. Characteristics of male and female workers in three Moscow factories, 1932 (percent)

	Hammer and Sickle plant		Stalin automobile plant		Tri-Mountain textile mill	
	Men (N=6,987)	Women (N=2,184)	Men (N=9,474)	Women (N=3,197)	Men (N=1,369)	Women (N=2,745)
Social origin						
Worker	44.9%	46.3%	44.8%	44.0%	49.5%	46.2%
Peasant	49.2	47.2	45.2	47.1	47.5	52.1
Age						
Under 17	10.2	16.7	7.4	13.6	6.6	5.7
18–19	14.3	22.2	13.4	20.6	5.8	8.7
20–23	16.4	24.7	23.7	29.5	9.6	16.3
24–29	23.0	17.4	30.8	20.4	13.3	16.6
30–39	20.3	13.0	15.7	11.5	23.1	22.2
40–49	10.5	4.4	6.6	3.6	21.4	21.6
50–59	4.7	1.5	2.0	0.7	18.0	8.7
60+	0.6	0.1	0.4	0.1	2.2	0.3
Years in production[a]						
Under 1	10.6	22.9	16.3	40.1	14.3	15.9
1–2	27.2	48.4	16.7	27.3	5.9	11.2
2–3	9.2	9.4	12.7	11.4	5.3	6.8
3–5	10.0	7.1	16.3	9.2	5.3	7.1
5–10	18.8	8.1	19.9	7.3	10.9	12.0
10–15	9.5	2.8	8.1	2.8	13.0	11.5
15+	14.7	3.3	10.0	1.9	45.3	35.5

[a]Stazh.

The diversity of the Moscow municipal economy (Table II.7) makes it difficult to discuss the workforce as a whole. Noteworthy, however, is the large percentage of workers of peasant origin, an indication that peasant in-migrants filled the expanding number of jobs in this sector and indeed outnumbered workers of urban origin by the end of the First Five-Year Plan. Some of these workers, however, had begun work before the 1930s.

Branches of light industry, exemplified by the flour, bread, and candy industry (Table II.7), did not expand much during the First Five-Year Plan, so the number of young and inexperienced workers was not nearly so great as in heavy industry. Nonetheless, the figures on social origin and years in production make it clear that former peasants were obtaining employment here, too.

The trade union census also collected data on Party and Komsomol membership and participation in shock work (see Tables II.8 and II.9).

Table II.7. Characteristics of male and female workers in three sectors of Moscow oblast economy, 1932 (percent)

	Flour, bread, candy industry		Construction		Municipal economy	
	Men (N=16,700)	Women (N=12,826)	Men (N=88,261)	Women (N=11,122)	Men (N=15,892)	Women (N=10,391)
Social origin						
Worker	37.8%	41.9%	23.6%	20.6%	43.0%	43.4%
Peasant	59.2	55.2	74.5	77.3	54.1	54.5
Age						
Under 17	2.9	4.3	4.4	5.9	1.2	0.6
18–19	9.3	12.7	13.7	20.1	6.6	8.7
20–23	18.3	22.9	23.5	31.8	15.5	20.4
24–29	20.1	20.0	22.1	20.4	21.6	22.5
30–39	23.8	23.5	17.8	13.8	21.9	29.1
40–49	16.8	13.0	11.5	6.0	21.3	15.9
50–59	7.6	3.4	5.7	1.8	10.4	2.6
60+	1.2	0.2	1.3	0.2	1.5	0.2
Years in production[a]						
Under 1	15.9	30.3	19.9	47.1	9.3	22.5
1–2	13.6	19.0	20.8	28.2	11.2	18.1
2–3	7.8	8.3	12.0	9.2	7.5	8.8
3–5	10.1	9.0	13.8	6.9	9.7	9.0
5–10	16.2	11.5	15.6	5.3	17.4	14.7
10–15	10.2	7.6	6.0	1.9	12.8	13.4
15+	26.2	14.3	11.9	1.4	32.1	13.5

[a]Stazh.

We may examine these statistics by cohorts (year work begun) in order to compare peasant in-migrants who recently arrived with workers who had been there for some time. As one might expect, in all these branches former peasants and other new workers had much lower rates of membership in the Communist Party and of participation in shock work. Of significance, however, is the fact that participation in shock work increased substantially within one year of arrival, especially at the Stalin automobile plant. First-generation workers apparently were quick to take advantage of the wage bonuses and material benefits that accompanied shock work.

Because the Komsomol was an organization for young people, only the cohorts that began work during or after 1928 had many eligible members. The large number of young workers at the Stalin automobile plant account in part for the relatively large percentage of Komso-

Table II.8. Shock workers and members of Komsomol and Communist Party among workers in two Moscow factories, by year work begun (percent)

Factory and year work begun	Shock workers	Komsomol members	Party members
Hammer and Sickle plant			
To 1917	82.9%	0.2%	32.0%
1918–21	75.0	0.2	28.8
1922–25	72.6	2.1	31.3
1926–27	66.0	6.4	25.3
1928–29	60.7	18.8	14.6
1930	59.3	27.3	11.5
1931	53.9	25.2	6.2
1932	44.8	11.6	1.7
Stalin automobile plant			
To 1917	88.2	0.3	30.8
1918–21	86.2	0.2	35.5
1922–25	84.6	5.7	34.3
1926–27	81.2	14.9	28.1
1928–29	77.4	28.9	17.9
1930	78.0	44.1	10.6
1931	74.7	29.7	7.1
1932	37.6	14.4	1.7

mol members there. The construction industry, however, employed an even greater percentage of young people, and Komsomol membership there was quite low. Urban youth employed at the automobile plant may account for part of the difference in Komsomol membership, but it also seems clear that peasant in-migrants employed in factories, either bowing to pressure or of their own accord, joined the Komsomol. Construction workers, because of their artels and their stronger ties with agriculture, much more commonly resisted joining the organization. The many construction workers who moved on to factory jobs in Moscow during the Second Five-Year Plan undoubtedly became more involved in official institutions, even as they continued to maintain their noninstitutional social networks.

Table II.9. Shock workers and members of Komsomol and Communist Party among workers in four sectors of Moscow oblast economy, by year work begun (percent)

Sector and year work begun	Shock workers	Komsomol members	Party members
Textile industry			
To 1917	63.6%	0.1%	11.8%
1918–21	60.5	0.3	12.3
1922–25	56.8	1.5	12.9
1926–27	52.6	5.9	9.9
1928–29	55.6	12.1	8.7
1930	51.1	23.9	5.2
1931	47.3	16.2	2.6
1932	37.6	9.2	1.3
Flour, bread, and candy industry			
To 1917	75.8	0.4	15.9
1918–21	72.1	0.5	14.6
1922–25	72.3	3.1	16.4
1926–27	67.8	7.2	9.6
1928–29	66.1	14.3	6.1
1930	66.8	13.3	4.8
1931	64.3	10.2	1.5
1932	37.0	4.3	0.5
Construction			
To 1917	54.6	0.3	7.1
1918–21	54.1	1.4	7.6
1922–25	55.6	3.1	7.9
1926–27	56.4	6.6	5.8
1928–29	54.0	8.8	2.9
1930	53.3	10.5	2.0
1931	48.6	8.8	1.7
1932	35.6	6.2	1.9
Municipal economy			
To 1917	79.9	0.2	19.8
1918–21	76.4	0.5	15.7
1922–25	73.1	2.7	15.8
1926–27	68.4	8.6	11.7
1928–29	65.0	5.0	6.8
1930	68.5	13.5	4.6
1931	61.8	9.7	2.0
1932	29.9	4.6	0.9

Bibliography

PRIMARY SOURCES

Archives

Arkhiv Akademii Nauk SSSR (AAN)
    f. 359 Materialy zavodov Moskvy: Stenograficheskie otchety Partiinykh i Komsomol'skikh konferentsii, dannye otdelov kadrov, avtobiografii rabochikh.
Arkhiv Museia Istorii Moskvy
    Sergei Sergeevich Davydov, lichnyi fond.
Arkhiv zavoda "Serp i molot," Moscow
Bakmeteff archives, Columbia University
    John Hazard Papers.
    Olga Rachinskaia, unpublished memoir.
Bancroft Library, University of California, Berkeley
    Robin Kinkead Papers.
British Foreign Office. Russia—Correspondence, 1930–1940.
    Available on microfilm, Scholarly Resources, Wilmington, Del., 1982.
Harvard Emigré Interview Project. Harvard University Russian Research Center, 1950.
Hoover Institution archives
    American Engineers in Russia, 1927–1933. Compiled by H. H. Fisher. Papers, correspondence, questionnaires, and articles.
    Horace Gilbert, "Russia's Industrialization Program."
    Boris Nikolaevsky Papers: correspondence, articles, documents.
    Clarence T. Starr Papers.
    Janucy K. Zawodny, "Twenty-six Interviews with Former Soviet Factory Workers."
Moskovskii Partiinyi Arkhiv (MPA)

f. 3 Moskovskii oblastnoi komitet VKP(b).

f. 4 Moskovskii gorodskoi komitet VKP(b).

f. 69 Krasnopresnenskii raionnyi komitet VKP(b).

f. 80 Proletarskii raionnyi komitet VKP(b).

f. 262 Partiinaia organizatsiia Pervoi sittsenabivnoi fabriki.

f. 429 Partiinaia organizatsiia zavoda Serp i Molot.

f. 432 Partiinaia organizatsiia zavoda Dinamo (im. Kirova).

f. 433 Partiinaia organizatsiia Pervogo gosudarstvennogo avtomobil'nogo zavoda (im. Stalina).

f. 468 Partiinaia organizatsiia Elektrozavoda (im. Kuibysheva).

f. 634 Moskovskii oblastnoi komitet VLKSM.

f. 635 Moskovskii gorodskoi komitet VLKSM.

f. 667 Krasnopresnenskii raionnyi komitet VLKSM.

Tsentral'nyi Gosudarstvennyi Arkhiv Moskovskoi Oblasti (TsGAMO)

f. 738 Moskovskii oblastnoi komitet profsoiuza transportnykh rabochikh.

f. 747 Moskovskii oblastnoi komitet profsoiuza rabotnikov kooperatsii i gostor-
govli.

f. 1310 Proletarskii raionnyi komitet VLKSM.

f. 1921 Upravlenie rabochego snabzheniia Moskovskogo oblastnogo otdela
snabzheniia.

f. 4775 Moskovskii oblastnoi statisticheskii otdel.

f. 4867 Moskovskii oblastnoi komitet profsoiuza stroitelei.

f. 6833 Stroitel'nyi otdel Mosoblispolkoma.

Tsentral'nyi Gosudarstvennyi Arkhiv Narodnogo Khoziaistva SSSR (TsGANKh)

f. 1562 Tsentral'noe statisticheskoe upravlenie.

f. 4086 Glavnoe upravlenie mashinostroitel'noi promyshlennosti Narkomtiazhproma.

f. 7566 Glavnoe upravlenie ugol'noi promyshlennosti Narkomtiazhproma.

f. 7604 Narkomat legkoi promyshlennosti.

f. 7622 Glavnoe upravlenie avtotraktornoi promyshlennosti Narkomtiazhproma.

f. 7995 Narkomat tiazheloi promyshlennosti.

Tsentral'nyi Gosudarstvennyi Arkhiv Oktiabr'skoi Revoliutsii SSSR (TsGAOR)

f. 382 Narkomat truda RSFSR.

f. 5451 Vsesoiuznyi tsentral'nyi sovet profsoiuzov.

f. 5469 Tsentral'nyi komitet soiuza rabochikh metallistov.

f. 5475 Tsentral'nyi komitet soiuza stroitelei.

f. 5515 Narkomat truda.

f. 5574 Vsesoiuznaia konferentsiia o tekhnicheskom obuchenii.

f. 5475 Tsentral'nyi komitet soiuza stroitel'nykh rabochikh.

f. 7676 Tsentral'nyi komitet soiuza rabochikh obshchego mashinostroeniia.

f. 7709 Tsentral'nyi komitet soiuza rabotnikov gosuchrezhdenii.

f. 7952 "Istoriia fabrik i zavodov."

Tsentral'nyi Gosudarstvennyi Arkhiv Oktiabr'skoi Revoliutsii goroda Moskvy
(TsGAORgM)

f. 100 Zavod "Dinamo" (im. Kirova).

f. 126 Moskovskoe gosudarstvennoe upravlenie narodnogo-khoziaistvennogo ucheta Gosplana.
f. 150 Moskovskii gorodskoi sovet (old fond number).
f. 168 Fabrika im. Frunze.
f. 176 Zavod "Serp i Molot."
f. 214 Moskovskii gorodskoi komitet soiuza rabochikh mashinostroeniia.
f. 415 Avtozavod (im. Stalina).
f. 453 Glavnoe upravlenie narodnogo pitaniia Moskvy.
f. 515 Pervyi gosudarstvennyi podshipnikovyi zavod (im. Kaganovicha).
f. 977 Elektrozavod (im. Kuibysheva).
f. 1289 Moskovskii komitet raboche-krest'ianskoi inspektsii (Rabkrin).
f. 2617 Moskovskii gorodskoi komitet soiuza rabochikh khimicheskoi promyshlennosti.
f. 2872 Moskovskii gorodskoi sovet (new fond number).
f. 5301 Moskovskii gorodskoi komitet soiuza stroitelei.
Tsentral'nyi Partiinyi Arkhiv (TsPA)
f. 17 Tsentral'nyi Komitet.
f. 77 Lichnyi fond Zhdanova.
f. 78 Lichnyi fond Kalinina.
f. 85 Lichnyi fond Ordzhonikidze.
f. 88 Lichnyi fond Shcherbakova.
f. 89 Lichnyi fond Iaroslavskogo.
f. 112 Politupravlenie Narkomzema.
f. 558 Lichnyi fond Stalina.
United States National Archives
Records of the Department of State relating to the internal affairs of the Soviet Union, 1930–1939.

Periodicals (published in Moscow unless otherwise noted)

Amostroika. Newspaper of the reconstruction project for the Stalin automobile plant.
AMOvets. Newspaper of the Stalin automobile plant, 1929–1931.
Aviamotor. Newspaper of the Frunze aviation engine plant.
Avral. Newspaper of the Moscow Oblast Water Transport Administration.
Bednota. Newspaper for peasants published by the Communist Party.
Biullenten' Moskovskoi oblastnoi soiuz potrebitel'skikh obshchestv. Bulletin of the Moscow Oblast Department of Trade and Union of Consumer Societies.
Biullenten' Narkomata kommunal'nogo khoziaistva. Bulletin of the Commissariat of the Municipal Economy.
Biullenten' Narkomata torgovli. Bulletin of the Commissariat of Trade.
Bol'shevik. Journal of the Central Committee of the Communist Party.
Bor'ba klassov. Journal of the Institute of History of the Academy of Sciences.
Bronnitskii kolkhoz (Bronnitsy). Newspaper of the Bronnitsy district Communist Party cell.
Dognat' i peregnat'. Newspaper of the Stalin automobile plant, 1933–1940.

Ekonomicheskoe stroitel'stvo. Journal of the Moscow City Council and the Moscow Oblast Planning Commission.

Elektrozavod. Newspaper of the Kuibyshev electronics factory.

Informatsionnyi biullenten' o sostoianii uchetno-statisticheskoi raboty v Moskovskoi oblasti. Bulletin of the Moscow Oblast Economic Accounting Administration.

Iunyi kommunist. Journal of the Central Committee and the Moscow Committee of the Komsomol.

Izvestiia: Ofitsial'noe izdanie Narkomata truda. Bulletin of decrees of the Commissariat of Labor.

Izvestiia Mosoblispolkoma, gorispolkoma i Moskovskogo soveta. Newspaper of the Moscow oblast and city executive committees and of the Moscow City Council.

Kirovets. Newspaper of the Kirov Dinamo engine plant.

Klub. Journal on cultural work published by the All-Union Central Council of Trade Unions.

Klub i revolutsiia. Journal of the mass-culture sector of the Commissariat of Education.

Komsomol'skaia pravda. Newspaper of the Central and Moscow committees of the Komsomol.

Kooperativnaia zhizn'. Newspaper of the Consumers' and Producers' Cooperative Association.

Krasnyi bogatyr'. Newspaper of the Red Hercules factory.

Krasnyi sport. Newspaper of the All-Union Council of Physical Culture.

Krest'ianskaia gazeta. Newspaper published for peasants by the Central Committee of the Communist Party.

Kul'turnaia revoliutsiia. Journal on cultural work published by the All-Union Central Council of Trade Unions.

Legkaia industriia. Newspaper of the Commissariat of Light Industry.

Martenovka. Newspaper of the Hammer and Sickle metallurgical plant.

Metro v srok. Newspaper of the Metro Construction Trust.

Molodaia gvardiia. Journal of the Central Committee of the Komsomol.

Molodoi bol'shevik. Journal of the Moscow oblast and Moscow city Komsomol.

Moskovskaia kolkhoznaia gazeta. Newspaper of the Moscow Oblast Committee of the Communist Party and the Moscow Oblast Executive Committee.

Moskovskaia oblast'. Journal of the Moscow Oblast Executive Committee.

Moskovskaia pravda. Newspaper of the Moscow City Committee of the Communist Party and the Moscow City Council.

Moskovskaia promyshlennaia kooperatsiia. Journal of the Moscow Council of Producers' Cooperation.

Moskovskii bol'shevik. Journal of the Moscow City Committee of the Communist Party.

Moskovskii kraeved. Journal of the Society for the Study of Moscow Oblast.

Moskovskii proletarii. Journal of the Moscow Oblast Council of Trade Unions.

Moskovskii transportnik. Newspaper of the Moscow Oblast Transport Workers' Union.

Moskovskoe obshchestvennoe pitanie. Journal of the Moscow Nutrition Association.

Na planovom fronte. Journal of the Presidium of Gosplan.

Narodnoe khoziaistvo. Journal of the Central Economic Accounting Administration.

Narodnoe tvorchestvo. Journal of the All-Union Committee for Artistic Affairs and the All-Union Council of Trade Unions.

Nashe stroitel'stvo. Journal of Gosplan.

Na strazhe. Newspaper of the Central and Moscow Aviation Councils.

Na trudovom fronte. Journal of the Commissariat of Labor.

Novyi mir. Journal of the Union of Soviet Writers.

Novyi proletarii. Newspaper for newly literate workers, published by the All-Union Council of Trade Unions.

Obshchestvennoe pitanie. Journal of the Commissariat of Trade.

Organizatsiia truda. Journal of the Central Institute of Labor.

Partiinoe stroitel'stvo. Journal of the Central Committee of the Communist Party.

Pishchevik. Newspaper of the Food-Processing Trade Union.

Plan. Journal of Gosplan and the Central Economic Accounting Administration.

Planovoe khoziaistvo. Journal of Gosplan.

Podmoskovskii gigant. Newspaper of the Bobrinovskii electric plant.

Podshipnik. Journal for ballbearing factories published by the Commissariat of Heavy Industry.

Postroika. Newspaper of the Construction Trade Union.

Pravda. Newspaper copublished by the Moscow Committee and the Central Committee of the Communist Party.

Problemy ekonomiki. Journal of the Economics Institute of the Communist Academy.

Puti industrializatsii. Journal of the All-Union Economic Council.

Rabochaia gazeta. Newspaper for workers published by the Central Committee of the Communist Party.

Rabochaia Moskva. Newspaper for workers published by the Moscow City Committee of the Communist Party and the Moscow City Council.

Rabochii narodnogo pitaniia. Journal of the Public Catering Trade Union.

Rabotnitsa. Journal for female workers published by the Communist Party.

Radio v derevne. Newspaper of the Society of Friends of Radio.

Sobranie zakonov i rasporiazhenii SSSR. Journal of the Council of People's Commissars.

Sovetskaia iustitsiia. Journal of the Commissariat of Justice.

Sovetskoe gosudarstvo i pravo. Journal of the Institute of State and Law of the Academy of Sciences.

Sovetskoe kraevedenie. Journal of the Society of Marxist Regional Studies of the Communist Academy.

Sputnik agitatora dlia goroda. Journal of the Central Committee of the Communist Party.

Sputnik kommunista. Journal of the Moscow Oblast Committee of the Communist Party.

Stalinskii udarnik. Newspaper of the Stalinskii District Committee of the Communist Party.

Statisticheskoe obozrenie. Journal of the Central Statistical Administration.

Stroitel'. Journal of the construction branch of the Commissariat of Heavy Industry.

Stroitel'naia gazeta. Newspaper of the State Construction Committee.

Stroitel'naia promyshlennost'. Technical journal of the Construction Council of the All-Union Economic Council.

Stroitel'stvo Moskvy. Journal of the Moscow City Council.

Sudebnaia praktika RSFSR. Journal of the Commissariat of Justice.

Sud idet (Leningrad). Journal of legal proceedings of Leningrad courts.

Trud. Newspaper of the All-Union Central Council of Trade Unions.

Udarnik. Journal of the All-Union Central Council of Trade Unions.

Ukhtomskii rabochii (Liubertsy). Newspaper of the Ukhtomskii District Committee of the Communist Party.

Vecherniaia Moskva. Newspaper of the Moscow City Committee of the Communist Party and the Moscow City Council.

Vlast' sovetov. Legal journal of the All-Russian Central Executive Committee.

Vodnyi transport. Newspaper of the Commissariat of Water Transport.

Voprosy profdvizheniia. Journal of the All-Union Council of Trade Unions.

Voprosy truda. Journal of the Commissariat of Labor.

Za Bol'shevistskie tempy. Newspaper of the Zamoskvoretskii District Committee of the Communist Party.

Za industrializatsiiu. Newspaper of the Commissariat of Heavy Industry.

Za kachestvo kadrov. Journal of the pedagogical-methodology sector of the Commissariat of Education.

Za novyi byt. Journal of the Moscow Oblast Department of Health.

Za ovladenie tekhnikoi: Stroiindustriia. Journal of the Glavstroiprom construction trust.

Za promyshlennye kadry. Journal of the All-Union Economic Council.

Za sotsialisticheskuiu rekonstruktsiiu gorodov. Journal of the All-Union Council on the Municipal Economy.

Za sovetskii podshipnik. Newspaper of the Kaganovich ballbearing plant.

Za udarnichestvo. Journal of the Moscow Oblast Council of Trade Unions.

Other Primary Publications

Administrativno-territorial'noe delenie Soiuza SSR. Moscow, 1929.

Atlas Moskovskoi oblasti. S. E. Guberman, ed. Moscow, 1934.

Avdienko, M. "Sdvigi v strukture proletariata v pervoi piatiletke." *Planovoe khoziaistvo* 1932 no. 6/7.

Bard, A. "Opyt raboty s nachinaiushchimi chitateliami." *Krasnyi bibliotekar'* 1937 no. 12.

Berlin, I., and Ia. Mebel'. "Strukturnye svidgi v naselenii i proletariata." *Voprosy truda* 1932 no. 11/12.

Bogushevskii, V., and A. Khavin. "God velikogo pereloma." In *God deviat'nadtsatyi: Al'manakh deviatyi.* Moscow, 1936.

Bokarev, Iu. P. *Biudzhetnye obsledovaniia krest'ianskikh khoziaistv 20-kh godov kak istoricheskii istochnik.* Moscow, 1981.

Bol'shaia Sovetskaia entsiklopediia. Vol. 40. Moscow, 1938.

Bol'shakov, A. M. *Derevnia, 1917–1927.* Moscow, 1927.

Bulatov, S. "Khuliganstvo i mery bor'by s nim v rekonstruktivnom periode." *Sovetskoe gosudarstvo i pravo* 1933 no. 4.

Burrell, George. *An American Engineer Looks at Russia.* Boston, 1932.

Busygin, Aleksandr Kh. *Moia zhizn' i moia rabota.* Leningrad, 1935.

——. *Zhizn' moia i moikh druzhei.* Moscow, 1939.

Byli industrial'nye: Ocherki i vospominaniia. Moscow, 1973.

Chaiko, S. E. *Kak vesti kul'trabotu sredi stroitelei.* Moscow, 1930.

Chastushki. L. A. Astaf'eva, comp. Moscow, 1987.

Chastushki. F. M. Selivanova, comp. Moscow, 1990.

Chastushki v zapisiakh sovetskogo vremeni. B. N. Putilov, ed. Moscow/Leningrad, 1965.

Chetvertaia Moskovskaia oblastnaia i III gorodskaia konferentsii VKP(b): Stenograficheskii otchet. Moscow, 1934.

Delo chesti. Moscow, 1934.

Desiat' tysiach anekdotov. Vyp. 1. Moscow, 1991.

Dokumenty trudovoi slavy Moskvichei, 1919–1965. D. V. Diagilev, ed. Moscow, 1967.

Dorofeev, Ia. *Derevnia Moskovskoi gubernii.* Moscow, 1923.

Ehrenburg, Ilia. *Out of Chaos.* Alexander Bakshy, trans. New York, 1934.

——. *A Street in Moscow.* Sonia Volochova, trans. New York, 1932.

Ekonomiko-statisticheskii spravochnik po raionam Moskovskoi oblasti. Moscow, 1934.

Ermilov, V. V. *Byt rabochei kazarmy.* Moscow/Leningrad, 1930.

Evreinov, N. N. "Novye kadry i zadachi profsoiuzov." *Voprosy profdvizheniia* 1933 no. 5.

Fabriki i zavody Moskovskoi oblasti. Moscow, 1931.

Fedorova, T. V. *Naverkhu—Moskva.* Moscow, 1975.

Filatov, S. *Partrabota na zavode "Serp i molot."* Moscow/Leningrad, 1931.

Gan, L. *V zavodskom kotle.* Leningrad, 1930.

Gastev, A. K. *Kak nado rabotat'.* Moscow, 1966.

General'nyi plan rekonstruktsii goroda Moskvy. Moscow, 1936.

Gershberg, S. R. *Rabota u nas takaia: Zapiski zhurnalista-pravdista 30-kh godov.* Moscow, 1971.

Gertsenzon, A. "Klassovaia bor'ba i perezhitki starogo byta." *Sovetskaia iustitsiia* 1934 no. 2.

Gol'tsman, M. T. "Sostav novykh rabochikh." *Udarnik* 1932 no. 3/4.

Gol'tsman, M. T., and L. M. Kogan. *Starye i novye kadry proletariata.* Moscow, 1934.

Gor'kii i sozdanie istorii fabrik i zavodov: Sbornik dokumentov. L. M. Zak and S. S. Zimina, eds. Moscow, 1959.

Govoriat stroiteli sotsializma: Vospominaniia uchastnikov sotsialisticheskogo stroitel'stva v SSSR. Moscow, 1959.

Grudkov, V. A. *Peredovoi opyt—vsem stalevaram: Rasskaz starshego mastera moskovskogo zavoda "Serp i molot."* Moscow, 1958.

Gudov, Ivan. *Put' stakhanovtsa: Rasskaz o moei zhizni.* Moscow, 1938.

——. *Sud'ba rabochego.* Moscow, 1974.

Hindus, Maurice. *Red Bread: Collectivization in a Russian Village.* Ronald G. Suny, ed. Bloomington, Ind., 1988.

Industrializatsiia SSSR: Dokumenty i materialy. Vols. 2 and 3. Moscow, 1970–1971.

Istochnikovedenie istorii sovetskogo obshchestva. Moscow, 1964.

Istoriia metro Moskvy: Rasskazy stroitelei metro. A. Kosarev, ed. Moscow, 1935.

Istoriia zavodov: Sbornik. Moscow, 1932.

Itogi vsesoiuznoi perepisi naseleniia 1959 goda. 16 vols. Moscow, 1963.

Iz istorii razvitiia metallugicheskoi promyshlennosti Moskvy, 1883–1932 gg.: Dokumenty i materialy. I. L. Kornakovskii, ed. Moscow, 1981.

Kadry tiazheloi promyshlennosti v tsifrakh. Moscow, 1936.

Kaganovich, L. M. *Kontrol'nye tsifry tret'ego goda piatiletki i zadachi Moskovskoi organizatsii: Rech' na V plenume MOK VKP(b), 19 fevralia 1931 g.* Moscow, 1931.

——. *O stroitel'stvo metropolitena i plane goroda Moskvy.* Moscow, 1934.

Kalistratov, Iu. A. *Za udarnyi proizvodstvennyi kollektiv.* Moscow, 1931.

Kats, Ia. "Tekuchest' rabochei sily v krupnoi promyshlennosti." *Plan* 1937 no. 9.

Khain, A., and V. Khandros. *Kto oni—novye liudi na proizvodstve?* Moscow, 1930.

Kheinman, S. A. "Sotsialisticheskoe sorevnovanie v promyshlennosti SSSR." In *Sotsialisticheskoe sorevnovanie v promyshlennosti SSSR: Sbornik statei.* Ia. M. Bineman, ed. Moscow, 1930.

Kholodny, T. *Moscow: Old and New.* Moscow, 1933.

Khriashcheva, A. I. "Drobinost' krest'ianskogo khoziaistva i differentsiia." *Ekonomicheskoe obozrenie* 1927 no. 6.

——. "Usloviia drobimosti krest'ianskikh khoziaistv." *Ekonomicheskoe obozrenie* 1928 no. 9.

Kingsbury, Susan M., and Mildred Fairchild. *Factory, Family, and Woman in the Soviet Union.* New York, 1935.

Klivanskii, S. "Otkhodnichestvo v SSSR v 1928/29–1931 gg." *Voprosy truda* 1932 no. 10.

Kokshaiskii, I. "Obespechenie kommunal'nym blagoustroistvom otdel'nykh sotsial'nykh grupp naseleniia g. Moskvy." *Kommunal'noe khoziaistvo* 1931 no. 19/20.

Kolkhozy Moskovskoi oblasti po materialam maiskogo sploshnogo ucheta kolkhozov. Moscow, 1930.

Kovalev, L. I., ed. *Metro: Sbornik posviashchennyi pusku moskovskogo metropolitena.* Moscow, 1935.

K probleme stroitel'stva sotsialisticheskogo goroda. Moscow, 1930.

KPSS v resoliutsiiakh i resheniiakh s''ezdov, konferentsii i plenumov TsK (Moscow, 1984).

Krasil'nikov, M. "Agrarnoe pereselenie v 1928/29 g." *Statisticheskoe obozrenie* 1930 no. 5.

——. "Sviaz' naseleniia g. Moskvy s nadel'noi zemlei." *Statisticheskoe obozrenie* 1928 no. 6.

Kravchenko, Victor. *I Chose Freedom*. New Brunswick, N.J., 1989.

Kritsman, L. N. *Klassovoe rassloenie v sovetskoi derevne*. Moscow, 1926.

——. "O statisticheskom izuchenii klassovoi struktury sovetskoi derevni." *Na agrarnom fronte* 1926 no. 2.

——, ed. *Materialy po istorii agrarnoi revoliutsii*. Moscow, 1928.

Krivitskii, M., ed. *Trud v pervoi piatiletke*. Moscow, 1934.

Kubanin, M. *Klassovaia sushchnost' protsessa drobleniia krest'ianskikh khoziaistv*. Moscow, 1929.

Kuz'minov, Iu. "Osvoenie novykh zavodov i novoi tekhniki i problema kadrov." *Problemy ekonomiki* 1935 no. 5.

Kvasha, Ia., and F. Shofman. "K kharakteristike sotsial'nogo sostava fabrichno-zavodskikh rabochikh SSSR." *Puti industrializatsii* 1930 no. 1/2.

Labour in the Land of the Soviets: Stakhanovites in Conference. Moscow, 1936.

Lapitskaia, S. *Byt rabochikh Trekhgornoi manufaktury*. Moscow, 1935.

Lekarenko, D., and V. A. Nevskii. "Chitatel'skii spros rabochei molodezhi." *Krasnyi bibliotekar'* 1935 no. 6.

Leonov, Leonid. *Soviet River*. Ivor Montagu and Sergei Nolbandov, trans. New York, 1932.

Malinkin, B. "Shkola FZU na avtozavode im. Stalina." *Voprosy profdvizheniia* 1935 no. 10.

Mandelstam, Nadezhda. *Hope against Hope*. Max Hayward, trans. New York, 1970.

Maslov, Pavel. *Perenaselenie russkoi derevni*. Moscow, 1930.

Massovye istochniki po sotsial'no-ekonomicheskoi istorii sovetskogo obshchestva. I. D. Koval'chenko, ed. Moscow, 1979.

Materialy k otchetu Egor'evskogo raikoma VKP(b): K IV Egor'evskoi raionnoi partkonferentsii. Egor'evsk, 1932.

Materialy k otchetu Moskovskogo oblastnogo i gorodskogo komitetov VLKSM 4-i oblastnoi i 3-i gorodskoi konferentsiiam VLKSM. Moscow, 1936.

Materialy k otchetu VTsSPS IX s''ezdu profsoiuzov. Moscow, 1932.

Materialy o khoziaistve Moskvy v itoge pervoi piatiletki. Moscow, 1934.

Materialy o rabote Moskovskogo Soveta rabochikh, krest'ianskikh i krasnoarmeiskikh deputatov za 1935–1936 gg. Moscow, 1936.

Mikhailov, N. *The Fight for Steel*. Moscow, 1931.

Mints, L. E. *Agrarnoe pereselenie i rynok truda SSSR*. Moscow, 1929.

——. "Otkhod krest'ian na zarabotki." In *Voprosy truda, 1926*. Moscow, 1926.

Mirer, S. I., and M. A. Mirer. *Delo chesti: Ustnye rasskazy rabochikh o sotssorevnovanii: Sbornik*. Moscow, 1931.

Mokhov, V. "Ot 'politiki' samoteka k organizovannomu naboru rabochei sily." *Voprosy truda* 1932 no. 8/9.

Molodaia gvardiia transporta. Moscow, 1936.

Monkhouse, Allan. *Moscow, 1911–1933: Being the Memoirs of Allan Monkhouse*. London, 1933.

Mordukhovich, Z. *Na bor'bu s tekuchest'iu rabochei sily*. Moscow/Leningrad, 1931.

Moskovskaia derevnia v ee dostizheniiakh: Sbornik statei. G. Lebedev, ed. Moscow, 1927.

Moskovskaia gorodskaia konferentsiia po zimnim rabotam 3–4 dekabria 1933 g.: Materialy konferentsii. Moscow, 1933.

Moskovskaia oblast' v tsifrakh. P. A. Pozdeev et al., eds. Moscow, 1939.

Moskovskaia oblast' za 50 let: Statisticheskii sbornik. E. I. Sukhova, ed. Moscow, 1967.

Moskovskie stakhanovtsy. Moscow, 1936.

Moskovskii mashinostroitel'nyi trest. Otchet. Moscow, 1929.

Moskovskoe metro. Moscow, 1980.

Moskva: Illiustrirovannaia istoriia. Vol. 2. V. S. Moldavan, ed. Moscow, 1986.

Moskva: Razvitie khoziaistva i kul'tury goroda. Moscow, 1958.

Moskva: Sbornik statei po sotsialistichekoi rekonstruktsii proletarskoi stolitsy. Ia. Brezanovskii, ed. Moscow, 1932.

Moskva i Moskovskaia oblast': Statistichesko-ekonomicheskii spravochnik po okrugam 1926/27–1928/29. Moscow, 1930.

Moskva i Moskovskaia oblast': Statistiko-ekonomicheskii spravochnik. Moscow, 1929.

Moskva rekonstruiuretsia: Al'bom diagramm. Moscow, 1938.

Moskva v novykh raionakh. Moscow, 1936.

Moskva v tsifrakh. Moscow, 1934.

Moskva v tsifrakh. I. A. Grakin and T. A. Selivanov, eds. Moscow, 1940.

Moskva v tsifrakh, 1917–1977. Moscow, 1977.

Moskva za 50 let Sovetskoi vlasti. Moscow, 1968.

Narodnoe khoziaistvo i kul'turnoe stroitel'stvo RSFSR: Statisticheskii spravochnik. Moscow, 1935.

Narodnoe khoziaistvo SSSR: Statisticheskii spravochnik, 1932. Moscow/Leningrad, 1932.

Neizvedannymi putiami: Vospominaniia uchastnikov sotsialisticheskogo stroitel'stva. V. A. Smyshliaev and V. F. Finogenov, eds. Leningrad, 1967.

Neizvestnaia Rossiia. V. A. Kozlov, ed. Moscow, 1992.

Newsholme, Arthur, and John A. Kingsbury. *Red Medicine: Socialized Health in Soviet Russia.* Garden City, N.Y., 1933.

Nezabyvaemye 30-e: Vospominaniia veteranov partii—moskvichei. Moscow, 1986.

Nikol'skii, V., and I. Vanshtein. "Rabota s otstalymi gruppami rabochikh." *Voprosy profdvizheniia* 1933 no. 9.

Novatory: Sbornik. L. Rogachevskaia, ed. Moscow, 1972.

Ob''edinennaia IV Moskovskaia oblastnaia i III gorodskaia konferentsiia VKP(b). Moscow, 1934.

Ognev, P. "Zarabotnaia plata stroitel'nykh rabochikh." *Voprosy profdvizheniia* 1934 no. 3.

Ordzhonikidze, G. K. *Report of the People's Commissariat of Heavy Industry.* Moscow/Leningrad, 1935.

——. *Stat'i i rechi.* Vol. 2. Moscow, 1957.

Osnovnye itogi vypolneniia plana po khoziaistvu Moskovskogo soveta za 1939 god. Moscow, 1940.

Ostroumov, Lev. "Kul'turno-bytovye usloviia truda na torforazrabotkakh." *Sovetskoe kraevedenie* 1932 no. 4.

Otkhod sel'skogo naseleniia na zarabotki v SSSR v 1926/27 g. Moscow, 1929.

Perepis' Moskvy, 1902 g. Ch. I, vol. 2. Moscow, 1906.

Perestroika zarabotnoi platy rabochikh Moskovskoi promyshlennosti. A. S. Putiatin, ed. Moscow, 1932.

Plan g. Moskvy. Moscow, 1935.

Platonov, Andrei. "Usomnivshiisia Makar." In *Gosudartvennyi zhitel': Proza, rannie sochineniia, pis'ma.* M. A. Platonova, comp. Moscow, 1988.

Polliak, G. S. "K voprosu ob urovne zhizni rabochego klassa SSSR." *Planovoe khoziaistvo* 1931 no. 5/6.

Polliak, G. S., et al. "Proizvodstvennye kollektivy i kommuny." In *Sotsialisticheskoe sorevnovanie v promyshlennosti SSSR: Sbornik statei.* Ia. M. Bineman, ed. Moscow, 1930.

Postanovleniia plenuma Moskovskogo oblastnogo komiteta VKP(b) (13–14 ianvaria 1939 g.). Moscow, 1939.

Profsoiuznaia perepis', 1932–1933 g. Moscow, 1934.

Profsoiuzy SSSR: Dokumenty i materialy, 1905–1963. 4 vols. Moscow, 1963–1974.

Rabochii klass SSSR. Moscow, 1937.

Rabotnitsa na sotsialisticheskoi stroike: Sbornik avtobiografii rabotnits. O. N. Chaadaeva, ed. Moscow, 1932.

Raduga trekh gor: Iz biografii odnogo rabochego kollektiva. P. Podliashuk, ed. Moscow, 1967.

Rakino, F. "Postanovka raboty s novymi sloiami rabochikh." *Partiinoe stroitel'stvo* 1931 no. 13.

Rashin, A. G. *Sostav fabrichno-zavodskogo proletariata SSSR.* Moscow, 1930.

Rasskazy stroitelei metro: Istoriia metro Moskvy. A. Kosarev, ed. Moscow, 1935.

Ratner, B., ed. *Istoriia Moskovskogo instrumental'nogo zavoda.* Moscow, 1934.

Resheniia Partii i pravitel'stva po khoziaistvennym voprosam: Sbornik dokumentov za 50 let, 1917–1966 gg. 15 vols. Moscow, 1967–1985.

Resoliutsii Moskovskoi ob''edinennoi IV oblastnoi i III gorodskoi konferentsii VKP(b). Moscow, 1934.

Romanovskii, I. S. *Moskva sotsialisticheskaia.* Moscow, 1940.

Rubtsov, O. *Stengazetu kazhdyi den'.* Moscow, 1931.

Salov, Aleksandr. *Organizatsiia rabochego snabzheniia i opyt perestroiki rabochego snabzheniia na avtozavode im. Stalina.* Moscow, 1933.

Sazonova, N. M. *Kuda idet derevnia (po pis'mam krest'ian Moskovskoi gubernii).* Moscow/Leningrad, 1928.

Sbornik dokumentov po istorii SSSR. Vol. 3 (1933–1941). V. Z. Drobizhev, ed. Moscow, 1980.

Sbornik vazhneishikh postanovlenii po trudu. Moscow, 1935.

Serebrennikov, G. N. *Zhenskii trud v SSSR.* Moscow/Leningrad, 1934.

Shapovalova, G. G. "Derevenskaia chastushka v gorode." In *Etnograficheskie issledovaniia Severo-Zapada SSSR.* Leningrad, 1977.

Shestnadtsat' zavodov. Moscow, 1933.

Shitts, I. I. Dnevnik "velikogo pereloma": Mart 1928–avgust 1931. Paris, 1991.

Shol'ts, S. V. Klassovaia struktura krest'ianstva Moskovskoi gubernii. Moscow, 1929.

Simon, E. D., et al. Moscow in the Making. London, 1937.

Slavnye traditsii: K 100-letiiu zavoda "Krasnyi proletarii" im. A. I. Efremova, 1857–1957: Sbornik. Moscow, 1957.

Smith, Andrew. I Was a Soviet Worker. New York, 1936.

Sokol'niki. V. Boborykin, ed. Moscow, 1967.

Sostav novykh millionov chlenov profsoiuzov. Moscow, 1933.

Sotsialisticheskoe sel'skoe khoziaistvo SSSR. Moscow, 1939.

Sotsialisticheskoe stroitel'stvo soiuza SSR, 1933–1938. Moscow, 1939.

Sotsialisticheskoe stroitel'stvo v SSSR: Statisticheskii ezhegodnik. Moscow, 1936.

Soveshchanie khoziaistvennikov, inzhenerov, tekhnikov, partiinykh i profsoiuznykh rabotnikov tiazheloi promyshlennosti: 20–22 sen. 1934. Moscow/Leningrad, 1935.

Spravochnik dlia vydachi zabornykh knizhek v Moskve s 1 oktiabria 1932 g. Moscow, 1932.

Spravochnik po partprosveshcheniiu na 1931–1932 uch. g. Noginsk, 1931.

Spravochnik proizvodstvennykh stroitel'nykh norm (novoe urochnoe polozhenie). Moscow, 1931.

Sputnik kul'trabotnika sredi sezonnikov. Moscow, 1930.

Stalin, I. V. Sochineniia. 13 vols. Moscow, 1953.

Statisticheskii biulleten' g. Moskvy i Moskovskoi gubernii. Moscow, 1928.

Statisticheskii spravochnik po raionam Moskovskoi oblasti. Moscow, 1931.

Statisticheskii spravochnik po zhilishchno-kommunal'nomu khoziaistvu g. Moskvy. Moscow, 1939.

Statisticheskii spravochnik VTsSPS: Otdel statistiki. Moscow, 1937.

Stepanov, I. P. Materialy po obsledovaniiu krest'ianskogo khoziaistva Moskovskoi gubernii 1924 goda. Moscow, 1925.

Strievskii, K. Material'noe i kul'turnoe polozhenie moskovskikh rabochikh: Doklad na IV ob''edinennom plenume MK i MKK VKP(b). Moscow, 1929.

Strumilin, S. G. Sotsial'nye problemy piatiletki. Moscow, 1929.

Sul'kevich, S. I. Territoriia i naselenie SSSR. Moscow, 1940.

Svet nad zastavoi: Iz istorii zavoda "Serp i molot": Sbornik. A. Klement'eva and M. Skorokhodov, eds. Moscow, 1959.

Tertz, Abram. "Tenants." In Fantastic Stories. New York, 1963.

Trud v SSSR. Moscow, 1936.

Trud v SSSR: Ekonomiko-statisticheskii spravochnik. Moscow, 1932.

Trud v SSSR: Ezhegodnik 1934 g. Moscow, 1935.

Uglanov, N. A., ed. Trud v SSSR: Sbornik statei. Moscow, 1930.

Vasilevskaia, V. "Kak chitaiut knigu malogramotnye." Krasnyi bibliotekar' 1931 no. 5/6.

Vavilov, D. P. "Tekuchest' rabochei sily i mery bor'by s neiu." Udarnik 1932 no. 13.

Vneshnee blagoustroistvo g. Moskvy: Statisticheskii spravochnik po sostoianiiu *na 1 ianvaria 1937 g.* Moscow, 1937.

Vo glave kul'turnogo stroitel'stva: Moskovskie kommunisty—organizatory i ruko-voditeli kul'turnogo stroitel'stva v stolitse, 1917–1941: Sbornik dokumentov. Moscow, 1983.

Vorontsov, V. P. *Sud'ba kapitalizma v Rossii.* St. Petersburg, 1882.

Vovsi, M., and R. Shostak. "K voprosu o tekuchesti rabochei sily v promyshlennosti: Po materialam Moskovskoi oblasti." *Puti industrializatsii* 1930 no. 14.

Vsesoiuznaia perepis' naseleniia 1926 goda. 66 vols. Moscow, 1928–1933.

Vsesoiuznaia perepis' naseleniia 1937 g. Moscow, 1991.

Vsesoiuznaia perepis' naseleniia 1939 g. Cheliabinsk, 1938.

Vsia Moskva: Adresnaia i spravochnaia kniga. Moscow, 1930.

Witkin, Zara. *An American Engineer in Stalin's Russia: The Memoirs of Zara Witkin, 1932–1934.* Michael Gelb, ed. Berkeley, 1991.

Zarkhii, S. *Kommuna v tseke.* Moscow/Leningrad, 1930.

Zavod sovetskogo khleba (Moskovskii khlebzavod no. 4): Sbornik. Moscow, 1932.

Zhbankov, D. N. *Bab'ia storona: Statistiko-etnograficheskii ocherk.* Kostroma, 1891.

Zhiga, I. *Novye rabochie.* Moscow, 1928.

Zhilishchno-kommunal'noe khoziaistvo gorodov i rabochikh poselkov Moskovskoi oblasti: Statisticheskii spravochnik. Moscow, 1936.

Zhilishchno-kommunal'noe khoziaistvo i stroitel'stvo RSFSR (1931–1934). Moscow, 1934.

Zhukov, Iu. *Liudi 30-kh godov.* Moscow, 1960.

Interviews

Interviews of elderly peasant in-migrants at Izmailovskii Park, Moscow, conducted by Natalia Degteva (1973–1988) for the documentary film *Piatachok*, directed by Aleksei Khaniutin, Moscow (1989). Additional interviews conducted by the author (1992).

Interviews of retired workers of peasant origin at the Hammer and Sickle metallurgical plant, Moscow, conducted by the author (1989).

Secondary Works

Abrosimova, M. V. "Rukovodstvo moskovskoi partiinoi organizatsii podgotovkoi molodykh rabochikh kadrov v gody stroitel'stva fundamenta sotsializma (1926–1932 gg.)." Dissertation, Lenin State Pedagogical Institute, Moscow, 1975.

Abu-Lughod, Janet. "Migrant Adjustment to City Life: The Egyptian Case." In *Arab Society in Transition*, Saad Eddin Ibrahim and Nicholas S. Hopkins, eds. Cairo, 1977.

"Aktual'nye zadachi izucheniia sovetskogo rabochego klass: 'Kruglyi stol.'" *Voprosy istorii* 1988 no. 1.

Aleksandrova, T. S. "Iz istorii osvoeniia novoi tekhniki rabochimi Moskvy v gody vtoroi piatiletki." *Istoriia SSSR* 1957 no. 2.

———. "Rabochii klass Moskvy v bor'be za razvitie tiazheloi promyshlennosti v gody vtoroi piatiletki." Dissertation, Academy of Social Sciences of the Communist Party, Moscow, 1957.

Anderson, Barbara A. *Internal Migration during Modernization in Late Nineteenth-Century Russia.* Princeton, 1980.

Andrle, Vladimir. *Workers in Stalin's Russia: Industrialization and Social Change in a Planned Economy.* New York, 1988.

Anokhina, L. A., and Shmeleva, M. N. *Byt gorodskogo naseleniia srednei polosy RSFSR v proshlom i nastoiashchem.* Moscow, 1977.

Anoshin, Eduard Aleksandrovich. "Promyshlennye rabochie Moskvy v gody predvoennykh piatiletok." Dissertation, Moscow State University, 1979.

Arutiunian, Iu. V. "Kollektivizatsiia sel'skogo khoziaistva i vysvobozhdenie rabochei sily dlia promyshlennosti." In *Formirovanie i razvitie sovetskogo rabochego klassa (1917–1961 gg.).* Moscow, 1964.

Babaev, M. M. "Kriminologicheskie issledovaniia problem migratsii naseleniia." *Sovetskoe gosudarstvo i pravo* 1968 no. 3.

Bacha, Edmar L., and Herbert S. Klein, eds. *Social Change in Brazil, 1945–1985.* Albuquerque, 1989.

Bailes, Kendall E. *Technology and Society under Lenin and Stalin.* Princeton, 1978.

Bakhtin, Mikhail M. *The Dialogic Imagination.* Caryl Emerson and Michael Holquist, trans. Austin, 1981.

———. "Zametki." In *Literaturno-kriticheskie stat'i.* Moscow, 1986.

Barber, John. "The Development of Soviet Employment and Labour Policy, 1930–1941." In *Labour and Employment in the USSR,* David Lane, ed. New York, 1986.

Bater, James. *The Soviet City: Ideal and Reality.* London, 1980.

Benson, Susan Porter. *Counter Cultures: Saleswomen, Managers, and Customers in American Department Stores, 1890–1940.* Urbana, Ill., 1986.

Benvenuti, Francesco. "Stakhanovism and Stalinism, 1934–1938." Discussion paper, Centre for Russian and East European Studies, Birmingham, 1989.

Bodnar, John. *The Transplanted: A History of Immigrants in Urban America.* Bloomington, Ind., 1985.

Boiko, Iu. "Leningradskii udel'nyi park." In *Traditsionnyi fol'klor v sovremennoi khudozhestvennoi zhizni: Sbornik nauchnykh trudov.* Leningrad, 1984.

Bokarev, Iu. P. *Biudzhetnye obsledovaniia krest'ianskikh khoziaistv 20-kh godov kak istoricheskii istochnik.* Moscow, 1981.

Bonnell, Victoria E. "The Representation of Women in Early Soviet Political Art." *Russian Review* 1991 no. 3.

———. *Roots of Rebellion: Workers' Politics and Organizations in St. Petersburg and Moscow, 1900–1914.* Berkeley, 1983.

Bordiugov, G. A. "Nekotorye problemy kul'tury byta v kontse 20-kh–30-e gody." In *Dukhovnyi potentsial SSSR nakanune velikoi otechestvennoi voiny: Sbornik statei,* I. S. Borisov, ed. Moscow, 1985.

Borisov, I. S. *Podgotovka proizvodstvennykh kadrov sel'skogo khoziaistva SSSR v rekonstruktivnyi period.* Moscow, 1960.

Bourdieu, Pierre. *In Other Words: Essays toward a Reflexive Sociology.* Matthew Adamson, trans. Stanford, 1990.

Bradley, Joseph. *Muzhik and Muscovite: Urbanization in Late Imperial Russia.* Berkeley, 1985.

Brooks, Jeffrey. "Revolutionary Lives: Public Identities in *Pravda* during the 1920s." In *New Directions in Soviet History,* Stephen White, ed. New York, 1992.

Bruner, Jerome. *Acts of Meaning.* Cambridge, Mass., 1990.

Burawoy, Michael. *The Politics of Production: Factory Regimes under Capitalism and Socialism.* London, 1985.

Burds, Jeffrey. "The Social Control of Peasant Labor in Russia: The Response of Village Communities to Labor Migration in the Central Industrial Region, 1861– 1906." In *Peasant Economy, Culture, and Politics of European Russia,* Esther Kingston-Mann and Timothy Mixter, eds. Princeton, 1991.

Chaianov, A. V. *The Theory of Peasant Economy.* David Thorner et al., eds. Homewood, Ill., 1966.

Chase, William J. *Workers, Society, and the Soviet State: Labor and Life in Moscow, 1918–1929.* Urbana, Ill., 1987.

Clements, Barbara Evans, et al., eds. *Russia's Women: Accommodation, Resistance, Transformation.* Berkeley, 1991.

Cooper, Frederick, ed. *Struggle for the City: Migrant Labor, Capital, and the State in Urban Africa.* Beverly Hills, Calif., 1983.

Cottereau, Alain. "The Distinctiveness of Working-Class Cultures in France, 1848– 1900." In *Working-Class Formation: Nineteenth-Century Patterns in Western Europe and the United States,* Aristide R. Zolberg and Ira Katznelson, eds. Princeton, 1986.

Dadykin, R. P. "O chislennosti i istochnikakh popolneniia rabochego klassa SSSR (1928–1937 gg.)." *Istoricheskie zapiski* no. 87 (1971).

Danilov, V. P. "Krest'ianskii otkhod na promysly v 1920-kh godakh." *Istoricheskie zapiski* no. 94 (1974).

——. *Sovetskaia dokolkhoznaia derevnia: Naselenie, zemlepol'zovanie, khoziaistvo.* Moscow, 1977.

——. *Sovetskaia dokolkhoznaia derevnia: Sotsial'naia struktura, sotsial'nye otnosheniia.* Moscow, 1979.

Davies, R. W. *The Socialist Offensive: The Collectivization of Soviet Agriculture, 1929–1930.* Cambridge, Mass., 1980.

——. *The Soviet Collective Farm, 1929–1930.* Cambridge, Mass., 1980.

——. *The Soviet Economy in Turmoil, 1929–1930.* Cambridge, Mass., 1989.

Davydova, N. S., and A. Ponomarev. *Velikii podvig: Bor'ba moskovskikh bol'shevikov za osushchestvlenie leninskogo plana sotsialisticheskoi industrializatsii.* Moscow, 1970.

Degteva, Natalia. "Fenomen bytovoi kul'tury sovremennogo goroda—parkovyi piatachok: Izmailovskii park v Moskve." In *Traditsionnyi fol'klor v sovremennoi khudozhestvennoi zhizni: Sbornik nauchnykh trudov.* Leningrad, 1984.

——. "Piatachok." Unpublished manuscript, 1989.

Dinamo v gody stroitel'stva sotsializma: Istoriia zavoda. I. M. Nekrasova, ed. Moscow, 1964.

Drobizhev, V. Z. *Problemy metodologii, istoriografii, istochnikovedeniia sovetskogo rabochego klassa.* Moscow, 1987.

Dunham, Vera S. *In Stalin's Time: Middleclass Values in Soviet Fiction.* New York, 1976.

Dvornikov, I. S. *Tovarishcheskie sudy i ikh rol' v bor'be za ukreplenie trudovoi distsipliny.* Moscow, 1956.

Eliseeva, M. I. "O sposobakh privlecheniia rabochei sily v promyshlennost' i stroitel'stvo v period sotsialisticheskoi industrializatsii SSSR (1926–1937)." In *Izvestiia Voronezhskogo gosudarstvennogo pedigogicheskogo instituta,* vol. 63. Voronezh, 1967.

Engelstein, Laura. *Moscow, 1905: Working-Class Organization and Political Conflict.* Stanford, 1982.

Fainsod, Merle. *Smolensk under Soviet Rule.* New York, 1958.

Fedorov, V. D. "Formirovanie rabochikh kadrov na novostroikakh pervoi piatiletki." Dissertation, Gorky State University, 1966.

Figes, Orlando. *Peasant Russia, Civil War: The Volga Countryside in Revolution.* New York, 1989.

Filtzer, Donald. *Soviet Workers and Stalinist Industrialization: The Formation of Modern Soviet Industrial Relations, 1928–1941.* New York, 1986.

Fitzpatrick, Sheila. *Education and Social Mobility in the Soviet Union, 1921–1934.* New York, 1979.

———. "The Great Departure: Rural-Urban Migration in the Soviet Union, 1929–1933." In *Social Dimensions of Soviet Industrialization,* William Rosenberg and Lewis Siegelbaum, eds. Bloomington, Ind., 1993.

———. "Klassy i problemy klassovoi prinadlezhnosti v Sovetskoi Rossii 20-kh godov." *Voprosy istorii* 1990 no. 8.

———. "L'Usage bolshévique de la 'classe': Marxisme et construction de l'identité individuelle." *Actes de la Recherche en Sciences Sociales* no. 85 (November 1990).

———, ed. *Cultural Revolution in Russia, 1928–1931.* Bloomington, Ind., 1978.

Foucault, Michel. "Truth and Power." In *Power/Knowledge.* New York, 1977.

Frierson, Cathy A. "Peasant Family Divisions and the Commune." In *Land Commune and Peasant Community in Russia,* Roger Bartlett, ed. New York, 1990.

Gasiorowska, Xenia. *Women in Soviet Fiction.* Madison, Wis., 1968.

Geertz, Clifford. *The Interpretation of Cultures.* New York, 1973.

Geiger, H. Kent. *The Family in Soviet Russia.* Cambridge, Mass., 1968.

Glickman, Rose L. *Russian Factory Women: Workplace and Society, 1880–1914.* Berkeley, 1984.

Goldman, Wendy. "Women, Abortion, and the State, 1917–1936." In *Russia's Women,* Barbara Evans Clements et al., eds. Berkeley, 1991.

Gol'tsman, M. T. "Kharakteristika kul'turnogo urovnia i obshchestvenno-politicheskoi aktivnosti stroitel'nykh rabochikh SSSR v gody pervoi piatiletki." In *Metodologicheskie voprosy v statisticheskikh issledovaniiakh.* Moscow, 1968.

———. "Sostav stroitel'nykh rabochikh SSSR v gody pervoi piatiletki." In *Izmeneniia v chislennosti i sostave sovetskogo rabochego klassa.* Moscow, 1961.

Gordon, L. A., and E. V. Klopov. *Chto eto bylo? Razmyshleniia o predposylkakh i itogakh togo, chto sluchilos' s nami v 30–40e gody.* Moscow, 1989.

Gordon, L. A., E. V. Klopov, and L. A. Onikov. *Cherty sotsialisticheskogo obraza zhizni: Byt gorodskikh rabochikh vchera, segodnia, zavtra*. Moscow, 1977.

Gringlas, Larry. "Shkraby ne Kraby: Rural Teachers and Bolshevik Power in the Russian Countryside, 1921–1928." Master's thesis, Columbia University, 1987.

Grunt, A. Ia. *Pobeda oktiabr'skoi revoliutsii v Moskve*. Moscow, 1961.

Hamilton, F. E. Ian. *The Moscow City Region*. London, 1976.

Hamm, Michael F. "The Modern Russian City: An Historiographical Analysis." *Journal of Urban History* 4 no. 1 (1977).

Hanagan, Michael, and Charles Stephenson, eds. *Proletarians and Protest: The Roots of Class Formation in an Industrializing World*. New York, 1986.

Hareven, Tamara K. *Family Time and Industrial Time: The Relationship between Family and Work in a New England Industrial Community*. New York, 1982.

Hatch, John B. "Labor and Politics in NEP Russia: Workers, Trade Unions, and the Communist Party in Moscow, 1921–1926." Dissertation, University of California, Irvine, 1985.

——. "The 'Lenin Levy' and the Social Origins of Stalinism: Workers and the Communist Party in Moscow, 1921–1928." *Slavic Review* 1989 no. 4.

Hazard, John N. *Soviet Housing Law*. New Haven, 1939.

Hosking, Geoffrey. *The First Socialist Society*. Cambridge, Mass., 1985.

Inkeles, Alex, and Raymond A. Bauer. *The Soviet Citizen*. New York, 1968.

Istoriia krest'ianstva SSSR. G. V. Sharapov and V. P. Danilov, eds. 2 vols. Moscow, 1986.

Istoriia Moskovskogo avtozavoda im. I. A. Likhacheva. Moscow, 1966.

Istoriia Moskvy. 6 vols. Moscow, 1952–1959.

Istoriia Moskvy: Kratkii ocherk. Moscow, 1974.

Istoriia rabochikh Moskvy, 1917–1945 gg. A. M. Sinitsyn, ed. Moscow, 1983.

Ivnitskii, N. A. *Klassovaia bor'ba v derevne i likvidatsiia kulachestva kak klassa (1929–1932 gg.)*. Moscow, 1972.

Iz istorii bor'by trudiashchikhsia Moskvy i Moskovskoi oblasti za ustanovlenie sovetskoi vlasti i sotsialisticheskoe stroitel'stvo: Sbornik trudov. Moscow, 1977.

Izmeneniia sotsial'noi struktury sovetskogo obshchestva, 1921–seredina '30-kh godov. Moscow, 1979.

Jansen, Clifford J., ed. *Readings in the Sociology of Migration*. Oxford, 1970.

Jasny, Naum. *Soviet Industrialization, 1928–1952*. Chicago, 1961.

Johnson, Robert E. "Family Life in Moscow during NEP." In *Russia in the Era of NEP*, Sheila Fitzpatrick et al., eds. Bloomington, Ind. 1991.

——. *Peasant and Proletarian: The Working Class of Moscow in the Late Nineteenth Century*. New Brunswick, N.J., 1979.

Kabanov, V. V. *Krest'ianskoe khoziaistvo v usloviiakh "voennogo kommunizma."* Moscow, 1988.

Kanatchikov, Semen Ivanovich. *A Radical Worker in Tsarist Russia: The Autobiography of Semen Ivanovich Kanatchikov*. Reginald E. Zelnik, ed. Stanford, 1986.

Karyshev, N. A. "Russkaia fabrichno-zavodskaia promyshlennost' v 1885–1891." *Russkoe bogatstvo*, November 1894.

Kattsen, I. *Metro Moskvy*. Moscow, 1947.

Kerblay, Basile. *Modern Soviet Society*. Rupert Swyer, trans. New York, 1983.

Khlevniuk, O. V. "26 Iunia 1940 goda: Illiuzii i real'nosti administrirovaniia." *Kommunist* 1989 no. 9.

——. "Izmenenie kul'turnogo oblika gorodskikh rabochikh SSSR, 1926–1939." Dissertation, Institute of History, Moscow, 1986.

——. "1937 god: Protivodeistvie repressiiam." *Kommunist* 1989 no. 18.

——. *1937-i: Stalin, NKVD, i sovetskoe obshchestvo.* Moscow, 1992.

——. "Prinuditel'nyi trud v ekonomike SSSR, 1929–1941 gody." *Svobodnaia mysl'* 1992 no. 13.

——. *Udarniki pervoi piatiletki.* Moscow, 1989.

Kinitskaia, S. V. "Obshchestvo 'Za ovladenie tekhnikoi' v 1933–1935 gg." In *Trudy Moskovskogo gosudarstvennogo istoriko-arkhivnogo instituta,* vol. 16. Moscow, 1961.

Kliamkin, Igor'. "Pochemu trudno govorit' pravdu." *Novyi mir* 1989 no. 2.

Koditschek, Theodore. *Class Formation and Urban-Industrial Society: Bradford, 1750–1850.* New York, 1990.

Koenker, Diane. *Moscow Workers and the 1917 Revolution.* Princeton, 1981.

——. "Urbanization and Deurbanization in the Russian Revolution and Civil War." In *Party, State, and Society in the Russian Civil War,* Koenker et al., eds. Bloomington, Ind., 1989.

Kogan, L. N., and B. S. Pavlov. *Molodoi rabochii: Vchera, segodnia.* Sverdlovsk, 1976.

"Kollektivizatsiia: Istoki, sushchnost', posledstviia: Beseda za 'kruglym stolom.'" *Istoriia SSSR* 1989 no. 3.

Kol'tsov, A. V. *Kul'turnoe stroitel'stvo v RSFSR v gody pervoi piatiletki.* Moscow, 1960.

Konstantinov, O. A. "Geograficheskie razlichiia v dinamike gorodskogo naseleniia SSSR." *Izvestiia Vsesoiuznogo Geograficheskogo Obshchestva* 1943 no. 6.

Kopp, Anatole. *Town and Revolution: Soviet Architecture and City Planning, 1917–1935.* Thomas E. Burton, trans. New York, 1970.

Kornakovskii, I. L. "Istoriia zavoda 'Serp i molot,' 1917–1932." Dissertation, Institute of History, Moscow, 1972.

Kotkin, Stephen. "Magnetic Mountain: City Building and City Life in the Soviet Union in the 1930s: A Study of Magnitogorsk." Dissertation, University of California, Berkeley, 1988.

Kozlov, V. A. *Kul'turnaia revoliutsiia i krest'ianstvo, 1921–1927.* Moscow, 1983.

Kozlov, V. A., and O. V. Khlevniuk. *Nachinaetsia s cheloveka: Chelovecheskii faktor v sotsialisticheskom stroitel'stve.* Moscow, 1988.

——. *Pervye piatiletki: Liudi, tempy, sversheniia.* Moscow, 1987.

Koznova, Irina E. "Krest'ianskaia pozemel'naia obshchina v 1921–1929 godakh." Dissertation, Moscow State University, 1981.

Kulischer, Eugene M. *Europe on the Move.* New York, 1948.

Kuromiya, Hiroaki. "The Crisis of Proletarian Identity in the Soviet Factory, 1928–1929." *Slavic Review* 1985 no. 2.

——. *Stalin's Industrial Revolution: Politics and Workers, 1928–1932.* New York, 1988.

——. "Workers' Artels and Soviet Production Relations." In *Russia in the Era of NEP*, Sheila Fitzpatrick et al., eds. Bloomington, Ind. 1991.

Laman, N. K., and Iu. I. Krechetnikova. *Istoriia zavoda "Elektrozavod."* Moscow, 1967.

Lane, Christel. *The Rites of Rulers*. New York, 1981.

Lapchenko, E. S. "Moskovskaia partiinaia organizatsiia v bor'be za likvidatsiiu negramotnosti sredi rabochikh-tekstil'shchikov v gody pervoi piatiletki." In *Partiia v period stroitel'stva sotsializma i kommunizma*. Moscow, 1977.

Lapidus, Gail Warshofsky. *Women in Soviet Society*. Berkeley, 1978.

Lee, Everett. "A Theory of Migration." *Demography* 1966 no. 1.

Lees, Lynn. *Exiles of Erin: Irish Migrants in Victorian London*. Ithaca, 1979.

Lel'chuk, V. S. *Industrializatsiia SSSR—istoriia, opyt, problemy*. Moscow, 1984.

Lewin, Moshe. *The Making of the Soviet System: Essays in the Social History of Interwar Russia*. New York, 1985.

——. *Russian Peasants and Soviet Power*. New York, 1968.

Lewis, Robert A. "Soviet Demographic Policy: How Comprehensive, How Effective?" In *Soviet Geography Studies in Our Time*, Lutz Holzner and Jeane M. Knapp, eds. Milwaukee, 1987.

Lewis, Robert A., and Richard H. Rowland. *Population Redistribution in the USSR*. New York, 1979.

Little, Kenneth. *Urbanization as a Social Process: An Essay on Movement and Change in Contemporary Africa*. Boston, 1974.

Livshits, Ia. Z. "Rabochie-metallisty Moskvy v bor'be za zavershenie pervoi piatiletki, 1931–1932 gg." In *Trudy Moskovskogo gosudarstvennogo istoriko-arkhivnogo instituta*, vol. 14. Moscow, 1960.

Lorimer, Frank. *Population of the Soviet Union*. Geneva, 1946.

McIntosh, Mary. "The Family, Regulation, and the Public Sphere." In *State and Society in Contemporary Britain: A Critical Introduction*, Gregor McLennan et al., eds. Cambridge, 1984.

Male, Donald. *Russian Peasant Organization before Collectivization: A Study of Commune and Gathering, 1925–1930*. Cambridge, 1971.

Mangin, William, ed. *Peasants in Cities: Readings in the Anthropology of Urbanization*. Boston, 1970.

Matthews, Mervyn. "The State Labor Reserves." *Slavonic and East European Review* 1983 no. 2.

Mel'nikov, V. V. *Kul'turnaia revoliutsiia i Komsomol*. Rostov, 1973.

Merridale, Catherine. *Moscow Politics and the Rise of Stalin: The Communist Party in the Capital, 1925–1932*. New York, 1990.

Meyerowitz, Joanne J. *Women Adrift: Independent Wage Earners in Chicago, 1880–1930*. Chicago, 1988.

Mialo, K. G. "Oborvannaia nit': Krest'ianskaia kul'tura i kul'turnaia revoliutsiia." *Novyi mir* 1988 no. 8.

Miller, Frank J. *Folklore for Stalin: Russian Folklore and Pseudofolklore of the Stalin Era*. Armonk, N.Y., 1990.

Mixter, Timothy. "The Hiring Market as Workers' Turf: Migrant Agricultural

Laborers and Mobilization of Collective Action in the Steppe Grainbelt of European Russia, 1853–1913." In *Peasant Economy, Culture, and Politics of European Russia*, Esther Kingston-Mann and Mixter, eds. Princeton, 1991.

Moch, Leslie Page. *Paths to the City.* Beverly Hills, Calif., 1983.

Naselenie SSSR za 70 let. L. L. Rybakovskii, ed. Moscow, 1988.

Nekrylova, A. F. "Ob izuchenii russkogo iarmarochnogo fol'klora." In *Aktual'nye problemy sovremennoi fol'kloristiki: Sbornik statei i materialov.* Leningrad, 1980.

——. *Russkie narodnye gorodskie prazdniki, uveseleniia i zrelishcha: Konets XVIII–nachalo XX veka.* Leningrad, 1984.

Nesushchii svet: Ocherk o delakh i liudiakh pervoi Moskovskoi gosudarstvennoi elektrostantsii. Moscow, 1969.

Nove, Alec. *An Economic History of the USSR.* New York, 1982.

Ocherki istorii Moskovskoi organizatsii VLKSM. E. V. Taranov, ed. Moscow, 1976.

Oestreicher, Richard. "Working-Class Political Behavior and Theories of American Politics." *Journal of American History* 1988 no. 4.

Osipova, T. "Komsomol Moskvy v gody pervoi piatiletki." *Molodoi kommunist* 1958 no. 4.

"Osnovnye etapy razvitiia sovetskogo obshchestva: 'Kruglyi stol.'" *Kommunist* 1987 no. 12.

Osokina, E. A. *Ierarkhiia potrebleniia: O zhizni liudei v usloviiakh Stalinskogo snabzheniia, 1928–1935 gg.* Moscow, 1993.

Pallot, Judith, and Denis J. B. Shaw. *Landscape and Settlement in Romanov Russia, 1613–1917.* New York, 1990.

Panfilova, A. M. *Formirovanie rabochego klassa SSSR v gody pervoi piatiletki (1928–1932).* Moscow, 1964.

Perlman, Janice E. *The Myth of Marginality: Urban Poverty and Politics in Rio de Janeiro.* Berkeley, 1976.

Pervyi podshipnikovyi: Istoriia pervogo gosudarstvennogo podshipnikovogo zavoda, 1932–1972. Moscow, 1973.

Plekhanov, Georgii. *Selected Philosophical Works.* Vol. 1. Moscow, 1977.

Poletaev, V. E. *Na putiakh k novoi Moskve, 1917–1935.* Moscow, 1964.

——. "Zhilishchnoe stroitel'stvo v Moskve v 1931–1934 gg." *Istoricheskie zapiski* 66 (1960).

Rabochii klass—vedushchaia sila v stroitel'stve sotsialisticheskogo obshchestva, 1921–1937 gg. L. S. Rogachevskaia and A. M. Sivolobov, eds. Moscow, 1984.

Rancière, Jacques. *The Nights of Labor: The Workers' Dream in Nineteenth-Century France.* John Drury, trans. Philadelphia, 1989.

Rashin, A. G. "Dinamika promyshlennykh kadrov SSSR za 1917–1958 gg." In *Izmeneniia v chislennosti i sostave sovetskogo rabochego klassa.* Moscow, 1961.

——. *Formirovanie rabochego klassa Rossii: Istoriko-ekonomicheskie ocherki.* Moscow, 1958.

Rassweiler, Anne D. *The Generation of Power: The History of Dneprostroi.* New York, 1988.

Rittersporn, Gabor. *Stalinist Simplifications and Soviet Complications: Social Tensions and Political Conflicts in the USSR, 1933–1953.* Philadelphia, 1991.

Roberts, Bryan. *Cities of Peasants: The Political Economy of Urbanization in the Third World.* London, 1978.

Rose, Arnold M., ed. *Human Behavior and Social Processes.* Boston, 1962.

Rosenberg, William, and Lewis Siegelbaum, eds. *Social Dimensions of Soviet Industrialization.* Bloomington, Ind., 1993.

Rothstein, Frances. "The New Proletarians: Third World Realities and First World Categories." *Comparative Studies in Society and History* 1986 no. 2.

Schwarz, Solomon. *Labor in the Soviet Union.* New York, 1951.

Scott, James. *Weapons of the Weak: Everyday Forms of Peasant Resistance.* New Haven, 1985.

Scott, Joan Wallach. "The Evidence of Experience." *Critical Inquiry* 1991 no. 4.

——. *Gender and the Politics of History.* New York, 1988.

Scott, John. *Behind the Urals.* Bloomington, Ind., 1973.

Selunskaia, V. M. *Sotsial'naia struktura sovetskogo obshchestva: Istoriia i sovremennost'.* Moscow, 1987.

Sewell, William H. "How Classes Are Made: Critical Reflections on E. P. Thompson's Theory of Working-Class Formation." In *E. P. Thompson: Critical Perspectives,* Harvey J. Kaye and Keith McClelland, eds. Philadelphia, 1990.

Shearer, David R. "The Language and Politics of Socialist Rationalization: Productivity, Industrial Relations, and the Social Origins of Stalinism at the End of NEP." Paper presented at the conference "The Making of the Soviet Working Class," Michigan State University, November 1990.

——. "Rationalization and Reconstruction in the Soviet Machine Building Industry, 1926–1934." Dissertation, University of Pennsylvania, 1988.

Shimotomai, Nobuo. *Moscow under Stalinist Rule.* New York, 1991.

Shiokawa, Nobuaki. "The Collectivization of Agriculture and *Otkhodnichestvo* in the USSR, 1930." In *Annals of the Institute of Social Science* no. 24. Tokyo, 1983.

——. "Labor Turnover in the USSR, 1929–1933: A Sectorial Analysis." In *Annals of the Institute of Social Science* no. 23. Tokyo, 1982.

——. "A 'Socialist State' and the Working Class: Labour Management in the Soviet Factory, 1929–1933." Unpublished summary of book in Japanese of same title.

——. "The Soviet Working Class under the Stalinist System, 1929–1933." Unpublished summary of book in Japanese of same title.

Shkaratan, O. I. *Problemy sotsial'noi struktury rabochego klassa SSSR.* Moscow, 1970.

Shomrakova, I. A. "Massovyi chitatel' pervoi poloviny 30-kh godov XX veka." In *Istoriia russkogo chitatelia.* Leningrad, 1982.

Shryock, Henry, and Jacob Siegel. *The Methods and Materials of Demography.* Washington, D.C., 1971.

Sieber, Sam. "Toward a Theory of Role Accumulation." *American Sociological Review* 39 (August 1974).

Siegelbaum, Lewis H. "Production Collectives and Communes and the 'Imperatives' of Soviet Industrialization, 1929–1931." *Slavic Review* 1986 no. 1.

——. "Soviet Norm Determination in Theory and Practice, 1917–1941." *Soviet Studies* 1984 no. 1.

——. *Stakhanovism and the Politics of Productivity in the USSR, 1935–1941.* New York, 1988.

Simic, Andrei. *The Peasant Urbanites: A Study of Rural-Urban Mobility in Serbia.* New York, 1973.

Sinha, V. N. P., and Md. Ataullah. *Migration: An Interdisciplinary Approach.* Delhi, 1987.

Slanskaia, M. D. *Pechat' delo partiinoe: Iz opyta partiinogo rukovodstva mnogoti-razhnymi gazetami Moskvy.* Moscow, 1978.

Slatter, John. "Communes with Communists: The *Sel'sovety* in the 1920s." In *Land Commune and Peasant Community in Russia,* Roger Bartlett, ed. New York, 1990.

Smith, Gregory M. "The Impact of World War II on Women, Family Life, and Mores in Moscow, 1941–1945." Dissertation, Stanford University, 1990.

Sokolov, Andrei K. "From the Countryside to the Cities: A Comparative Historical Analysis of Rural-Urban Migration in Russia and the Soviet Union during the Industrialization Drive." *Historical Social Research* 1991 no. 2.

Sokolov, Iurii M. *Russian Folklore.* Catherine Ruth Smith, trans. New York, 1950.

Sonin, M. Ia. *Vosproizvodstvo rabochei sily v SSSR i balans truda.* Moscow, 1959.

Sosnovy, T. *The Housing Problem in the Soviet Union.* New York, 1954.

Starodubtsev, V. F. "Deiatel'nost' moskovskoi partiinoi organizatsii po razvitiiu obshchestvenno-politicheskoi aktivnosti rabochego klassa v gody pervoi piati-letki, 1928–1932 gg." Dissertation, Moscow Oblast Pedagogical Institute, Moscow, 1972.

Starr, S. Frederick. "Visionary Town Planning during the Cultural Revolution." In *Cultural Revolution in Russia, 1928–1931,* Sheila Fitzpatrick, ed. Bloomington, Ind., 1978.

Stedman Jones, Gareth. *Languages of Class: Studies in English Working-Class History, 1832–1932.* London, 1980.

Steinberg, Mark. *Moral Communities: The Culture of Class Relations in the Russian Printing Industry, 1867–1907.* Berkeley, 1992.

Stites, Richard. *Revolutionary Dreams.* New York, 1989.

Stone, Gregory. "Appearance and the Self." In *Human Behavior and Social Processes,* Arnold M. Rose, ed. Boston, 1962.

Straus, Kenneth. "From Heroic Class to Worker-Hero: Shock Work and Stakhanovism as Strategies for Increasing Labor Productivity, 1929–1941." Unpublished paper, 1988.

Strigin, A. S. "Deiatel'nost' moskovskoi partiinoi organizatsii po razvitiiu tru-dovoi aktivnosti molodezhi na stroikakh pervoi piatiletki." *Uchenye zapiski Moskovskogo pedagogicheskogo instituta* 1969 no. 357.

Tarle, G. Ia. "Razvertyvanie tekhnicheskoi ucheby rabochikh tiazheloi pro-myshlennosti SSSR v kontse 1935–nachale 1936 gg." *Trudy Moskovskogo gosudarstvennogo istoriko-arkhivnogo instituta* 1957 no. 10.

Thompson, E. P. *The Making of the English Working Class.* New York, 1963.

——. "Time, Work-Discipline, and Industrial Capitalism." *Past and Present* 1967 no. 38.

Tilly, Charles. "The Chaos of the Living City." In *An Urban World*, Tilly, ed. Boston, 1974.

——. "Demographic Origins of the European Proletariat." In *Proletarianization and Family History*. New York, 1984.

Timasheff, Nicholas S. *The Great Retreat: The Growth and Decline of Communism in Russia*. New York, 1945.

Troger, Annemarie. "The Creation of a Female Assembly-Line Proletariat." In *When Biology Became Destiny: Women in Weimar and Nazi Germany*, Renate Bridenthal et al., eds. New York, 1984.

Tsentral'nyi institut truda i ego metody NOT. Moscow, 1970.

Tugan-Baranovsky, Mikhail. *The Russian Factory in the Nineteenth Century*. Arthur and Clara Levin, trans. Homewood, Ill., 1970.

Tumarkin, Nina. *Lenin Lives: The Lenin Cult in Soviet Russia*. Cambridge, Mass., 1983.

Tverdokhleb, A. A. "Chislennost' i sostav rabochego klassa Moskvy v 1917–1939 gg." *Vestnik Moskovskogo universiteta* ser. 9, 1970 no. 1.

——. "Material'noe blagosostoianie rabochego klassa Moskvy v 1917–1937 gg." Dissertation, Moscow State University, 1970.

Vakar, Nicholas. *The Taproot of Soviet Society*. New York, 1961.

Vdovin, A. I., and V. Z. Drobizhev. *Rost rabochego klassa SSSR, 1917–1940 gg.* Moscow, 1976.

Viola, Lynne. *The Best Sons of the Fatherland: Workers in the Vanguard of Soviet Collectivization*. New York, 1987.

Von Hagen, Mark. *Soldiers in the Proletarian Dictatorship: The Red Army and the Soviet Socialist State, 1917–1930*. Ithaca, 1990.

Vse dorogi vedut v Moskvu: O proshlom i nastoiashchem moskovskoi zheleznoi dorogi. Moscow, 1971.

Vyas, Arvind. *Consumption in a Socialist Economy: The Soviet Industrialization Experience, 1929–1937*. New Delhi, 1978.

Walder, Andrew G. *Communist Neo-Traditionalism: Work and Authority in Chinese Industry*. Berkeley, 1986.

Ward, Chris. *Russia's Cotton Workers and the New Economic Policy*. New York, 1990.

Waters, Elizabeth. "The Female Form in Soviet Political Iconography, 1917–1932." In *Russia's Women*, Barbara Evans Clements et al., eds. Berkeley, 1991.

Weber, Adna Ferrin. *The Growth of Cities in the Nineteenth Century*. Ithaca, 1963.

Willems, Emilio. "Peasantry and City: Cultural Persistence and Change in European Perspective." *American Anthropologist* 72 (1970).

Wood, Elizabeth. "Gender and Politics in Soviet Russia: Working Women under the New Economic Policy, 1918–1928." Dissertation, University of Michigan, 1991.

Zaleski, Eugene. *Planning for Economic Growth in the Soviet Union, 1918–1932*. Marie-Christine MacAndrew and G. Warren Nutter, eds. Chapel Hill, N.C., 1971.

Zurcher, Louis A. *Social Roles: Conformity, Conflict, and Creativity*. Beverly Hills, Calif., 1983.

Index

Studies of the Harriman Institute

Soviet National Income in 1937, by Abram Bergson, Columbia University Press, 1953.

Through the Glass of Soviet Literature: Views of Russian Society, edited by Ernest Simmons Jr., Columbia University Press, 1953.

Polish Postwar Economy, by Thad Paul Alton, Columbia University Press, 1954.

Management of the Industrial Firm in the USSR: A Study in Soviet Economic Planning, by David Granick, Columbia University Press, 1954.

Soviet Policies in China, 1917–1924, by Allen S. Whiting, Columbia University Press, 1954; paperback, Stanford University Press, 1968.

Literary Politics in the Soviet Ukraine, 1917–1934, by George S. N. Luckyj, Columbia University Press, 1956.

The Emergence of Russian Panslavism, 1856–1870, by Michael Boro Petrovich, Columbia University Press, 1956.

Lenin on Trade Unions and Revolution, 1893–1917, by Thomas Taylor Hammond, Columbia University Press, 1956.

The Last Years of the Georgian Monarchy, 1658–1832, by David Marshall Lang, Columbia University Press, 1957.

The Japanese Thrust into Siberia, 1918, by James William Morley, Columbia University Press, 1957.

Bolshevism in Turkestan, 1917–1927, by Alexander G. Park, Columbia University Press, 1957.

Soviet Marxism: A Critical Analysis, by Herbert Marcuse, Columbia University Press, 1958; paperback, Columbia University Press, 1985.

Soviet Policy and the Chinese Communists, 1931–1946, by Charles B. McLane, Columbia University Press, 1958.

The Agrarian Foes of Bolshevism: Promise and Defeat of the Russian Socialist Revolutionaries, February to October, 1917, by Oliver H. Radkey, Columbia University Press, 1958.

Pattern for Soviet Youth: A Study of the Congresses of the Komsomol, 1918–1954, by Ralph Talcott Fisher, Jr., Columbia University Press, 1959.

The Emergence of Modern Lithuania, by Alfred Erich Senn, Columbia University Press, 1959.

The Soviet Design for a World State, by Elliot R. Goodman, Columbia University Press, 1960.

Settling Disputes in Soviet Society: The Formative Years of Legal Institutions, by John N. Hazard, Columbia University Press, 1960.

Soviet Marxism and Natural Science, 1917–1932, by David Joravsky, Columbia University Press, 1961.

Russian Classics in Soviet Jackets, by Maurice Friedberg, Columbia University Press, 1962.

Stalin and the French Communist Party, 1941–1947, by Alfred J. Rieber, Columbia University Press, 1962.

Sergei Witte and the Industrialization of Russia, by Theodore K. Von Laue, Columbia University Press, 1962.

Ukranian Nationalism, by John H. Armstrong, Columbia University Press, 1963.

The Sickle under the Hammer: The Russian Socialist Revolutionaries in the Early Months of Soviet Rule, by Oliver H. Radkey, Columbia University Press, 1963.

Comintern and World Revolution, 1928–1943: The Shaping of Doctrine, by Kermit E. McKenzie, Columbia University Press, 1964.

Weimar Germany and Soviet Russia, 1926–1933: A Study in Diplomatic Instability, by Harvey L. Dyck, Columbia University Press, 1966.

Financing Soviet Schools, by Harold J. Noah, Teachers College Press, 1966.

Russia, Bolshevism, and the Versailles Peace, by John M. Thompson, Princeton University Press, 1966.

The Russian Anarchists, by Paul Avrich, Princeton University Press, 1967.

The Soviet Academy of Sciences and the Communists Party, 1927–1932, by Loren R. Graham, Princeton University Press, 1967.

Red Virgin Soil: Soviet Literature in the 1920s, by Robert A. Maguire, Princeton University Press, 1968; paperback, Cornell University Press, 1987.

Communist Party Membership in the U.S.S.R., 1917–1967, by T. H. Rigby, Princeton University, 1968.

Soviet Ethics and Morality, by Richard T. De George, University of Michigan Press, 1969; paperback, Ann Arbor Paperbacks, 1969.

Vladimir Akimov on the Dilemmas of Russian Marxism, 1895–1903, by Jonathan Frankel, Cambridge University Press, 1969.

Soviet Perspectives on International Relations, 1956–1967, by William Zimmerman, Princeton University Press, 1969.

Krondstadt, 1921, by Paul Avrich, Princeton University Press, 1970.

Class Struggle in the Pale: The Formative Years of the Jewish Workers' Movement in Tsarist Russia, by Ezra Mendelsohn, Cambridge University Press, 1970.

The Proletarian Episode in Russian Literature, by Edward J. Brown, Columbia University Press, 1971.

Labor and Society in Tsarist Russia: The Factory Workers of St. Petersburg, 1855–1870, by Reginald E. Zelnik, Stanford University Press, 1971.

Archives and Manuscript Repositories in the U.S.S.R.: Moscow and Leningrad, by Patricia K. Grimsted, Princeton University Press, 1972.

The Baku Commune, 1917–1918, by Ronald G. Suny, Princeton University Press, 1972.

Mayakovsky: A Poet in the Revolution, by Edward J. Brown, Princeton University Press, 1973.

Oblomov and His Creator: The Life and Art of Ivan Goncharov, by Milton Ehre, Princeton University Press, 1973.

German Politics under Soviet Occupation, by Henry Krisch, Columbia University Press, 1974.

Soviet Politics and Society in the 1970s, edited by Henry W. Morton and Rudolph L. Tokes, Free Press, 1974.

Liberals in the Russia Revolution, by William G. Rosenberg, Princeton University Press, 1974.

Famine in Russia, 1891–1892, by Richard G. Robbins, Jr., Columbia University Press, 1975.

In Stalin's Time: Middleclass Values in Soviet Fiction, by Vera Dunham, Cambridge University Press, 1976.

The Road to Bloody Sunday, by Walter Sablinsky, Princeton University Press, 1976; paperback, Princeton University Press, 1986.

The Familiar Letter as a Literary Genre in the Age of Pushkin, by William Mills Todd III, Princeton University Press, 1976.

Russian Realist Art. The State and Society: The Peredvizhniki and Their Tradition, by Elizabeth Valkenier, Ardis Publishers, 1977; paperback, Columbia University Press, 1989.

The Soviet Agrarian Debate, by Susan Solomon, Westview Press, 1978.

Cultural Revolution in Russia, 1928–1931, edited by Sheila Fitzpatrick, Indiana University Press, 1978; paperback, Midland Books, 1984.

Soviet Criminologists and Criminal Policy: Specialists in Policy-Making, by Peter Solomon, Columbia University Press, 1978.

Technology and Society under Lenin and Stalin: Origins of the Soviet Technical Intelligentsia, by Kendall E. Bailes, Princeton University Press, 1978.

The Politics of Rural Russia, 1905–1914, edited by Leopold H. Haimson, Indiana University Press, 1979

Political Participation in the U.S.S.R., by Theodore H. Friedgut, Princeton University Press, 1979; paperback, Princeton University Press, 1982.

Education and Social Mobility in the Soviet Union, 1921–1934, by Sheila Fitzpatrick, Cambridge University Press, 1979.

The Soviet Marriage Market: Mate Selection in Russia and the USSR, by Wesley Andrew Fisher, Praeger Publishers, 1980.

Prophecy and Politics: Socialism, Nationalism, and the Russian Jews, 1862–1917, by Jonathan Frankel, Cambridge University Press, 1981.

Dostoevsky and The Idiot: *Author, Narrator, and Reader*, by Robin Feuer Miller, Harvard University Press, 1981.

Moscow Workers and the 1917 Revolution, by Diane Koenker, Princeton University Press, 1981; paperback, Princeton University Press, 1986.

Archives and Manuscript Repositories in the USSR: Estonia, Latvia, Lithuania, and Belorussia, by Patricia K. Grimsted, Princeton University Press, 1981.

Zionism in Poland: The Formative Years, 1915–1926, by Ezra Mendelsohn, Yale University Press, 1982.

Soviet Risk-Taking and Crisis Behavior, by Hannes Adomeit, George Allen and Unwin Publishers, 1982.

Russia at the Crossroads: The 26th Congress of the CPSU, edited by Seweryn Bialer and Thane Gustafson, George Allen and Unwin Publishers, 1982.

The Crisis of the Old Order in Russia: Gentry and Government, by Roberta Thompson Manning, Princeton University Press, 1983; paperback, Princeton University Press, 1986.

Sergei Aksakov and Russian Pastoral, by Andrew A. Durkin, Rutgers University Press, 1983.

Politics and Technology in the Soviet Union, by Bruce Parrott, MIT Press, 1983.

The Soviet Union and the Third World: An Economic Bind, by Elizabeth Kridl Valkenier, Praeger Publishers, 1983.

Russian Metaphysicial Romanticism: The Poetry of Tiutchev and Boratynskii, by Sarah Pratt, Stanford University Press, 1984.

Ruling Russia: Politics and Administration in the Age of Absolutism, 1762–1796, by John LeDonne, Princeton University Press, 1984.

Insidious Intent: A Structural Analysis of Fedor Sologub's Petty Demon, by Diana Greene, Slavica Publishers, 1986.

Leo Tolstoy: Resident and Stranger, by Richard Gustafson, Princeton University Press, 1986.

Workers, Society, and the State: Labor and Life in Moscow, 1918–1929, by William Chase, University of Illinois Press, 1987.

Andrey Bely: Spirit of Symbolism, edited by John Malmstad, Cornell University Press, 1987.

Government and Peasant in Russia, 1861–1906: The Prehistory of the Stolypin Reforms, by David A. J. Macey, Northern University Press, 1987.

The Making of Three Russian Revolutionaries: Voices from the Menshevik Past, edited by Leopold H. Haimson in collaboration with Ziva Galili y García and Richard Wortman, Cambridge University Press, 1988.

Revolution and Culture: The Bogdanov-Lenin Controversy, by Zenovia A. Sochor, Cornell University Press, 1988.

A Handbook of Russian Verbs, by Frank Miller, Ardis Publishers, 1989.

1905 in St. Petersburg: Labor, Society, and Revolution, by Gerald D. Surh, Stanford University Press, 1989.

Alien Tongues: Bilingual Russian Writers of the "First" Emigration, by Elizabeth Klosty Beaujour, Cornell University Press, 1989.

Iuzovka and Revolution, Volume I: Life and Work in Russia's Donbass, 1869–1924, by Theodore H. Friedgut, Princeton University Press, 1989.

The Menshevik Leaders in the Russian Revolution: Social Realities and Political Strategies, by Ziva Galili, Princeton University Press, 1989.

Russian Literary Politics and the Pushkin Celebration of 1880, by Marcus C. Levitt, Cornell University Press, 1989.

Russianness: In Honor of Rufus Mathewson, edited by Robert L. Belknap, Ardis Publishers, 1990.

Soldiers in the Proletarian Dictatorship: The Red Army and the Soviet Socialist State, 1917–1930, by Mark von Hagen, Cornell University Press, 1990.

Ilya Repin and the World of Russian Art, by Elizabeth Valkenier, Columbia University Press, 1990.

The Genesis of "The Brothers Karamazov," by Robert L. Belknap, Northwestern University Press, 1990.

Autobiographical Statements in Twentieth-Century Russian Literature, edited by Jane Gary Harris, Princeton University Press, 1990.

Folklore for Stalin, by Frank Miller, M. E. Sharpe, 1990.

Vasilii Trediakovsky: The Fool of the "New" Russian Literature, by Irina Reyfman, Stanford University Press, 1990.

Russia, Germany, and the West from Khrushchev to Gorbachev, by Michael Sodaro, Cornell University Press, 1990.

Reforming Rural Russia: State, Local Society, and National Politics, 1855–1914, by Francis William Wcislo, Princeton University Press, 1990.

Remizov's Fictions, 1900–1921, by Greta N. Slobin, Northern Illinois University Press, 1991.

The Corporation under Russian Law, 1800–1917: A Study in Tsarist Economic Policy, by Thomas C. Owen, Cambridge University Press, 1991.

Physics and Politics in Revolutionary Russia, by Paul R. Josephson, University of California Press, 1991.

The Paradise Myth in Eighteenth-Century Russia: Utopian Patterns in Early Secular Russian Literature and Culture, by Stephen Lessing Baehr, Stanford University Press, 1991.

Thinking Theoretically about Soviet Nationalities: Concepts, History, and

Comparison in the Study of the USSR, edited by Alexander J. Motyl, Columbia University Press, 1992.

The Post-Soviet Nations: Perspectives on the Demise of the USSR, edited by Alexander J. Motyl, Columbia University Press, 1992.

Andrei Bitov: The Ecology of Inspiration, by Ellen Chances, Cambridge University Press, 1993.

The Revolution of 1905 in Odessa: Blood on the Steps, by Robert Weinberg, Indiana University Press, 1993.

The Pragmatics of Insignificance: Chekhov, Zoshchenko, Gogol, by Cathy Popkin, Stanford University Press, 1993.

Forging Revolution: Metalworkers, Managers, and the State in St. Petersburg, 1890–1914, by Heather Hogan, Indiana University Press, 1993.

Iuzovka and Revolution, Volume II: Politics and Revolution in Russia's Donbass, 1869–1924, by Theodore H. Friedgut, Princeton University Press, 1994.

Peasant Metropolis: Social Identities in Moscow, 1929–1941, by David L. Hoffmann, Cornell University Press, 1994.